A Devil and Her Love Song

Story & Art by
Miyoshi Tomori

Volume 12

A Devil and Her Love Song

Volume 12
CONTENTS

The devil makes me LOVELY!!!

STORY THUS FAR

Maria and Shin are finally a couple after affirming their love for one another. But unfortunately, Maria loses her voice, and Shin suffers an injury to his right hand. In a bid to help Maria regain her voice, Maria, Shin and Yusuke visit Yokosuka, the place where Maria grew up. There, they meet Maria's father, John. Initially, Maria only has hatred toward her father because of what transpired between him and her mother in the past. She gradually learns to forgive him, however, and they reconcile. With that, Maria also gets her voice back. But in the meantime, Shin's injury gets worse...

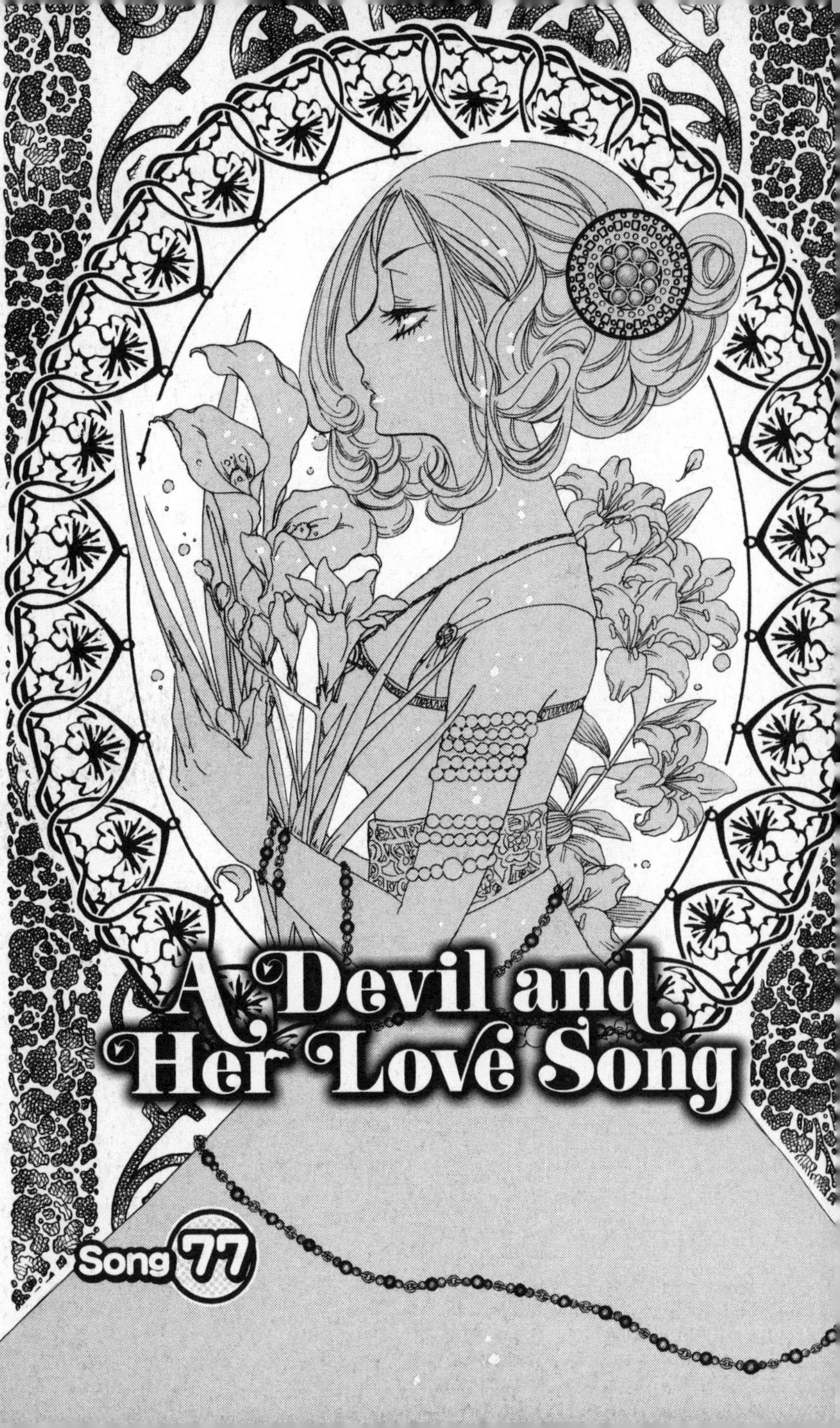
A Devil and
Her Love Song
Song 77

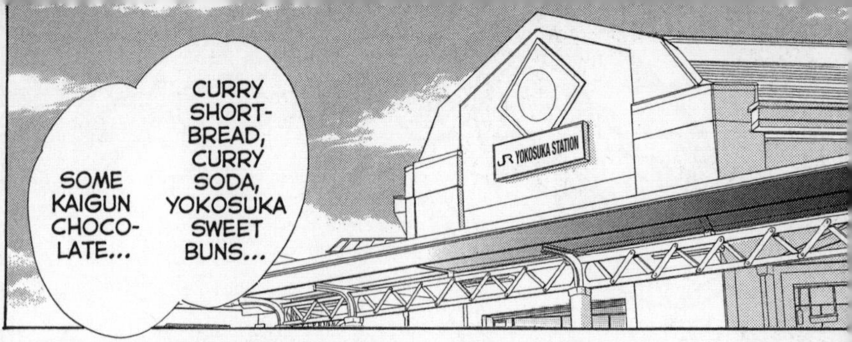
JR YOKOSUKA STATION
CURRY SHORT-BREAD, CURRY SODA, YOKOSUKA SWEET BUNS...
SOME KAIGUN CHOCO-LATE...

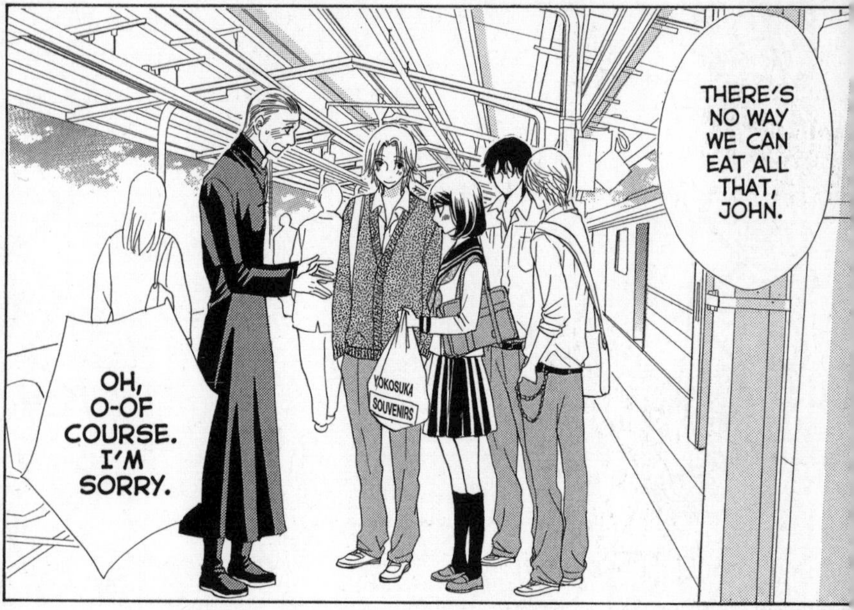
THERE'S NO WAY WE CAN EAT ALL THAT, JOHN.
YOKOSUKA SOUVENIRS
OH, O-OF COURSE. I'M SORRY.

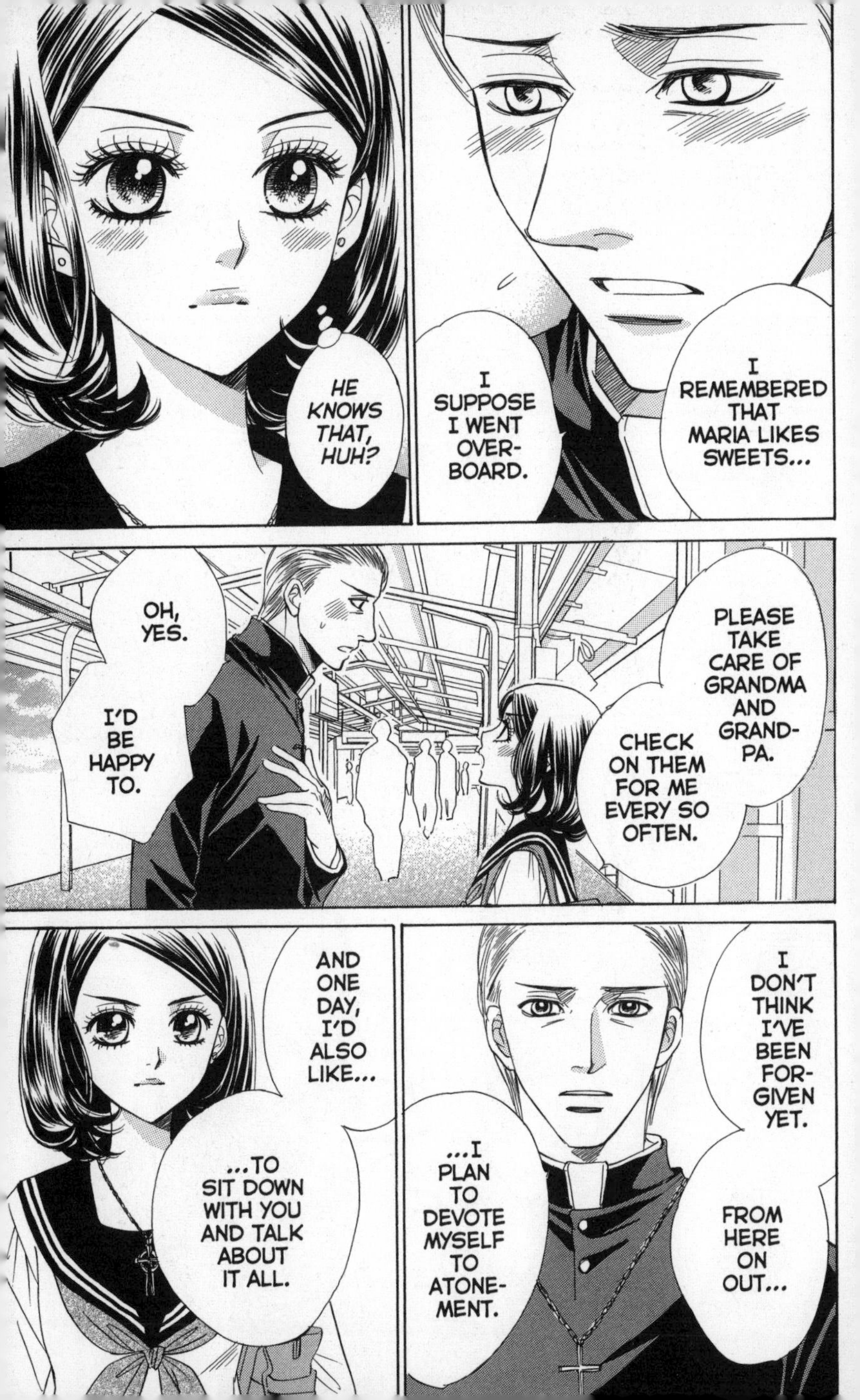
I REMEMBERED THAT MARIA LIKES SWEETS...
I SUPPOSE I WENT OVERBOARD.
HE KNOWS THAT, HUH?
PLEASE TAKE CARE OF GRANDMA AND GRANDPA.
CHECK ON THEM FOR ME EVERY SO OFTEN.
OH, YES.
I'D BE HAPPY TO.
I DON'T THINK I'VE BEEN FORGIVEN YET.
FROM HERE ON OUT...
...I PLAN TO DEVOTE MYSELF TO ATONEMENT.
AND ONE DAY, I'D ALSO LIKE...
...TO SIT DOWN WITH YOU AND TALK ABOUT IT ALL.

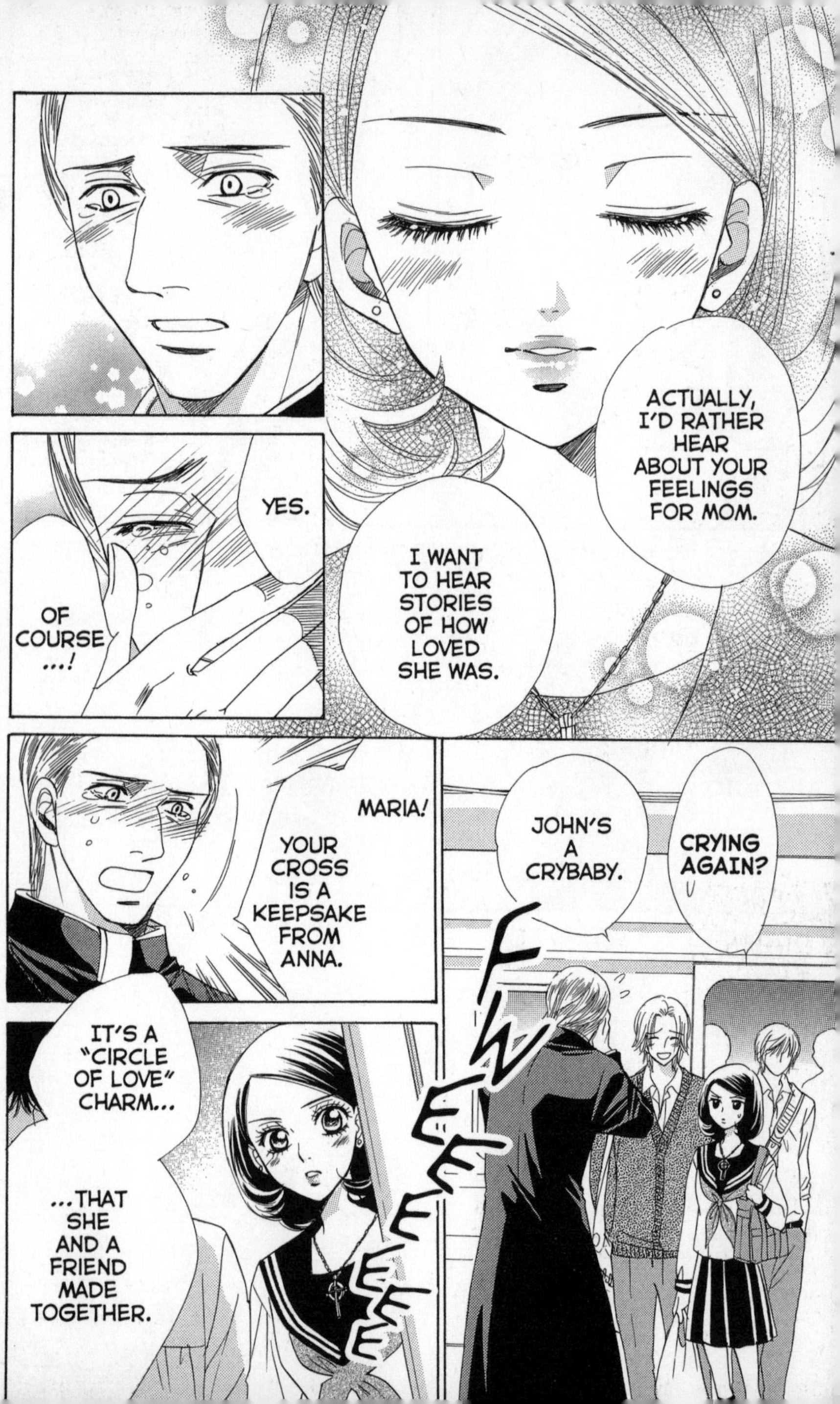
ACTUALLY, I'D RATHER HEAR ABOUT YOUR FEELINGS FOR MOM.
I WANT TO HEAR STORIES OF HOW LOVED SHE WAS.
YES.
OF COURSE ...!
CRYING AGAIN?
JOHN'S A CRYBABY.
FWEEEEEEE
MARIA!
YOUR CROSS IS A KEEPSAKE FROM ANNA.
IT'S A "CIRCLE OF LOVE" CHARM...
...THAT SHE AND A FRIEND MADE TOGETHER.

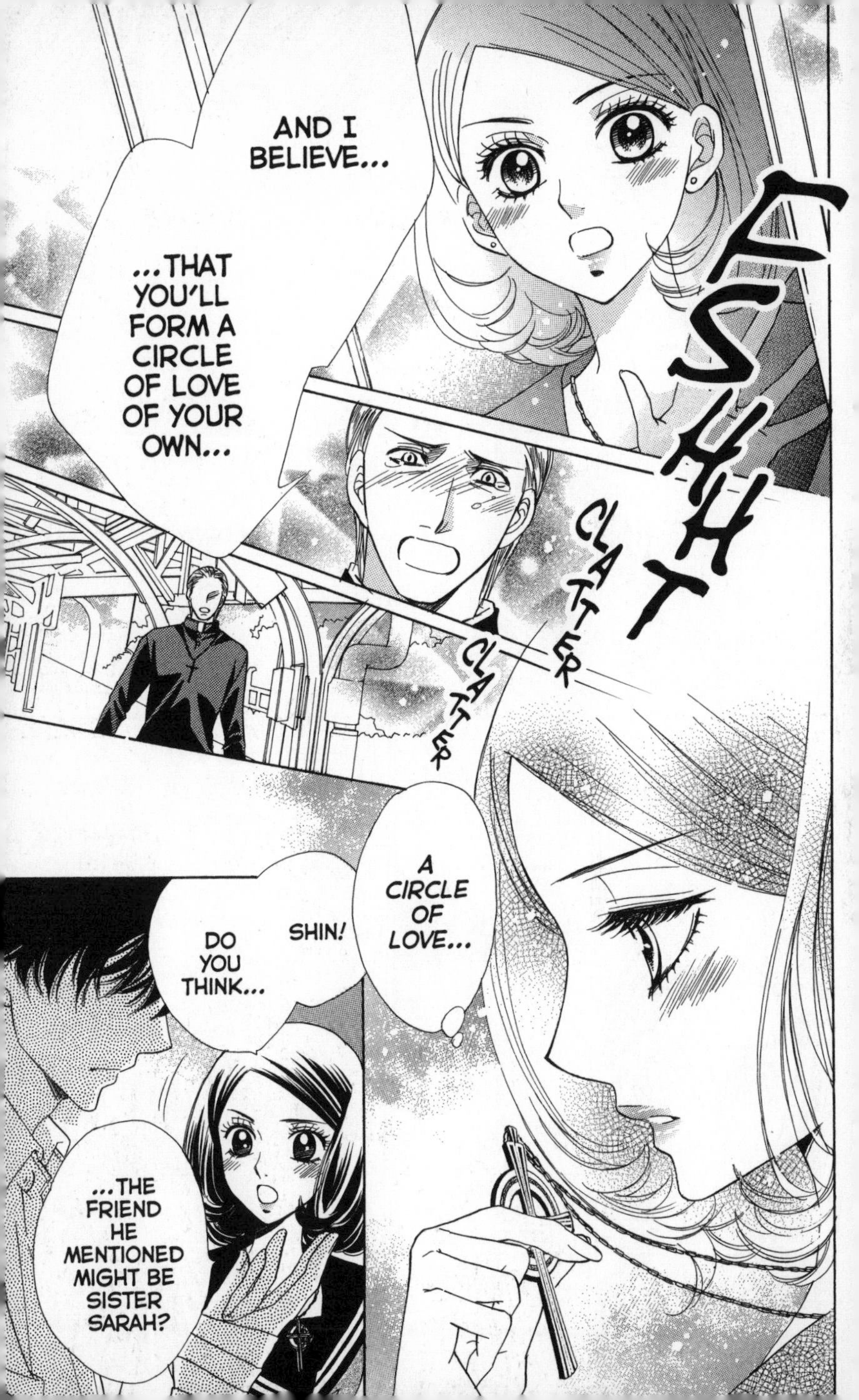
AND I BELIEVE...
...THAT YOU'LL FORM A CIRCLE OF LOVE OF YOUR OWN...
FSSHHT
CLATTER
CLATTER
A CIRCLE OF LOVE...
SHIN!
DO YOU THINK...
...THE FRIEND HE MENTIONED MIGHT BE SISTER SARAH?

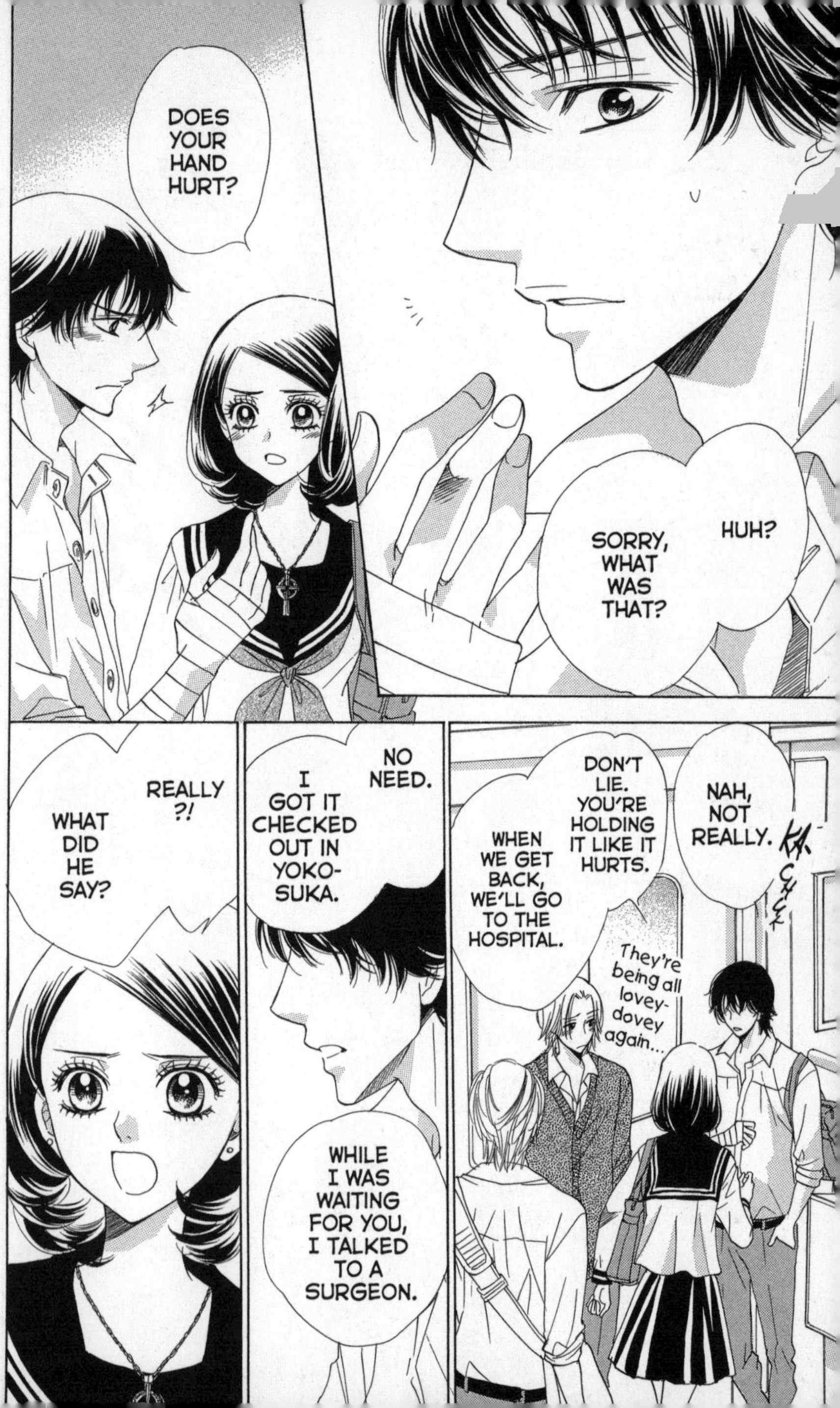
HUH?
SORRY, WHAT WAS THAT?
DOES YOUR HAND HURT?
NAH, NOT REALLY.
KA-CHUK
DON'T LIE. YOU'RE HOLDING IT LIKE IT HURTS.
WHEN WE GET BACK, WE'LL GO TO THE HOSPITAL.
They're being all lovey-dovey again...
NO NEED.
I GOT IT CHECKED OUT IN YOKO-SUKA.
WHILE I WAS WAITING FOR YOU, I TALKED TO A SURGEON.
REALLY?!
WHAT DID HE SAY?

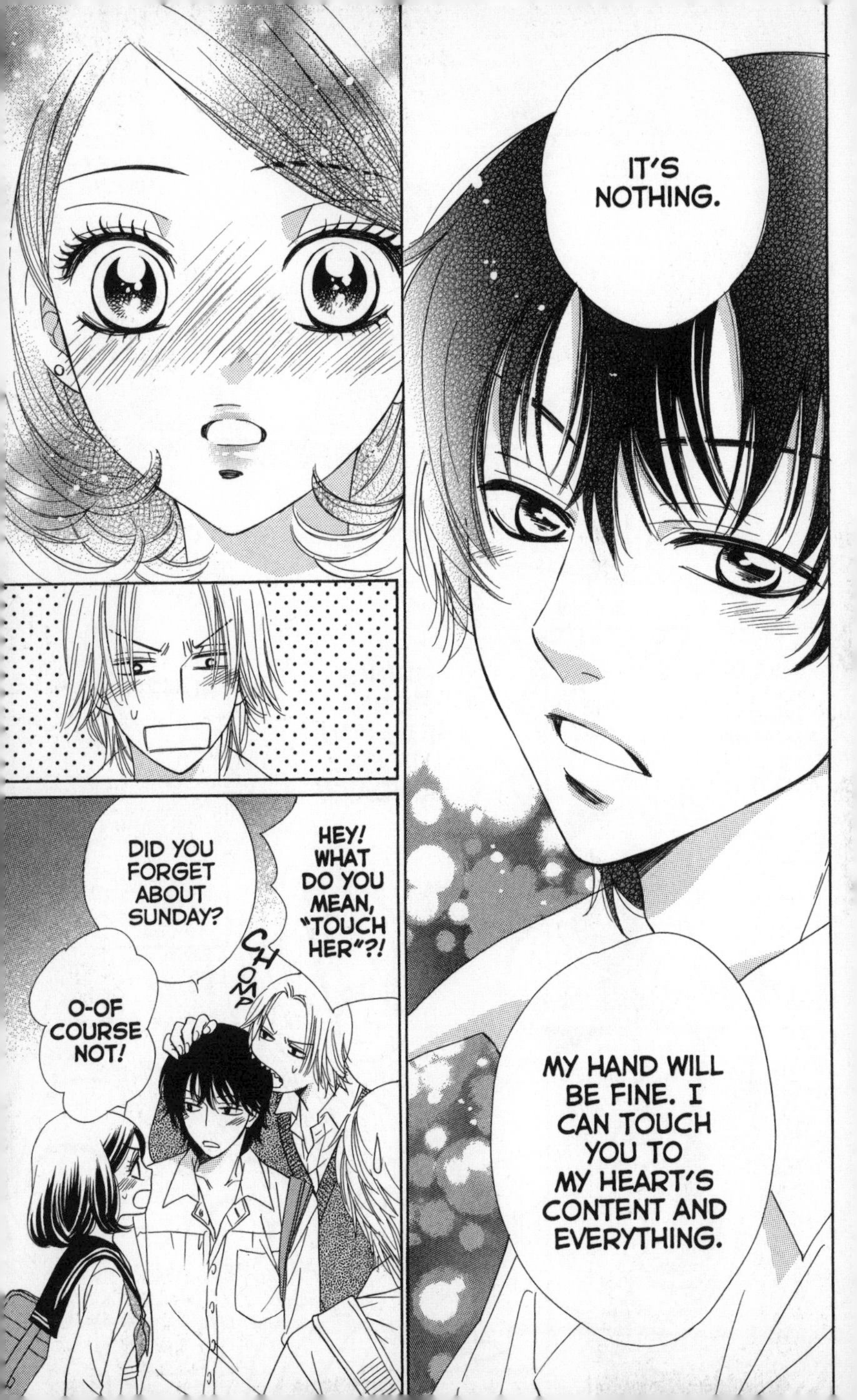
IT'S NOTHING.
MY HAND WILL BE FINE. I CAN TOUCH YOU TO MY HEART'S CONTENT AND EVERYTHING.
HEY! WHAT DO YOU MEAN, "TOUCH HER"?!
DID YOU FORGET ABOUT SUNDAY?
CHOMP
O-OF COURSE NOT!

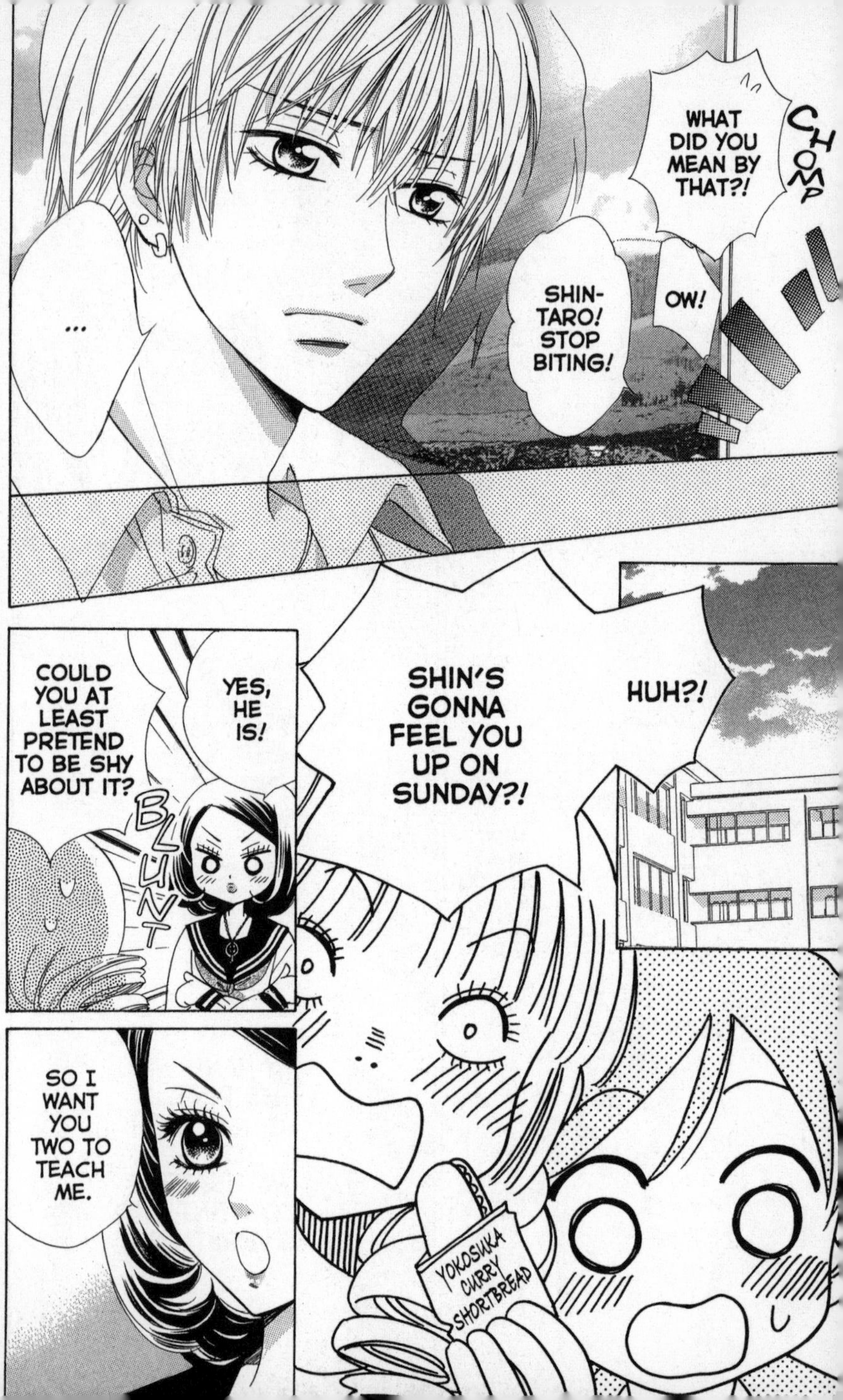
WHAT DID YOU MEAN BY THAT?!
CHOMP
OW!
SHIN-TARO! STOP BITING!
...
HUH?!
SHIN'S GONNA FEEL YOU UP ON SUNDAY?!
YOKOSUKA CURRY SHORTBREAD
YES, HE IS!
COULD YOU AT LEAST PRETEND TO BE SHY ABOUT IT?
BLUNT
SO I WANT YOU TWO TO TEACH ME.

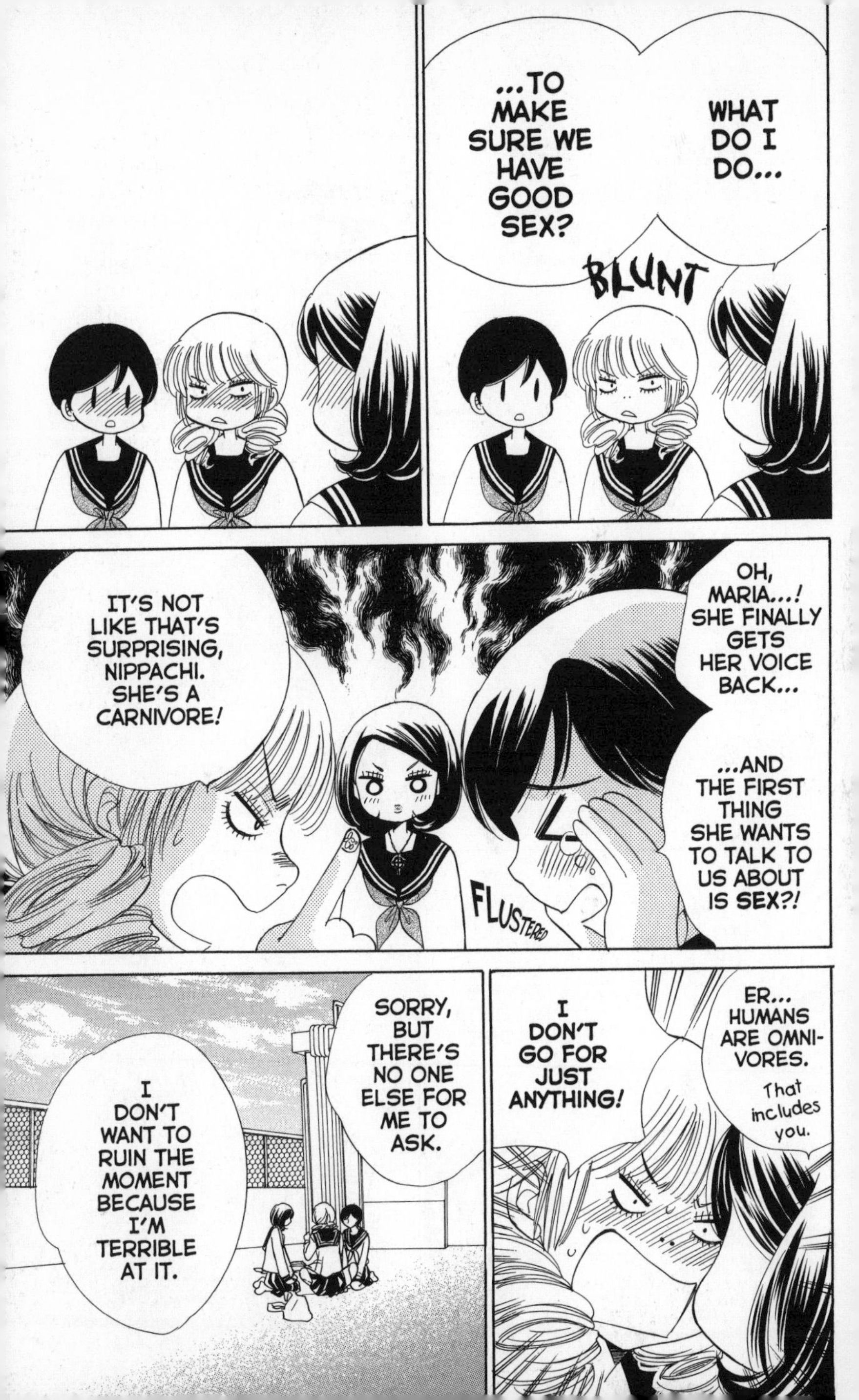
WHAT DO I DO...
...TO MAKE SURE WE HAVE GOOD SEX?
BLUNT
OH, MARIA...! SHE FINALLY GETS HER VOICE BACK...
...AND THE FIRST THING SHE WANTS TO TALK TO US ABOUT IS SEX?!
FLUSTERED
IT'S NOT LIKE THAT'S SURPRISING, NIPPACHI. SHE'S A CARNIVORE!
ER... HUMANS ARE OMNI-VORES.
That includes you.
I DON'T GO FOR JUST ANYTHING!
SORRY, BUT THERE'S NO ONE ELSE FOR ME TO ASK.
I DON'T WANT TO RUIN THE MOMENT BECAUSE I'M TERRIBLE AT IT.

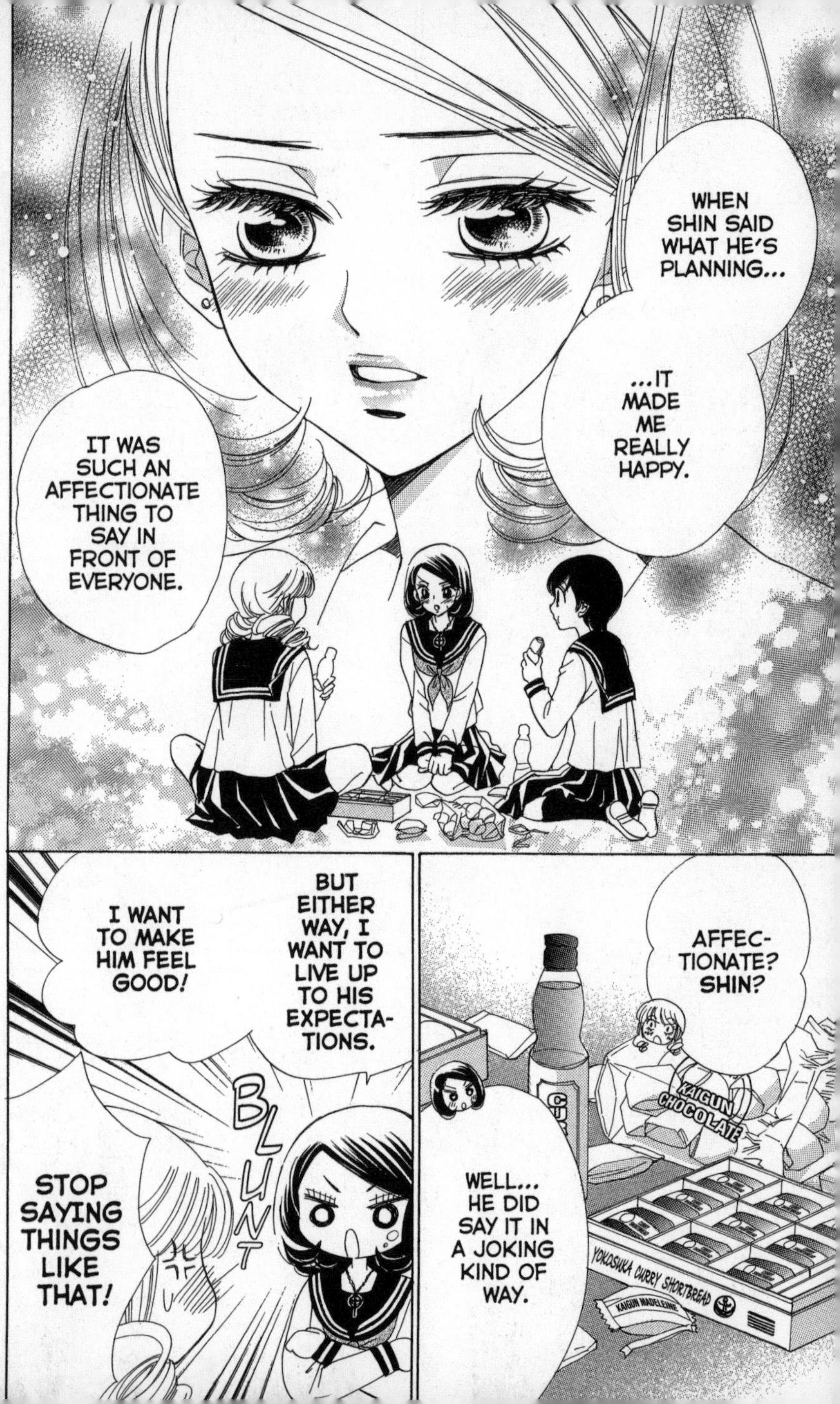
WHEN SHIN SAID WHAT HE'S PLANNING...
...IT MADE ME REALLY HAPPY.
IT WAS SUCH AN AFFECTIONATE THING TO SAY IN FRONT OF EVERYONE.
AFFEC-TIONATE? SHIN?
KAIGUN CHOCOLATE
WELL... HE DID SAY IT IN A JOKING KIND OF WAY.
YOKOSUKA CURRY SHORTBREAD
KAIGUN MADELEINE
BUT EITHER WAY, I WANT TO LIVE UP TO HIS EXPECTA-TIONS.
I WANT TO MAKE HIM FEEL GOOD!
BLUNT
STOP SAYING THINGS LIKE THAT!

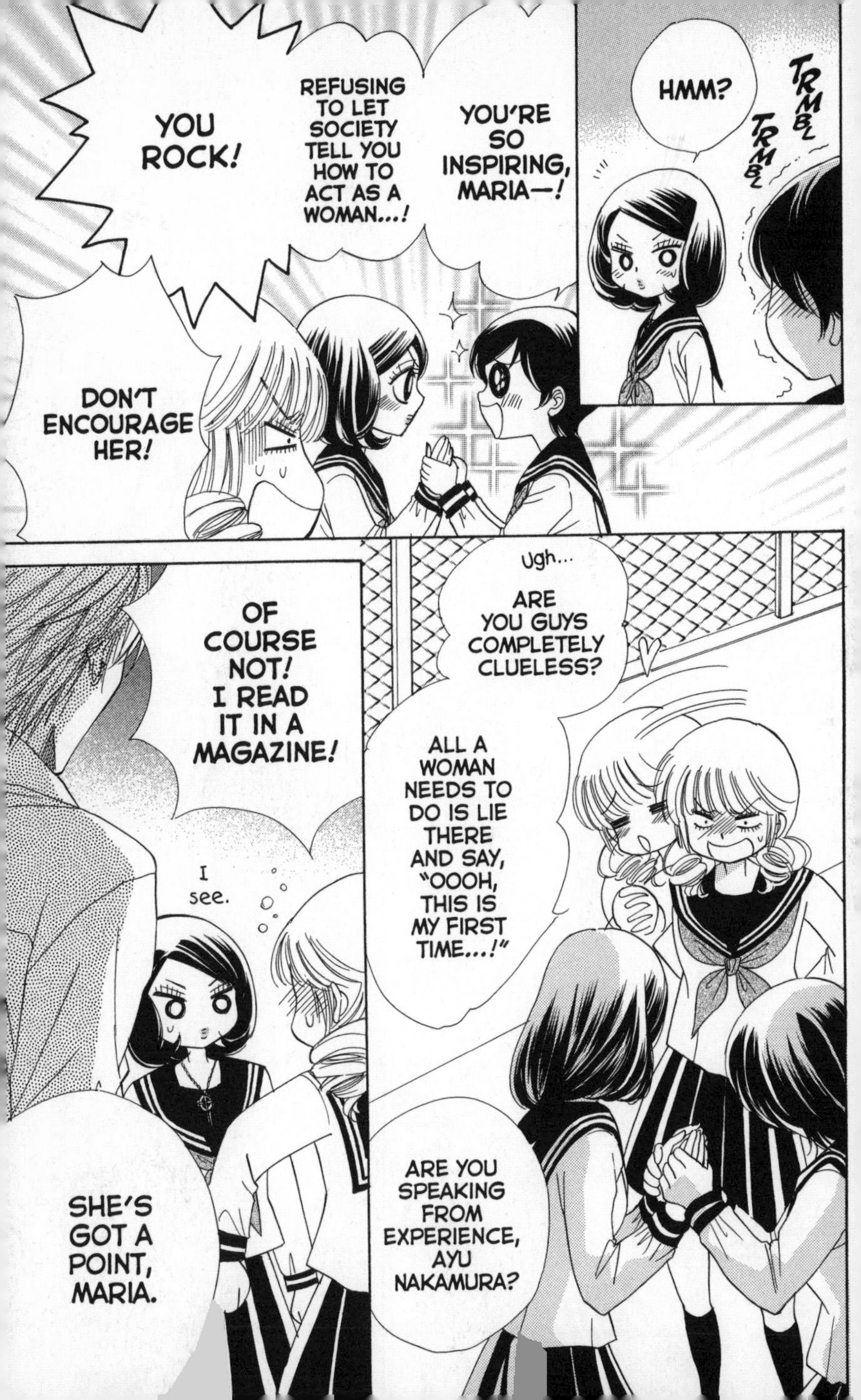
TRMBL
TRMBL
HMM?
YOU'RE SO INSPIRING, MARIA—!
REFUSING TO LET SOCIETY TELL YOU HOW TO ACT AS A WOMAN...!
YOU ROCK!
DON'T ENCOURAGE HER!
Ugh...
ARE YOU GUYS COMPLETELY CLUELESS?
ALL A WOMAN NEEDS TO DO IS LIE THERE AND SAY, "OOOH, THIS IS MY FIRST TIME...!"
ARE YOU SPEAKING FROM EXPERIENCE, AYU NAKAMURA?
OF COURSE NOT! I READ IT IN A MAGAZINE!
I see.
SHE'S GOT A POINT, MARIA.

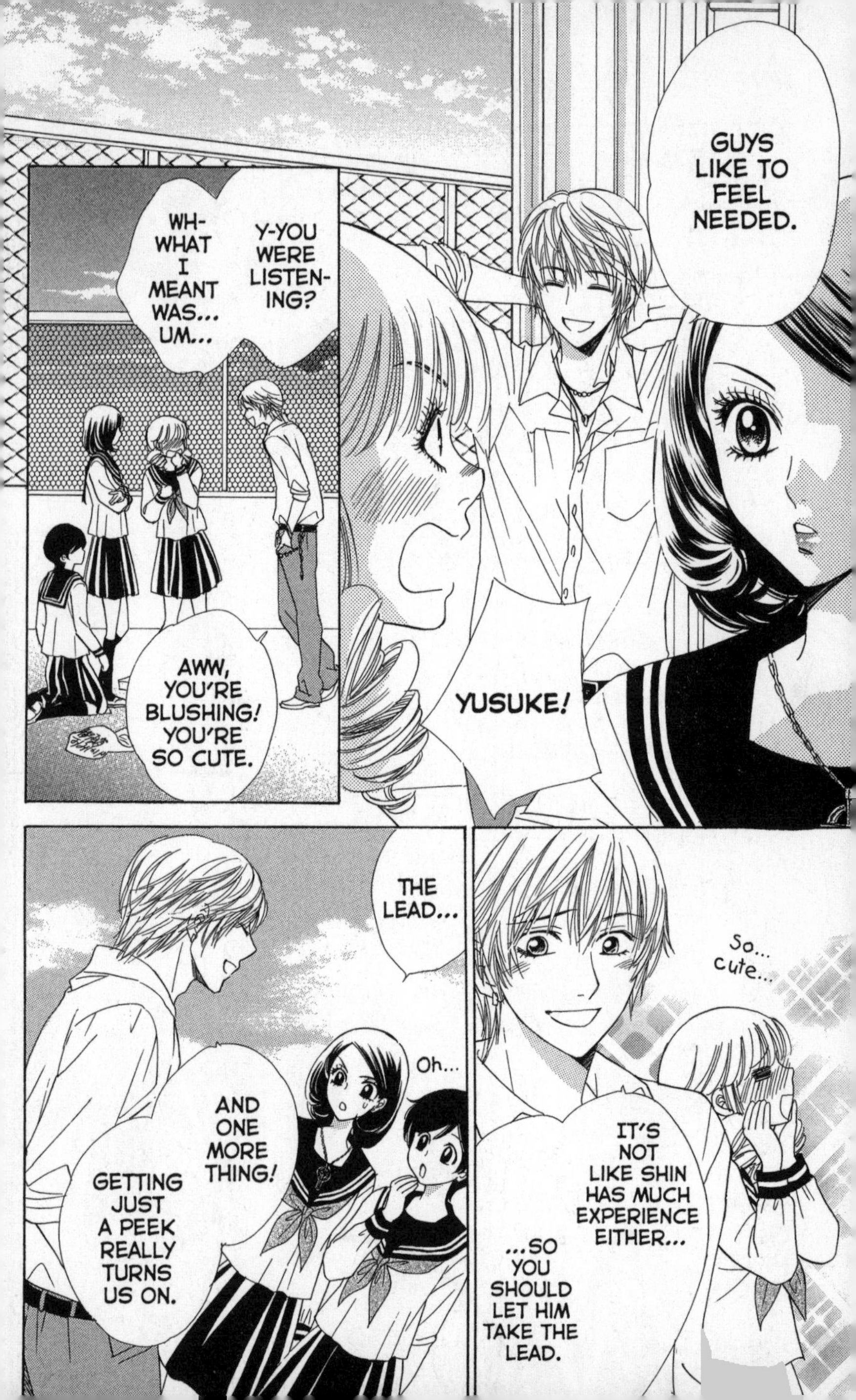
GUYS LIKE TO FEEL NEEDED.
YUSUKE!
Y-YOU WERE LISTENING?
WH-WHAT I MEANT WAS... UM...
AWW, YOU'RE BLUSHING! YOU'RE SO CUTE.
So... cute...
IT'S NOT LIKE SHIN HAS MUCH EXPERIENCE EITHER...
...SO YOU SHOULD LET HIM TAKE THE LEAD.
THE LEAD...
Oh...
AND ONE MORE THING!
GETTING JUST A PEEK REALLY TURNS US ON.

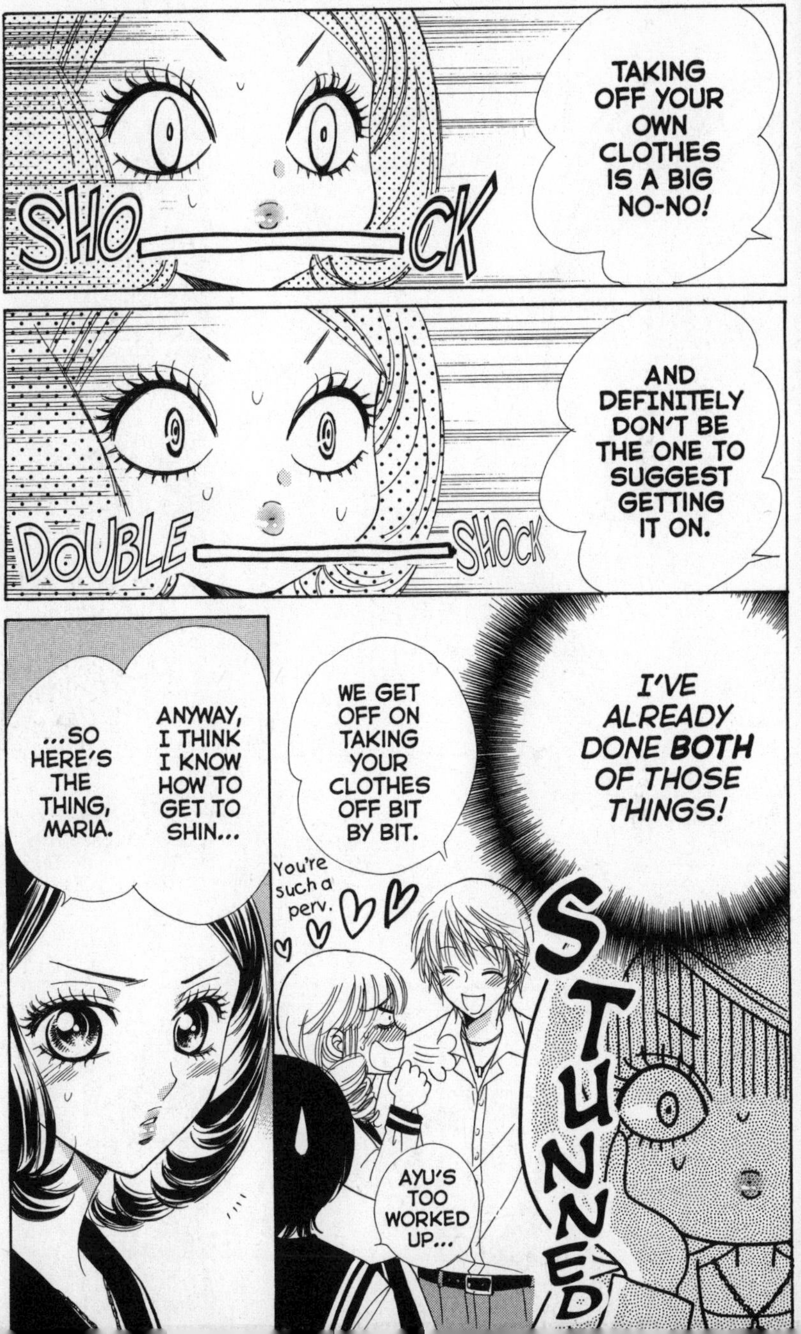
TAKING OFF YOUR OWN CLOTHES IS A BIG NO-NO!
SHOCK
AND DEFINITELY DON'T BE THE ONE TO SUGGEST GETTING IT ON.
DOUBLE SHOCK
*I'VE ALREADY DONE **BOTH** OF THOSE THINGS!*
STUNNED
WE GET OFF ON TAKING YOUR CLOTHES OFF BIT BY BIT.
You're such a perv.
AYU'S TOO WORKED UP...
ANYWAY, I THINK I KNOW HOW TO GET TO SHIN...
...SO HERE'S THE THING, MARIA.

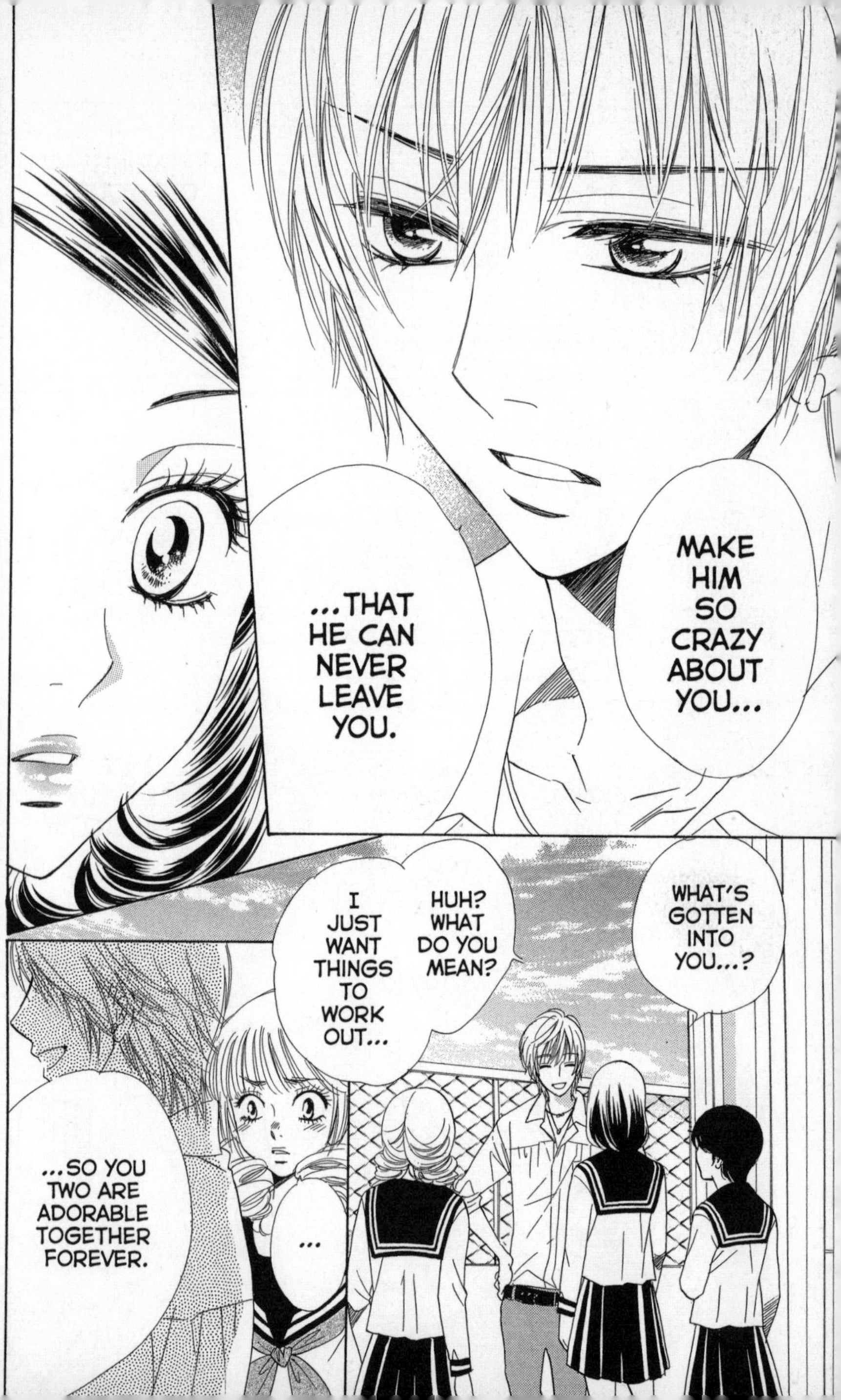
MAKE HIM SO CRAZY ABOUT YOU...
...THAT HE CAN NEVER LEAVE YOU.
WHAT'S GOTTEN INTO YOU...?
HUH? WHAT DO YOU MEAN?
I JUST WANT THINGS TO WORK OUT...
...
...SO YOU TWO ARE ADORABLE TOGETHER FOREVER.

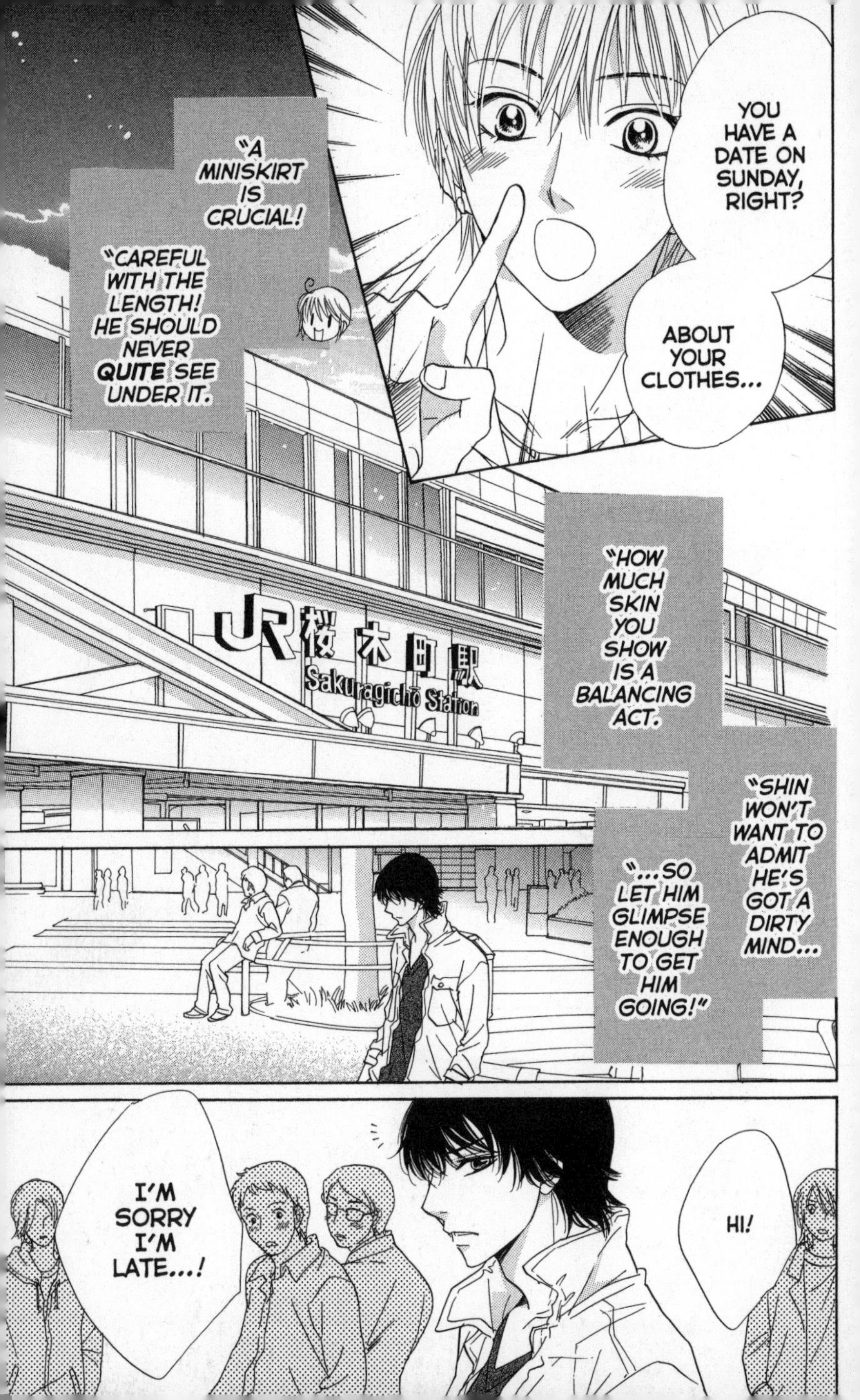
YOU HAVE A DATE ON SUNDAY, RIGHT?
ABOUT YOUR CLOTHES...
"A MINISKIRT IS CRUCIAL!
"CAREFUL WITH THE LENGTH! HE SHOULD NEVER QUITE SEE UNDER IT.
JR 桜木町駅
Sakuragichō Station
"HOW MUCH SKIN YOU SHOW IS A BALANCING ACT.
"SHIN WON'T WANT TO ADMIT HE'S GOT A DIRTY MIND...
"...SO LET HIM GLIMPSE ENOUGH TO GET HIM GOING!"
HI!
I'M SORRY I'M LATE...!

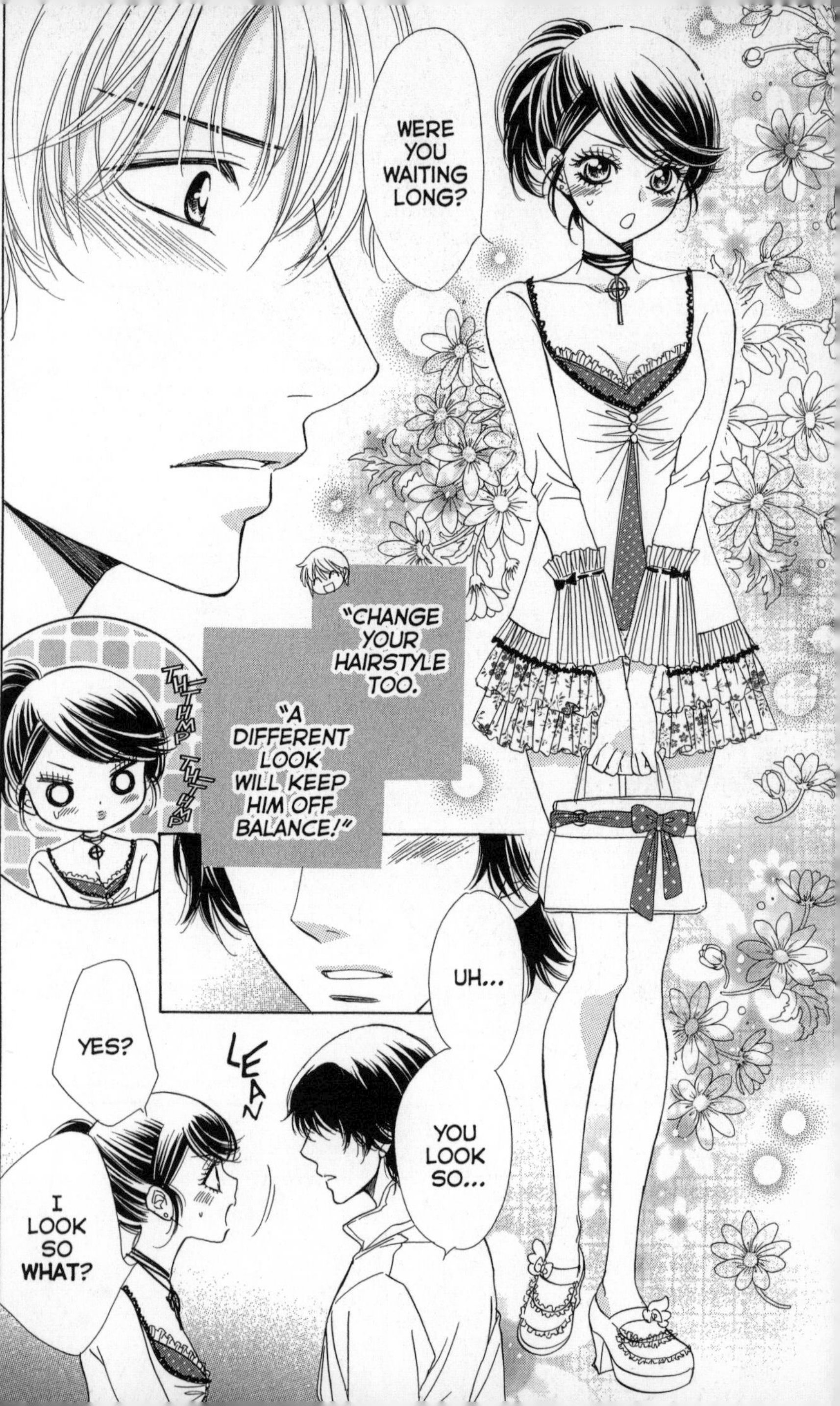
WERE YOU WAITING LONG?
"CHANGE YOUR HAIRSTYLE TOO.
"A DIFFERENT LOOK WILL KEEP HIM OFF BALANCE!"
TH-THUMP TH-THUMP
UH...
YOU LOOK SO...
YES?
LEAN
I LOOK SO WHAT?

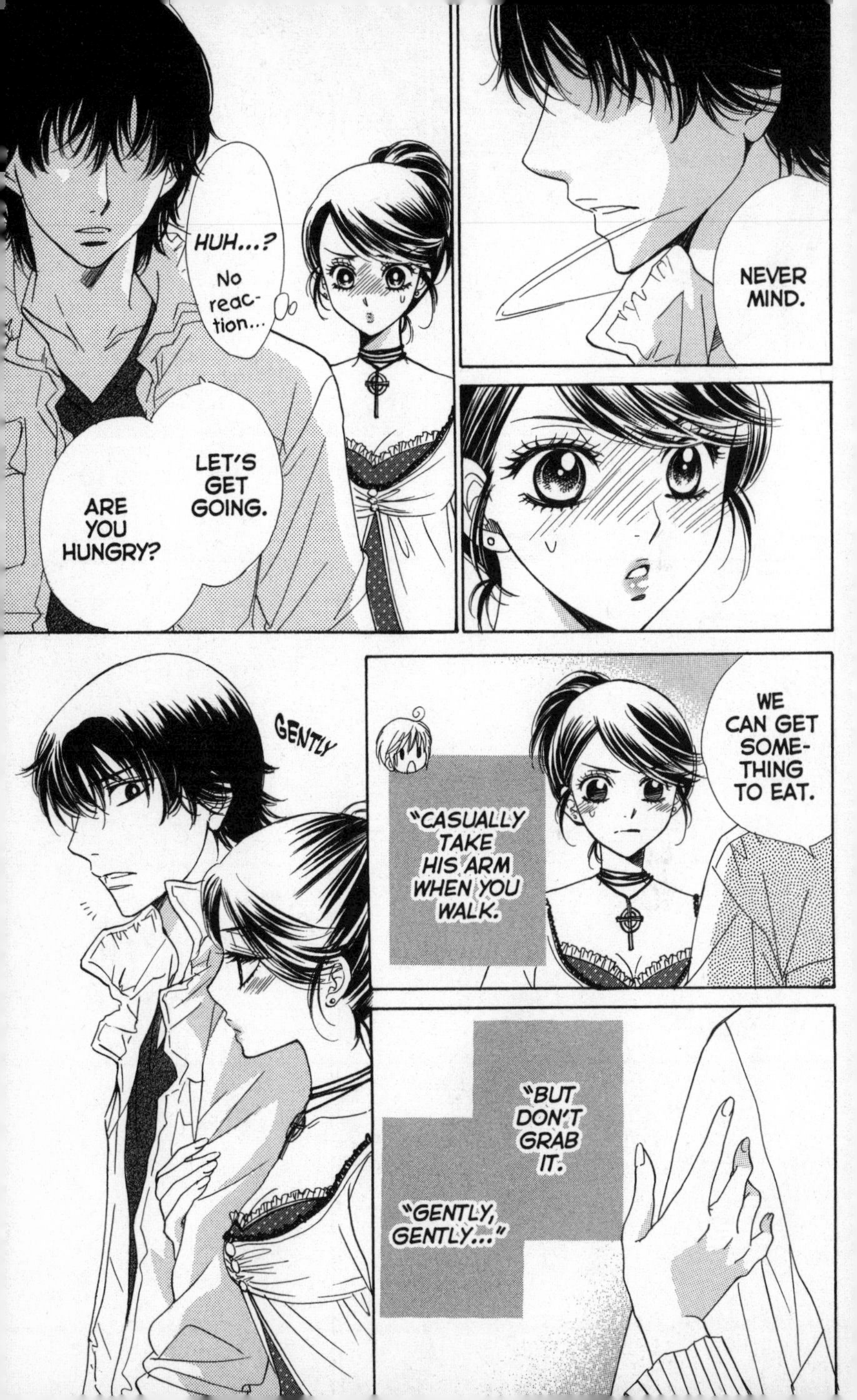
NEVER MIND.
HUH...? No reaction...
LET'S GET GOING.
ARE YOU HUNGRY?
WE CAN GET SOMETHING TO EAT.
"CASUALLY TAKE HIS ARM WHEN YOU WALK.
"BUT DON'T GRAB IT.
"GENTLY, GENTLY..."
GENTLY

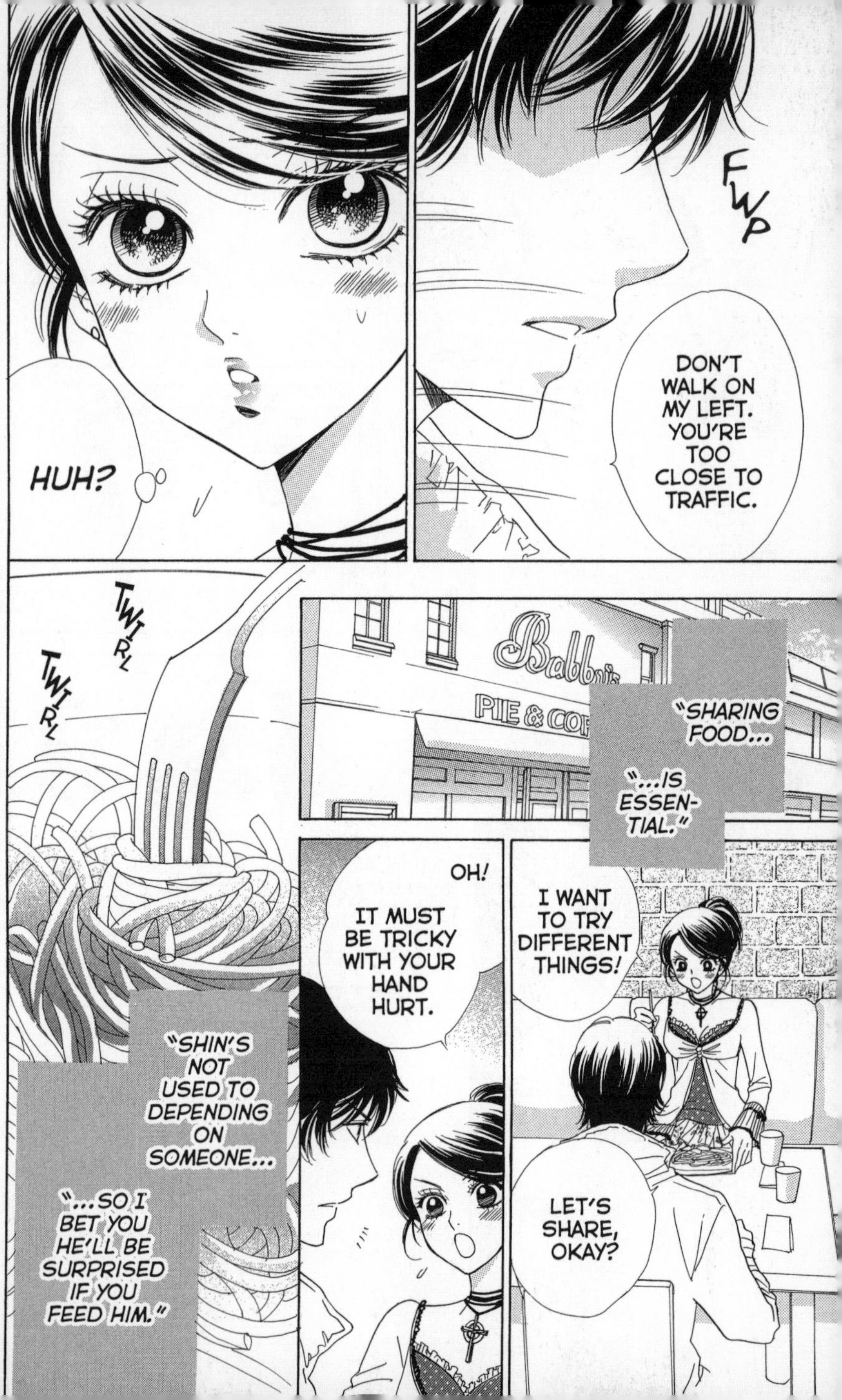
FWP
DON'T WALK ON MY LEFT. YOU'RE TOO CLOSE TO TRAFFIC.
HUH?
"SHARING FOOD...
"...IS ESSEN-TIAL."
I WANT TO TRY DIFFERENT THINGS!
LET'S SHARE, OKAY?
OH!
IT MUST BE TRICKY WITH YOUR HAND HURT.
TWIRL
TWIRL
"SHIN'S NOT USED TO DEPENDING ON SOMEONE...
"...SO I BET YOU HE'LL BE SURPRISED IF YOU FEED HIM."

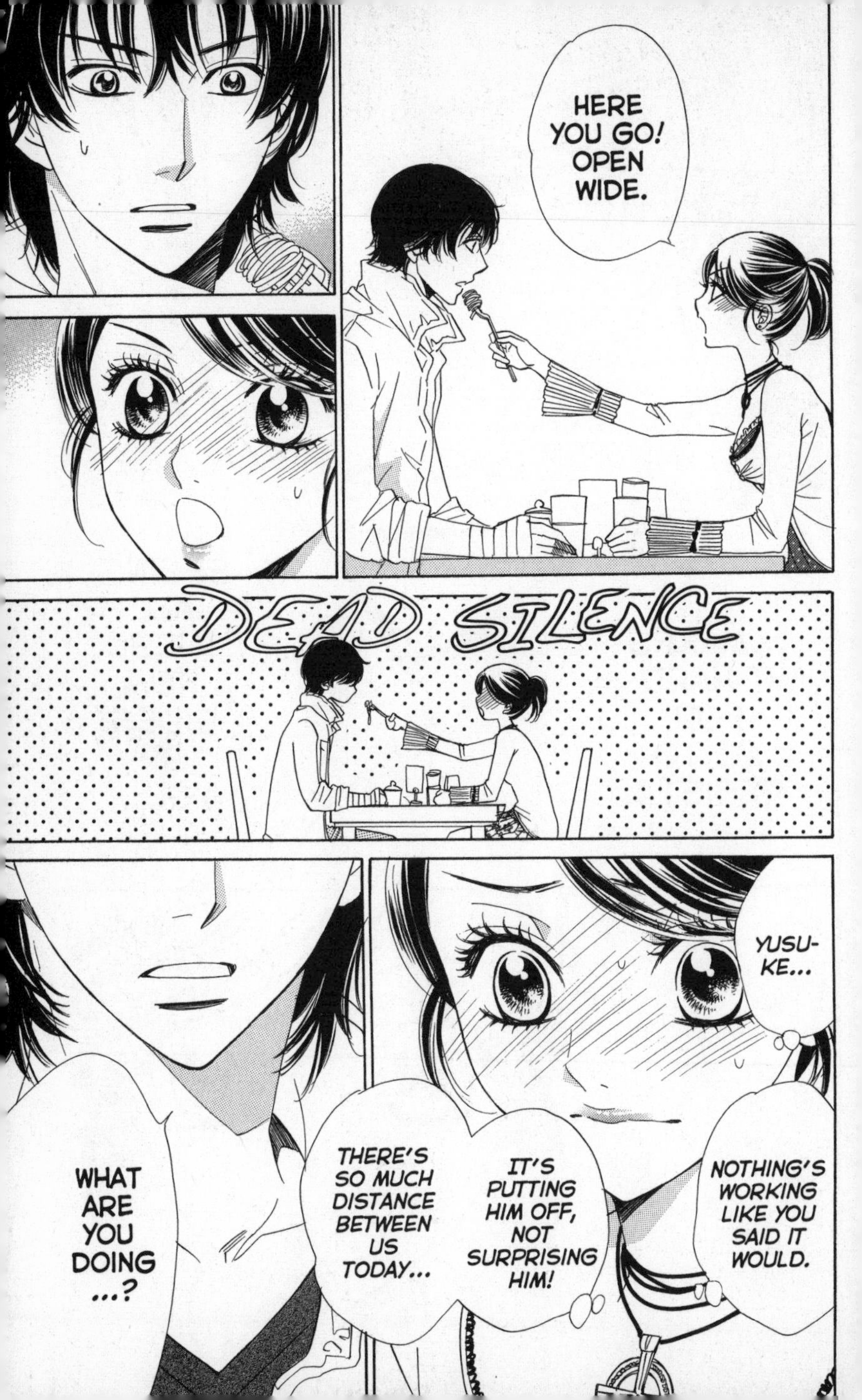
HERE YOU GO! OPEN WIDE.
DEAD SILENCE
YUSU-KE...
NOTHING'S WORKING LIKE YOU SAID IT WOULD.
IT'S PUTTING HIM OFF, NOT SURPRISING HIM!
THERE'S SO MUCH DISTANCE BETWEEN US TODAY...
WHAT ARE YOU DOING ...?

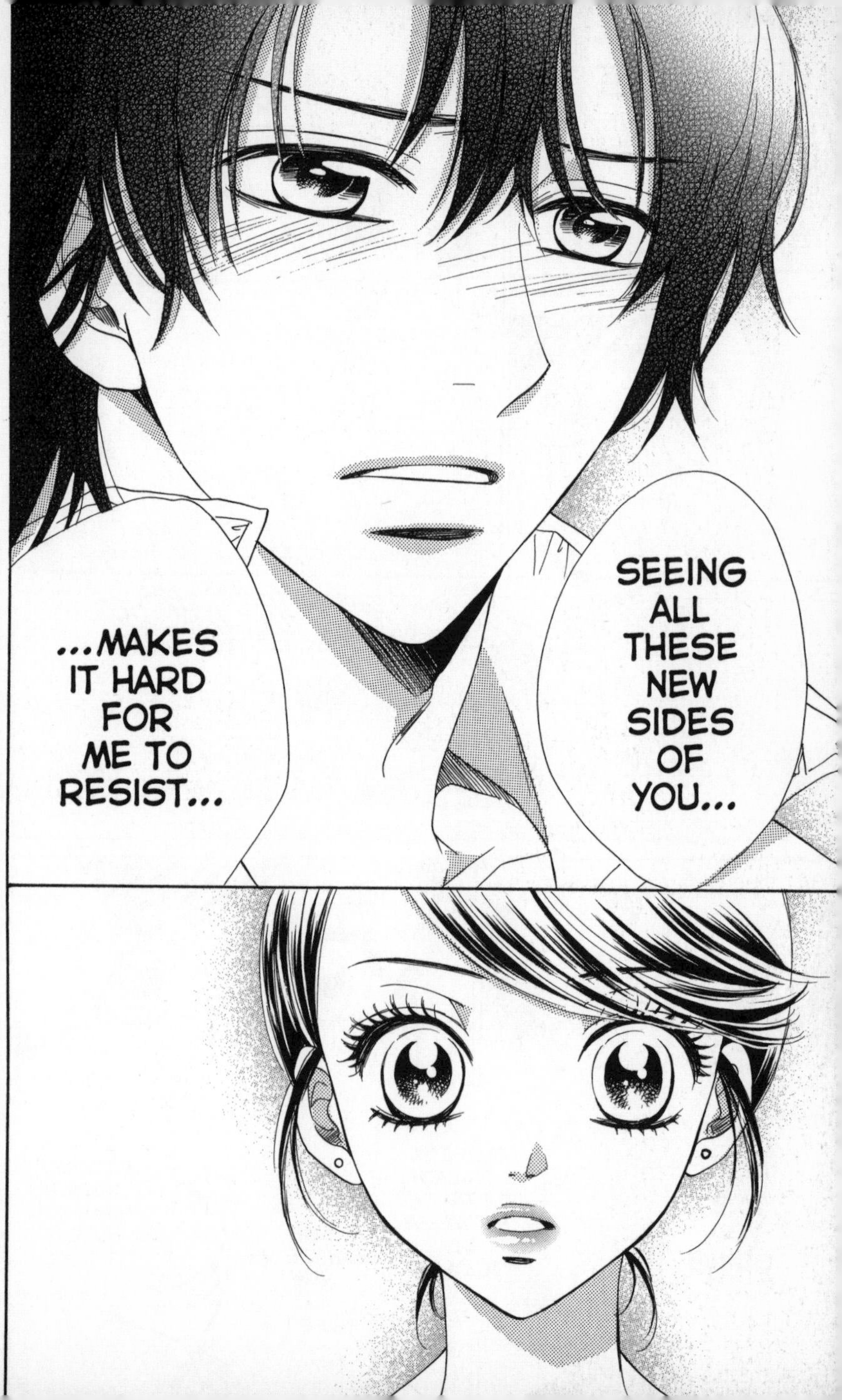
SEEING ALL THESE NEW SIDES OF YOU...
...MAKES IT HARD FOR ME TO RESIST...

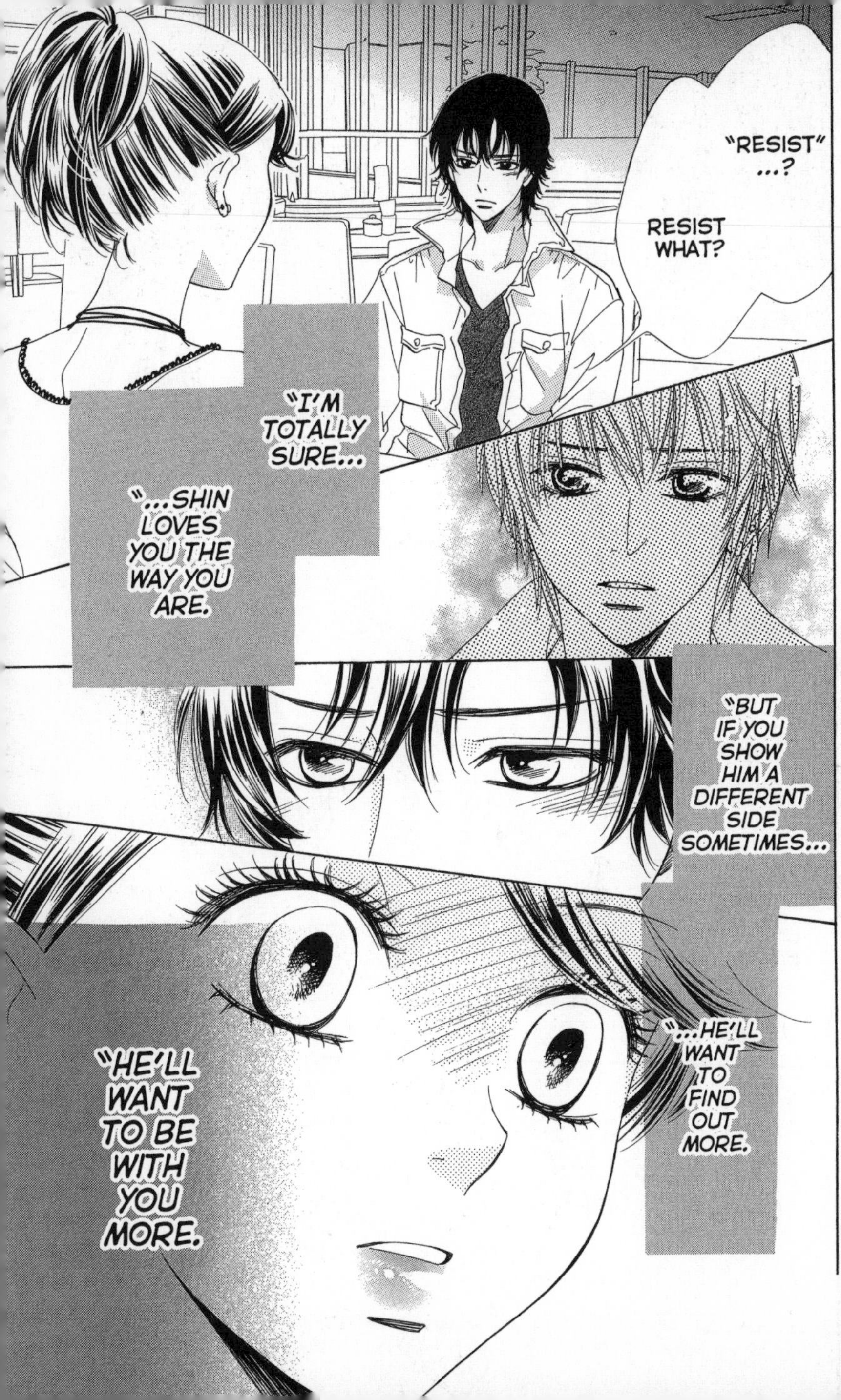
"RESIST" ...?
RESIST WHAT?
"I'M TOTALLY SURE...
"...SHIN LOVES YOU THE WAY YOU ARE.
"BUT IF YOU SHOW HIM A DIFFERENT SIDE SOMETIMES...
"...HE'LL WANT TO FIND OUT MORE.
"HE'LL WANT TO BE WITH YOU MORE.

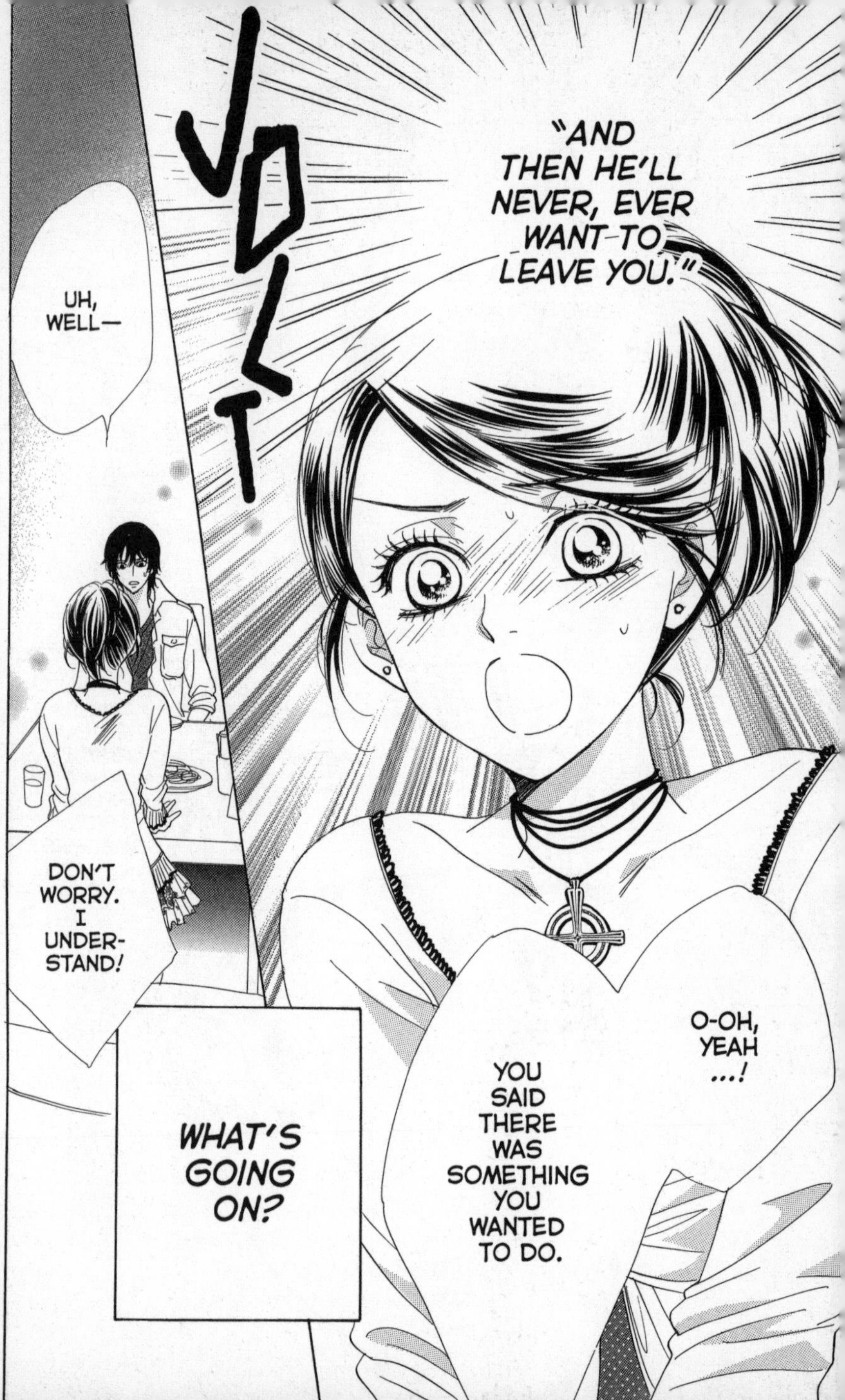
"AND THEN HE'LL NEVER, EVER WANT TO LEAVE YOU."
JOLT
O-OH, YEAH ...!
YOU SAID THERE WAS SOMETHING YOU WANTED TO DO.
UH, WELL—
DON'T WORRY. I UNDER-STAND!
WHAT'S GOING ON?

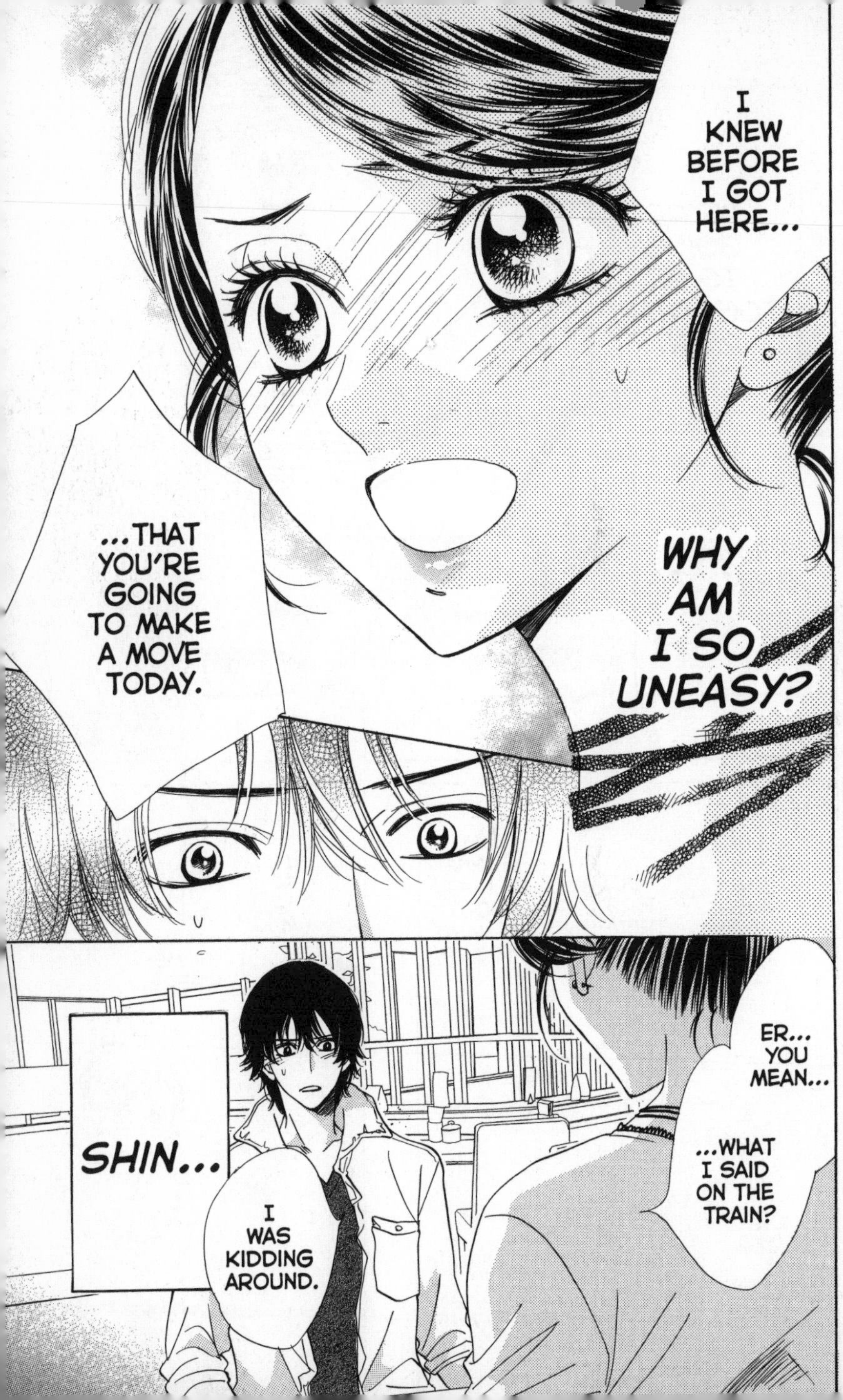
I KNEW BEFORE I GOT HERE...
...THAT YOU'RE GOING TO MAKE A MOVE TODAY.
WHY AM I SO UNEASY?
ER... YOU MEAN...
...WHAT I SAID ON THE TRAIN?
SHIN...
I WAS KIDDING AROUND.

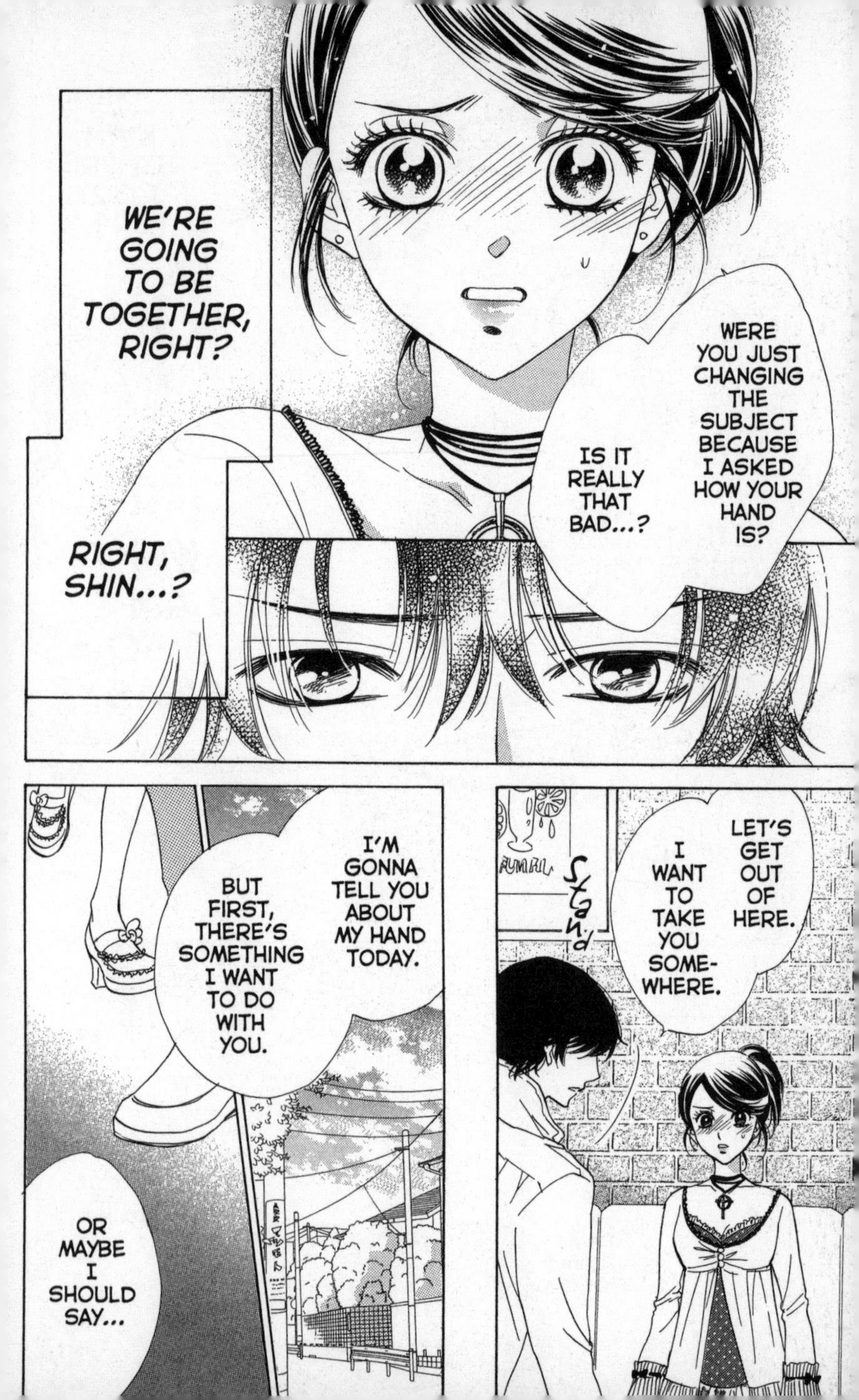
WERE YOU JUST CHANGING THE SUBJECT BECAUSE I ASKED HOW YOUR HAND IS?
IS IT REALLY THAT BAD...?
WE'RE GOING TO BE TOGETHER, RIGHT?
RIGHT, SHIN...?
Stand
LET'S GET OUT OF HERE.
I WANT TO TAKE YOU SOME-WHERE.
I'M GONNA TELL YOU ABOUT MY HAND TODAY.
BUT FIRST, THERE'S SOMETHING I WANT TO DO WITH YOU.
OR MAYBE I SHOULD SAY...

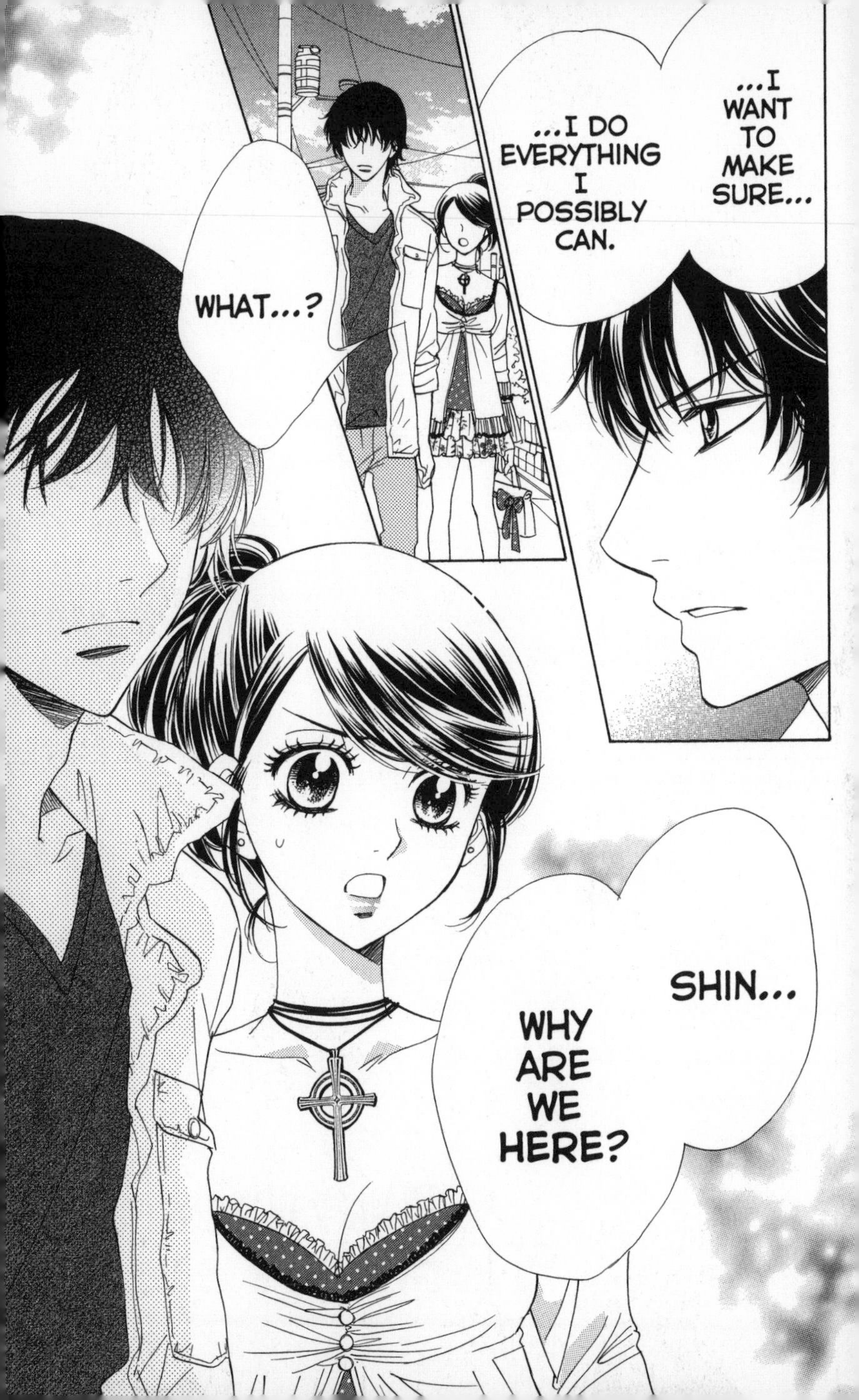
...I WANT TO MAKE SURE...
...I DO EVERYTHING I POSSIBLY CAN.
WHAT...?
SHIN...
WHY ARE WE HERE?

A Devil and Her Love Song

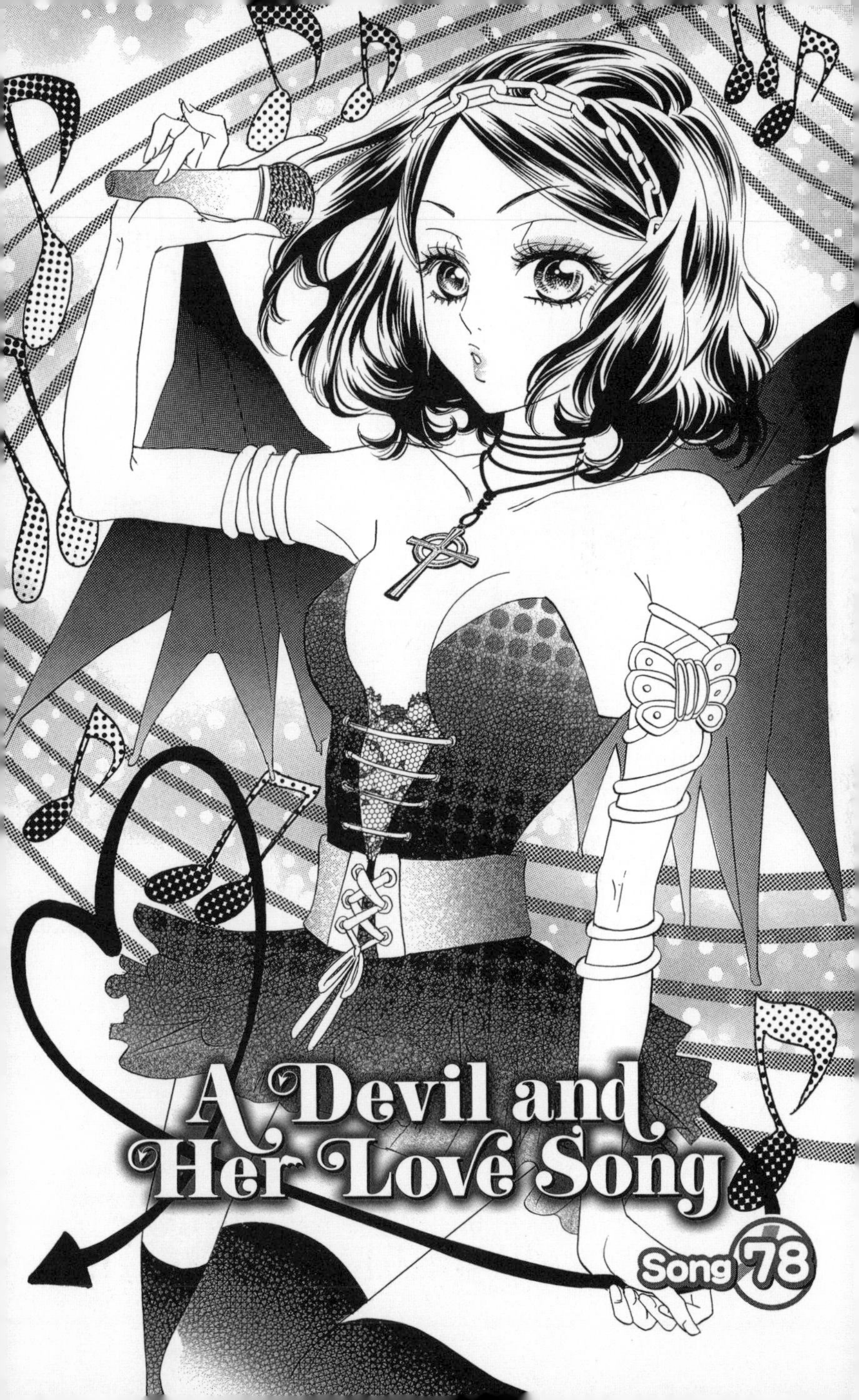
A Devil and Her Love Song
Song 78

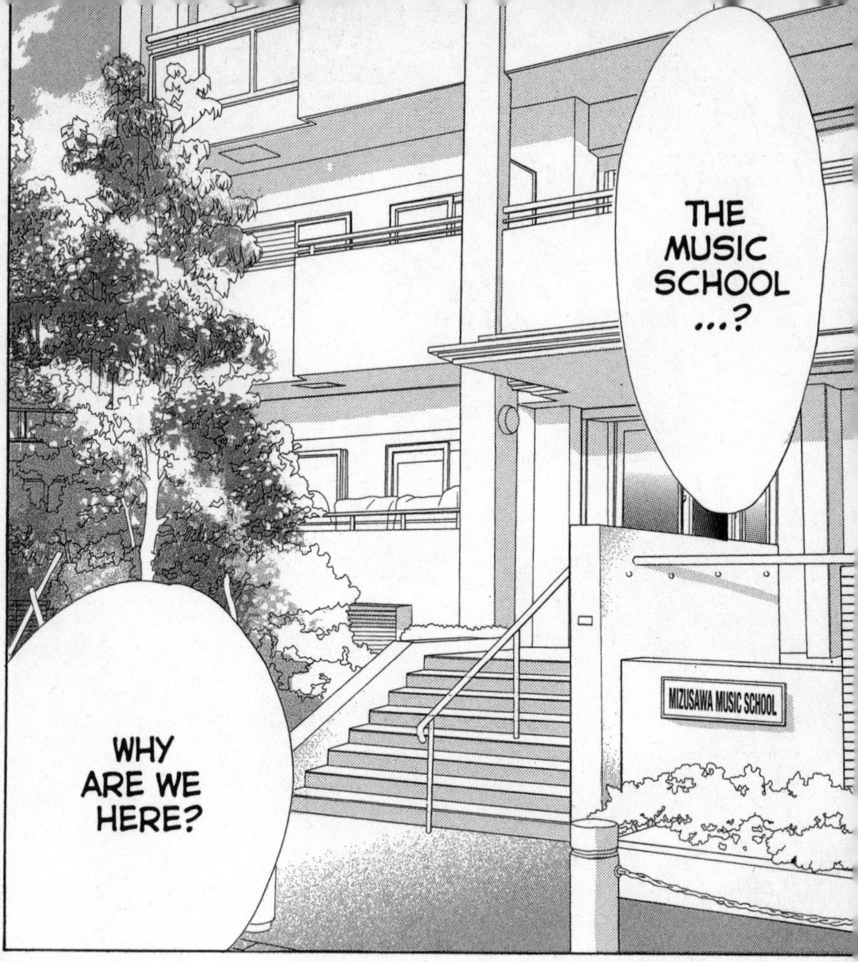
THE MUSIC SCHOOL ...?
MIZUSAWA MUSIC SCHOOL
WHY ARE WE HERE?

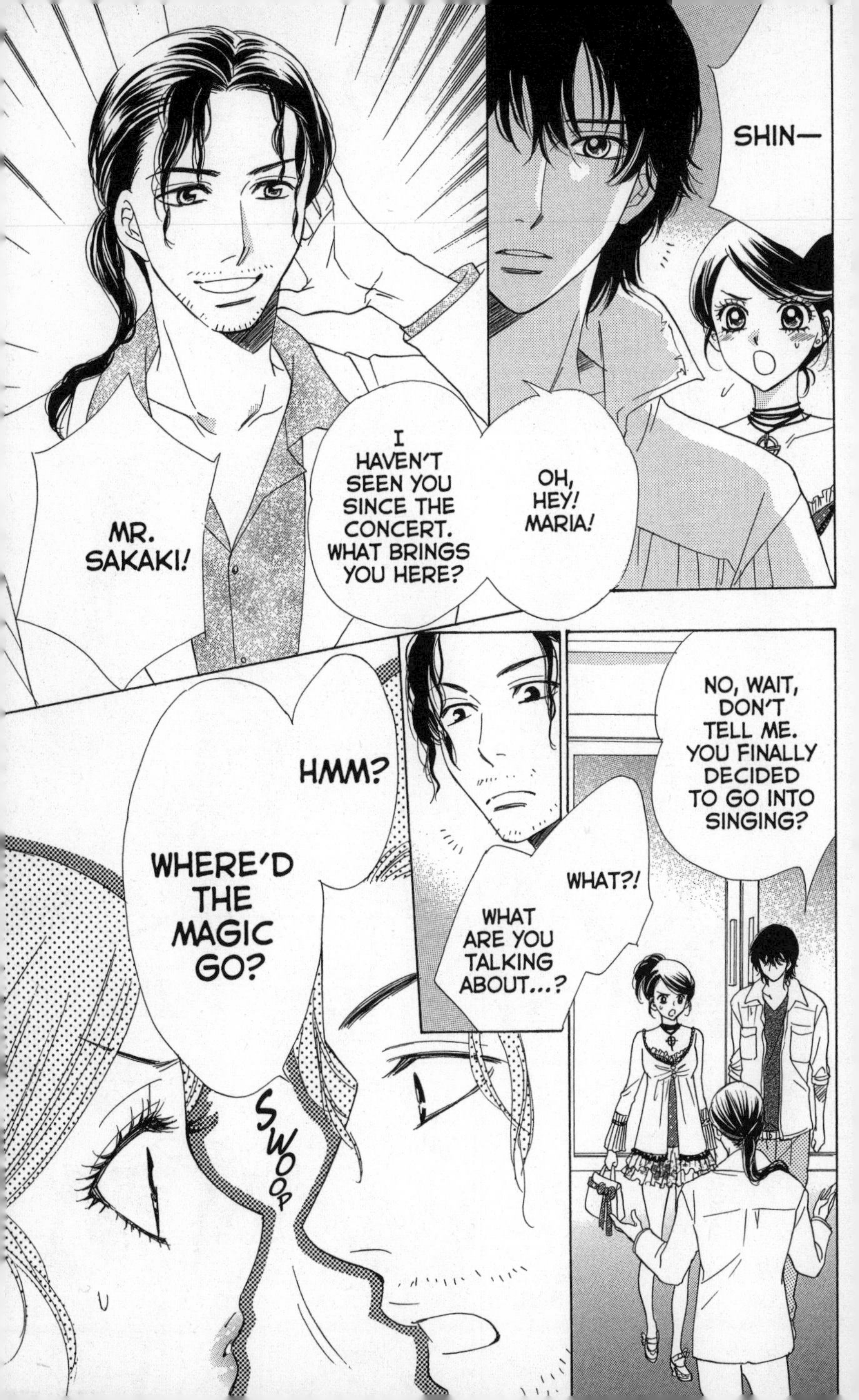

SHIN—
OH, HEY! MARIA!
I HAVEN'T SEEN YOU SINCE THE CONCERT. WHAT BRINGS YOU HERE?
MR. SAKAKI!
NO, WAIT, DON'T TELL ME. YOU FINALLY DECIDED TO GO INTO SINGING?
WHAT?!
WHAT ARE YOU TALKING ABOUT...?
HMM?
WHERE'D THE MAGIC GO?
SWOOP

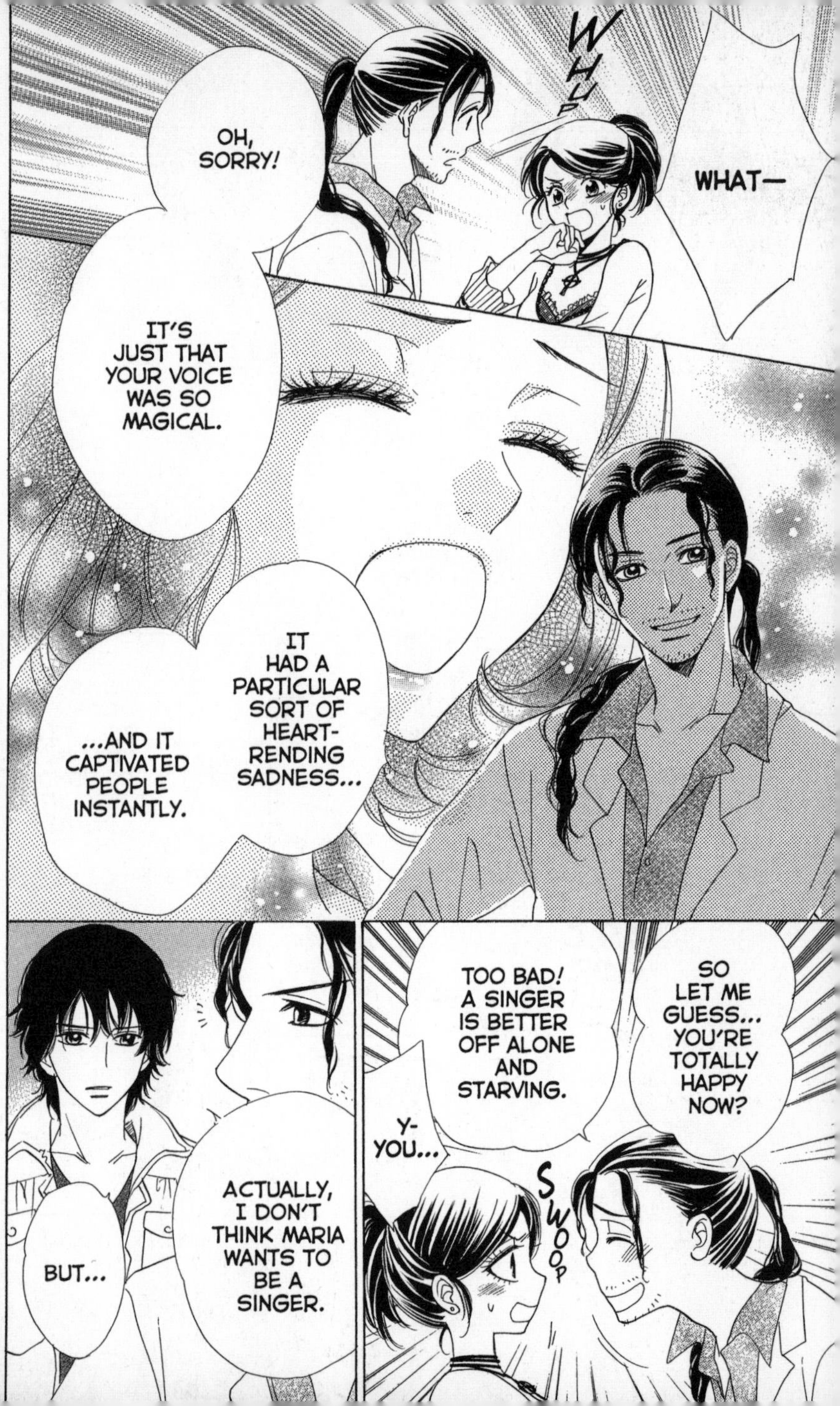
WHAT—
WHUP
OH, SORRY!
IT'S JUST THAT YOUR VOICE WAS SO MAGICAL.
IT HAD A PARTICULAR SORT OF HEART-RENDING SADNESS...
...AND IT CAPTIVATED PEOPLE INSTANTLY.
SO LET ME GUESS... YOU'RE TOTALLY HAPPY NOW?
TOO BAD! A SINGER IS BETTER OFF ALONE AND STARVING.
Y-YOU...
SWOOP
ACTUALLY, I DON'T THINK MARIA WANTS TO BE A SINGER.
BUT...

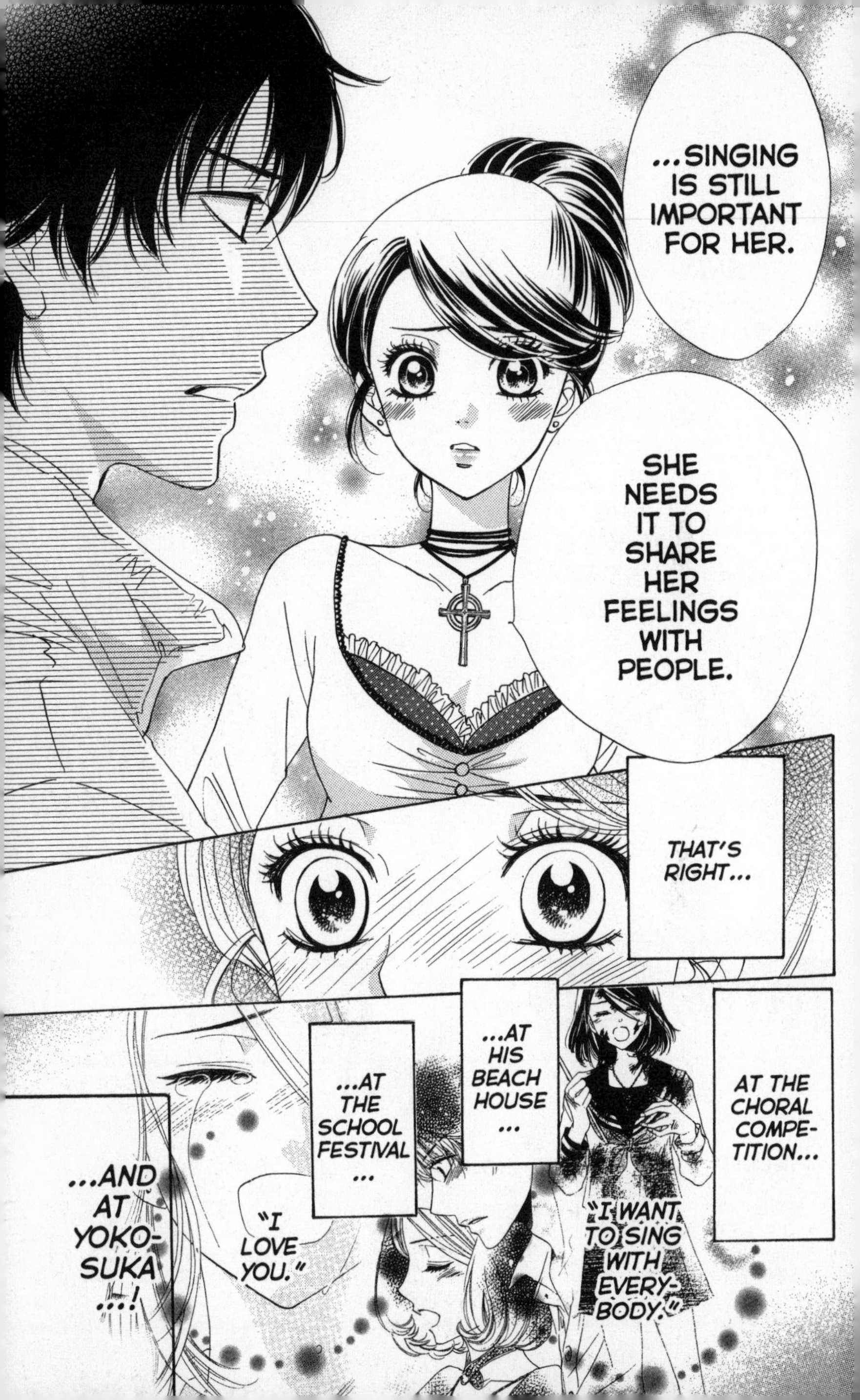
...SINGING IS STILL IMPORTANT FOR HER.
SHE NEEDS IT TO SHARE HER FEELINGS WITH PEOPLE.
THAT'S RIGHT...
AT THE CHORAL COMPE-TITION...
"I WANT TO SING WITH EVERY-BODY."
...AT HIS BEACH HOUSE ...
...AT THE SCHOOL FESTIVAL ...
"I LOVE YOU."
...AND AT YOKO-SUKA ...!

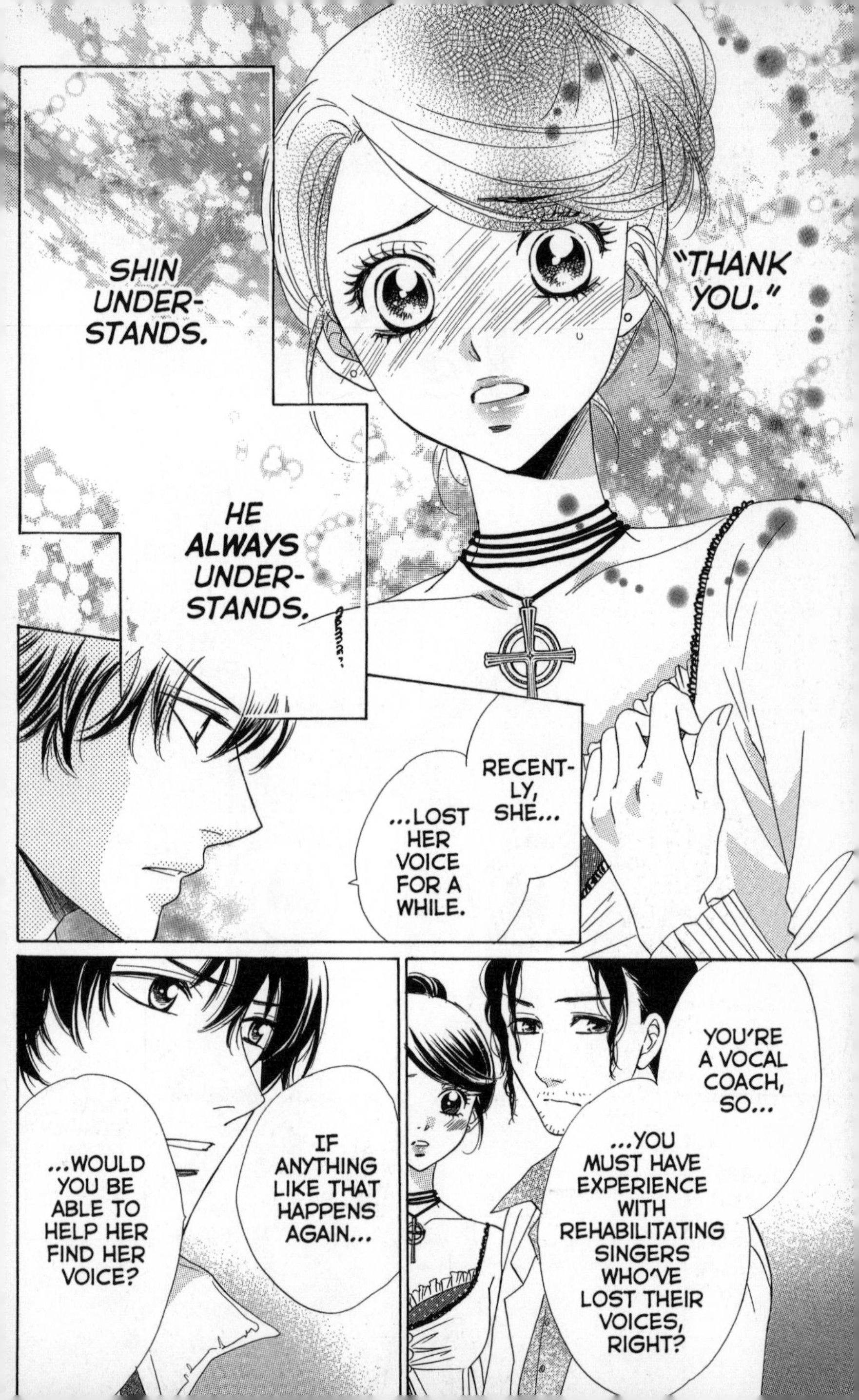
"THANK YOU."
SHIN UNDERSTANDS.
HE ALWAYS UNDERSTANDS.
RECENTLY, SHE...
...LOST HER VOICE FOR A WHILE.
YOU'RE A VOCAL COACH, SO...
...YOU MUST HAVE EXPERIENCE WITH REHABILITATING SINGERS WHO'VE LOST THEIR VOICES, RIGHT?
IF ANYTHING LIKE THAT HAPPENS AGAIN...
...WOULD YOU BE ABLE TO HELP HER FIND HER VOICE?

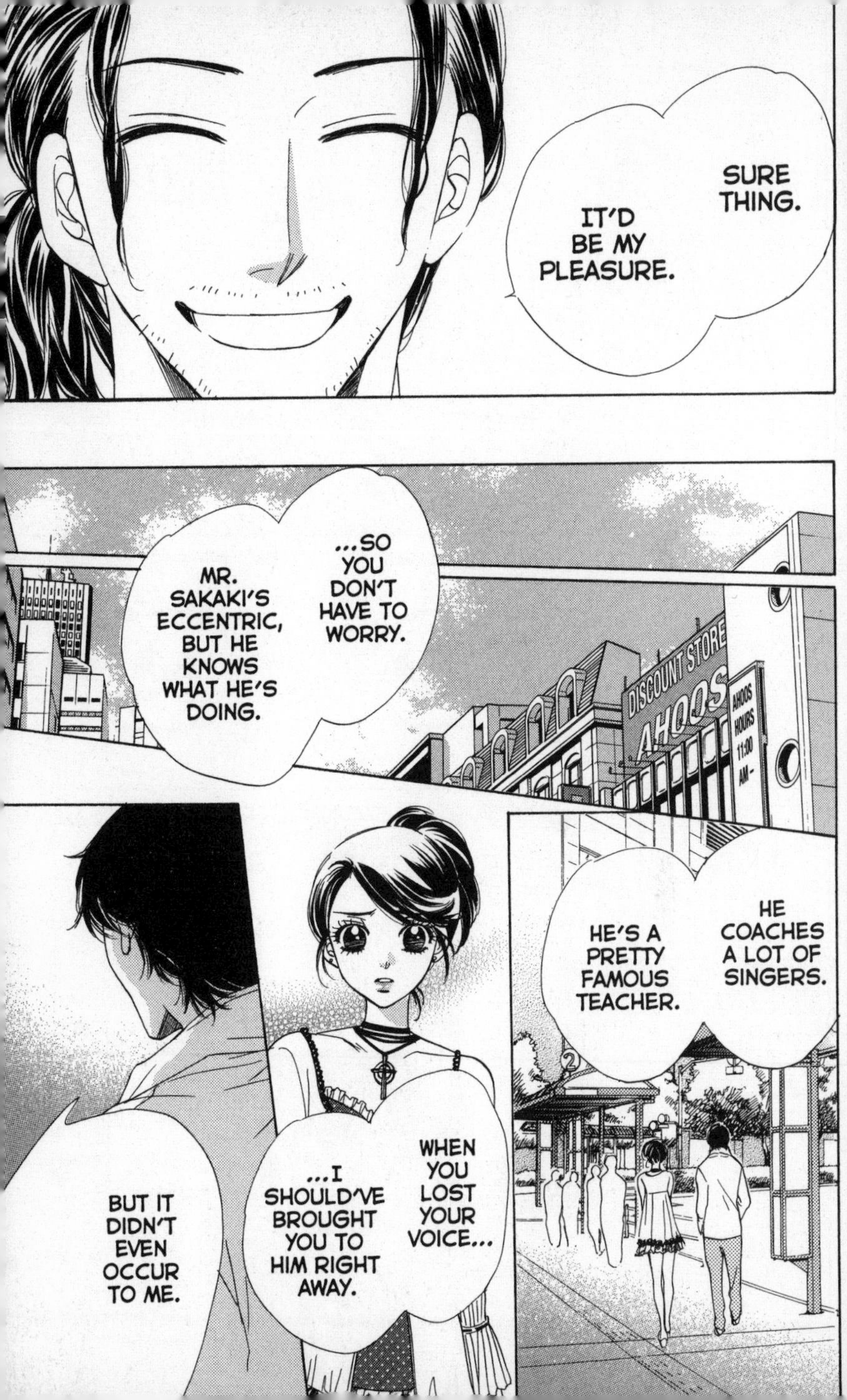
SURE THING.
IT'D BE MY PLEASURE.
MR. SAKAKI'S ECCENTRIC, BUT HE KNOWS WHAT HE'S DOING.
...SO YOU DON'T HAVE TO WORRY.
DISCOUNT STORE AHOOS
AHOOS HOURS 11:00 AM-
HE COACHES A LOT OF SINGERS.
HE'S A PRETTY FAMOUS TEACHER.
WHEN YOU LOST YOUR VOICE...
...I SHOULD'VE BROUGHT YOU TO HIM RIGHT AWAY.
BUT IT DIDN'T EVEN OCCUR TO ME.

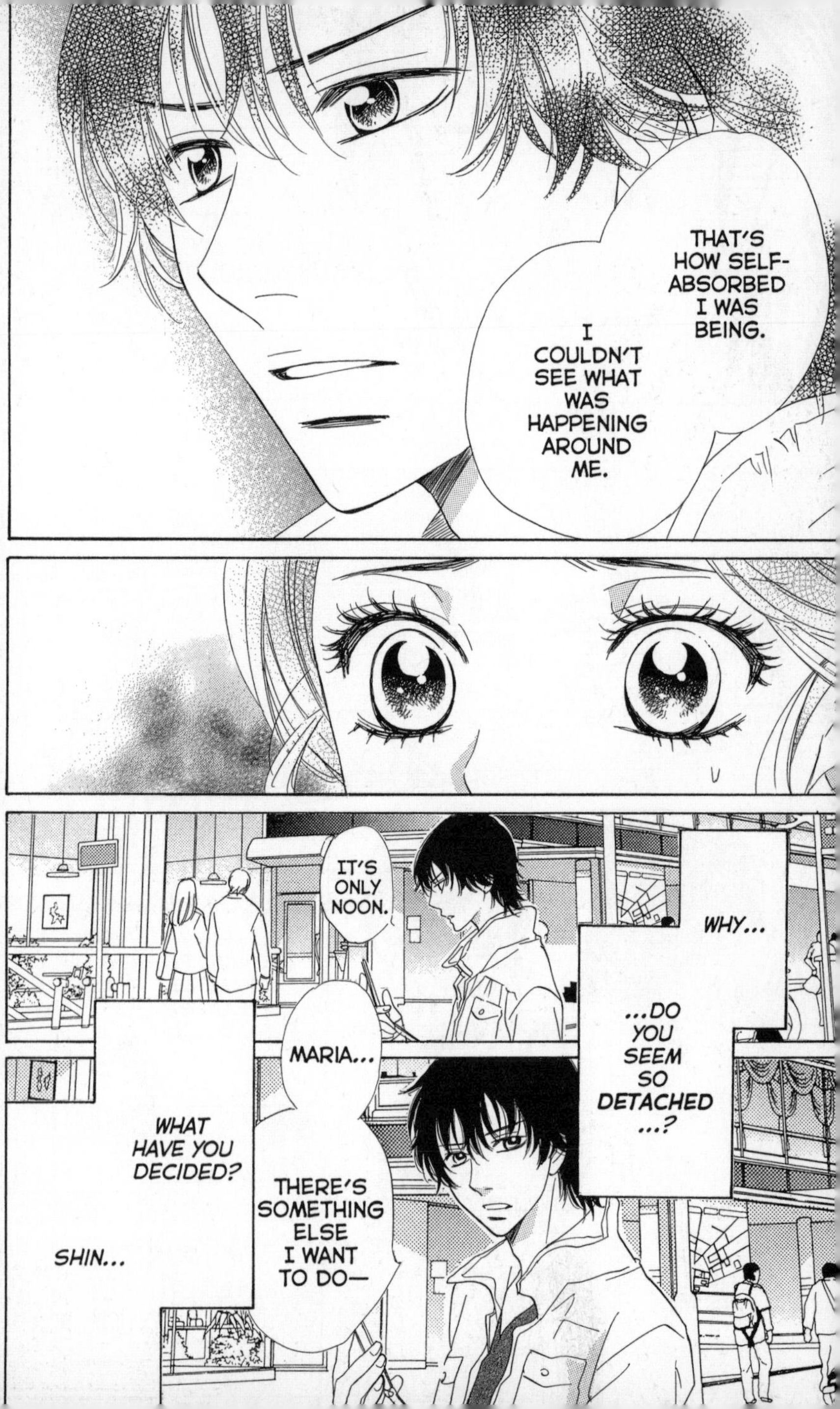
THAT'S HOW SELF-ABSORBED I WAS BEING.
I COULDN'T SEE WHAT WAS HAPPENING AROUND ME.
IT'S ONLY NOON.
WHY...
...DO YOU SEEM SO DETACHED ...?
MARIA...
THERE'S SOMETHING ELSE I WANT TO DO—
WHAT HAVE YOU DECIDED?
SHIN...

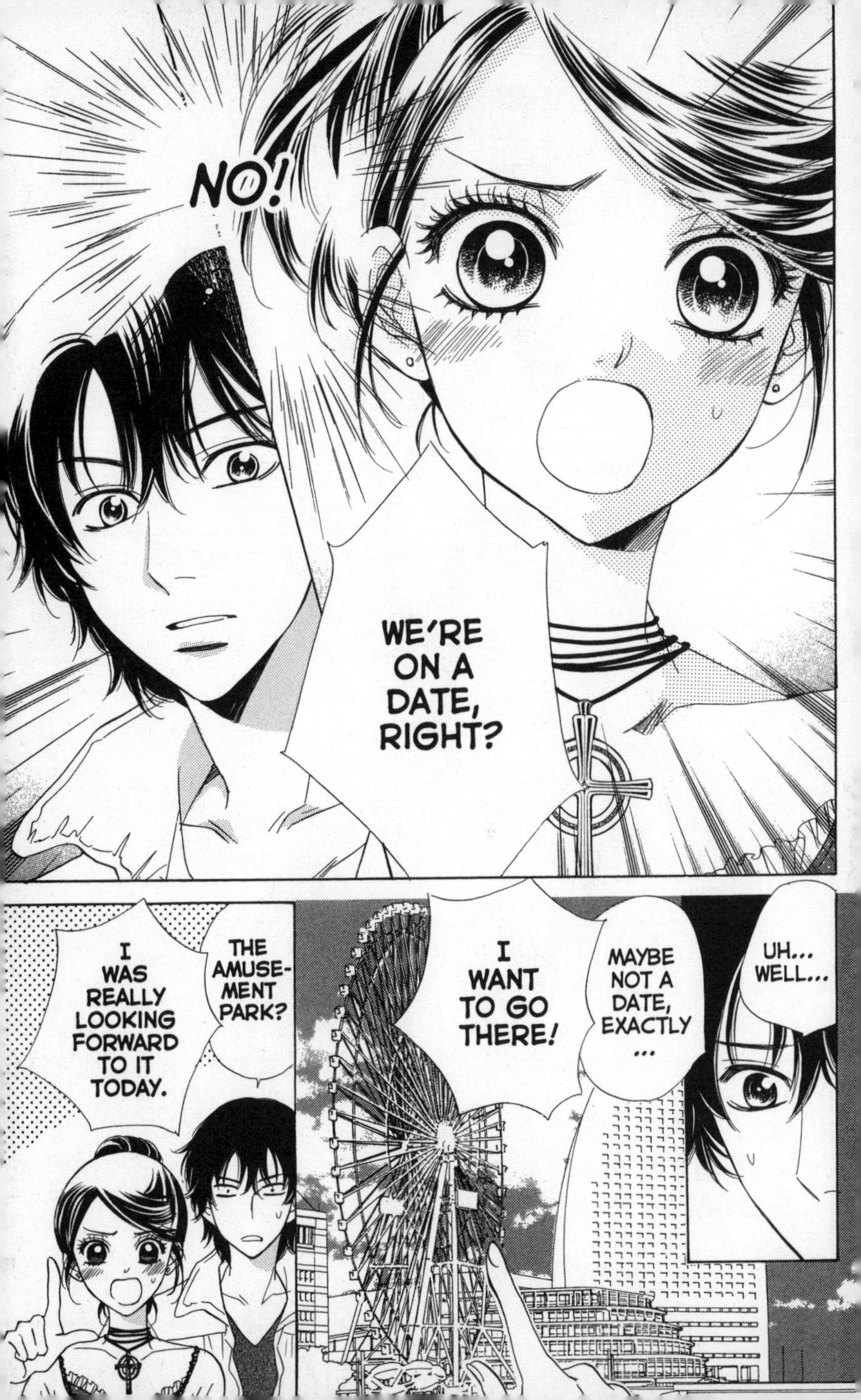
NO!
WE'RE ON A DATE, RIGHT?
UH... WELL...
MAYBE NOT A DATE, EXACTLY ...
I WANT TO GO THERE!
THE AMUSEMENT PARK?
I WAS REALLY LOOKING FORWARD TO IT TODAY.

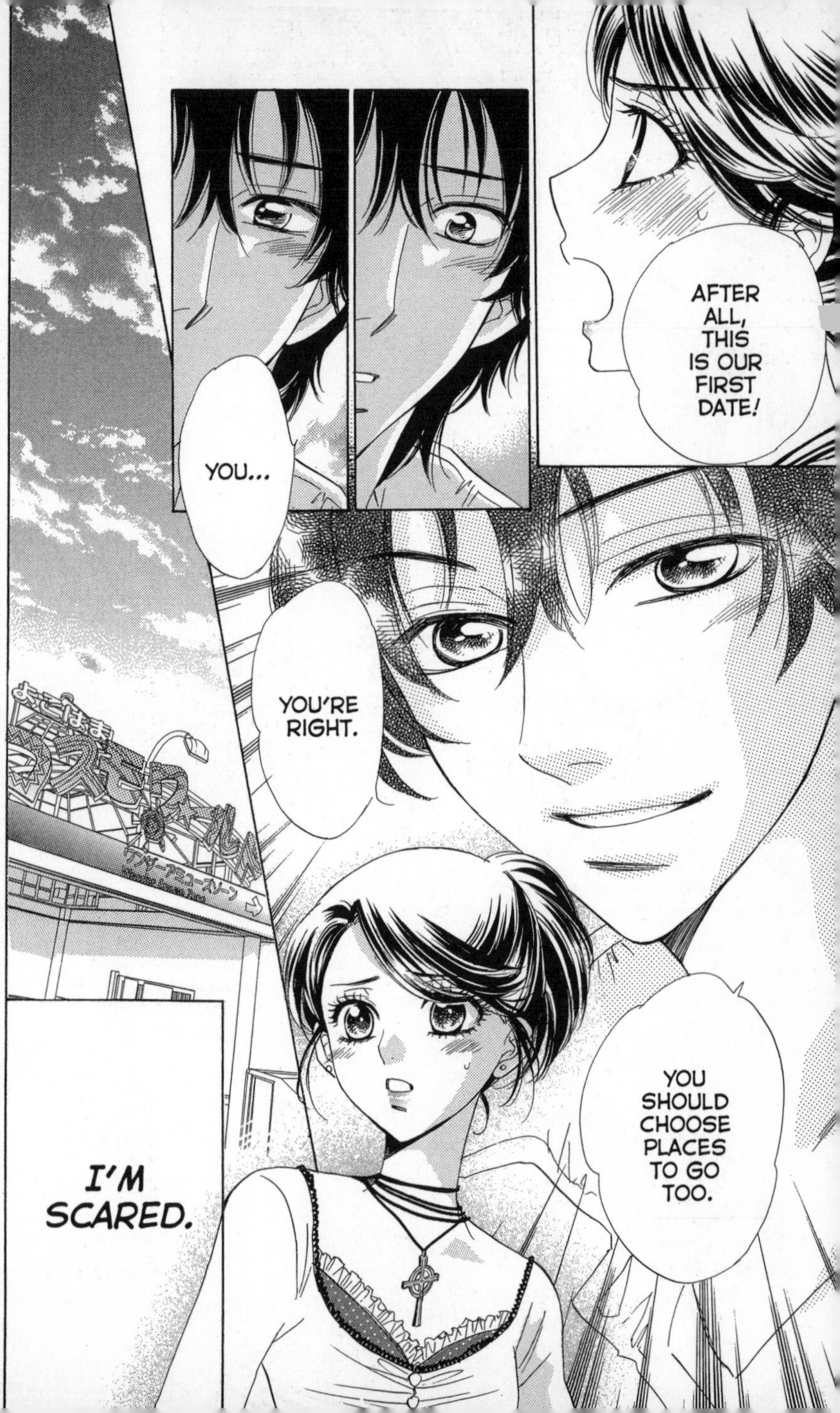
AFTER ALL, THIS IS OUR FIRST DATE!
YOU...
YOU'RE RIGHT.
YOU SHOULD CHOOSE PLACES TO GO TOO.
よこはま
ワンダーアミューズゾーン
I'M SCARED.

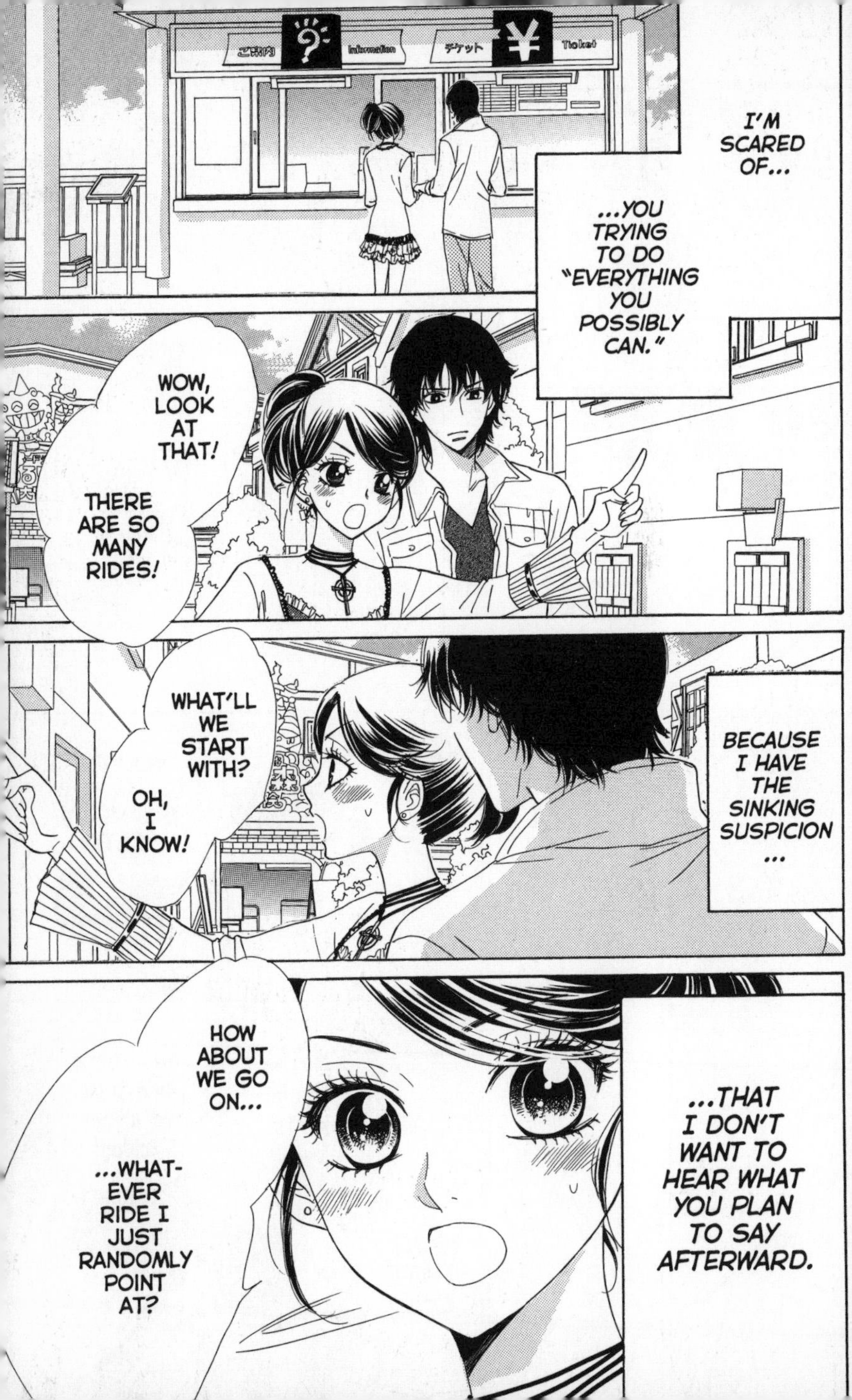
I'M SCARED OF...
...YOU TRYING TO DO "EVERYTHING YOU POSSIBLY CAN."
Ticket
チケット
Information
ご案内
WOW, LOOK AT THAT!
THERE ARE SO MANY RIDES!
BECAUSE I HAVE THE SINKING SUSPICION ...
WHAT'LL WE START WITH?
OH, I KNOW!
...THAT I DON'T WANT TO HEAR WHAT YOU PLAN TO SAY AFTERWARD.
HOW ABOUT WE GO ON...
...WHAT-EVER RIDE I JUST RANDOMLY POINT AT?

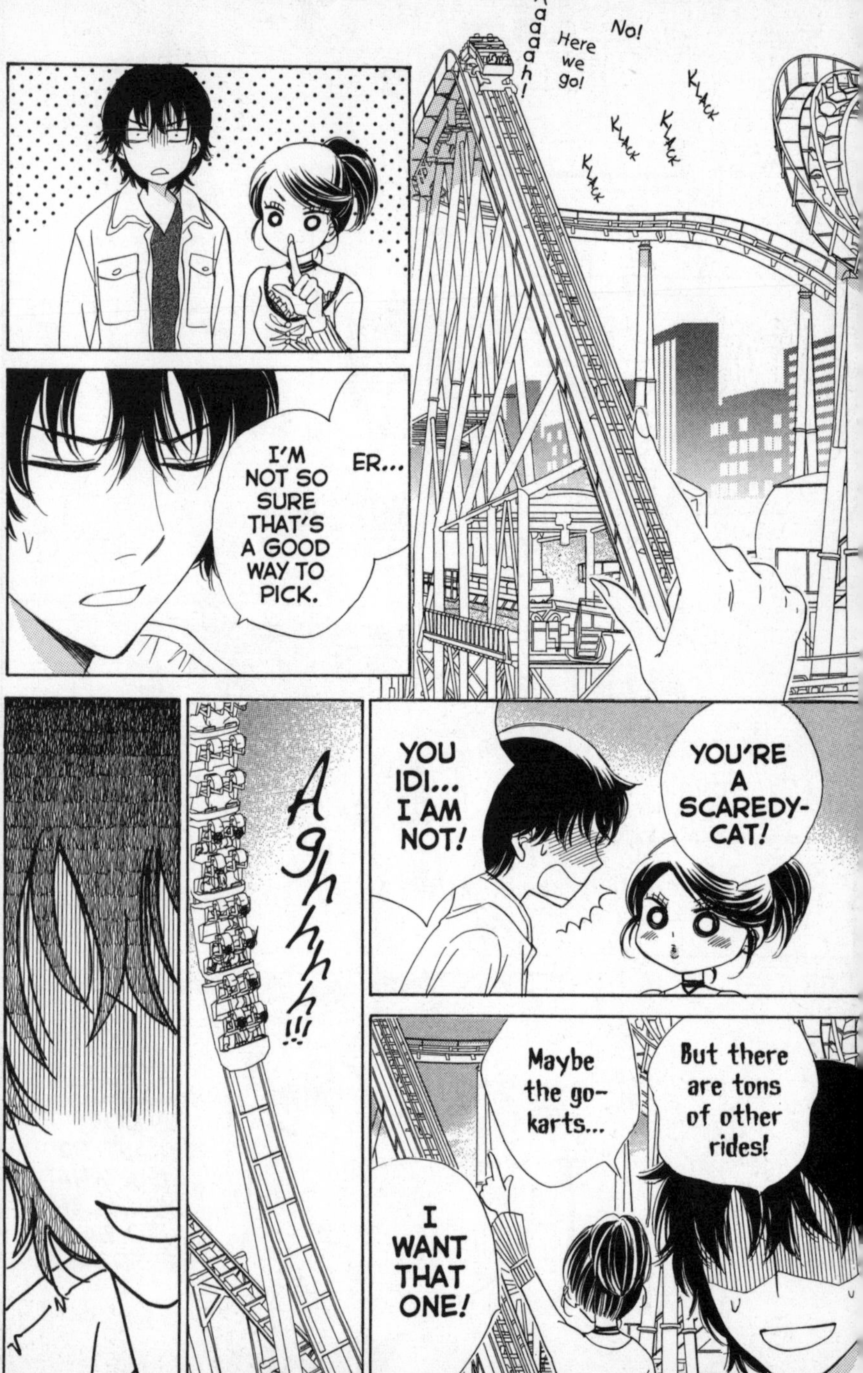
No!
Here we go!
Aaaaah!
KLACK
KLACK
KLACK
KLACK
ER...
I'M NOT SO SURE THAT'S A GOOD WAY TO PICK.
YOU'RE A SCAREDY-CAT!
YOU IDI... I AM NOT!
But there are tons of other rides!
Maybe the go-karts...
I WANT THAT ONE!
Aghhhh!!!

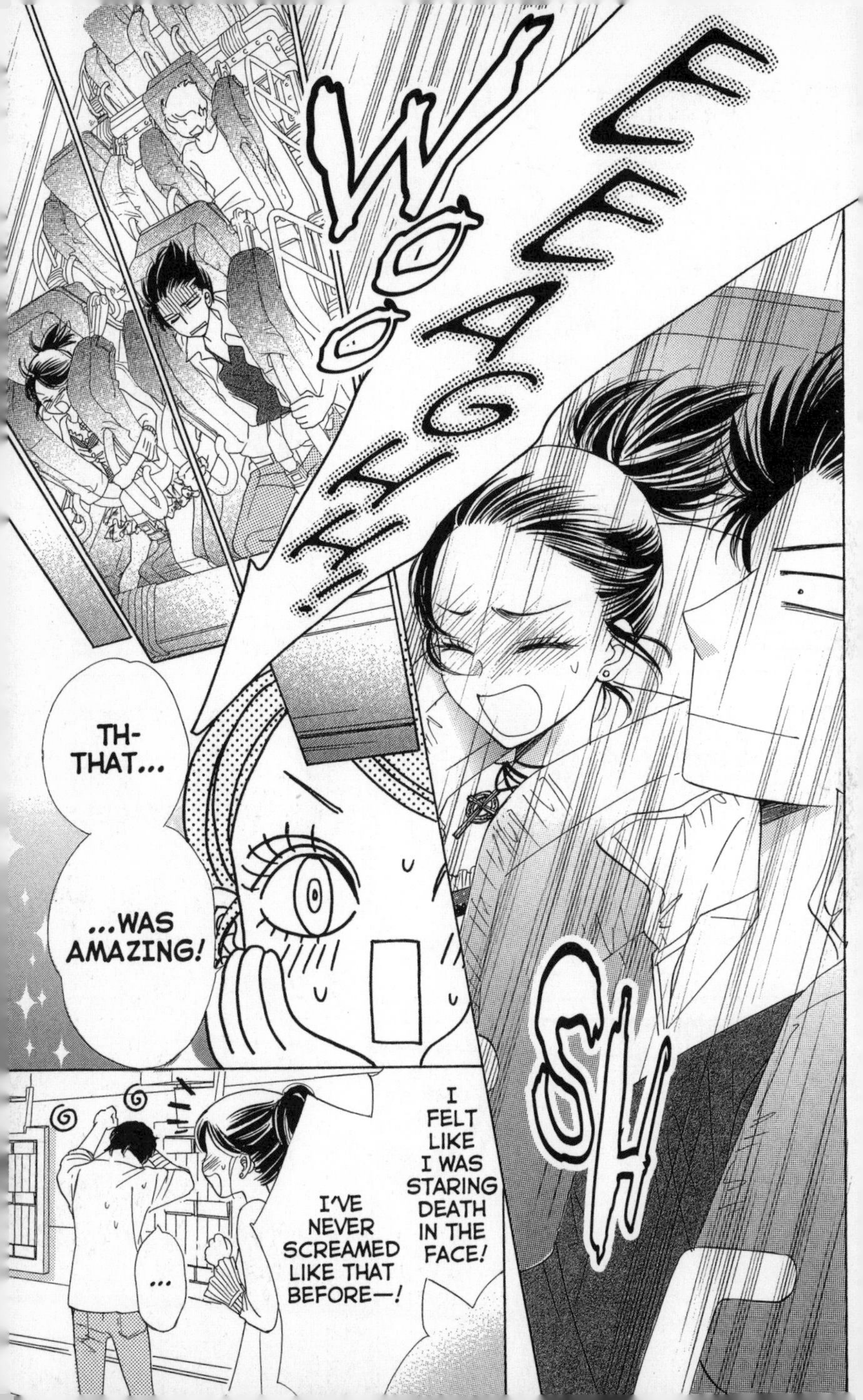
EEEAGHH!
WOO
SH
TH-THAT...
...WAS AMAZING!
I FELT LIKE I WAS STARING DEATH IN THE FACE!
I'VE NEVER SCREAMED LIKE THAT BEFORE—!
...

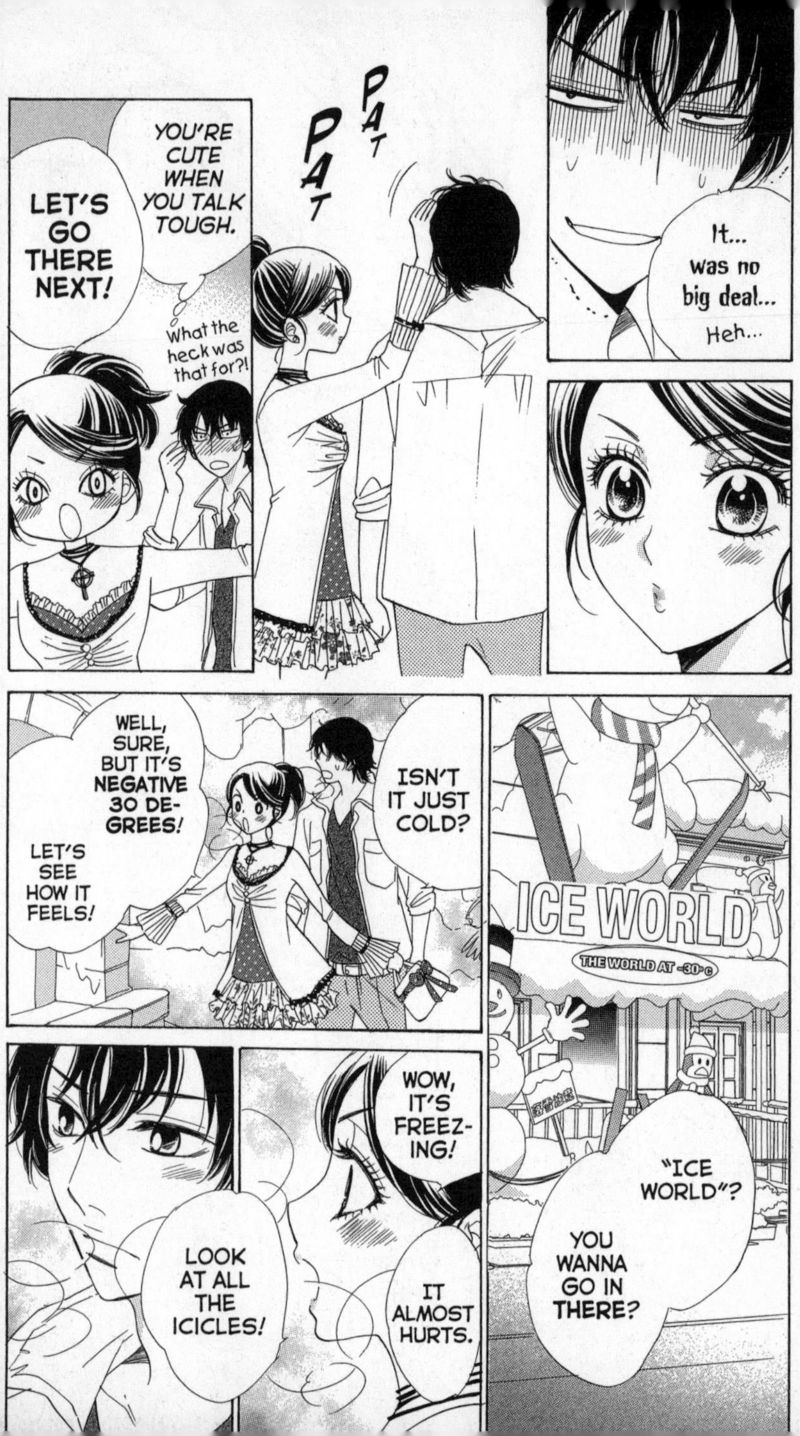
It... was no big deal... Heh...
PAT PAT
YOU'RE CUTE WHEN YOU TALK TOUGH.
What the heck was that for?!
LET'S GO THERE NEXT!
ICE WORLD
THE WORLD AT -30°C
"ICE WORLD"? YOU WANNA GO IN THERE?
ISN'T IT JUST COLD?
WELL, SURE, BUT IT'S NEGATIVE 30 DEGREES!
LET'S SEE HOW IT FEELS!
WOW, IT'S FREEZING!
IT ALMOST HURTS.
LOOK AT ALL THE ICICLES!

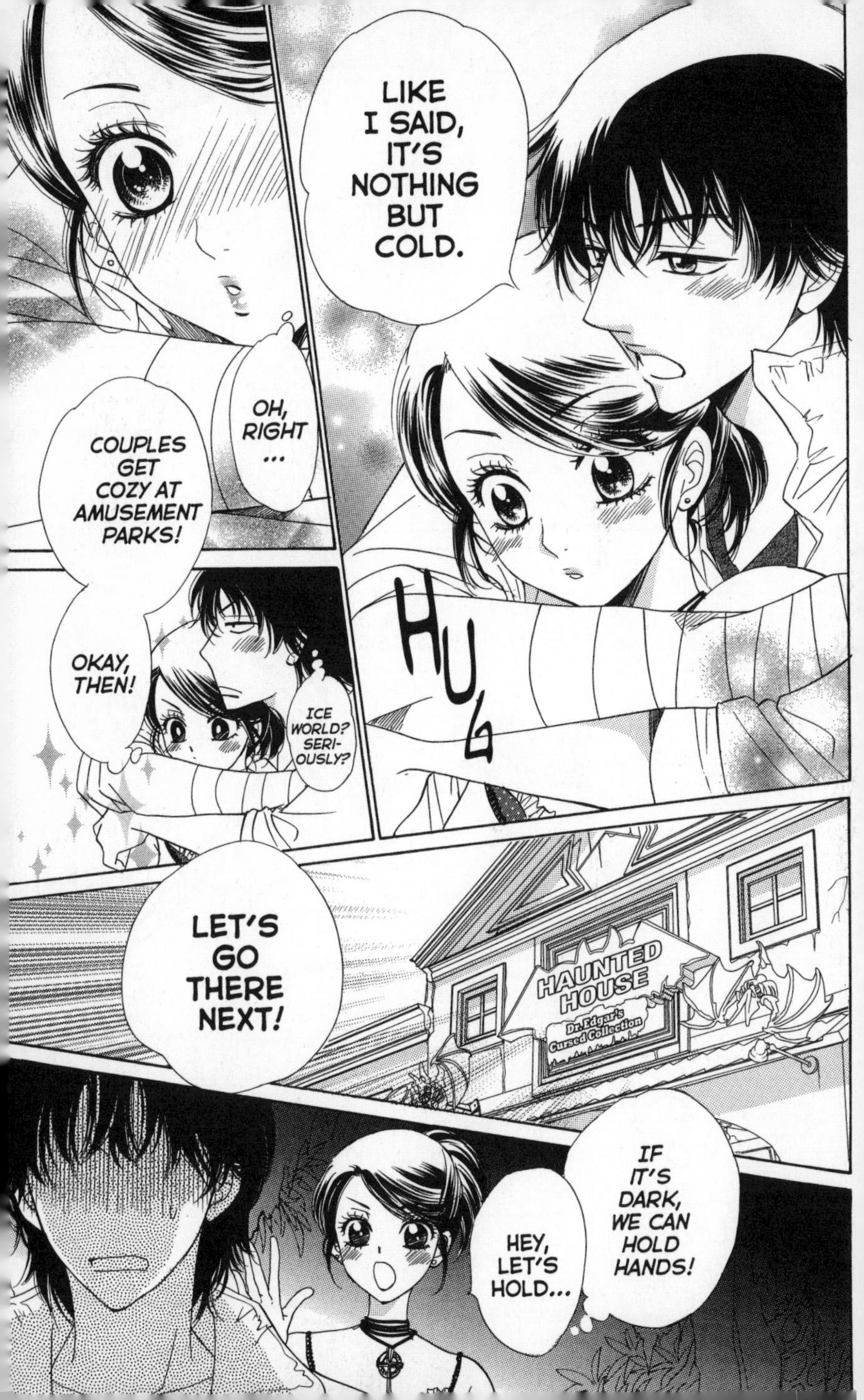
LIKE I SAID, IT'S NOTHING BUT COLD.
HUG
OH, RIGHT...
COUPLES GET COZY AT AMUSEMENT PARKS!
ICE WORLD? SERIOUSLY?
OKAY, THEN!
HAUNTED HOUSE
Dr. Edgar's Cursed Collection
LET'S GO THERE NEXT!
IF IT'S DARK, WE CAN HOLD HANDS!
HEY, LET'S HOLD...

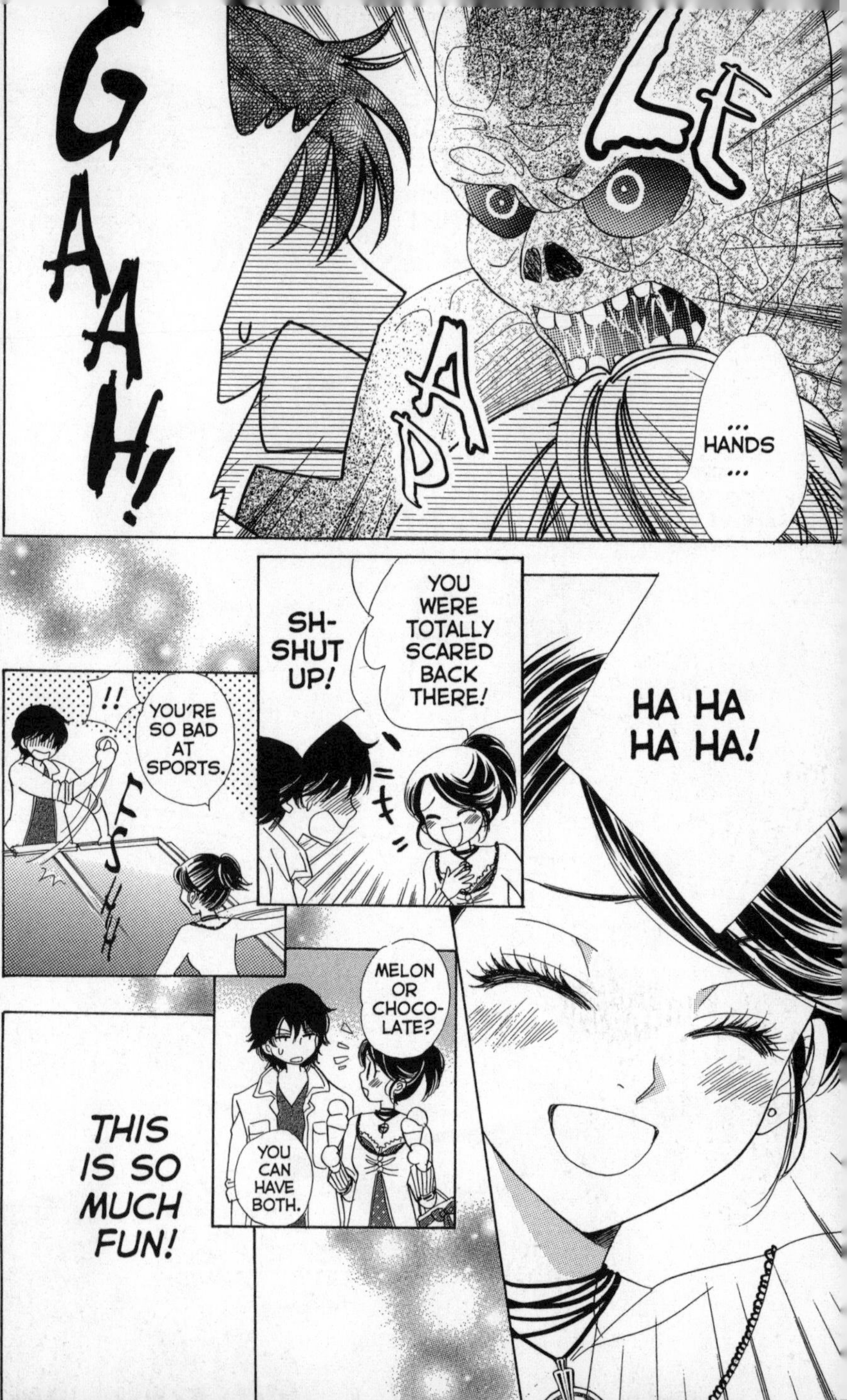
LE
... HANDS ...
AP
GAAH!
HA HA HA HA!
YOU WERE TOTALLY SCARED BACK THERE!
SH-SHUT UP!
!!
YOU'RE SO BAD AT SPORTS.
MELON OR CHOCO-LATE?
YOU CAN HAVE BOTH.
THIS IS SO MUCH FUN!

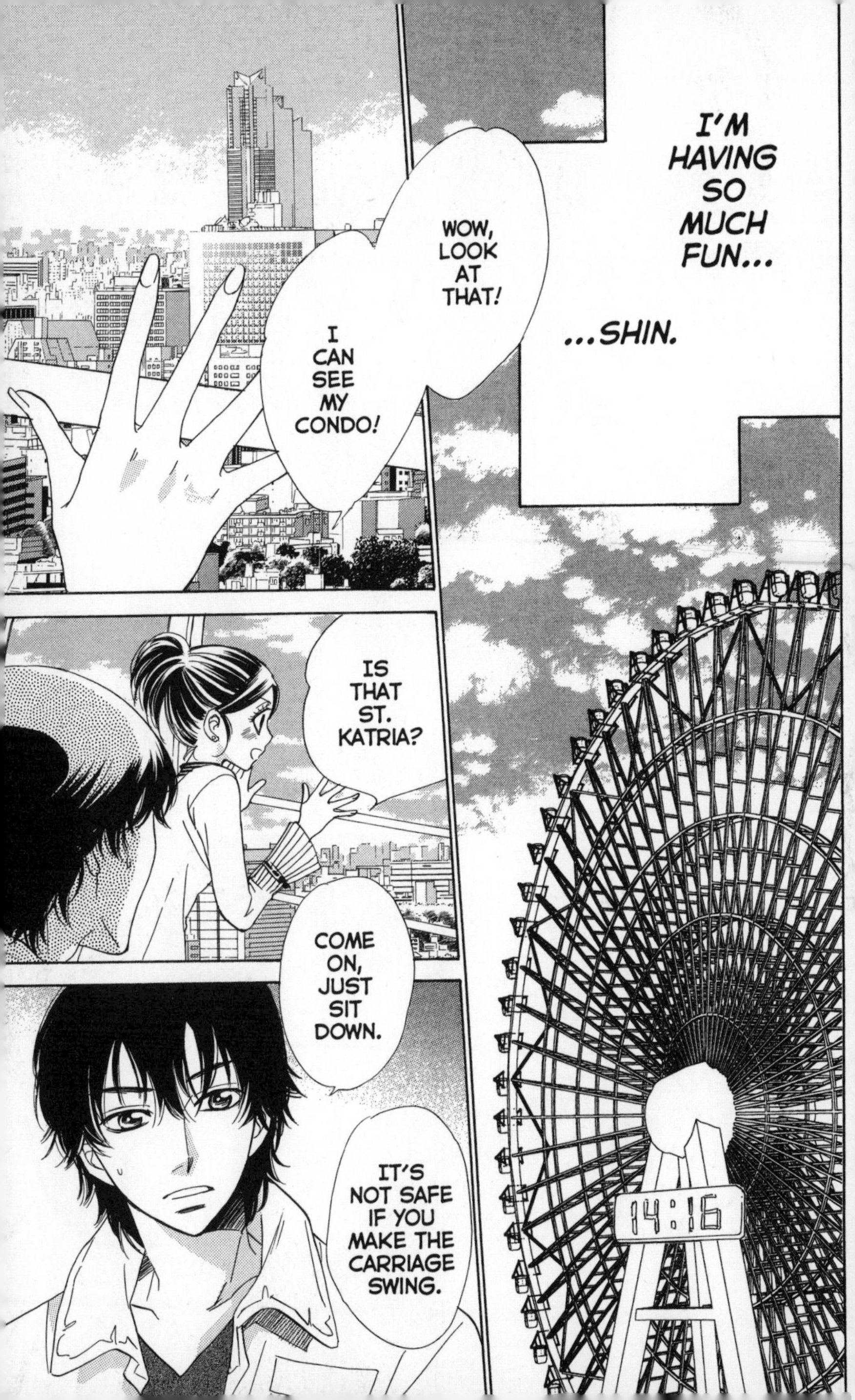
I'M HAVING SO MUCH FUN...
...SHIN.
14:16
WOW, LOOK AT THAT!
I CAN SEE MY CONDO!
IS THAT ST. KATRIA?
COME ON, JUST SIT DOWN.
IT'S NOT SAFE IF YOU MAKE THE CARRIAGE SWING.

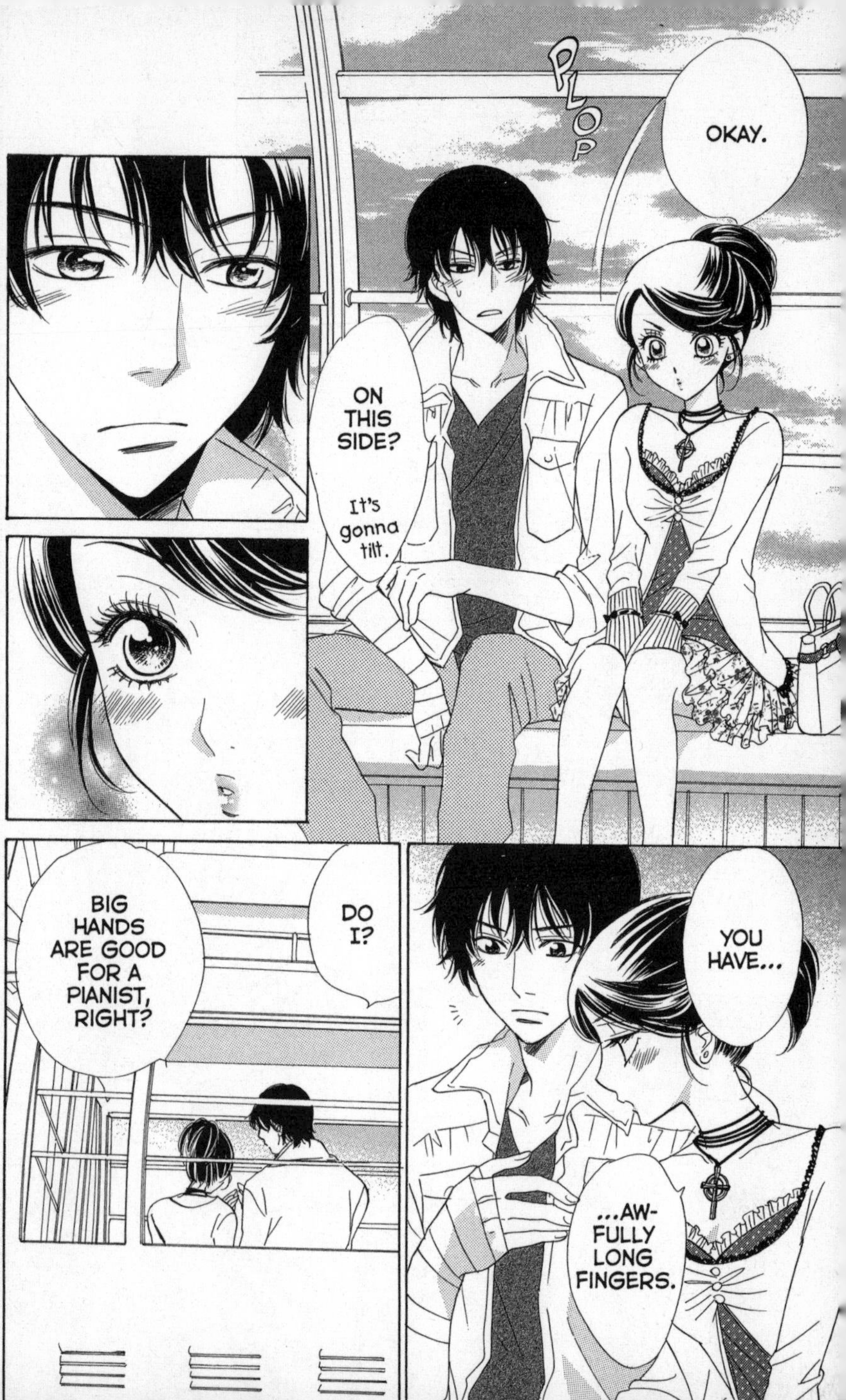
OKAY.
PLOP
ON THIS SIDE?
It's gonna tilt.
YOU HAVE...
...AW-FULLY LONG FINGERS.
DO I?
BIG HANDS ARE GOOD FOR A PIANIST, RIGHT?

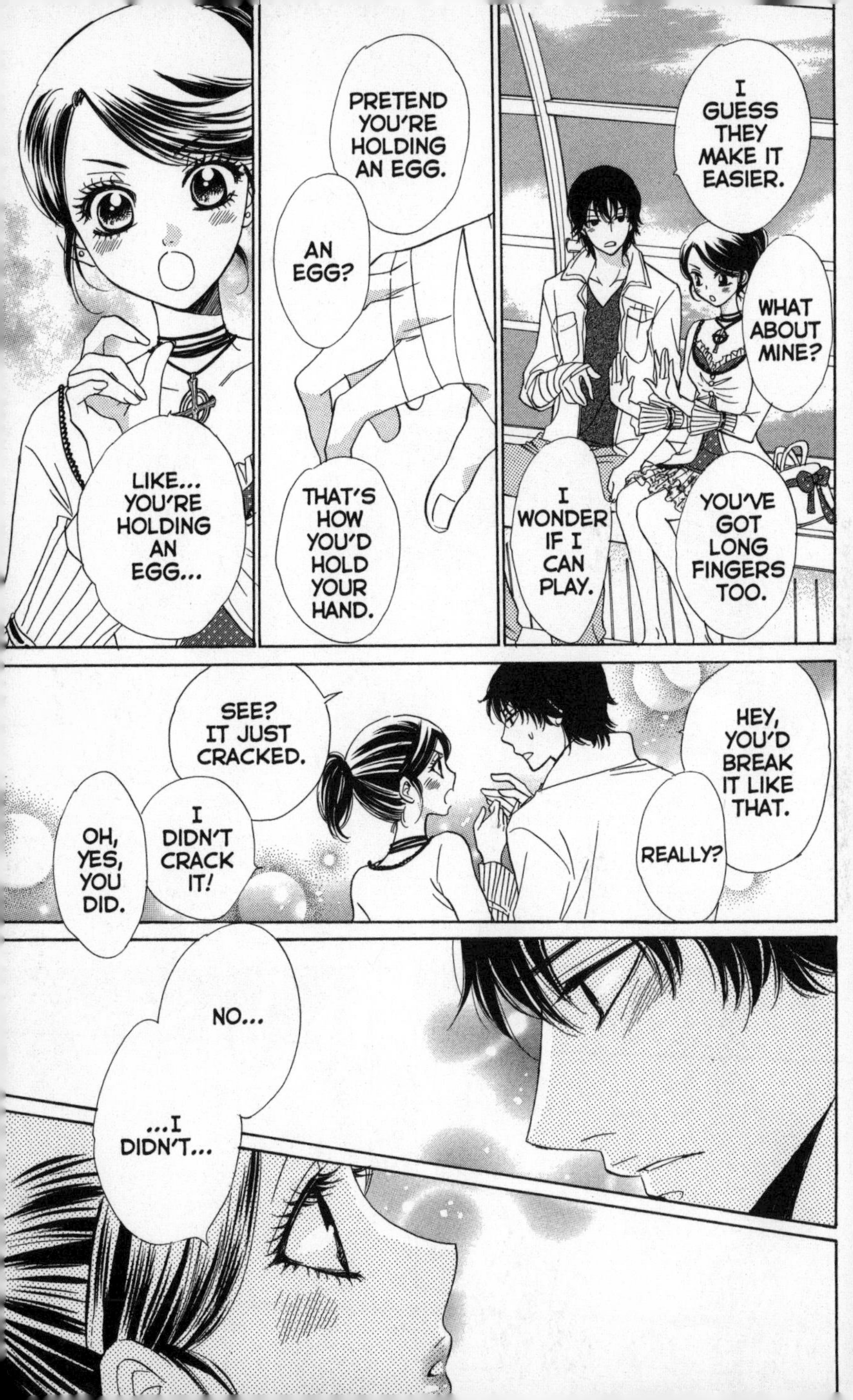
I GUESS THEY MAKE IT EASIER.
WHAT ABOUT MINE?
YOU'VE GOT LONG FINGERS TOO.
I WONDER IF I CAN PLAY.
PRETEND YOU'RE HOLDING AN EGG.
AN EGG?
THAT'S HOW YOU'D HOLD YOUR HAND.
LIKE... YOU'RE HOLDING AN EGG...
HEY, YOU'D BREAK IT LIKE THAT.
REALLY?
SEE? IT JUST CRACKED.
I DIDN'T CRACK IT!
OH, YES, YOU DID.
NO...
...I DIDN'T...

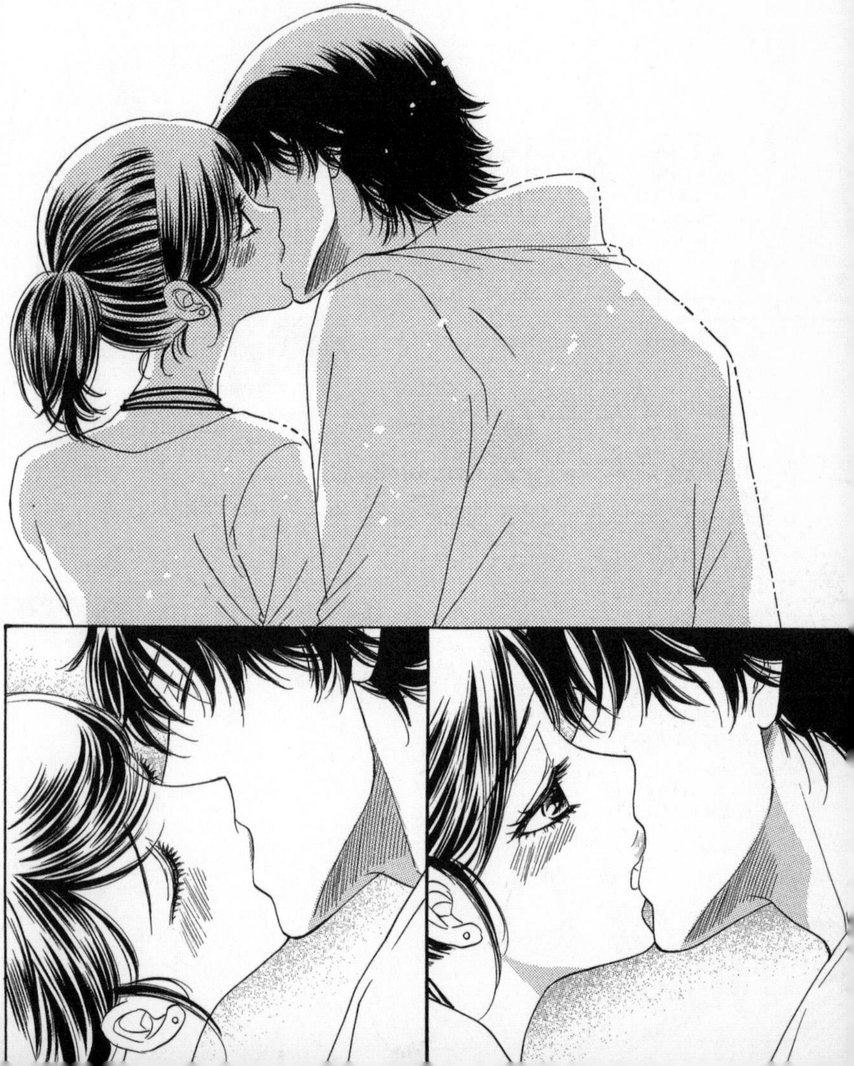

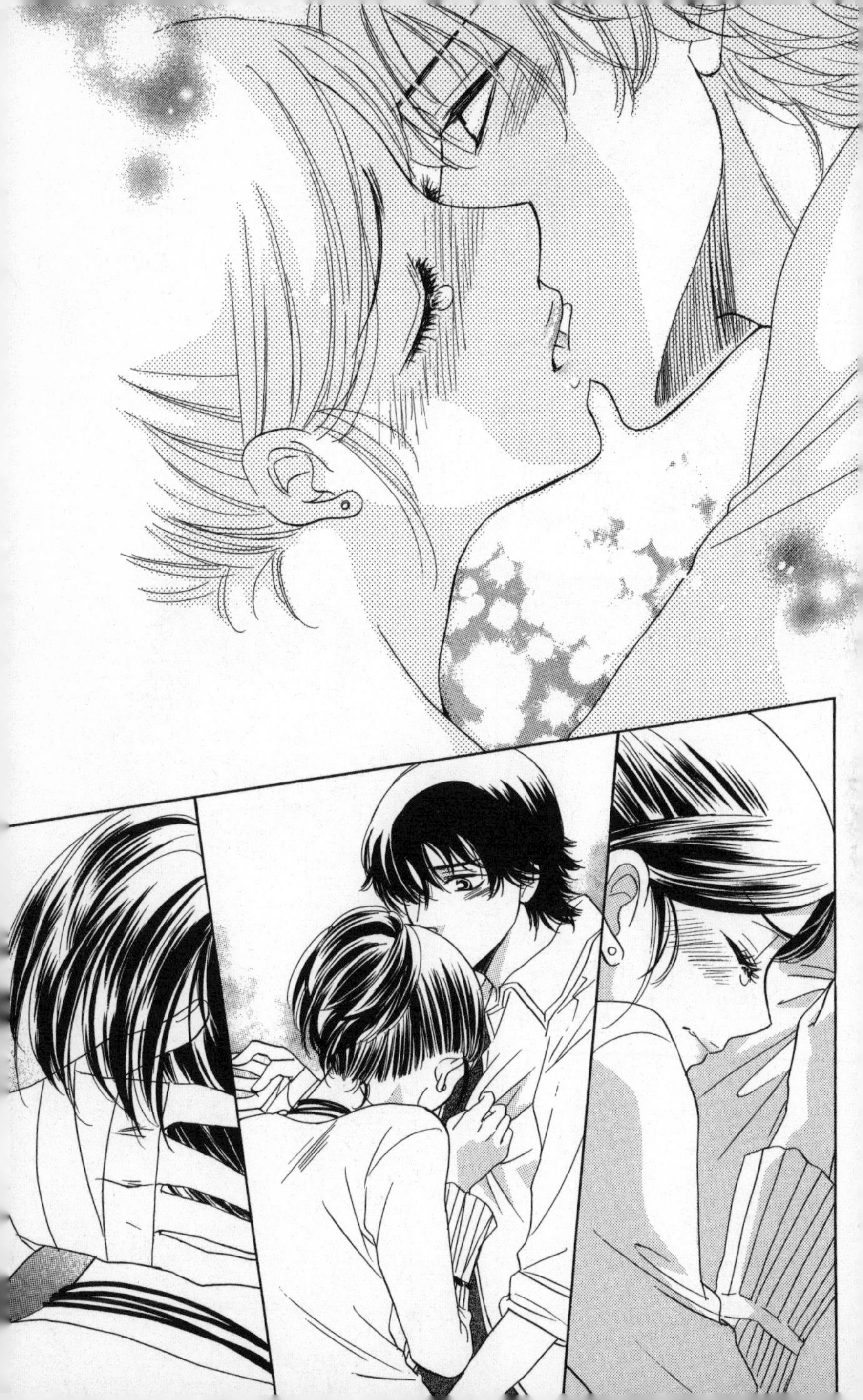

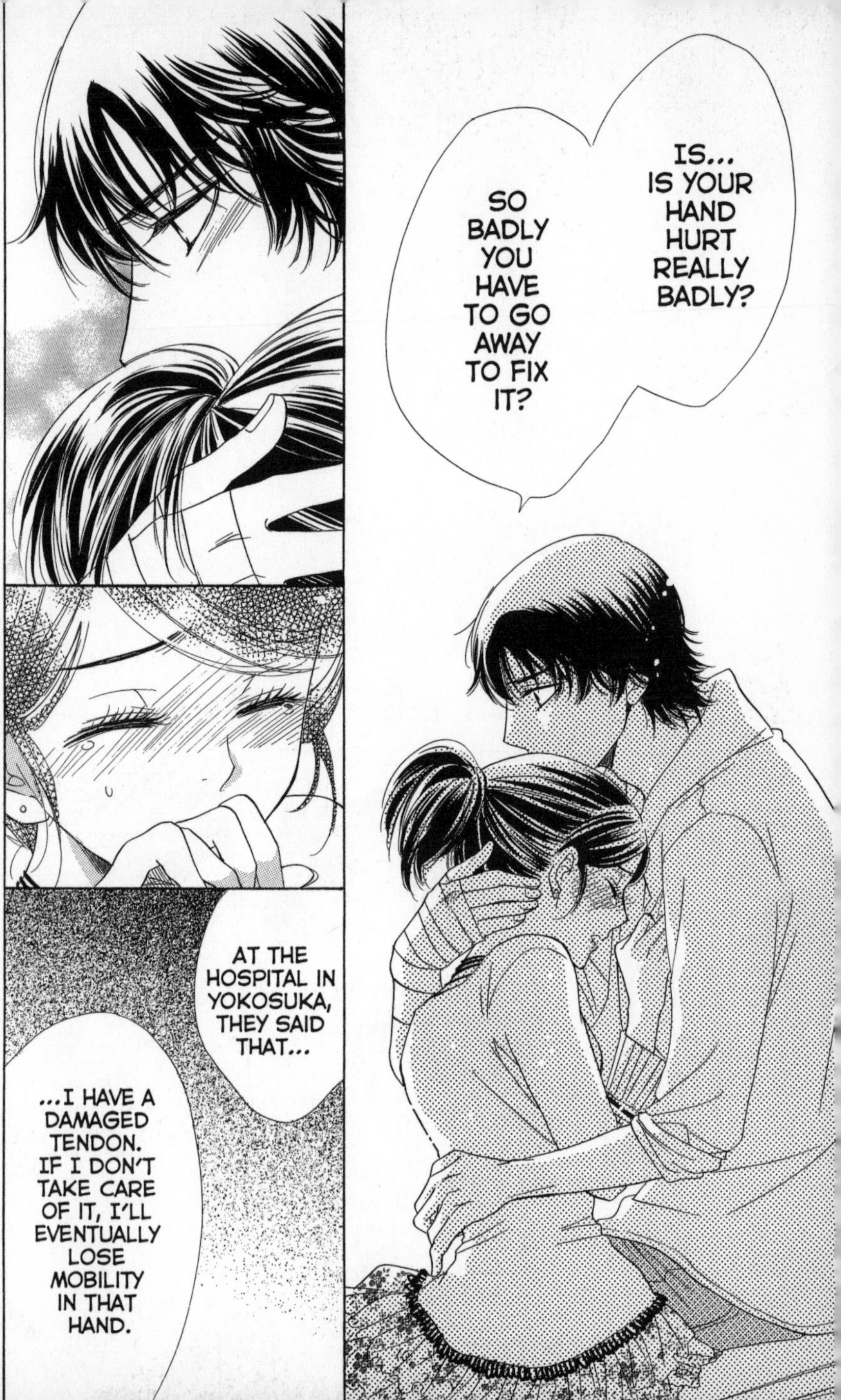
IS... IS YOUR HAND HURT REALLY BADLY? SO BADLY YOU HAVE TO GO AWAY TO FIX IT?
AT THE HOSPITAL IN YOKOSUKA, THEY SAID THAT...
...I HAVE A DAMAGED TENDON. IF I DON'T TAKE CARE OF IT, I'LL EVENTUALLY LOSE MOBILITY IN THAT HAND.

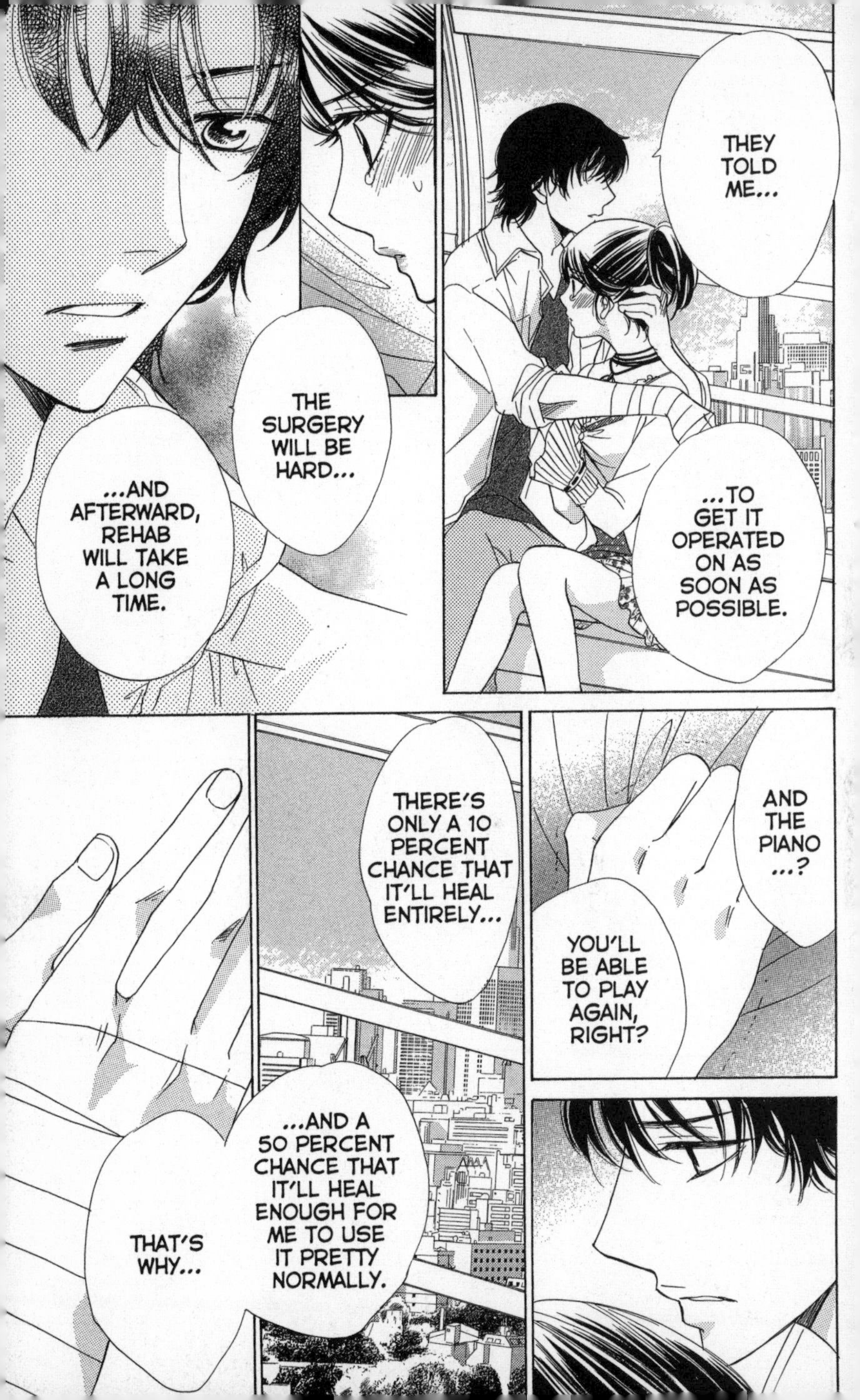
THEY TOLD ME...
...TO GET IT OPERATED ON AS SOON AS POSSIBLE.
THE SURGERY WILL BE HARD...
...AND AFTERWARD, REHAB WILL TAKE A LONG TIME.
AND THE PIANO ...?
YOU'LL BE ABLE TO PLAY AGAIN, RIGHT?
THERE'S ONLY A 10 PERCENT CHANCE THAT IT'LL HEAL ENTIRELY...
...AND A 50 PERCENT CHANCE THAT IT'LL HEAL ENOUGH FOR ME TO USE IT PRETTY NORMALLY.
THAT'S WHY...

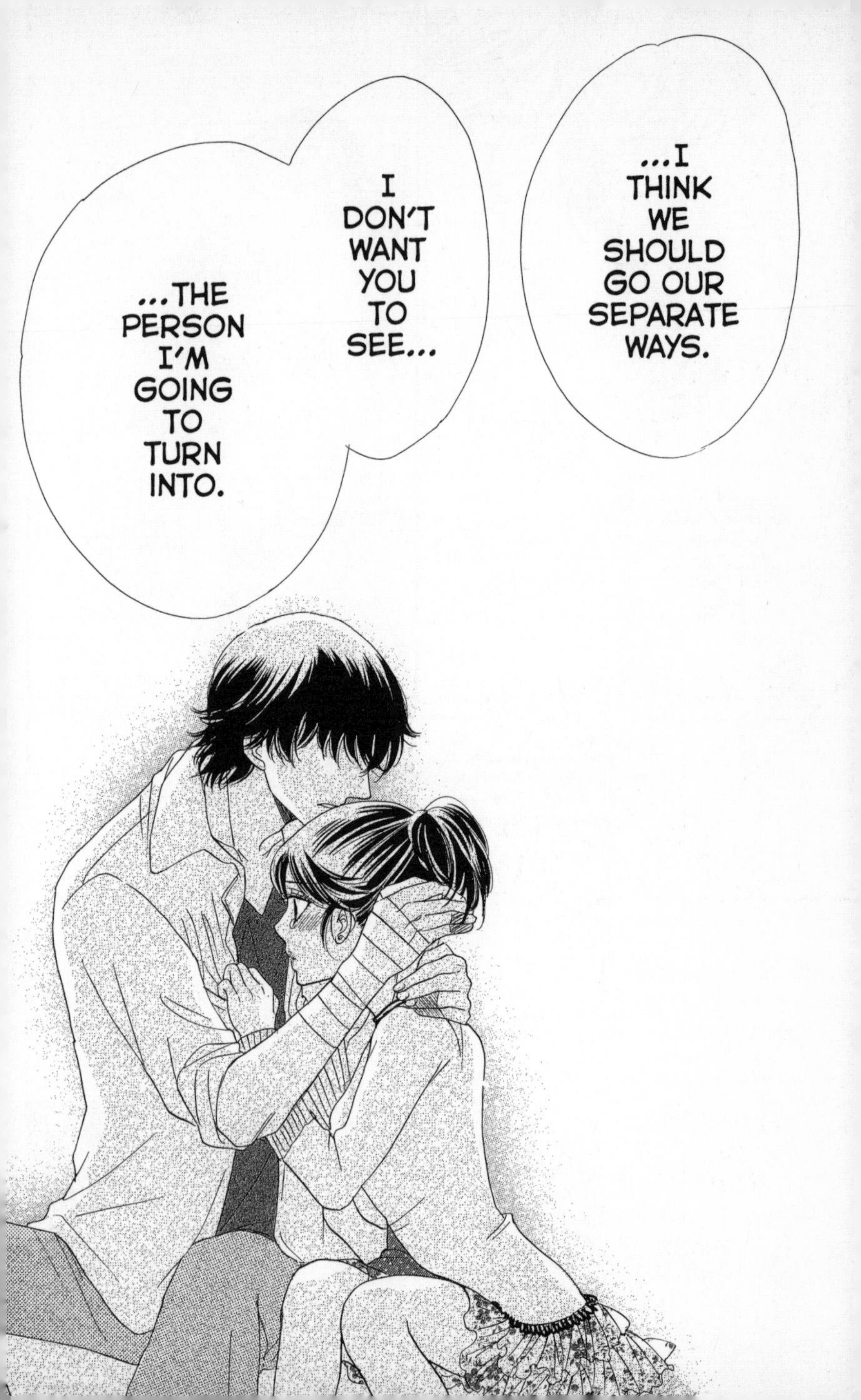
...I THINK WE SHOULD GO OUR SEPARATE WAYS.
I DON'T WANT YOU TO SEE...
...THE PERSON I'M GOING TO TURN INTO.

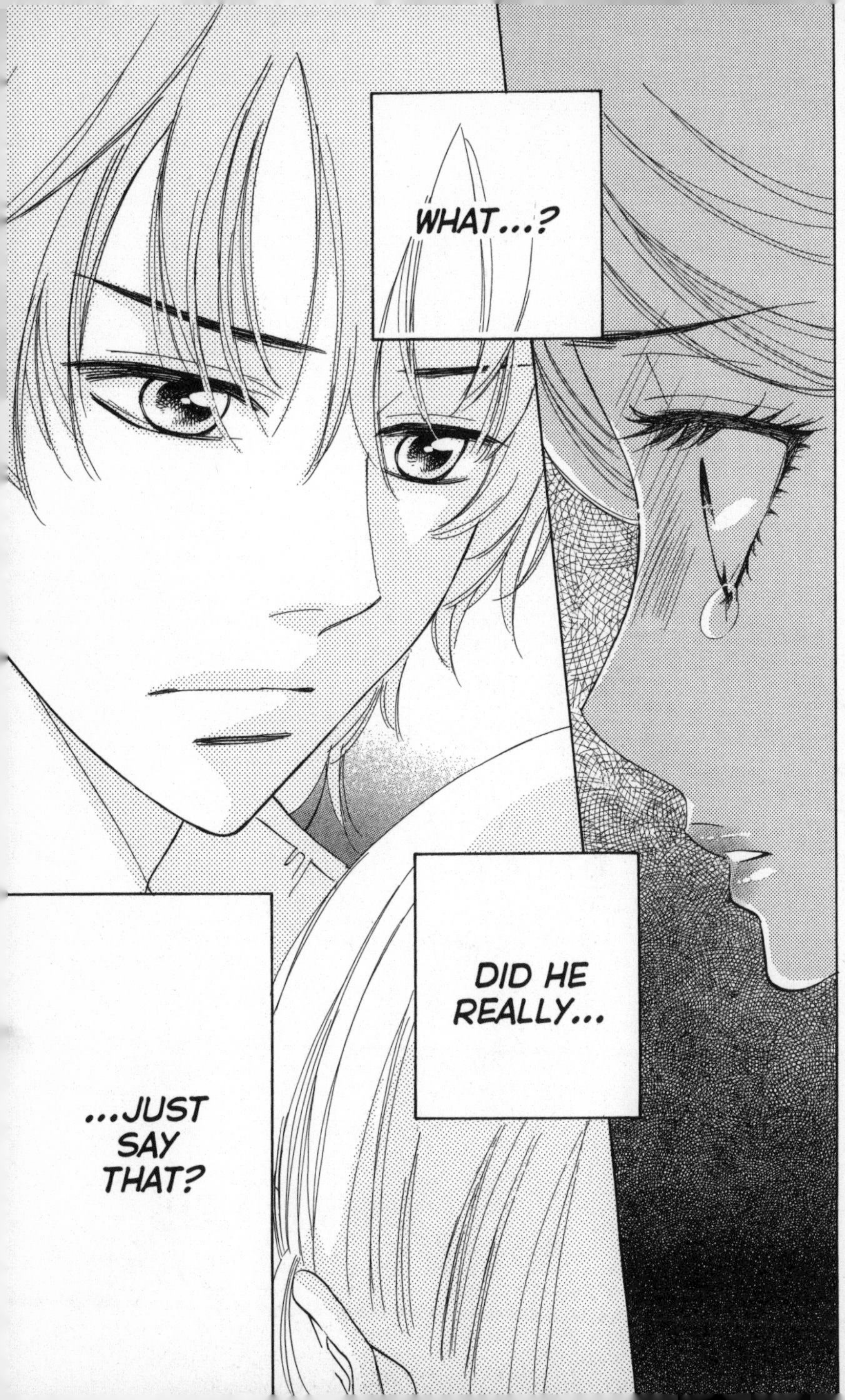
WHAT...?
DID HE REALLY...
...JUST SAY THAT?

A Devil and
Her Love Song

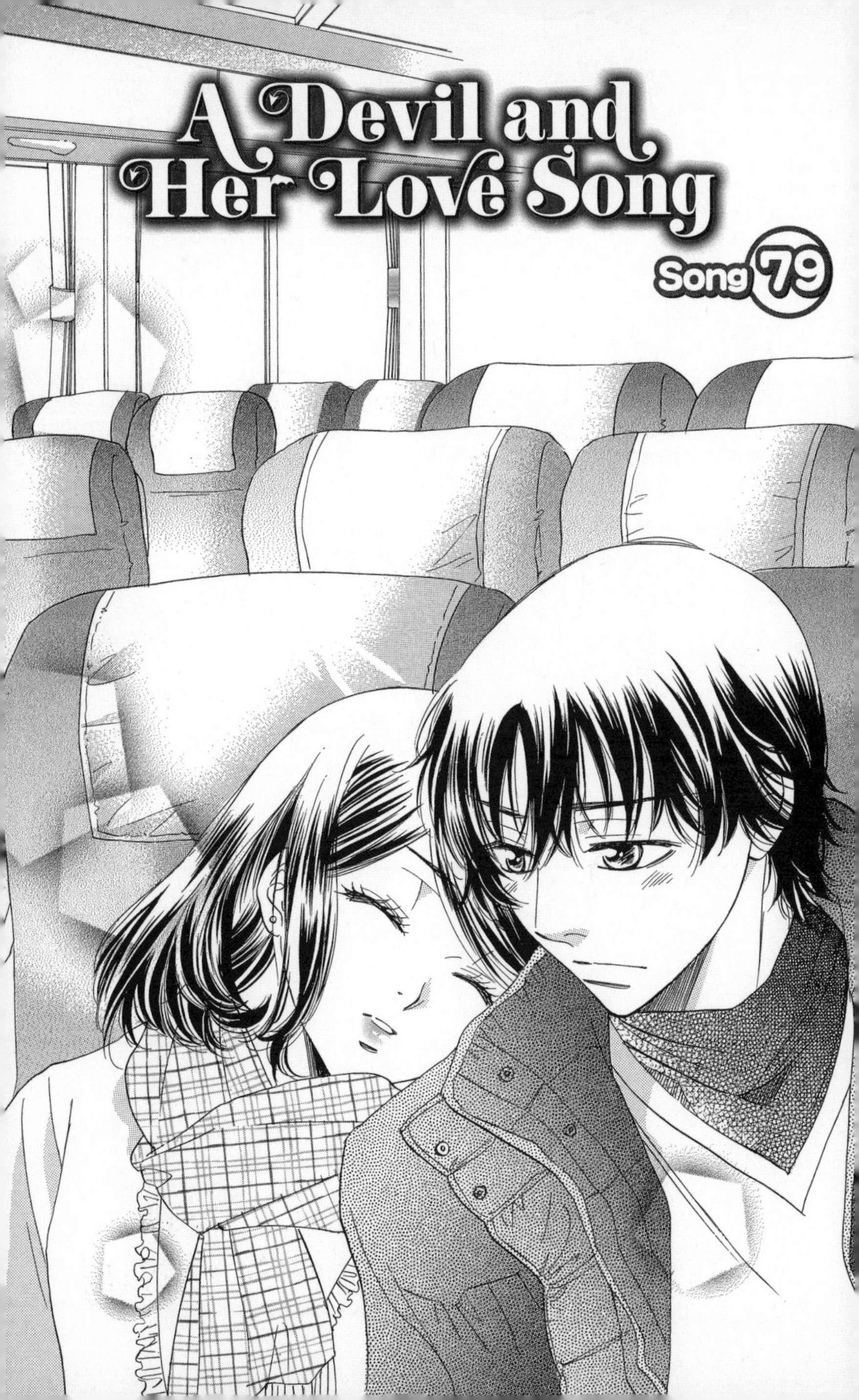
A Devil and Her Love Song
Song 79

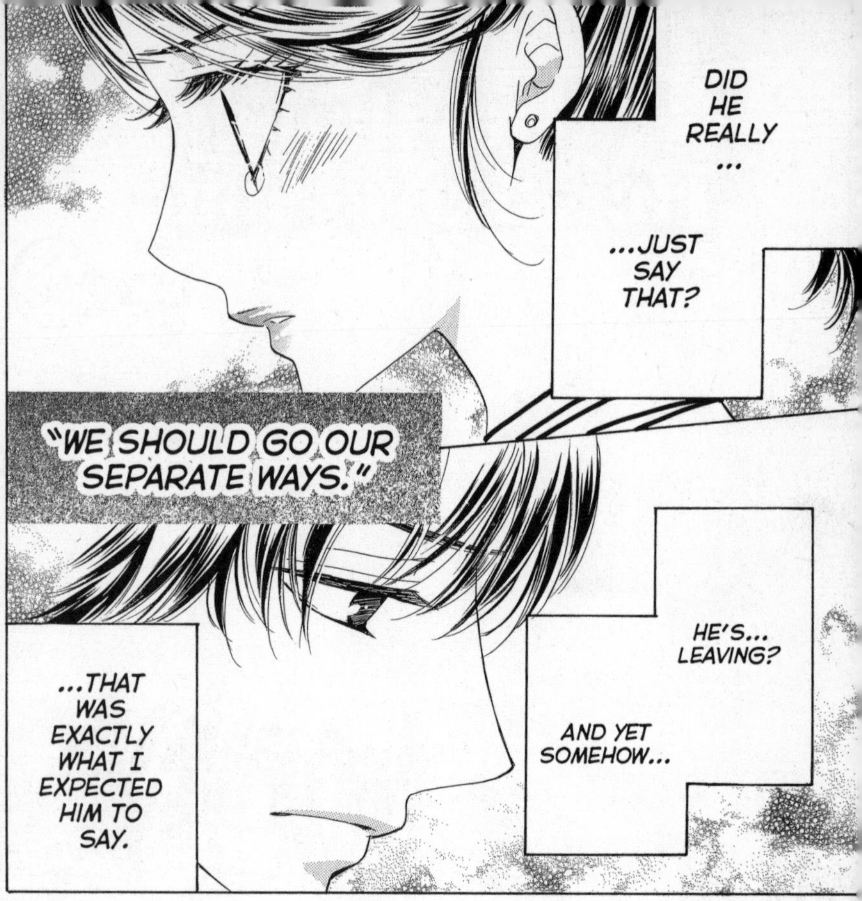
DID HE REALLY ...
...JUST SAY THAT?
"WE SHOULD GO OUR SEPARATE WAYS."
HE'S... LEAVING?
AND YET SOMEHOW...
...THAT WAS EXACTLY WHAT I EXPECTED HIM TO SAY.

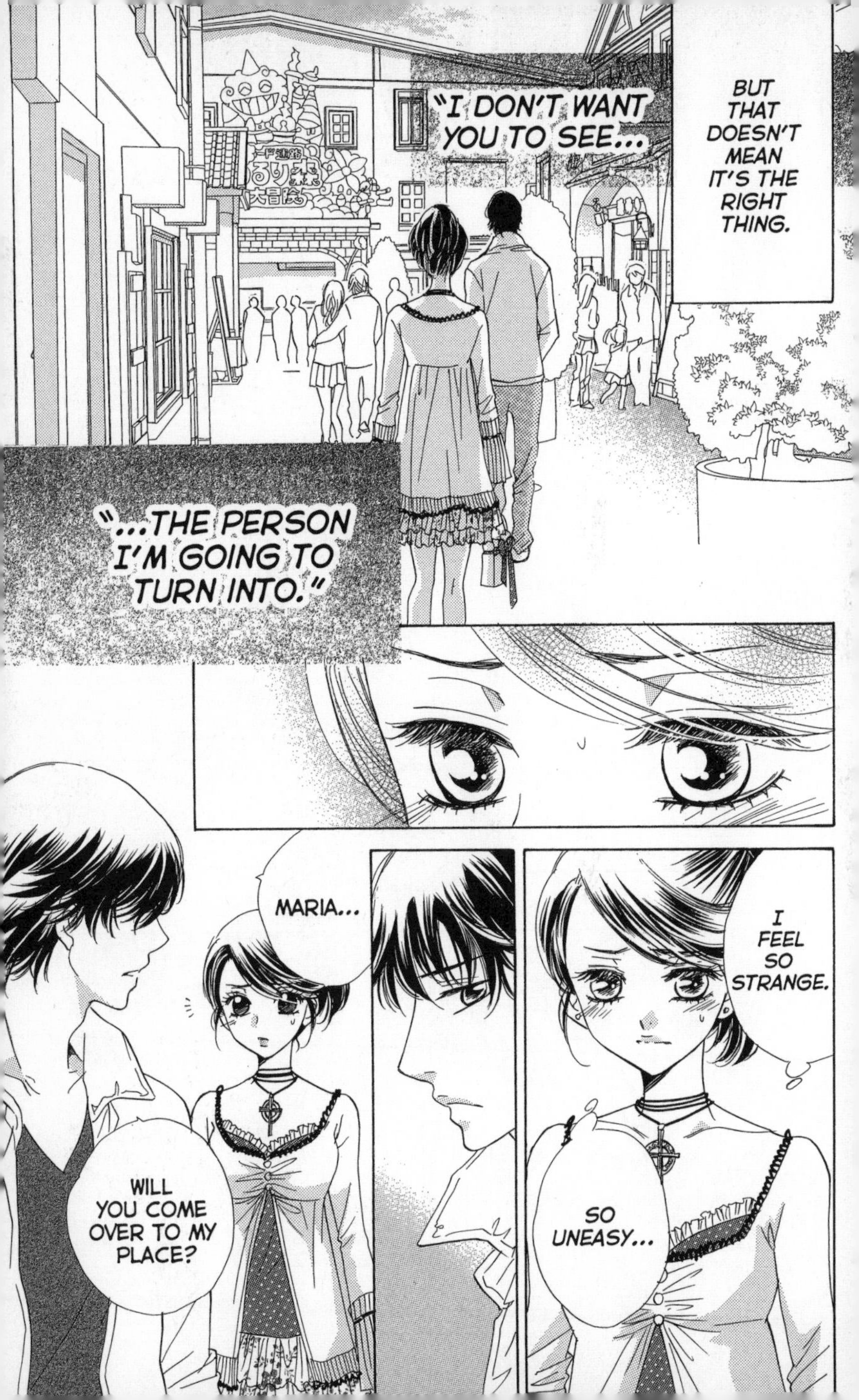

BUT THAT DOESN'T MEAN IT'S THE RIGHT THING.
"I DON'T WANT YOU TO SEE...
"...THE PERSON I'M GOING TO TURN INTO."
I FEEL SO STRANGE.
SO UNEASY...
MARIA...
WILL YOU COME OVER TO MY PLACE?

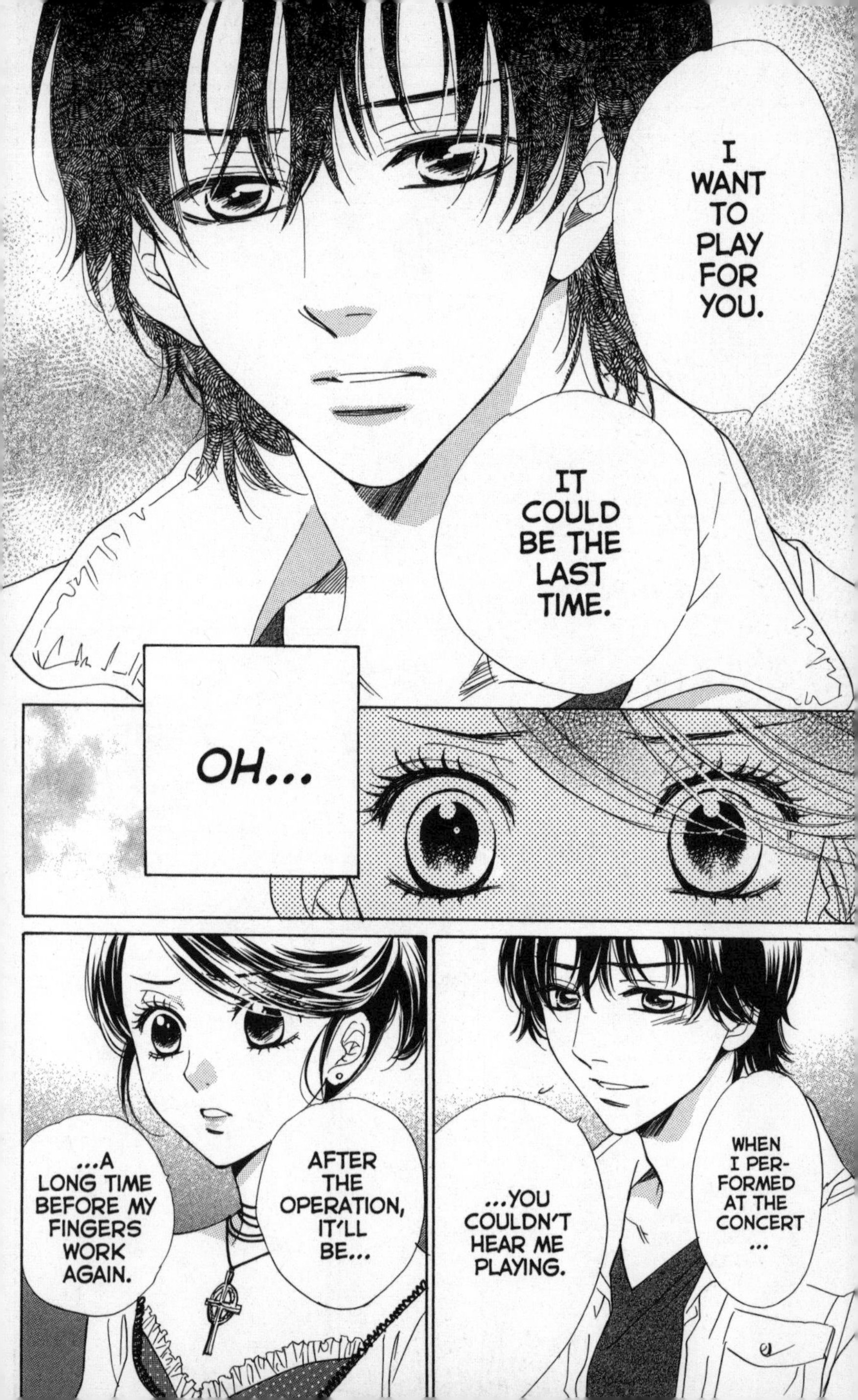
I WANT TO PLAY FOR YOU.
IT COULD BE THE LAST TIME.
OH...
WHEN I PER-FORMED AT THE CONCERT ...
...YOU COULDN'T HEAR ME PLAYING.
AFTER THE OPERATION, IT'LL BE...
...A LONG TIME BEFORE MY FINGERS WORK AGAIN.

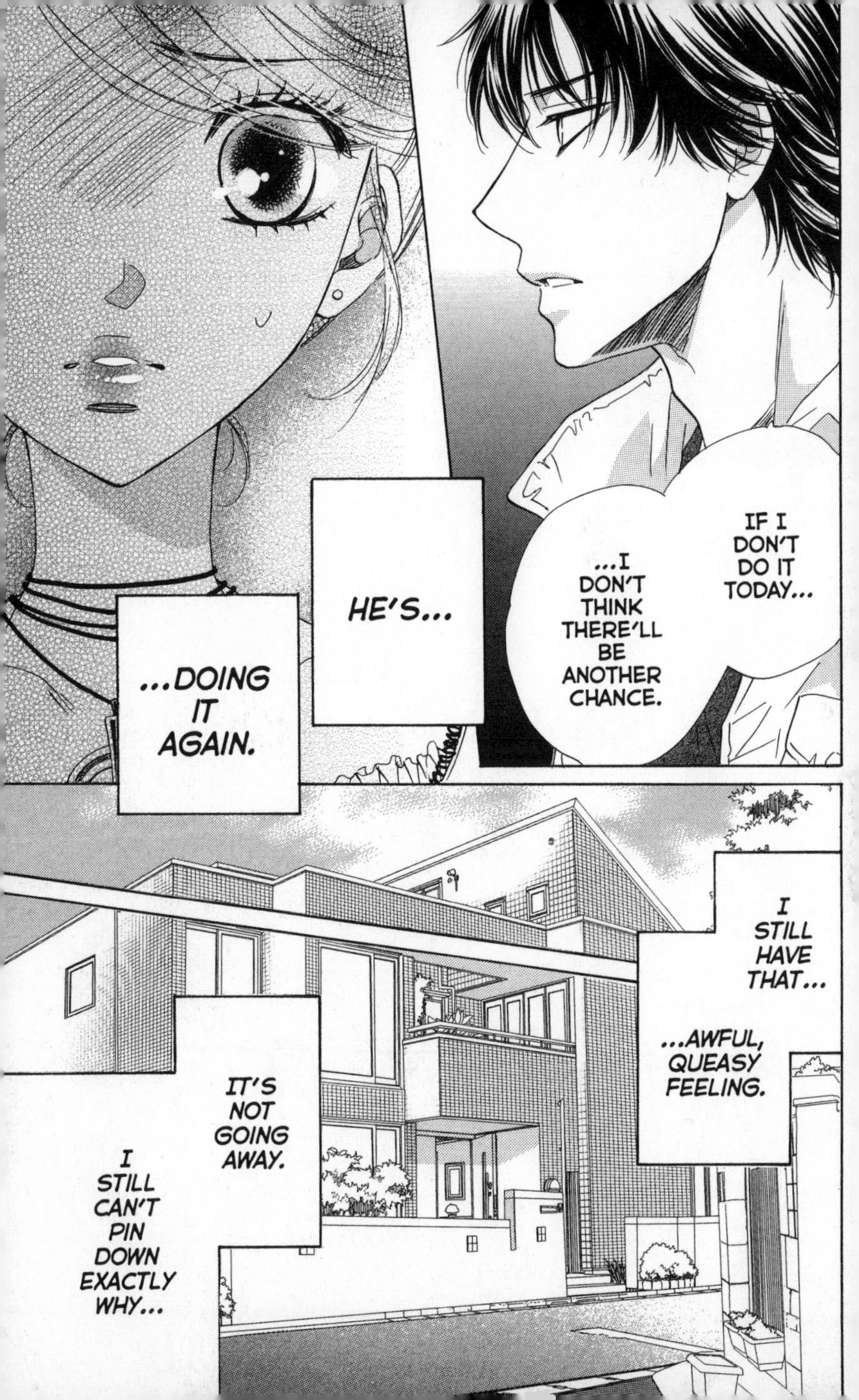
IF I DON'T DO IT TODAY...
...I DON'T THINK THERE'LL BE ANOTHER CHANCE.
HE'S...
...DOING IT AGAIN.
I STILL HAVE THAT...
...AWFUL, QUEASY FEELING.
IT'S NOT GOING AWAY.
I STILL CAN'T PIN DOWN EXACTLY WHY...

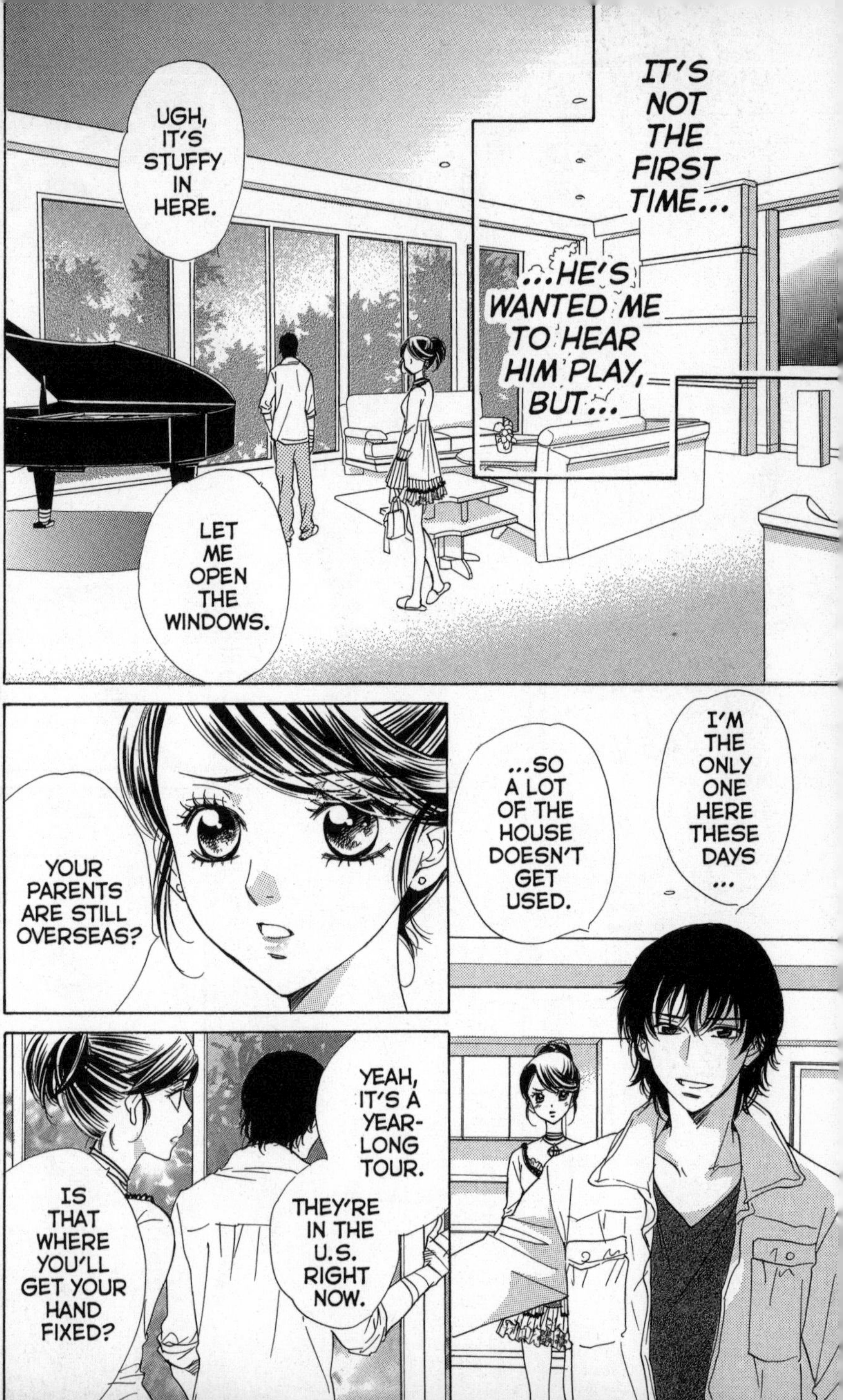
IT'S NOT THE FIRST TIME...
...HE'S WANTED ME TO HEAR HIM PLAY, BUT...
UGH, IT'S STUFFY IN HERE.
LET ME OPEN THE WINDOWS.
I'M THE ONLY ONE HERE THESE DAYS...
...SO A LOT OF THE HOUSE DOESN'T GET USED.
YOUR PARENTS ARE STILL OVERSEAS?
YEAH, IT'S A YEAR-LONG TOUR.
THEY'RE IN THE U.S. RIGHT NOW.
IS THAT WHERE YOU'LL GET YOUR HAND FIXED?

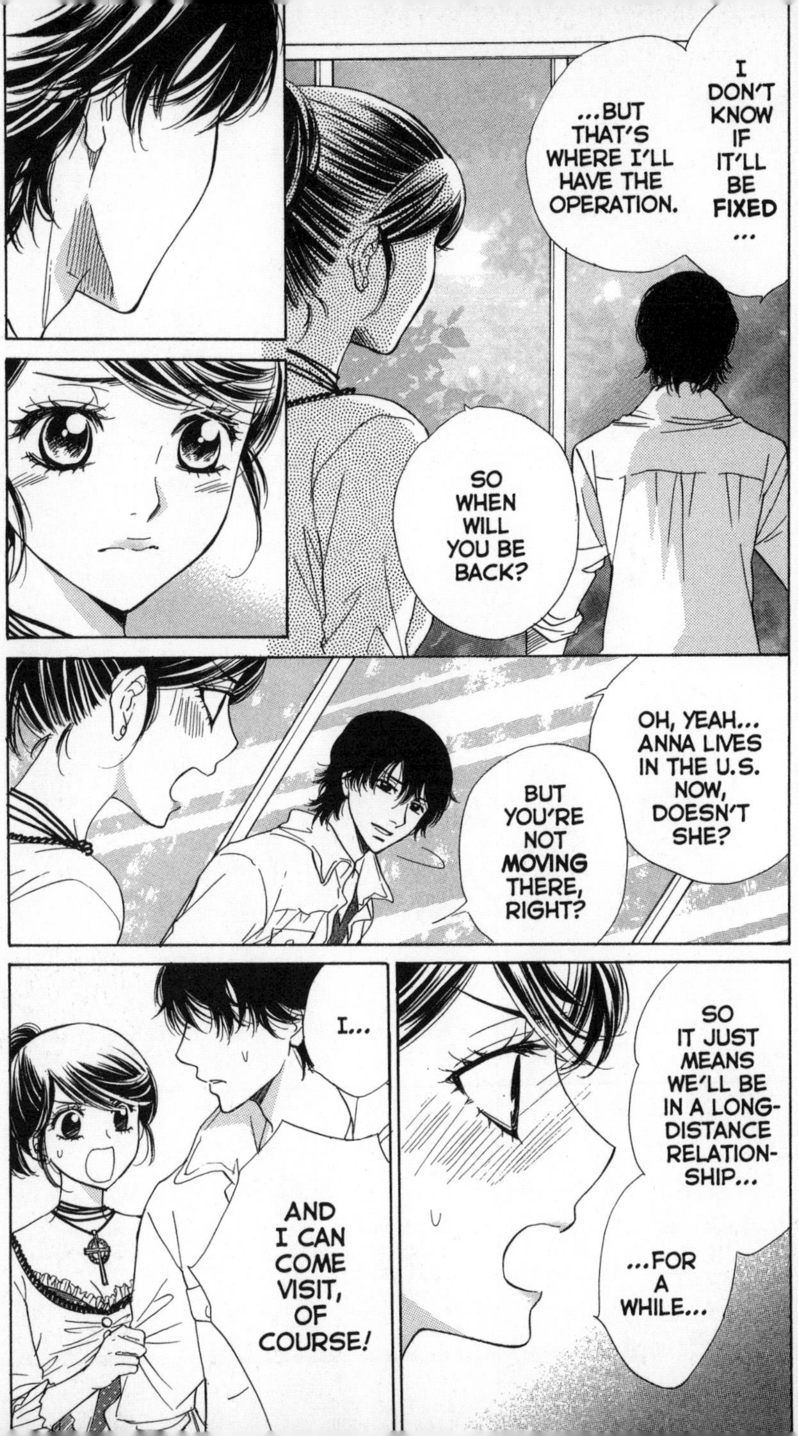
I DON'T KNOW IF IT'LL BE FIXED...
...BUT THAT'S WHERE I'LL HAVE THE OPERATION.
SO WHEN WILL YOU BE BACK?
OH, YEAH... ANNA LIVES IN THE U.S. NOW, DOESN'T SHE?
BUT YOU'RE NOT MOVING THERE, RIGHT?
SO IT JUST MEANS WE'LL BE IN A LONG-DISTANCE RELATIONSHIP...
...FOR A WHILE...
I...
AND I CAN COME VISIT, OF COURSE!

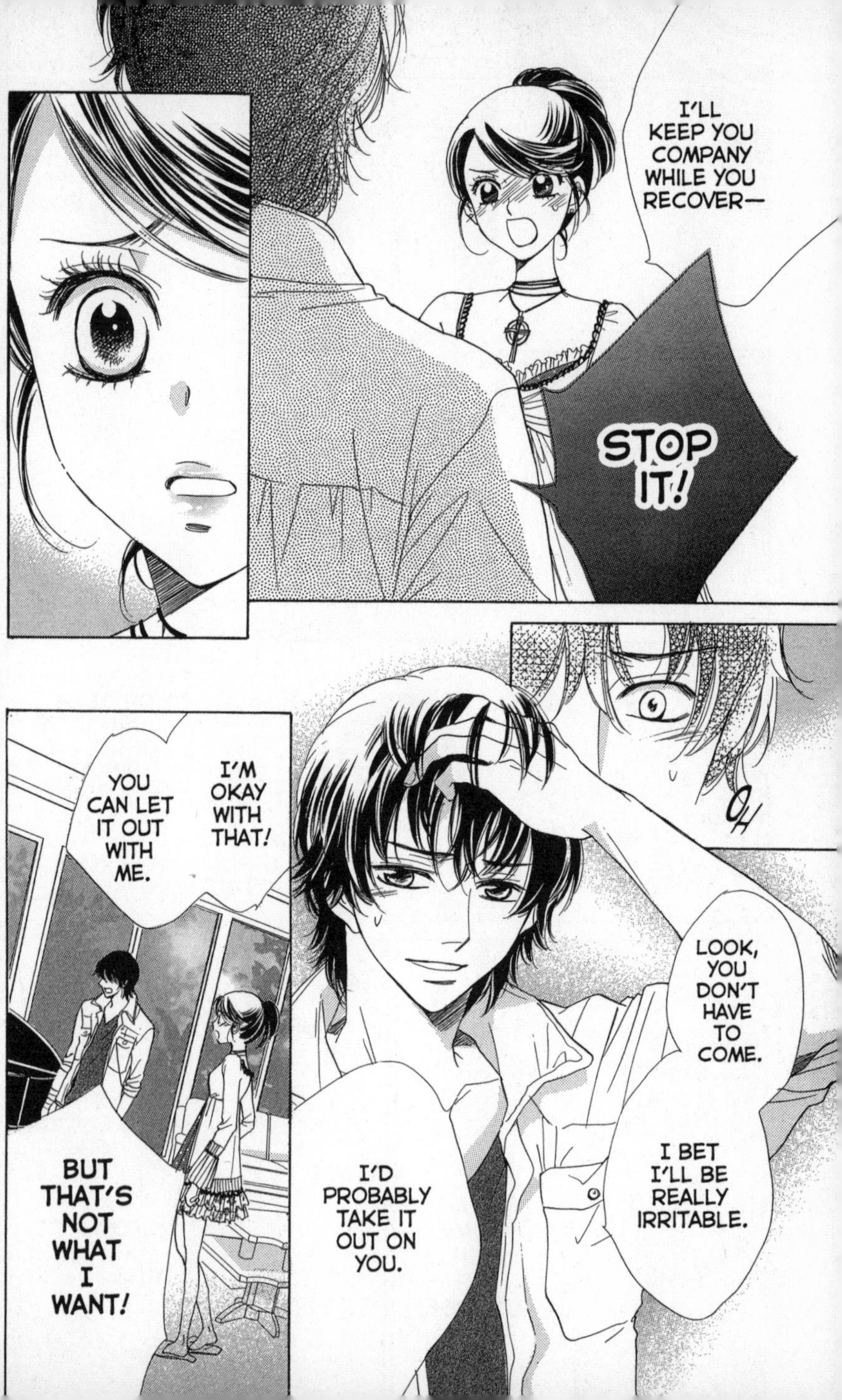

I'LL KEEP YOU COMPANY WHILE YOU RECOVER—
STOP IT!
OH
LOOK, YOU DON'T HAVE TO COME.
I BET I'LL BE REALLY IRRITABLE.
I'D PROBABLY TAKE IT OUT ON YOU.
I'M OKAY WITH THAT!
YOU CAN LET IT OUT WITH ME.
BUT THAT'S NOT WHAT I WANT!

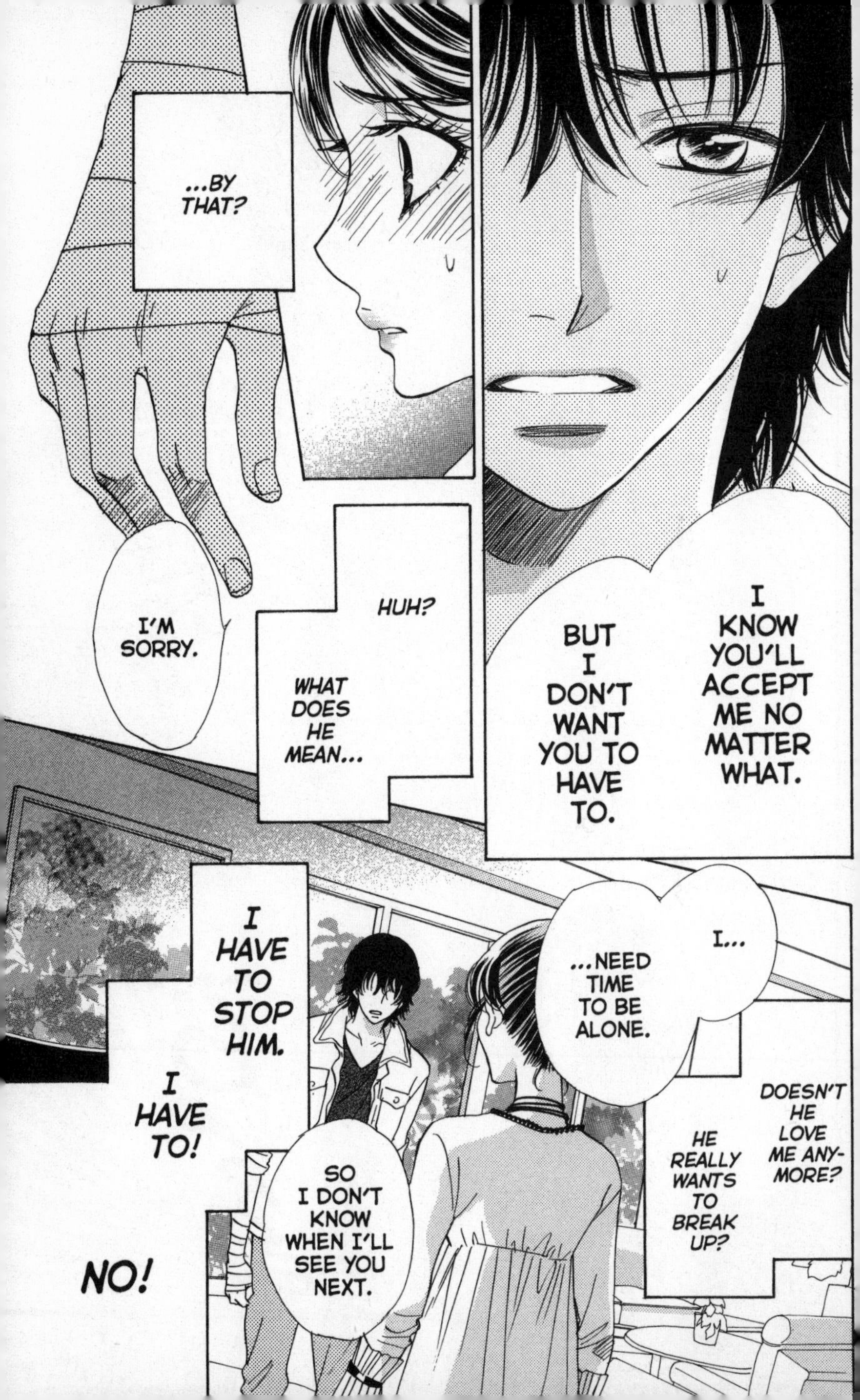
I KNOW YOU'LL ACCEPT ME NO MATTER WHAT.
BUT I DON'T WANT YOU TO HAVE TO.
I'M SORRY.
HUH?
WHAT DOES HE MEAN...
...BY THAT?
I...
...NEED TIME TO BE ALONE.
SO I DON'T KNOW WHEN I'LL SEE YOU NEXT.
DOESN'T HE LOVE ME ANY-MORE?
HE REALLY WANTS TO BREAK UP?
I HAVE TO STOP HIM.
I HAVE TO!
NO!

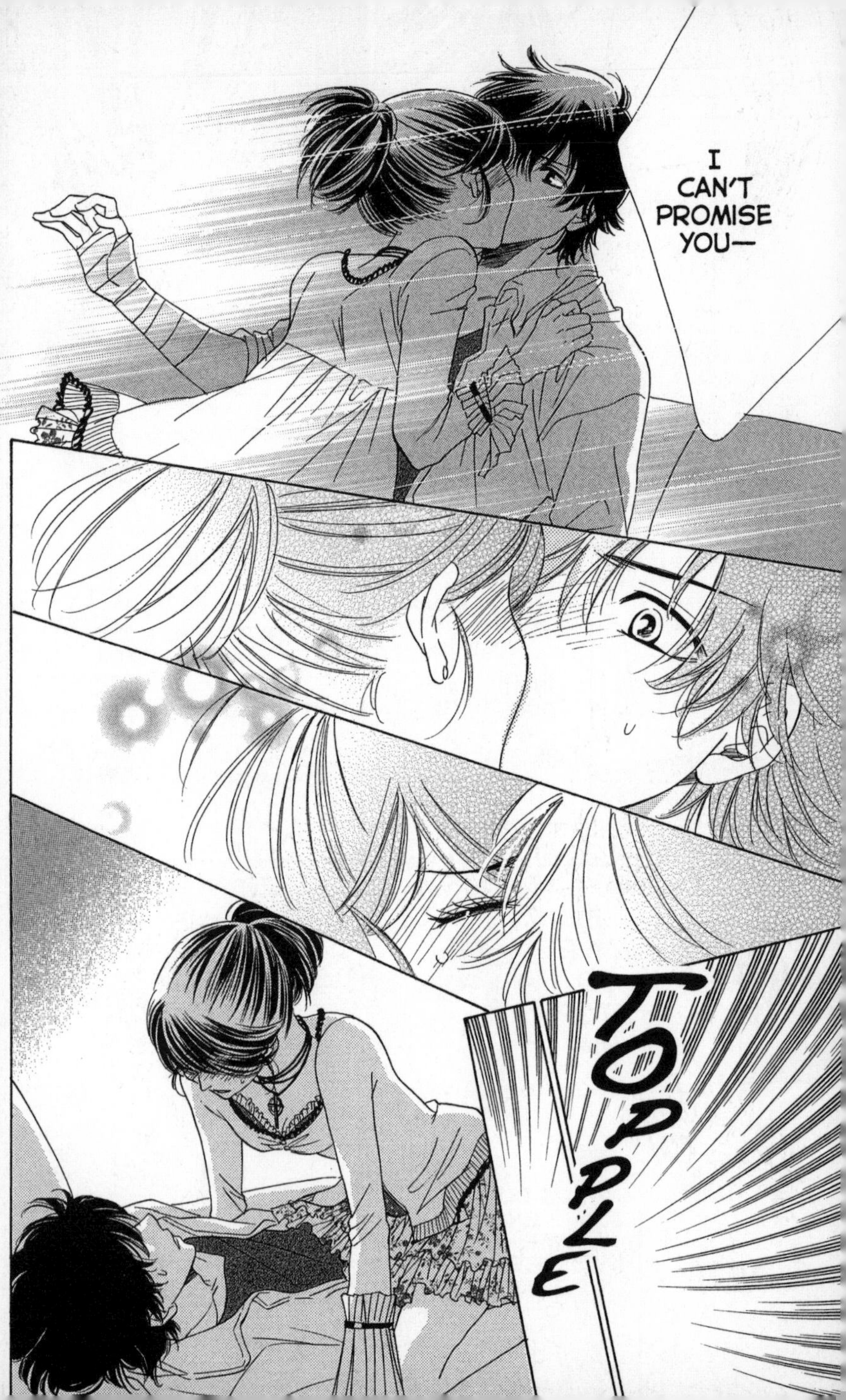
I CAN'T PROMISE YOU—
TOPPLE

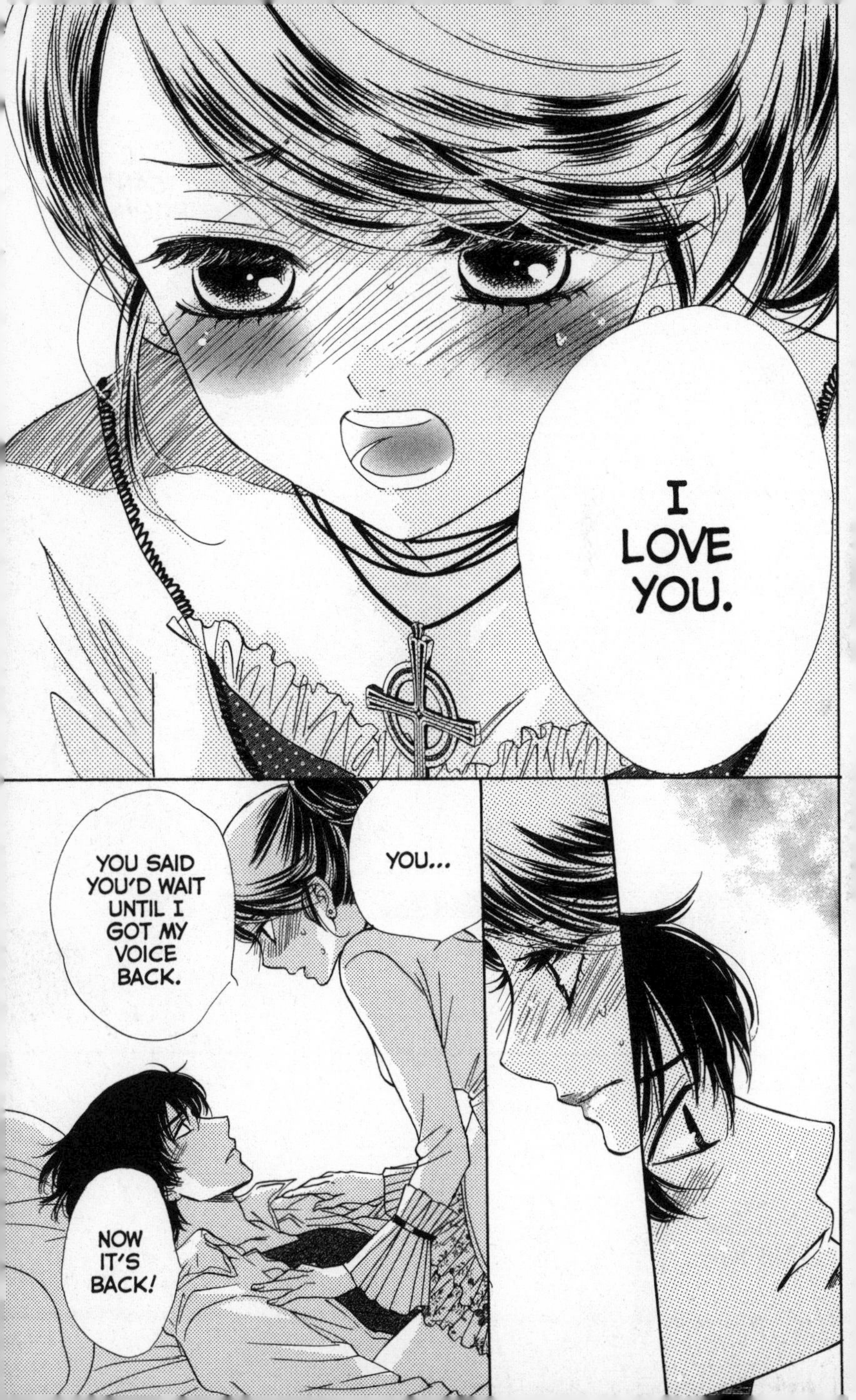
I LOVE YOU.
YOU...
YOU SAID YOU'D WAIT UNTIL I GOT MY VOICE BACK.
NOW IT'S BACK!

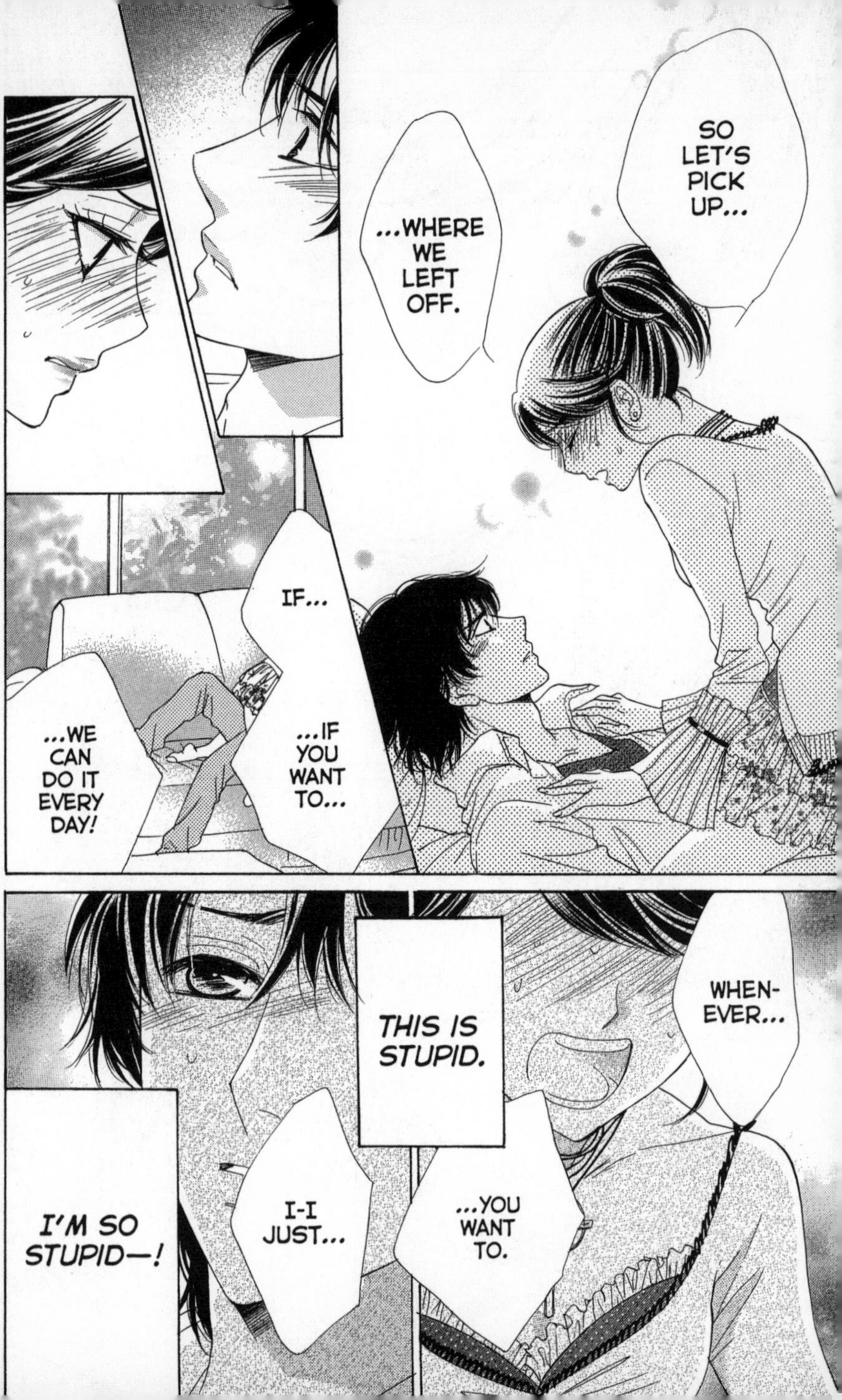
SO LET'S PICK UP...
...WHERE WE LEFT OFF.
IF...
...IF YOU WANT TO...
...WE CAN DO IT EVERY DAY!
WHEN-EVER...
...YOU WANT TO.
THIS IS STUPID.
I-I JUST...
I'M SO STUPID—!

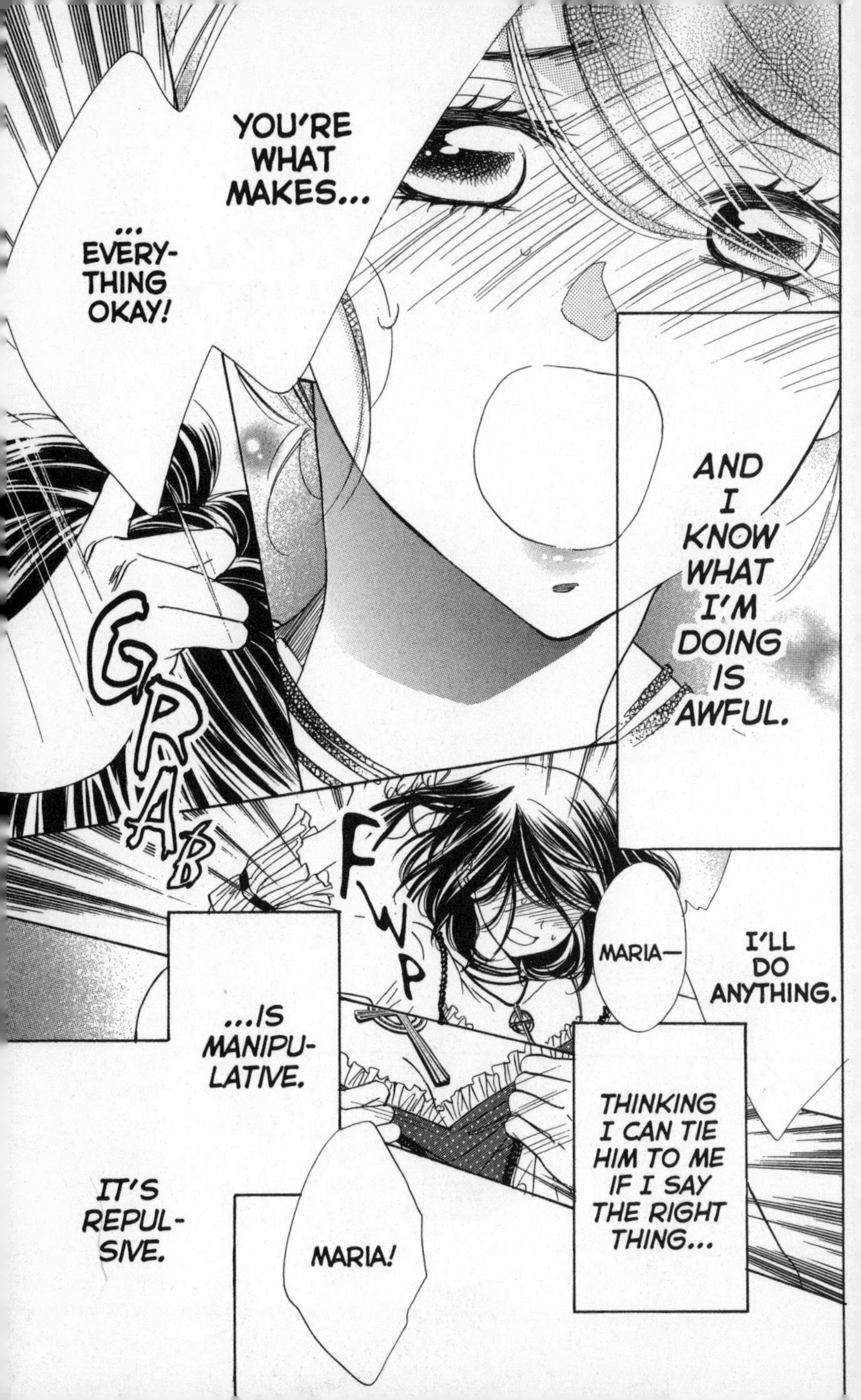
YOU'RE WHAT MAKES...
...EVERY-THING OKAY!
AND I KNOW WHAT I'M DOING IS AWFUL.
GRAB
I'LL DO ANYTHING.
MARIA—
FWP
...IS MANIPU-LATIVE.
THINKING I CAN TIE HIM TO ME IF I SAY THE RIGHT THING...
MARIA!
IT'S REPUL-SIVE.

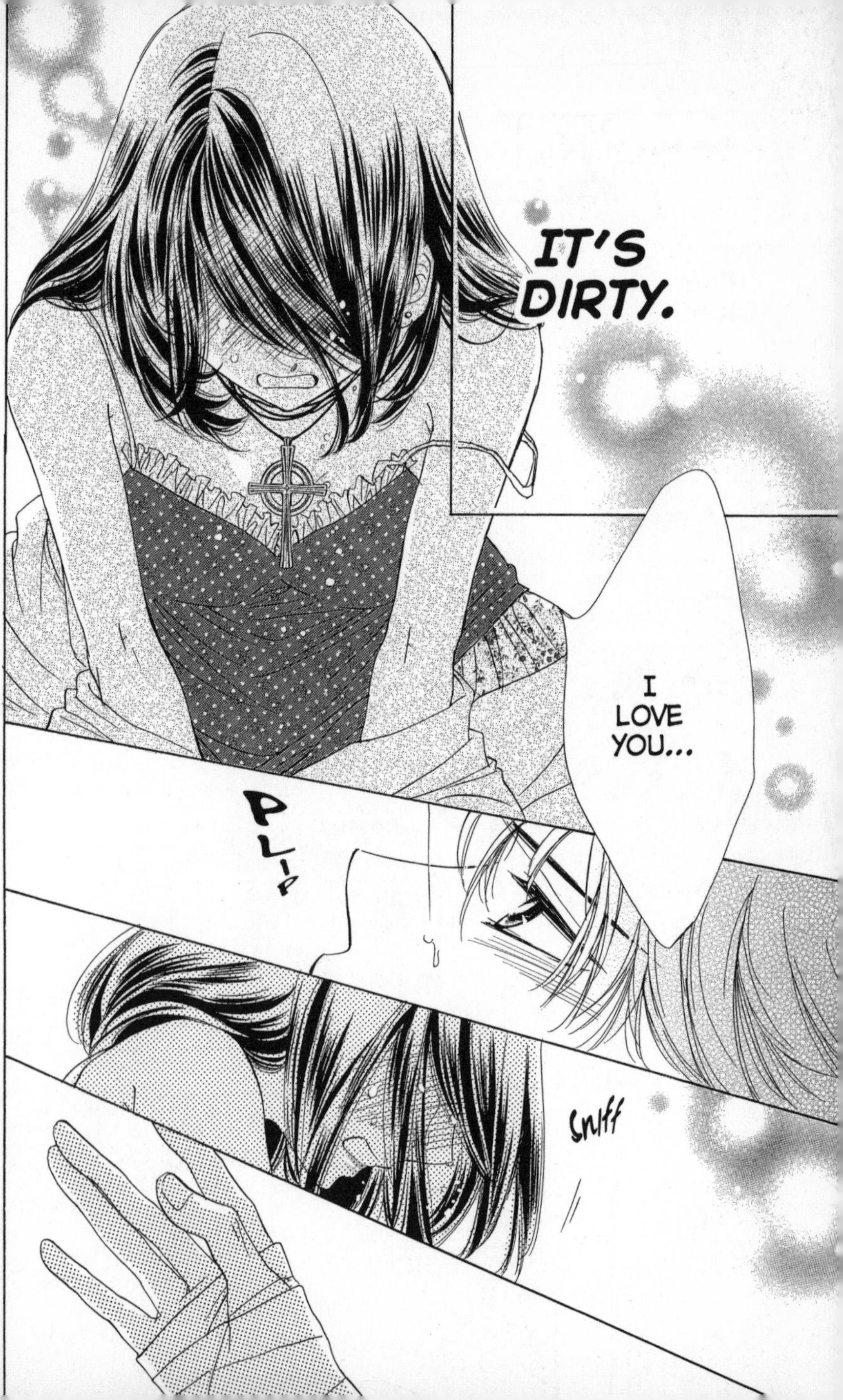
IT'S DIRTY.
I LOVE YOU...
PLIP
SNIFF

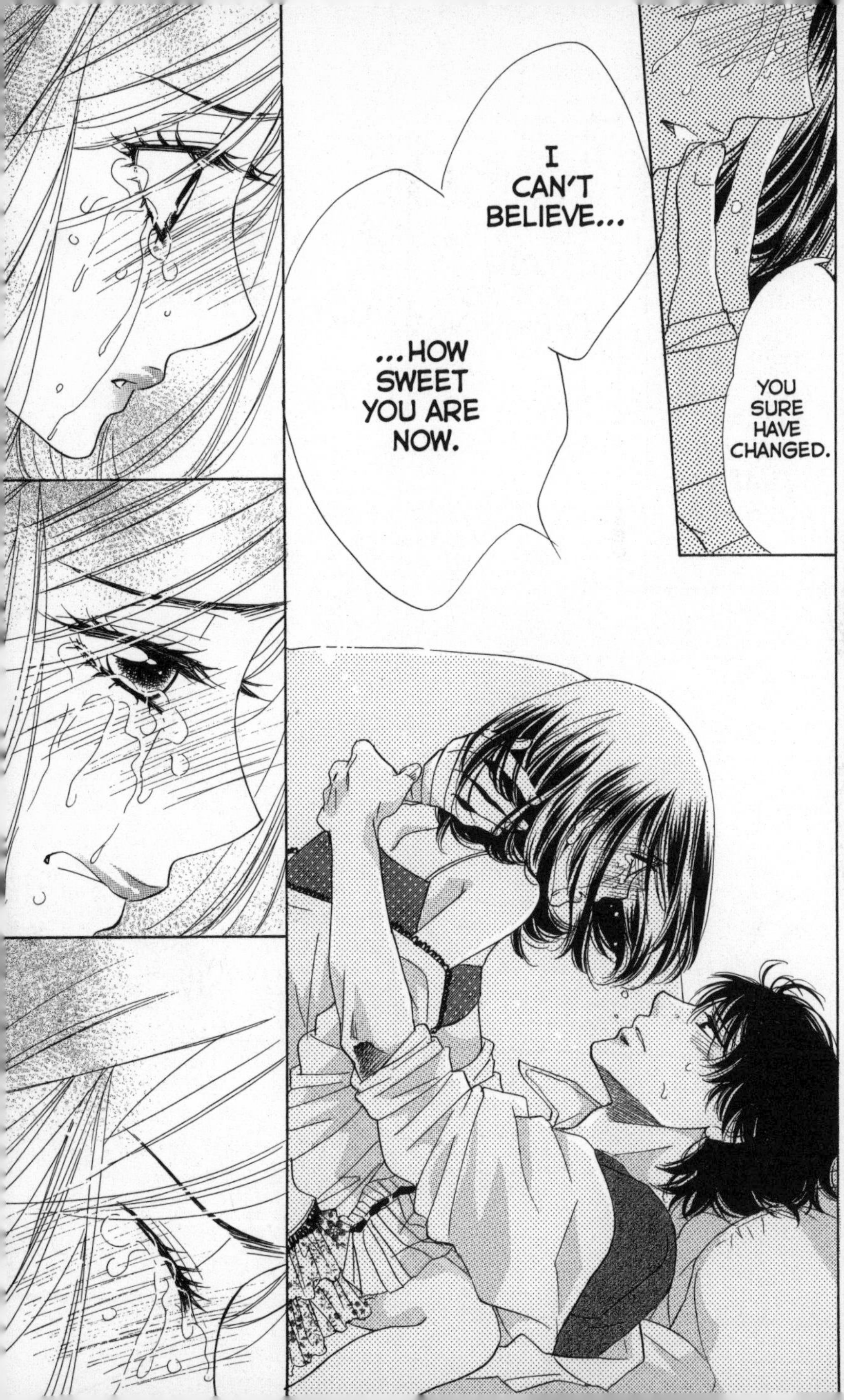
YOU SURE HAVE CHANGED.
I CAN'T BELIEVE...
...HOW SWEET YOU ARE NOW.

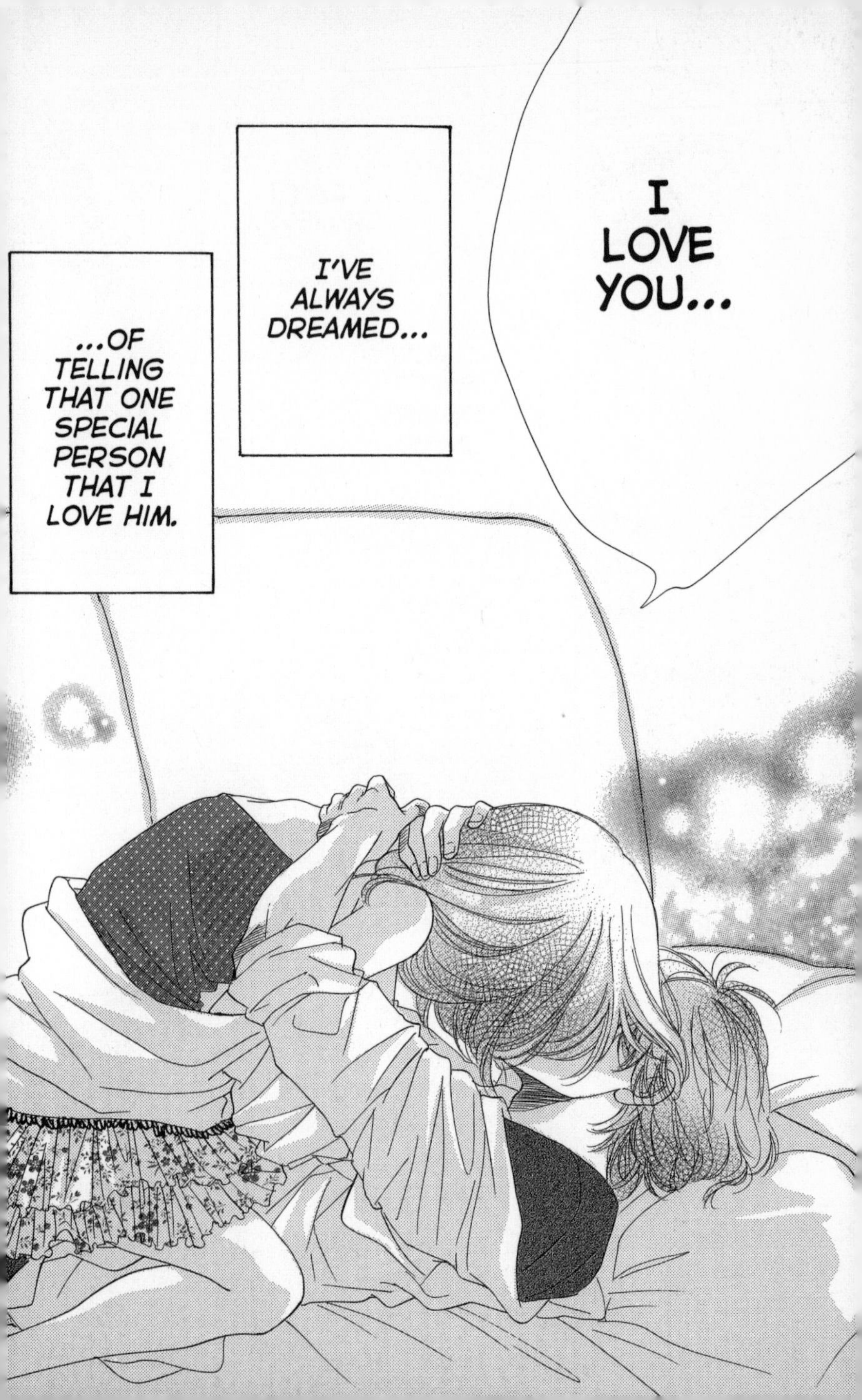
I LOVE YOU...
I'VE ALWAYS DREAMED...
...OF TELLING THAT ONE SPECIAL PERSON THAT I LOVE HIM.

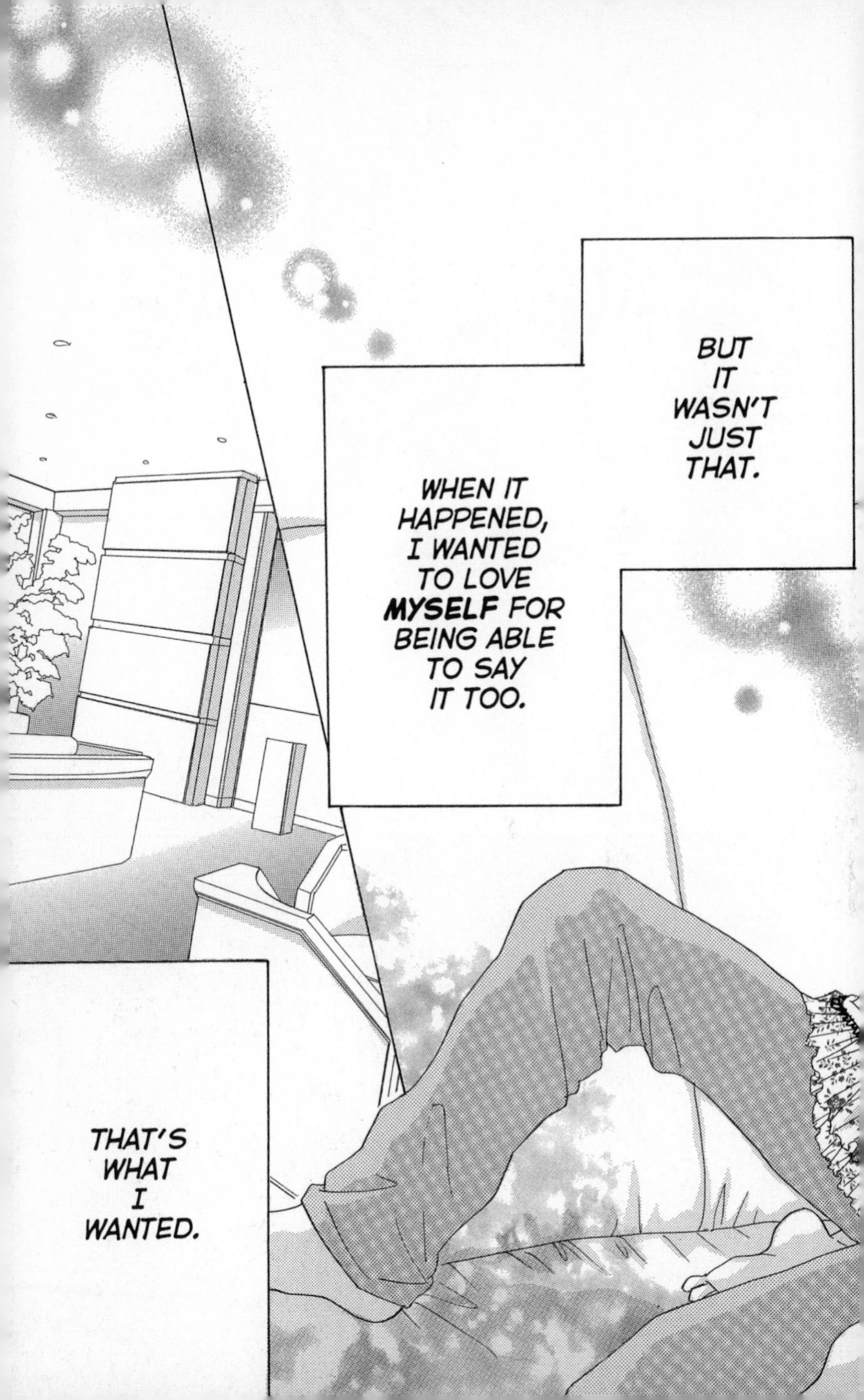
BUT IT WASN'T JUST THAT.
WHEN IT HAPPENED, I WANTED TO LOVE **MYSELF** FOR BEING ABLE TO SAY IT TOO.
THAT'S WHAT I WANTED.

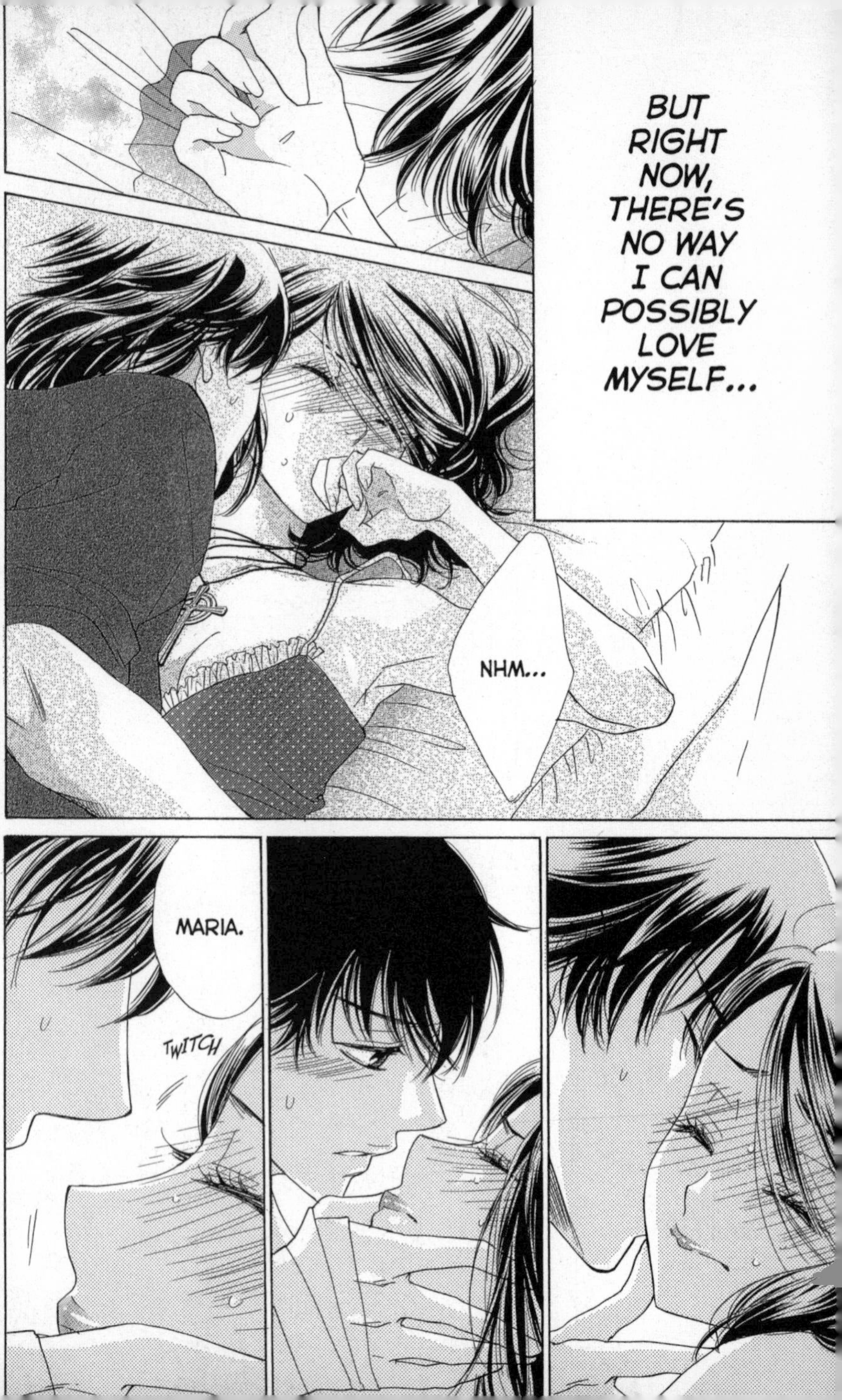
BUT RIGHT NOW, THERE'S NO WAY I CAN POSSIBLY LOVE MYSELF...
NHM...
MARIA.
TWITCH

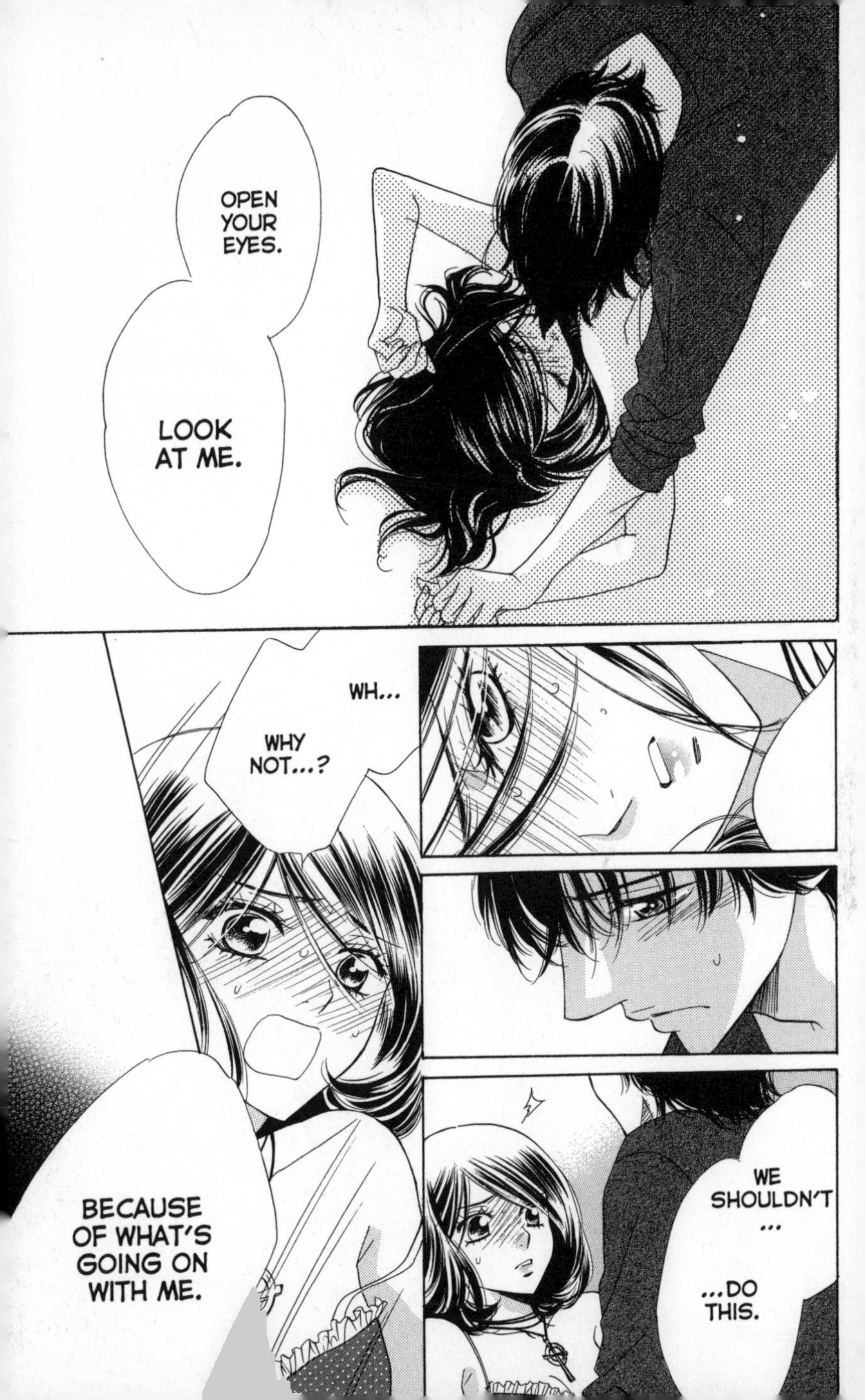
OPEN YOUR EYES.
LOOK AT ME.
WE SHOULDN'T ...
...DO THIS.
WH...
WHY NOT...?
BECAUSE OF WHAT'S GOING ON WITH ME.

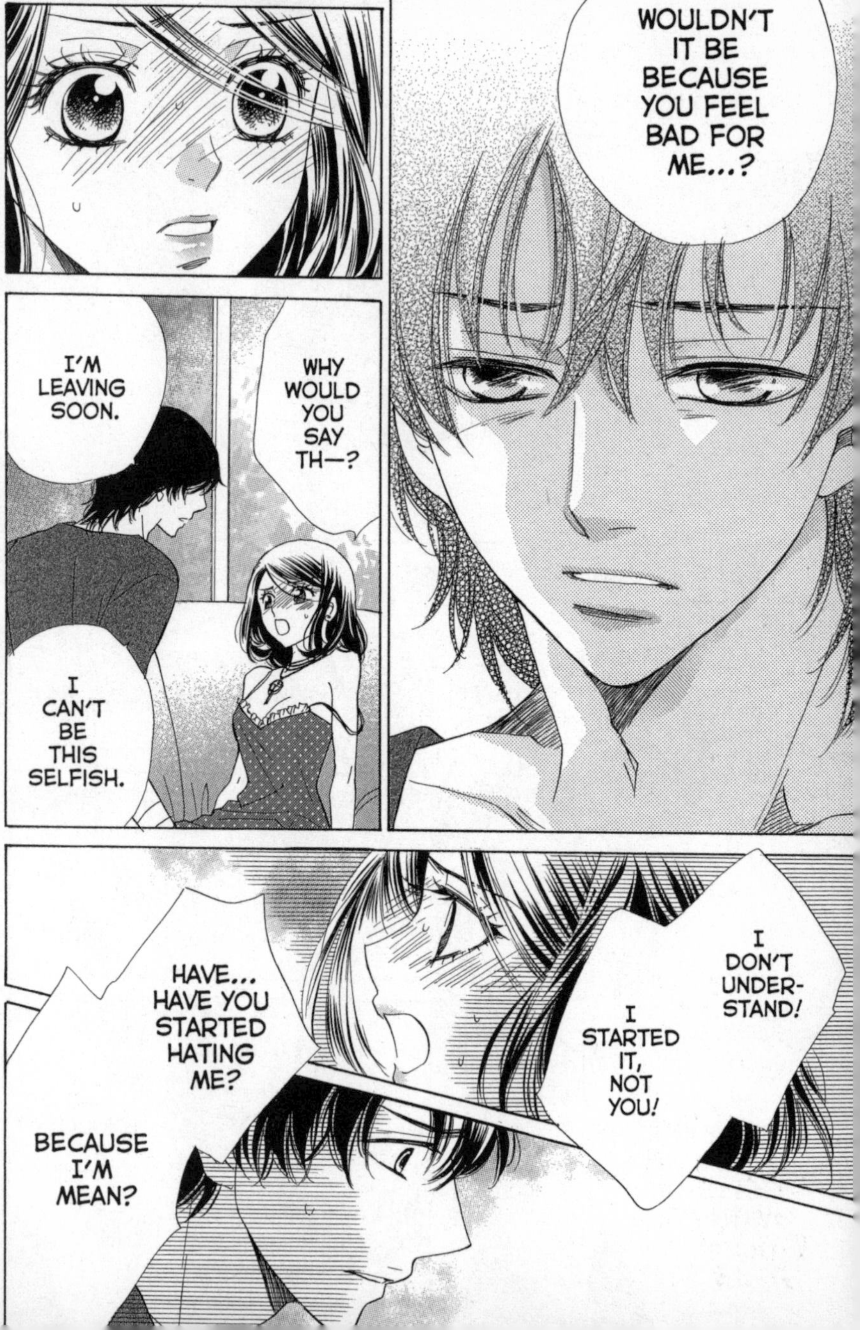
WOULDN'T IT BE BECAUSE YOU FEEL BAD FOR ME...?
WHY WOULD YOU SAY TH—?
I'M LEAVING SOON.
I CAN'T BE THIS SELFISH.
I DON'T UNDER-STAND!
I STARTED IT, NOT YOU!
HAVE... HAVE YOU STARTED HATING ME?
BECAUSE I'M MEAN?

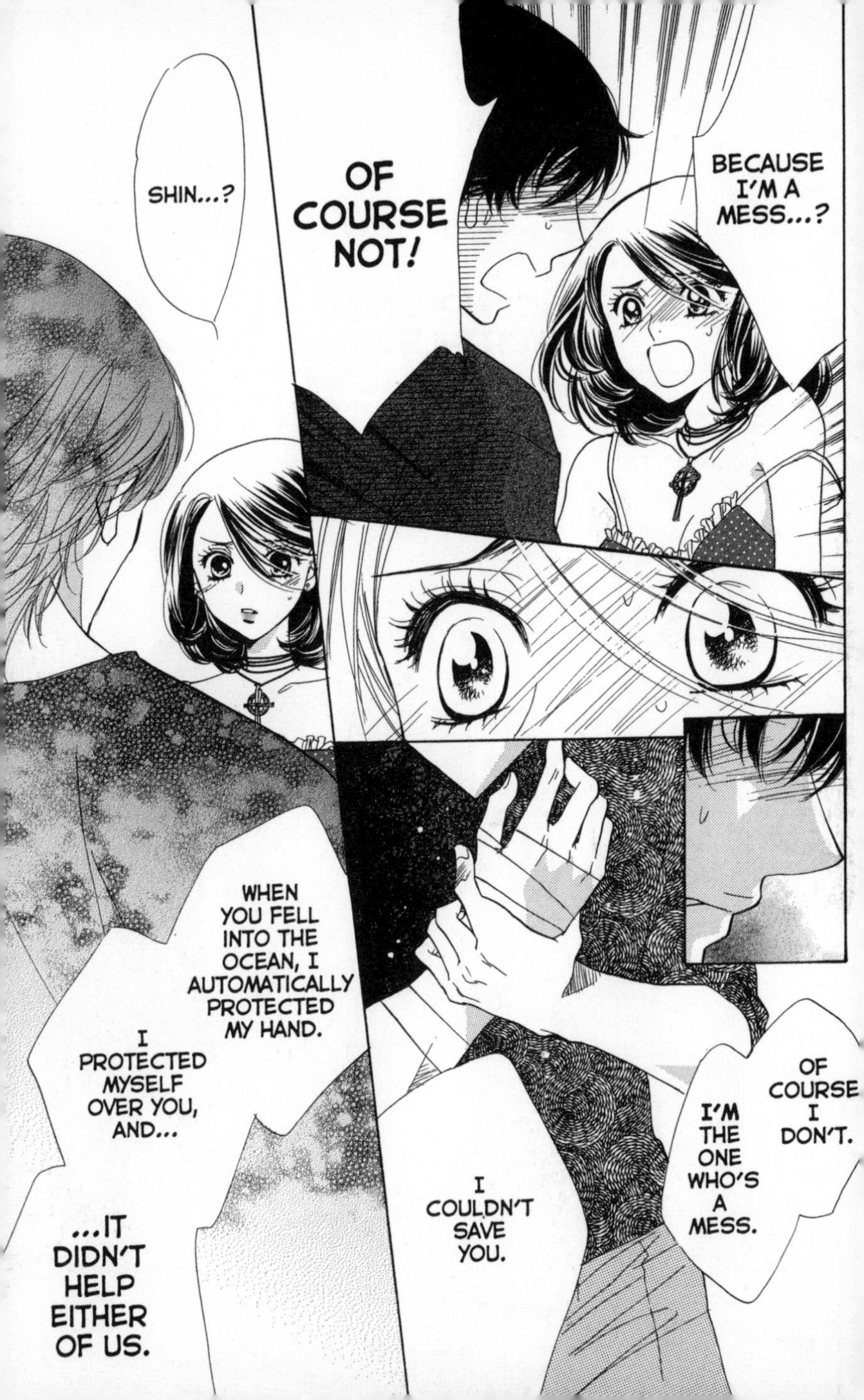
BECAUSE I'M A MESS...?
OF COURSE NOT!
SHIN...?
OF COURSE I DON'T.
I'M THE ONE WHO'S A MESS.
I COULDN'T SAVE YOU.
WHEN YOU FELL INTO THE OCEAN, I AUTOMATICALLY PROTECTED MY HAND.
I PROTECTED MYSELF OVER YOU, AND...
...IT DIDN'T HELP EITHER OF US.

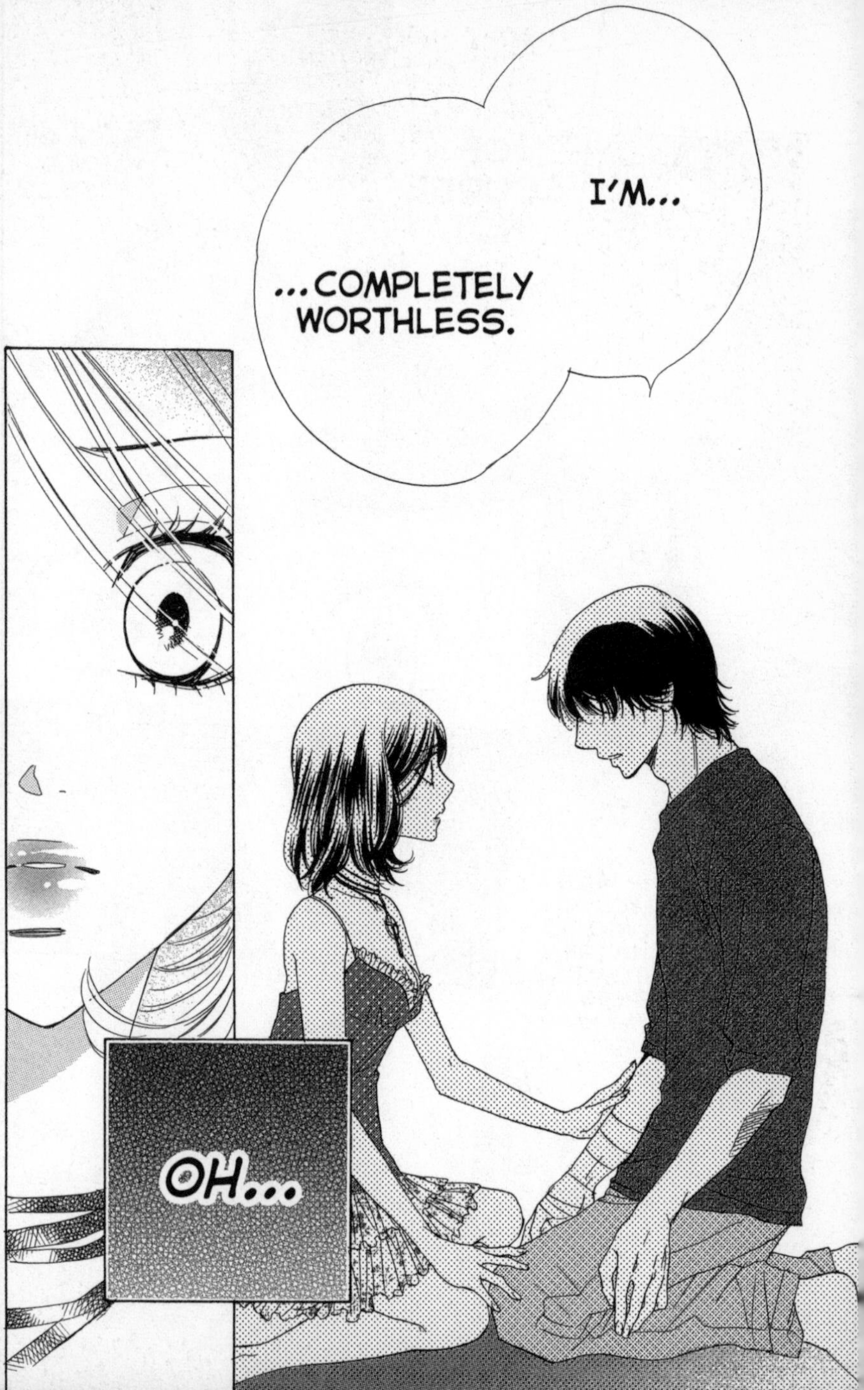
I'M...
...COMPLETELY WORTHLESS.
OH...

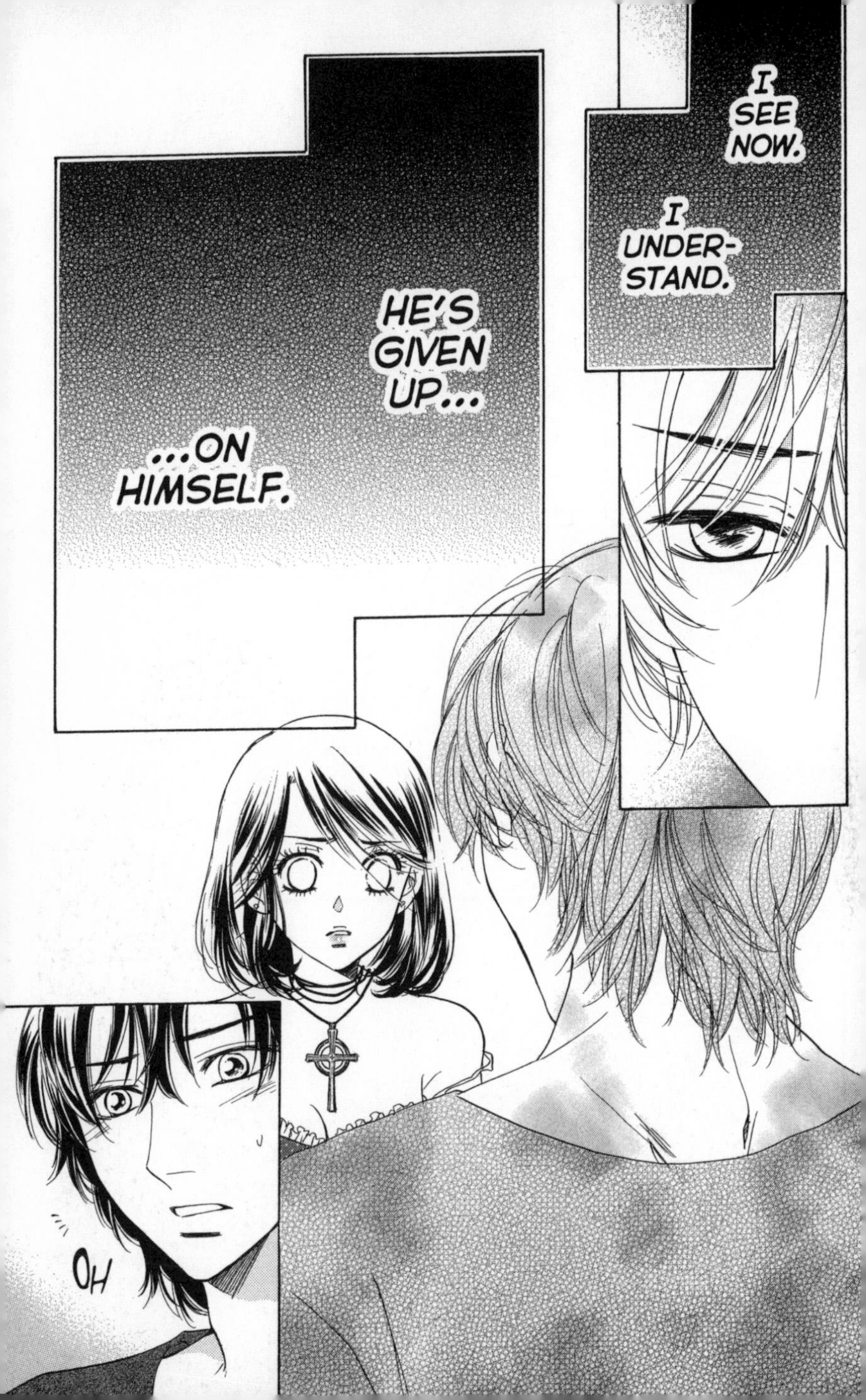
I SEE NOW.
I UNDER-STAND.
HE'S GIVEN UP...
...ON HIMSELF.
OH

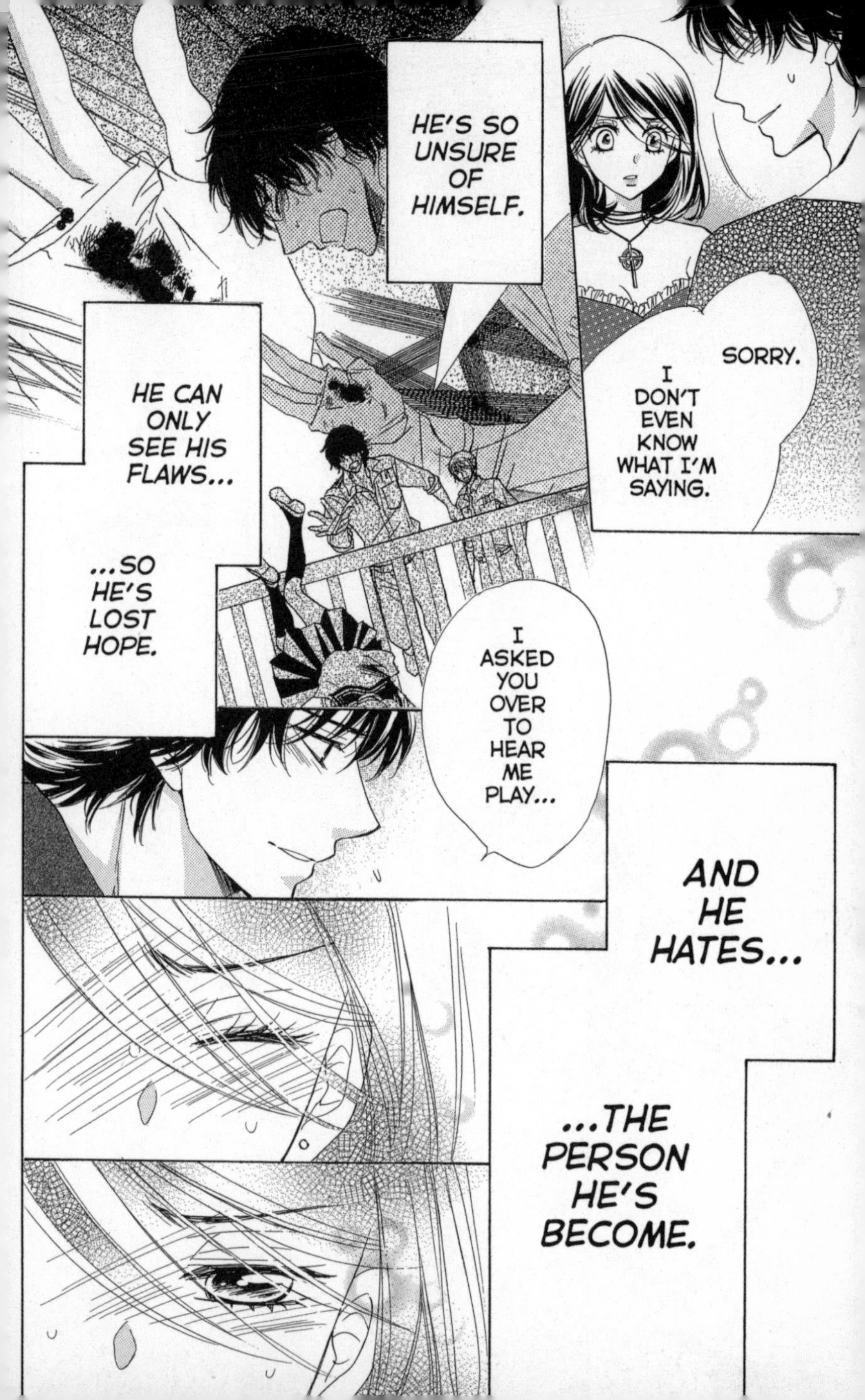
SORRY.
I DON'T EVEN KNOW WHAT I'M SAYING.
HE'S SO UNSURE OF HIMSELF.
HE CAN ONLY SEE HIS FLAWS...
...SO HE'S LOST HOPE.
I ASKED YOU OVER TO HEAR ME PLAY...
AND HE HATES...
...THE PERSON HE'S BECOME.

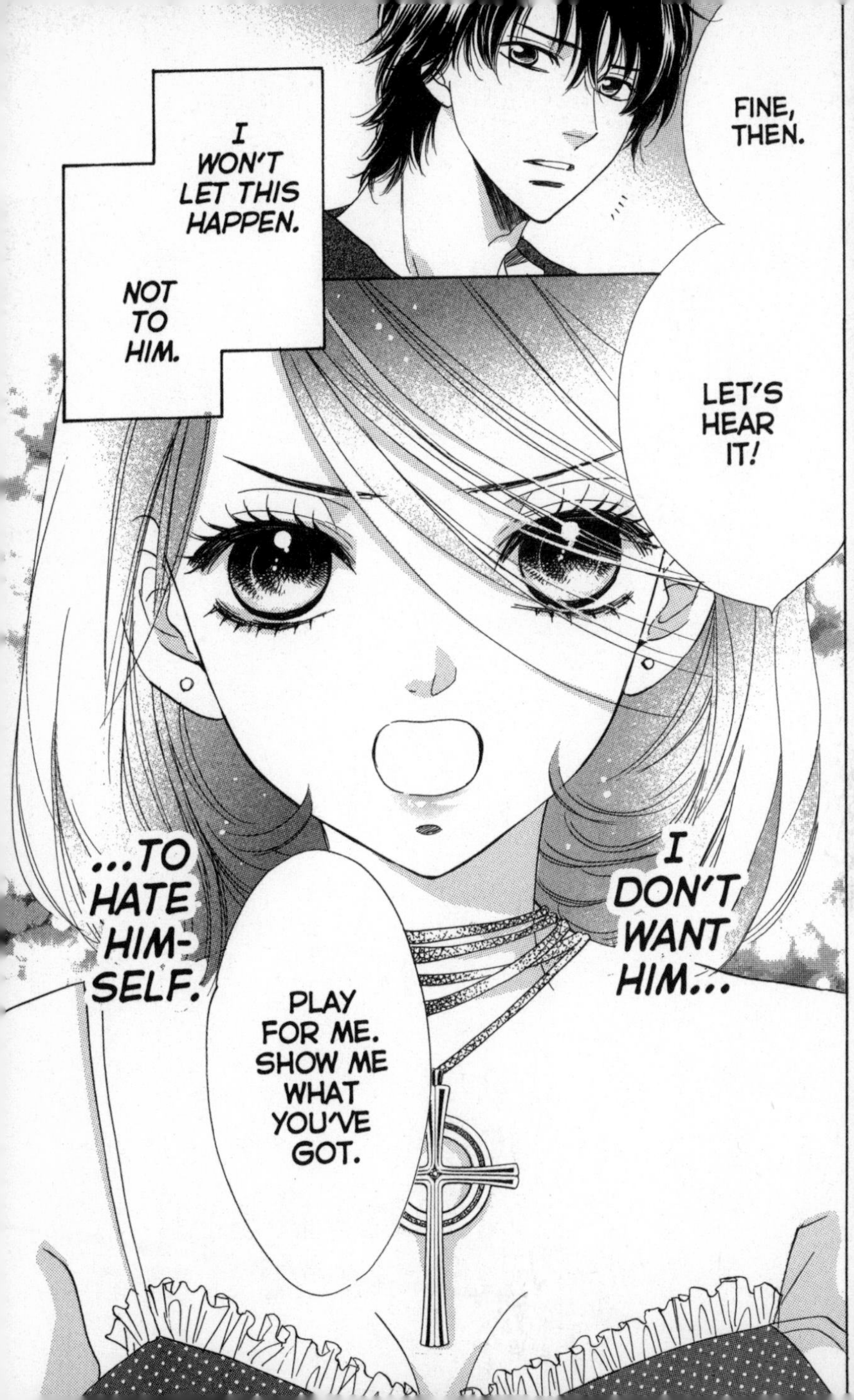
FINE, THEN.
I WON'T LET THIS HAPPEN.
NOT TO HIM.
LET'S HEAR IT!
I DON'T WANT HIM...
...TO HATE HIM-SELF.
PLAY FOR ME. SHOW ME WHAT YOU'VE GOT.

A Devil and
Her Love Song

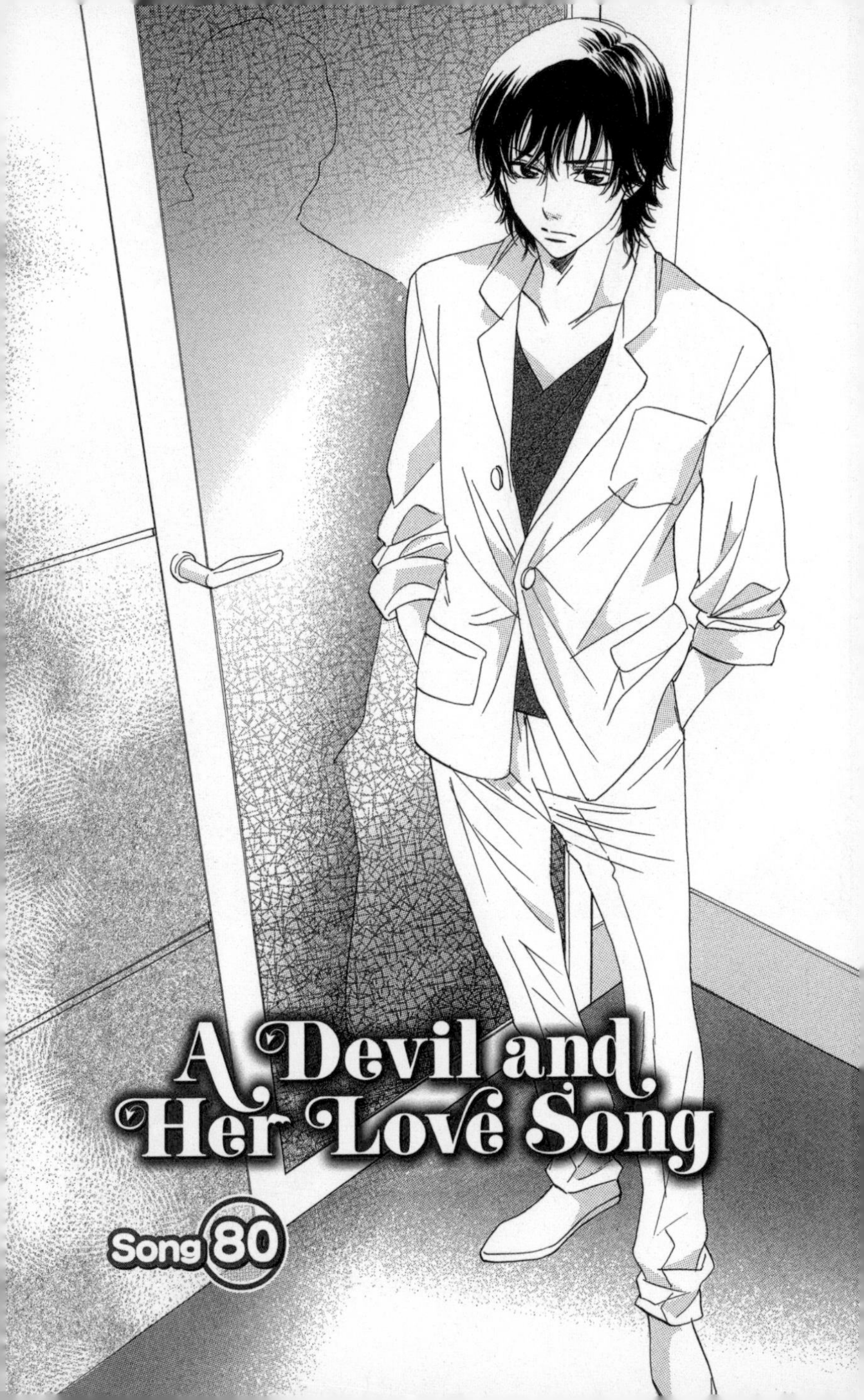
A Devil and Her Love Song
Song 80

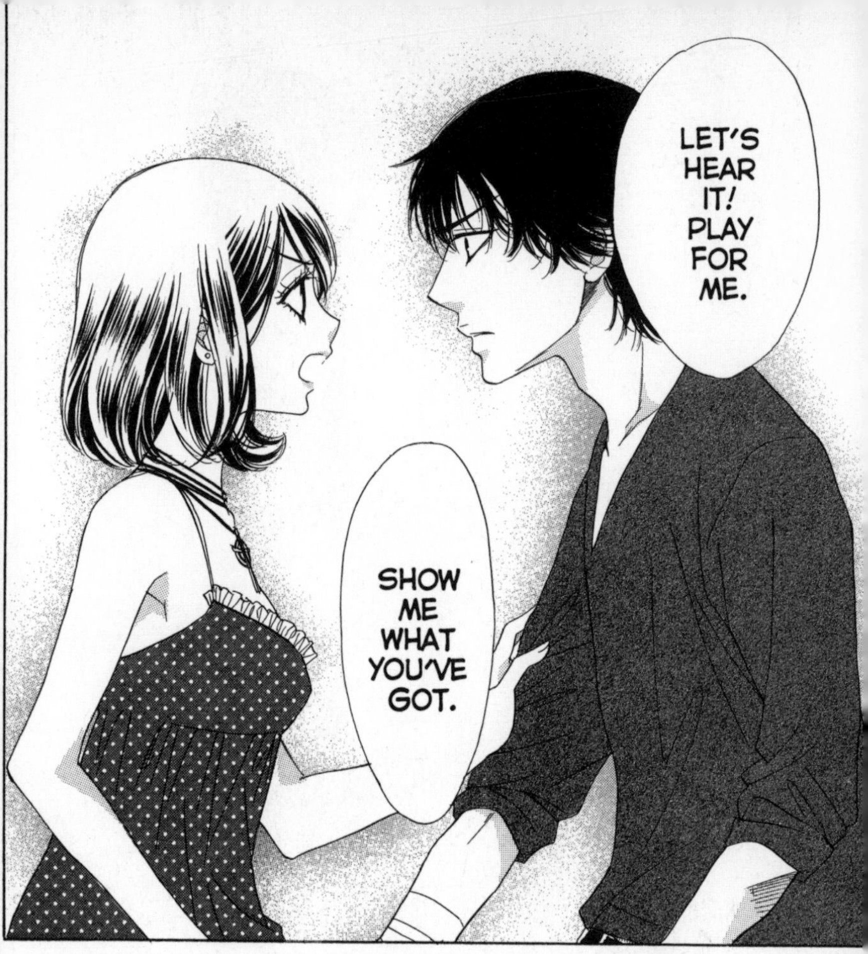
LET'S HEAR IT! PLAY FOR ME.
SHOW ME WHAT YOU'VE GOT.

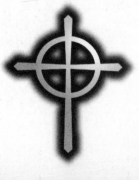

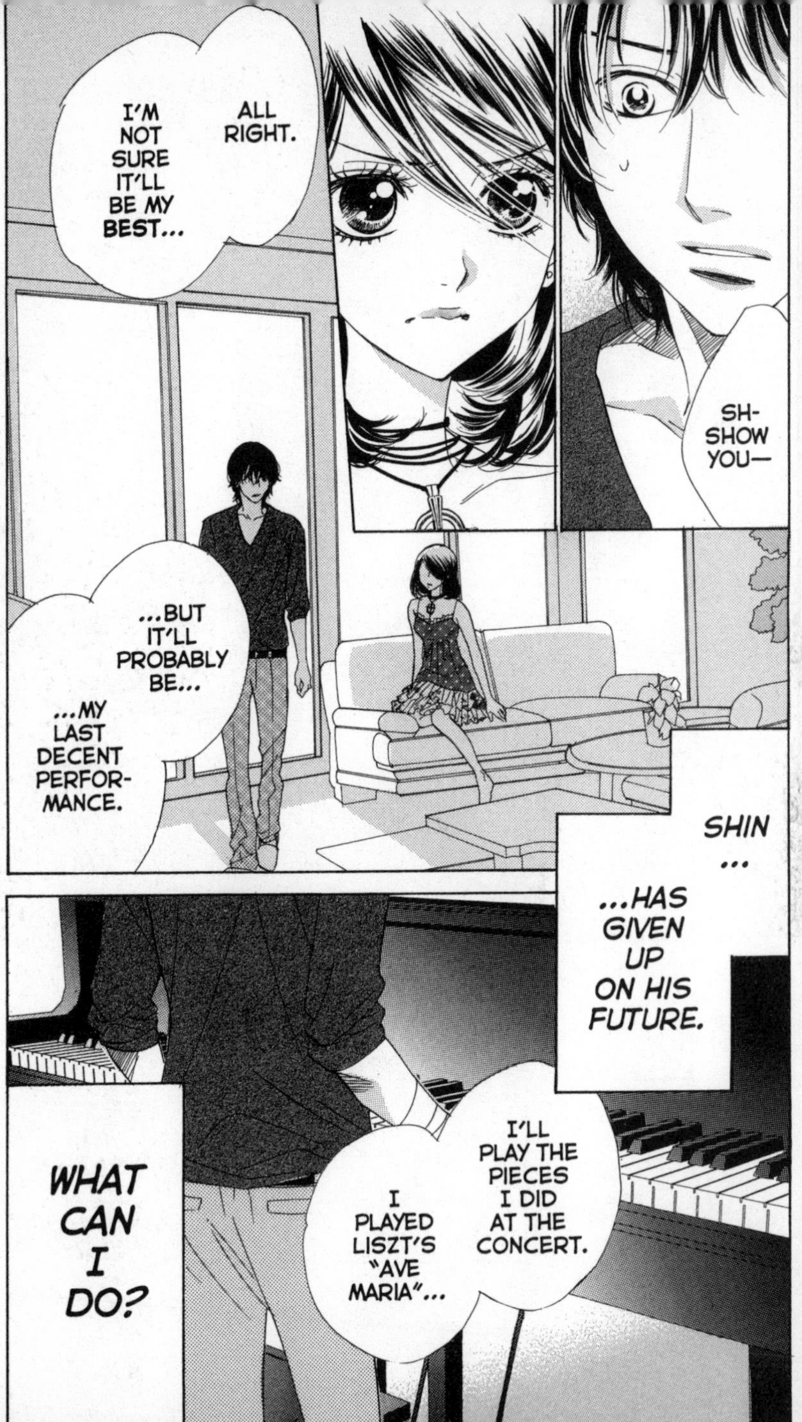
SH-SHOW YOU—
ALL RIGHT.
I'M NOT SURE IT'LL BE MY BEST...
...BUT IT'LL PROBABLY BE...
...MY LAST DECENT PERFORMANCE.
SHIN...
...HAS GIVEN UP ON HIS FUTURE.
I'LL PLAY THE PIECES I DID AT THE CONCERT.
I PLAYED LISZT'S "AVE MARIA"...
WHAT CAN I DO?

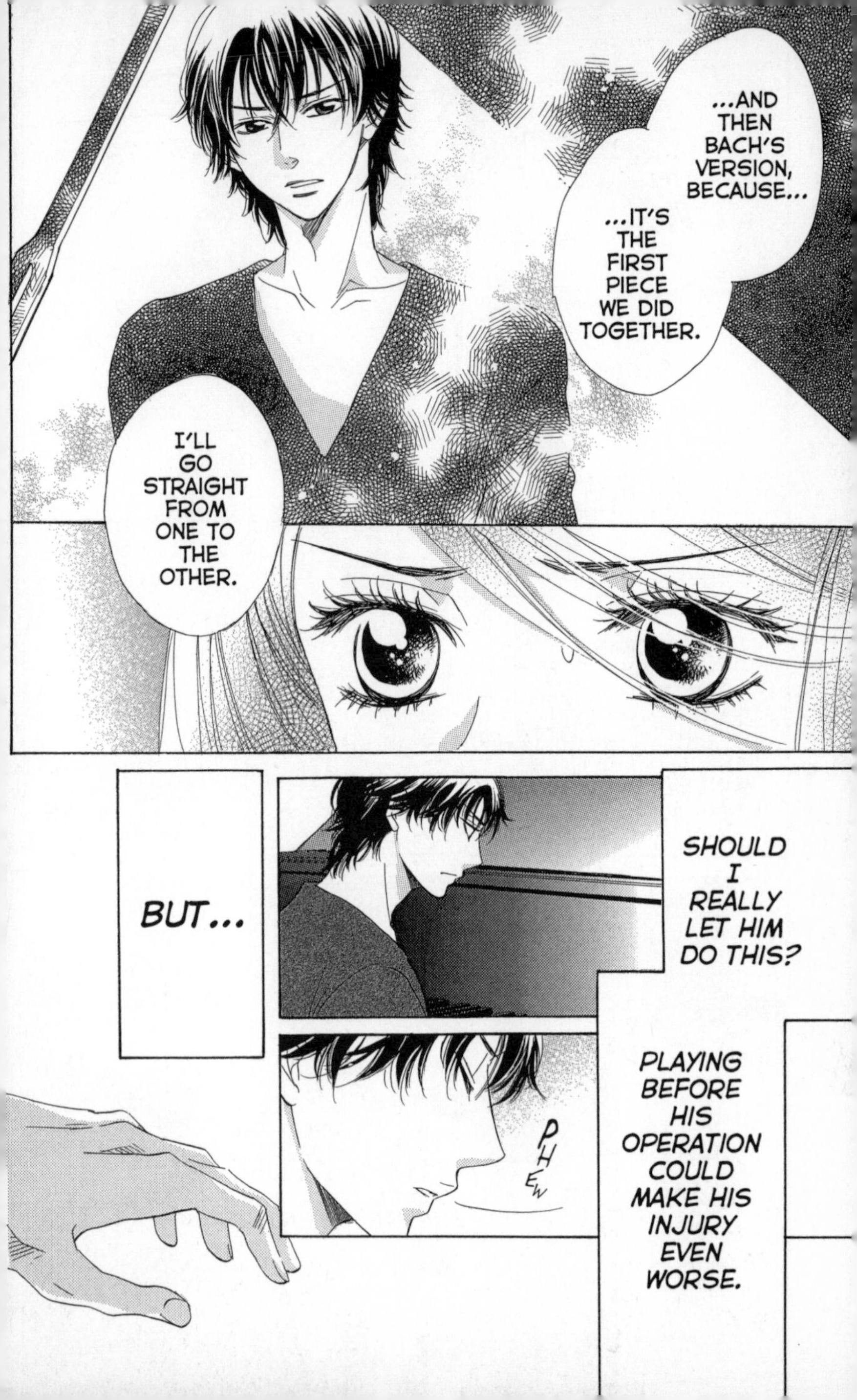
...AND THEN BACH'S VERSION, BECAUSE...
...IT'S THE FIRST PIECE WE DID TOGETHER.
I'LL GO STRAIGHT FROM ONE TO THE OTHER.
SHOULD I REALLY LET HIM DO THIS?
BUT...
PLAYING BEFORE HIS OPERATION COULD MAKE HIS INJURY EVEN WORSE.
PHEW

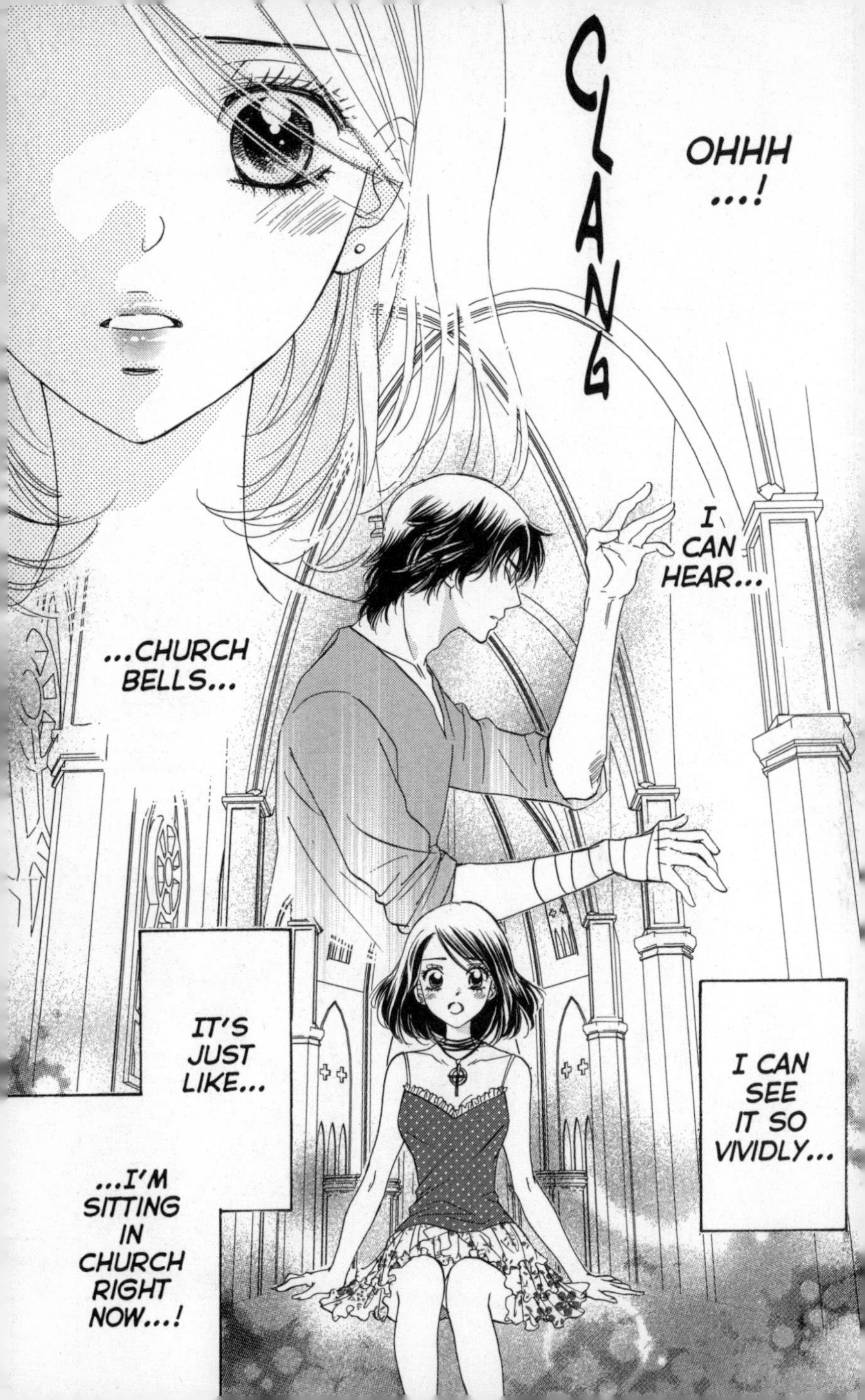
CLANG
OHHH ...!
I CAN HEAR...
...CHURCH BELLS...
I CAN SEE IT SO VIVIDLY...
IT'S JUST LIKE...
...I'M SITTING IN CHURCH RIGHT NOW...!

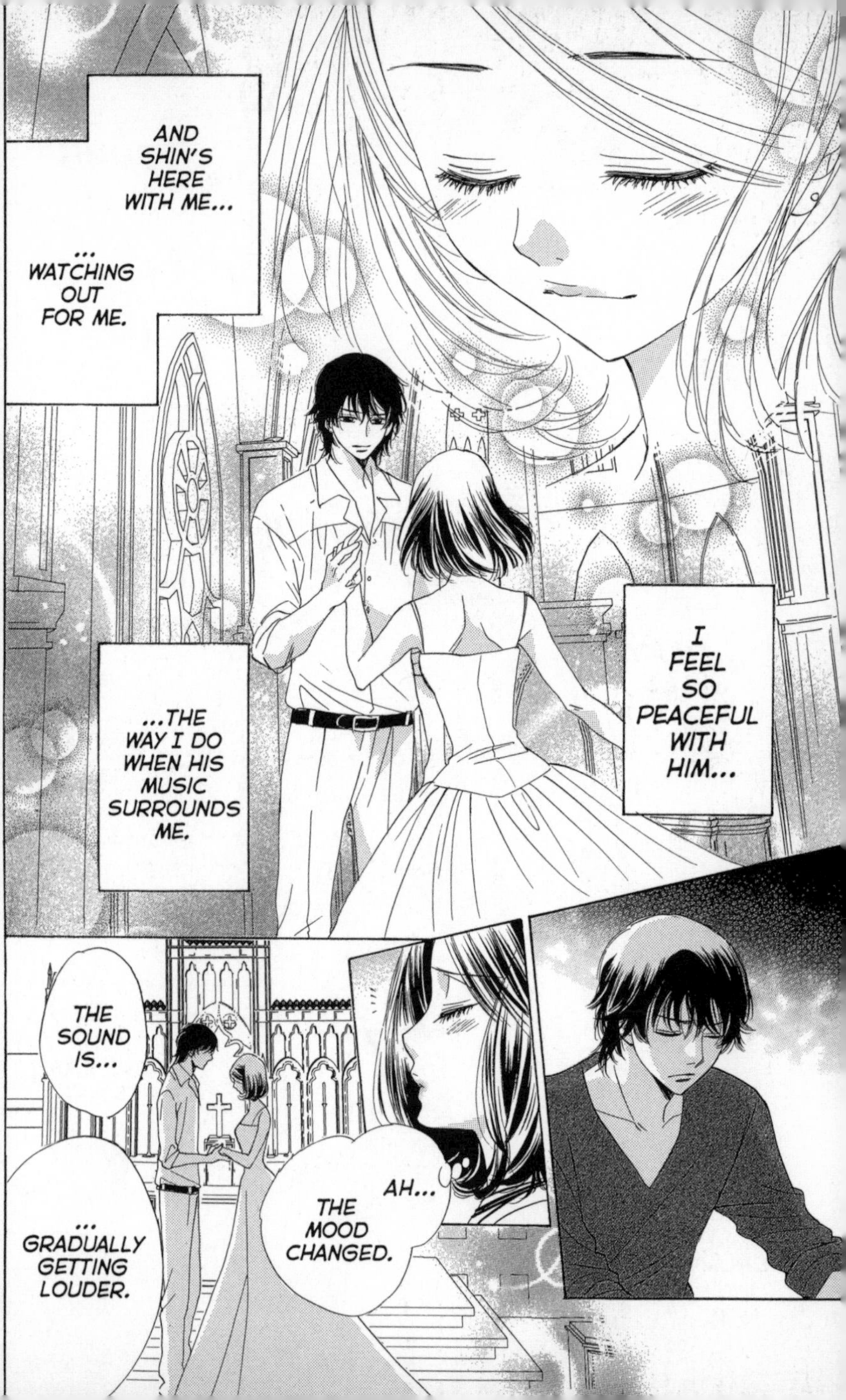
AND SHIN'S HERE WITH ME...
...WATCHING OUT FOR ME.
I FEEL SO PEACEFUL WITH HIM...
...THE WAY I DO WHEN HIS MUSIC SURROUNDS ME.
AH... THE MOOD CHANGED.
THE SOUND IS...
...GRADUALLY GETTING LOUDER.

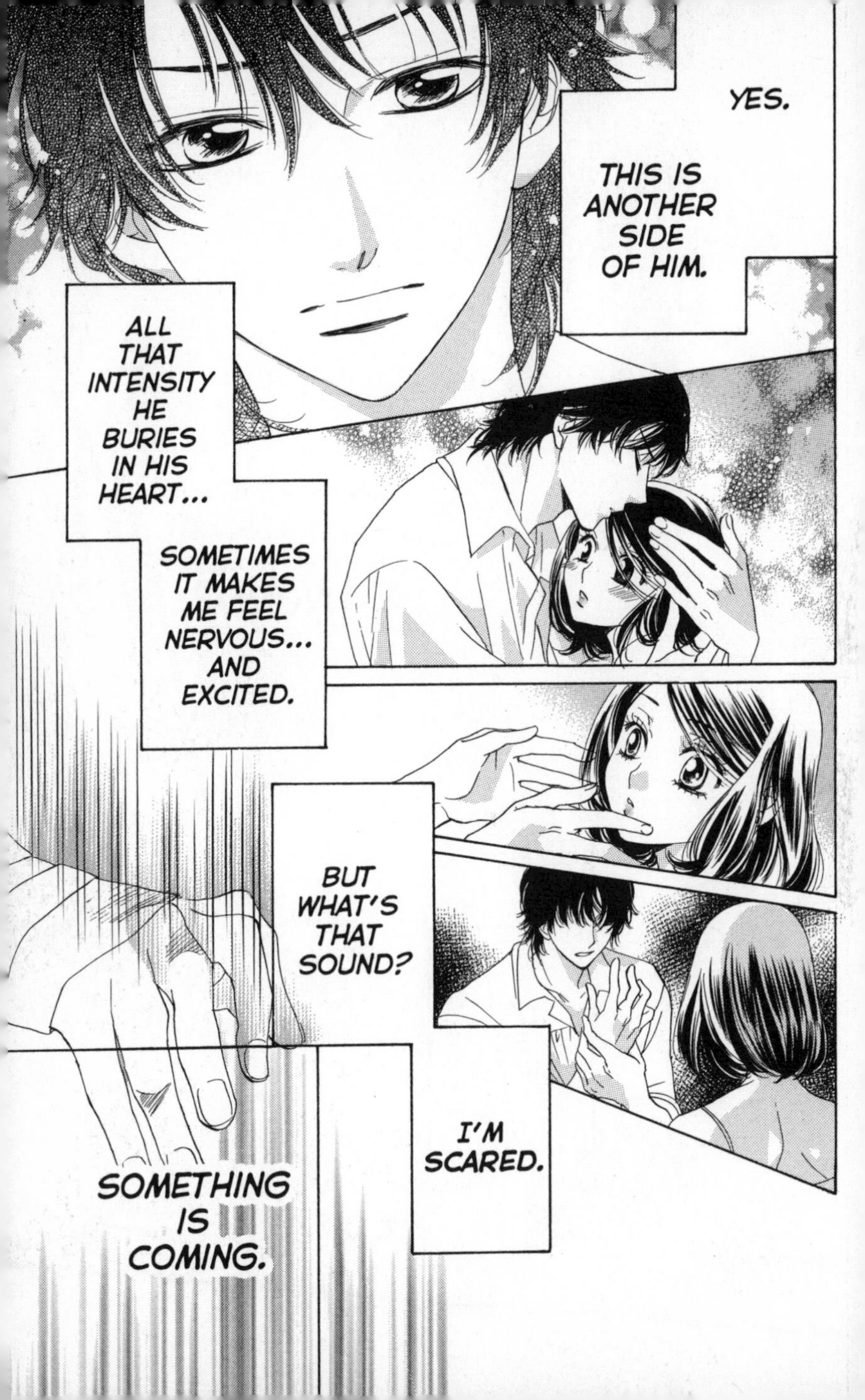
YES.
THIS IS ANOTHER SIDE OF HIM.
ALL THAT INTENSITY HE BURIES IN HIS HEART...
SOMETIMES IT MAKES ME FEEL NERVOUS... AND EXCITED.
BUT WHAT'S THAT SOUND?
I'M SCARED.
SOMETHING IS COMING.

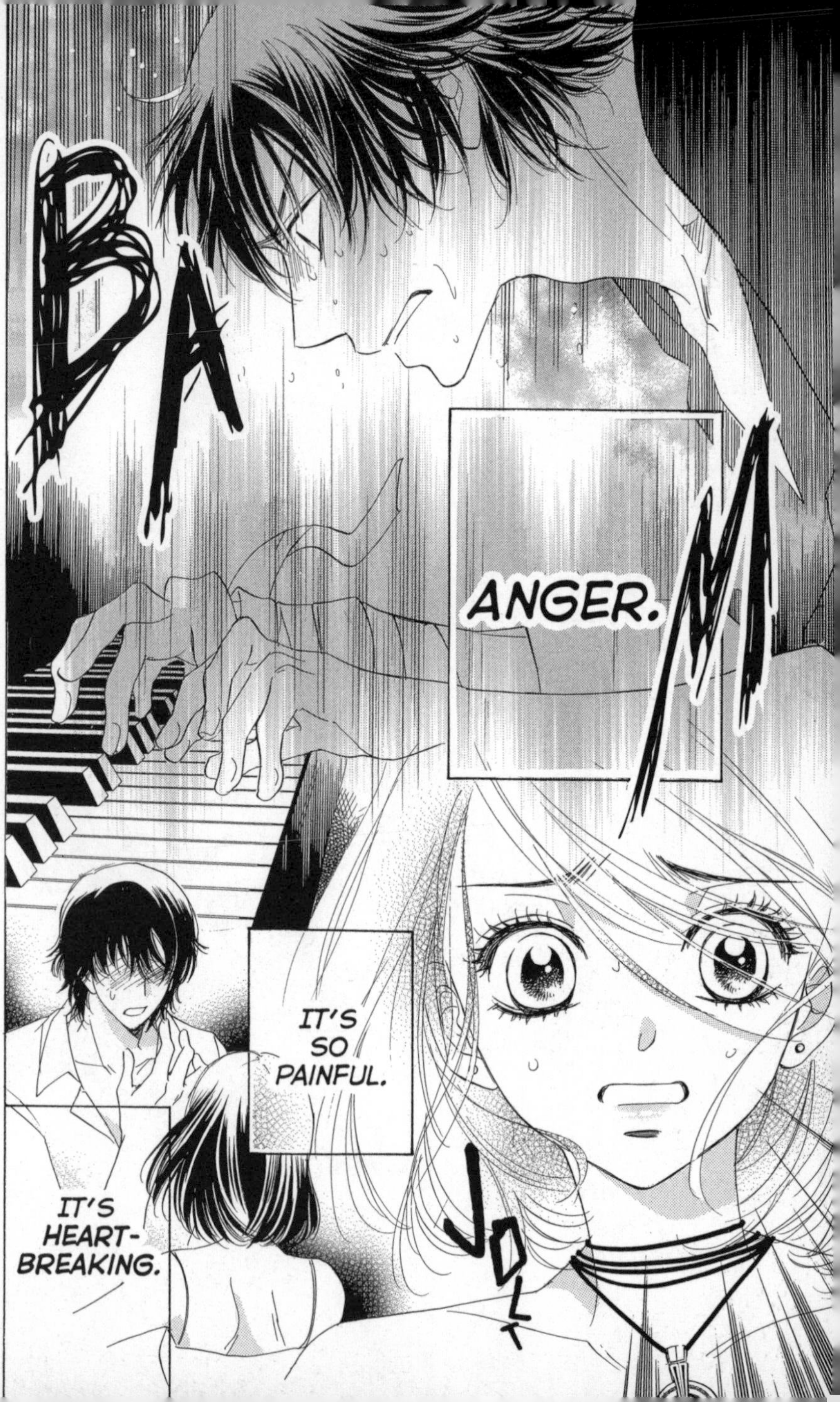
BAM
ANGER.
JOLT
IT'S SO PAINFUL.
IT'S HEART-BREAKING.

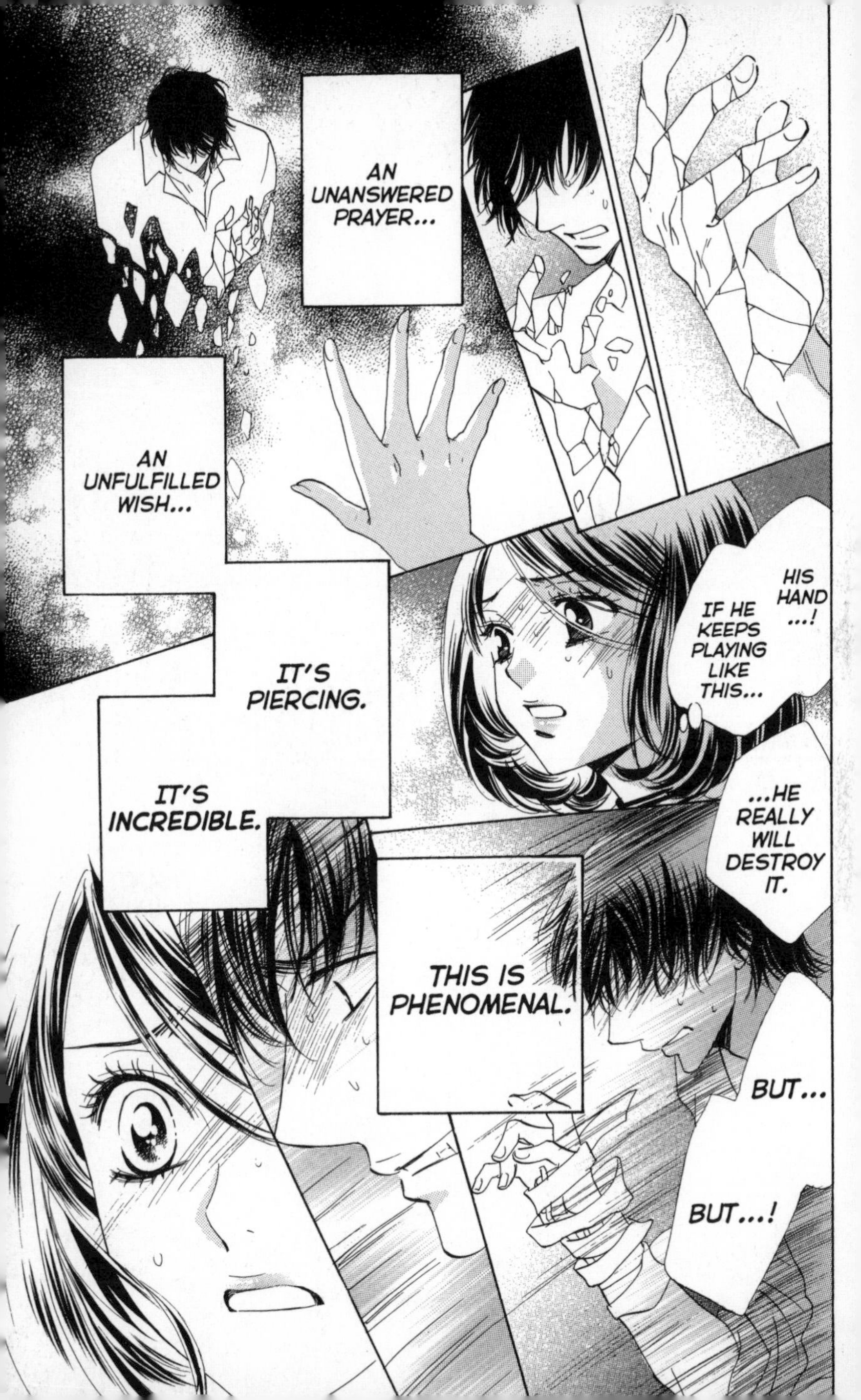
AN UNANSWERED PRAYER...
AN UNFULFILLED WISH...
HIS HAND ...!
IF HE KEEPS PLAYING LIKE THIS...
...HE REALLY WILL DESTROY IT.
IT'S PIERCING.
IT'S INCREDIBLE.
BUT...
BUT...!
THIS IS PHENOMENAL.

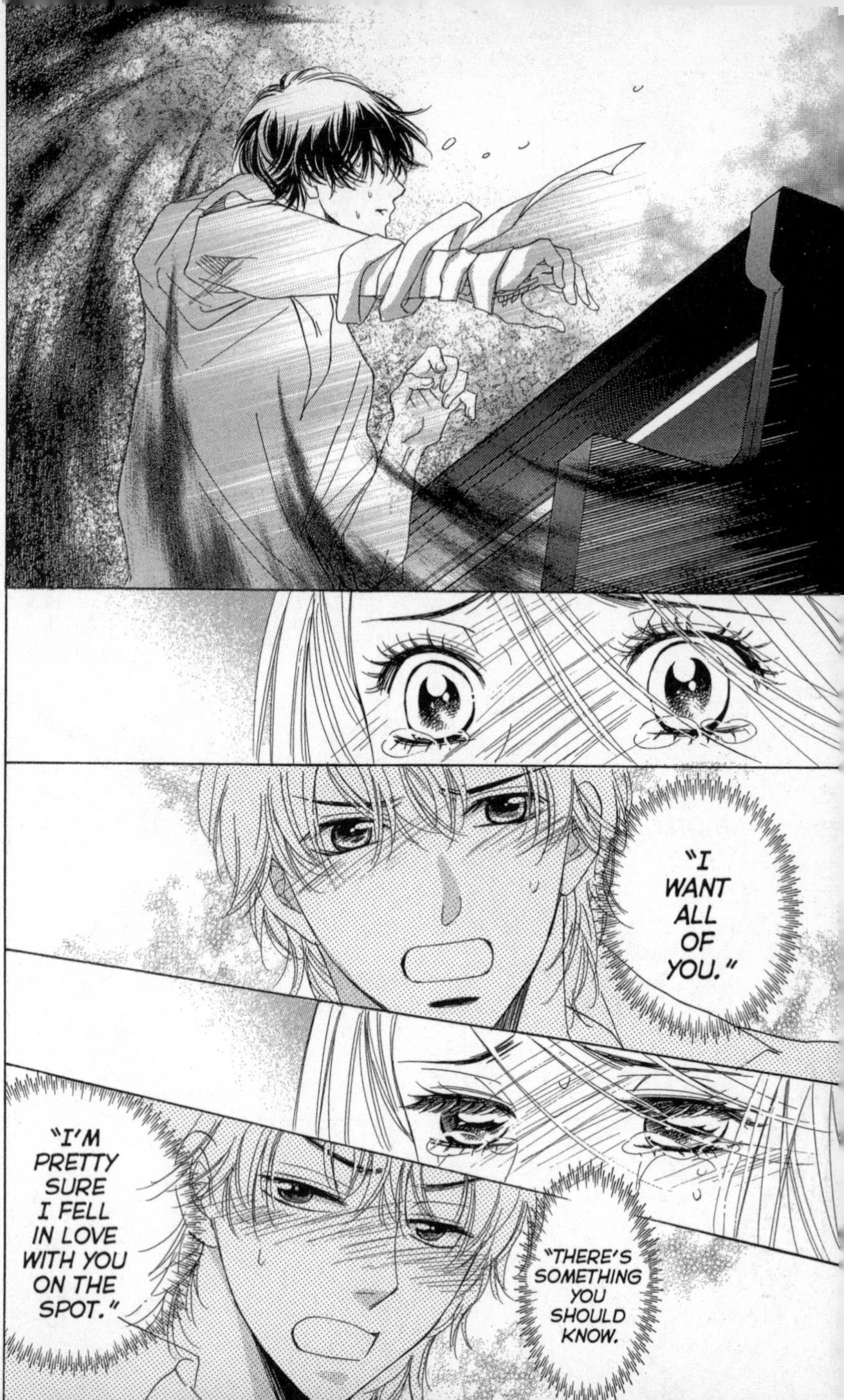
"I WANT ALL OF YOU."
"THERE'S SOMETHING YOU SHOULD KNOW.
"I'M PRETTY SURE I FELL IN LOVE WITH YOU ON THE SPOT."

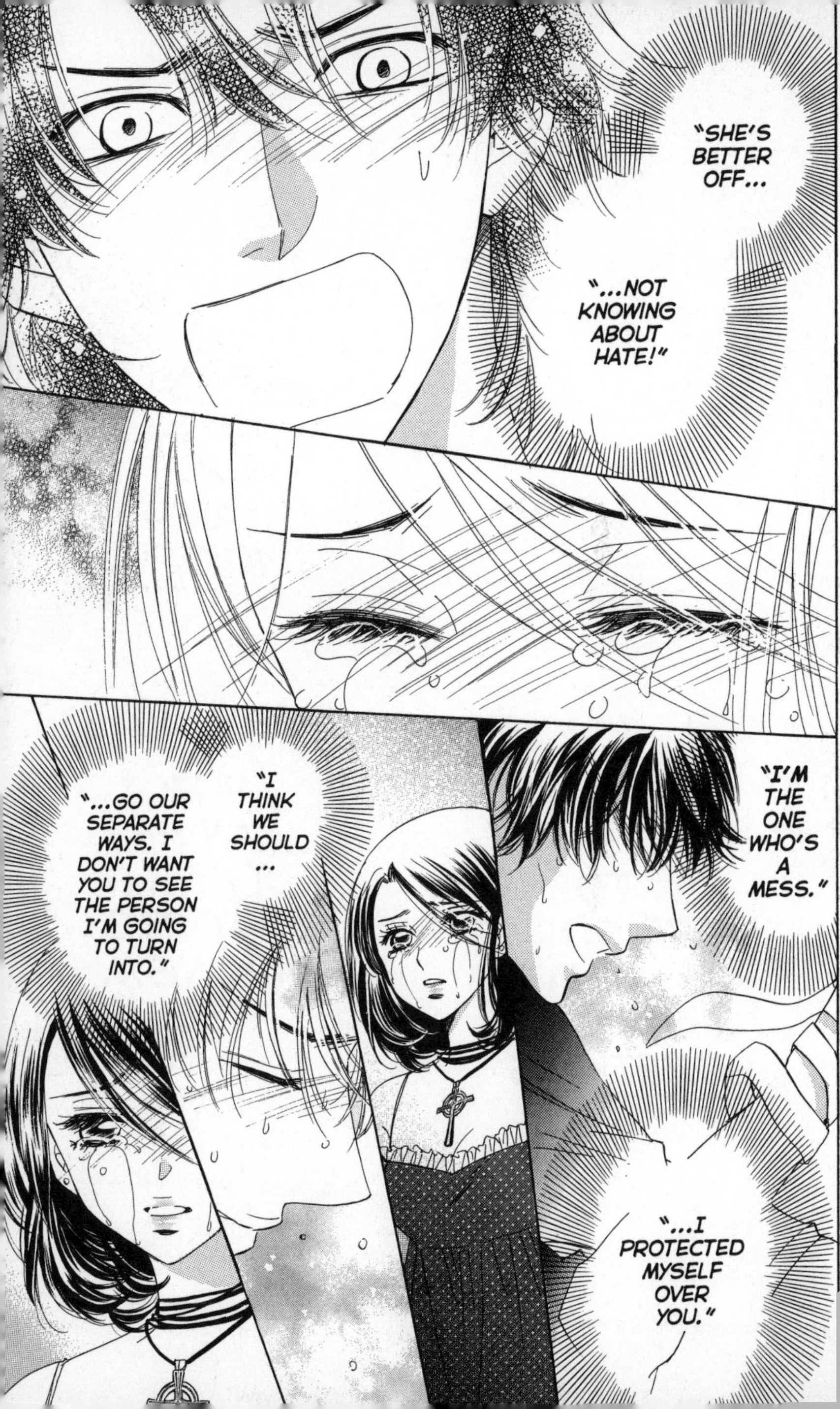
"SHE'S BETTER OFF...
"...NOT KNOWING ABOUT HATE!"
"I'M THE ONE WHO'S A MESS."
"...I PROTECTED MYSELF OVER YOU."
"I THINK WE SHOULD ...
"...GO OUR SEPARATE WAYS. I DON'T WANT YOU TO SEE THE PERSON I'M GOING TO TURN INTO."

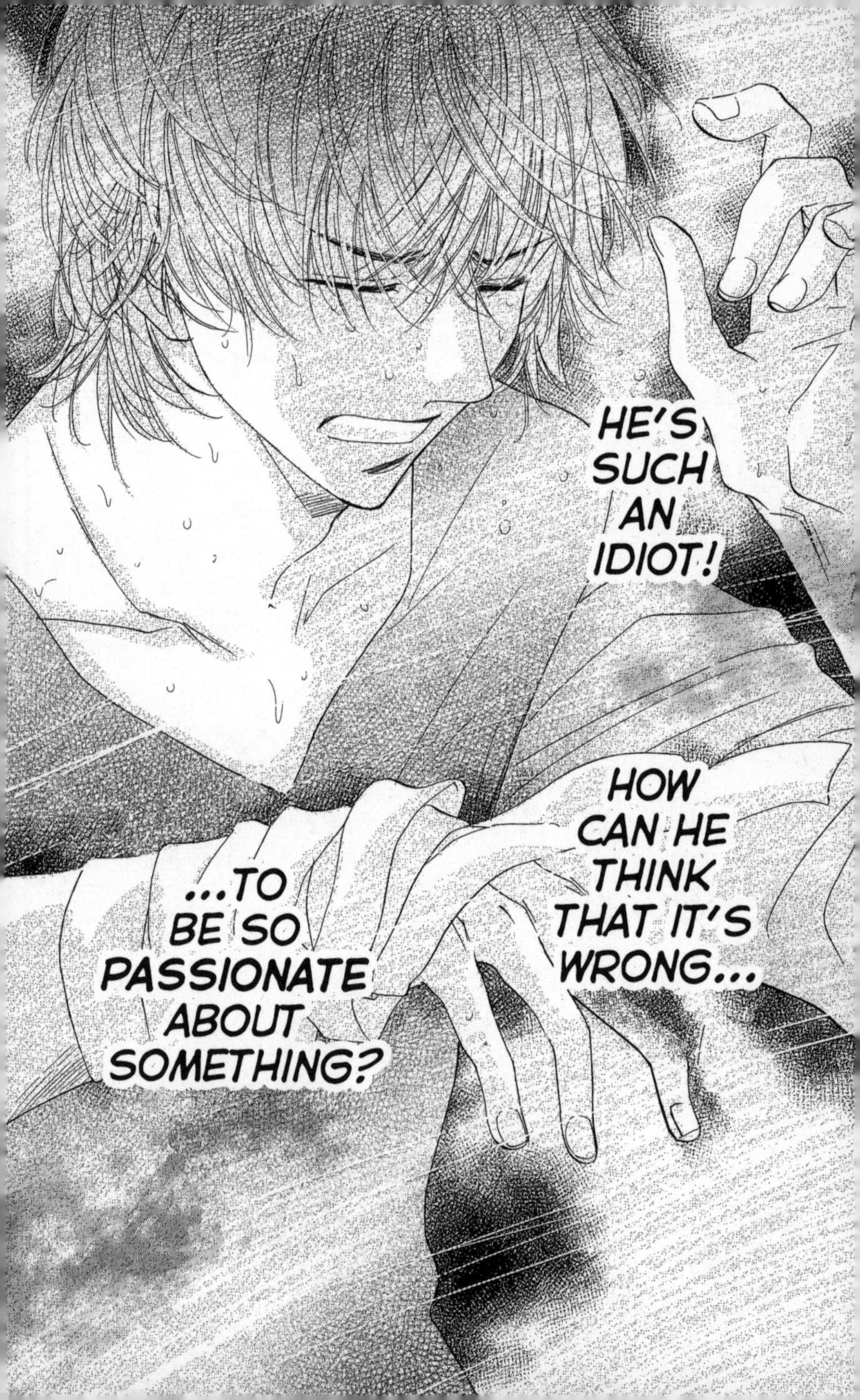
HE'S SUCH AN IDIOT!
HOW CAN HE THINK THAT IT'S WRONG...
...TO BE SO PASSIONATE ABOUT SOMETHING?

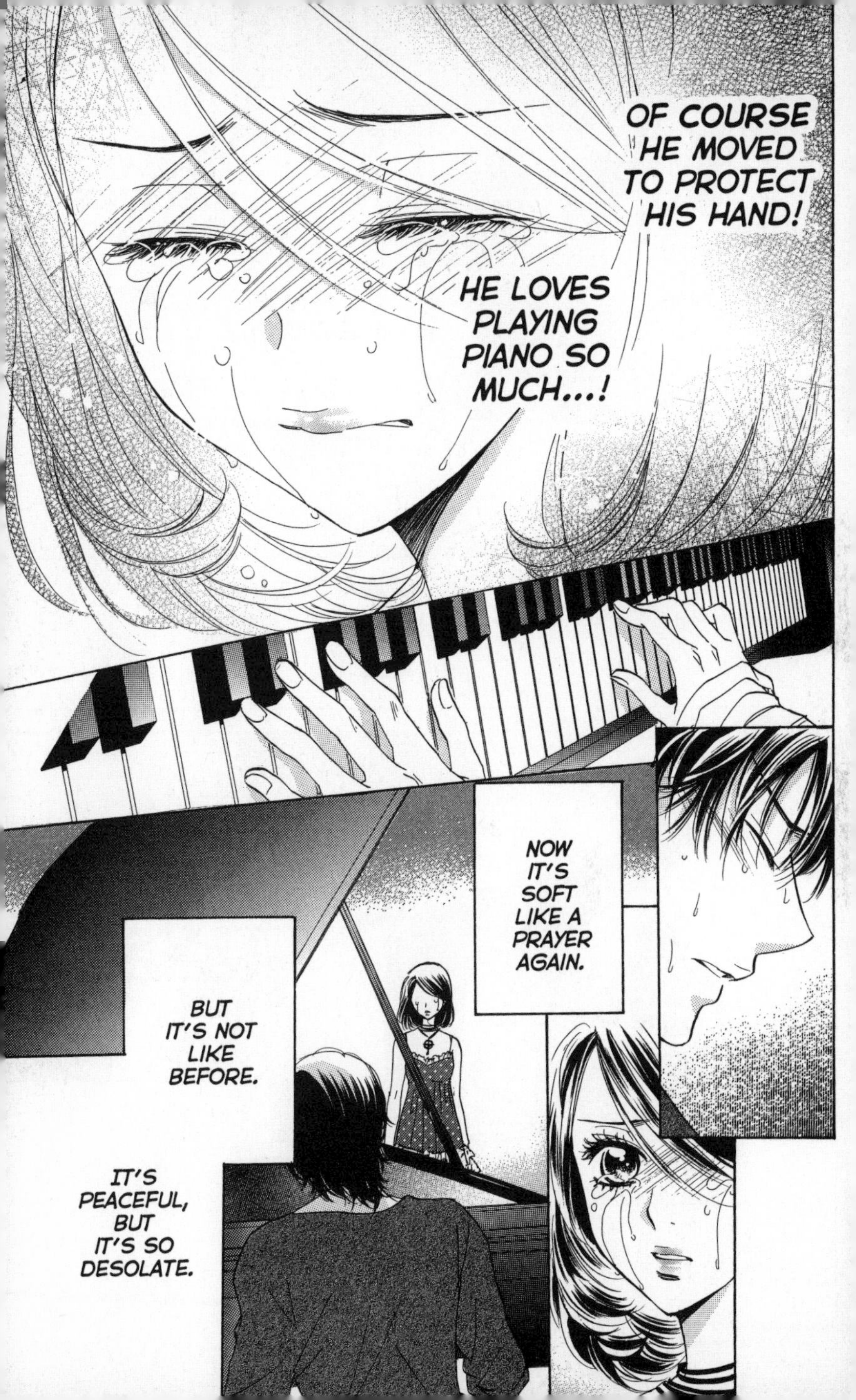
OF COURSE HE MOVED TO PROTECT HIS HAND!
HE LOVES PLAYING PIANO SO MUCH...!
NOW IT'S SOFT LIKE A PRAYER AGAIN.
BUT IT'S NOT LIKE BEFORE.
IT'S PEACEFUL, BUT IT'S SO DESOLATE.

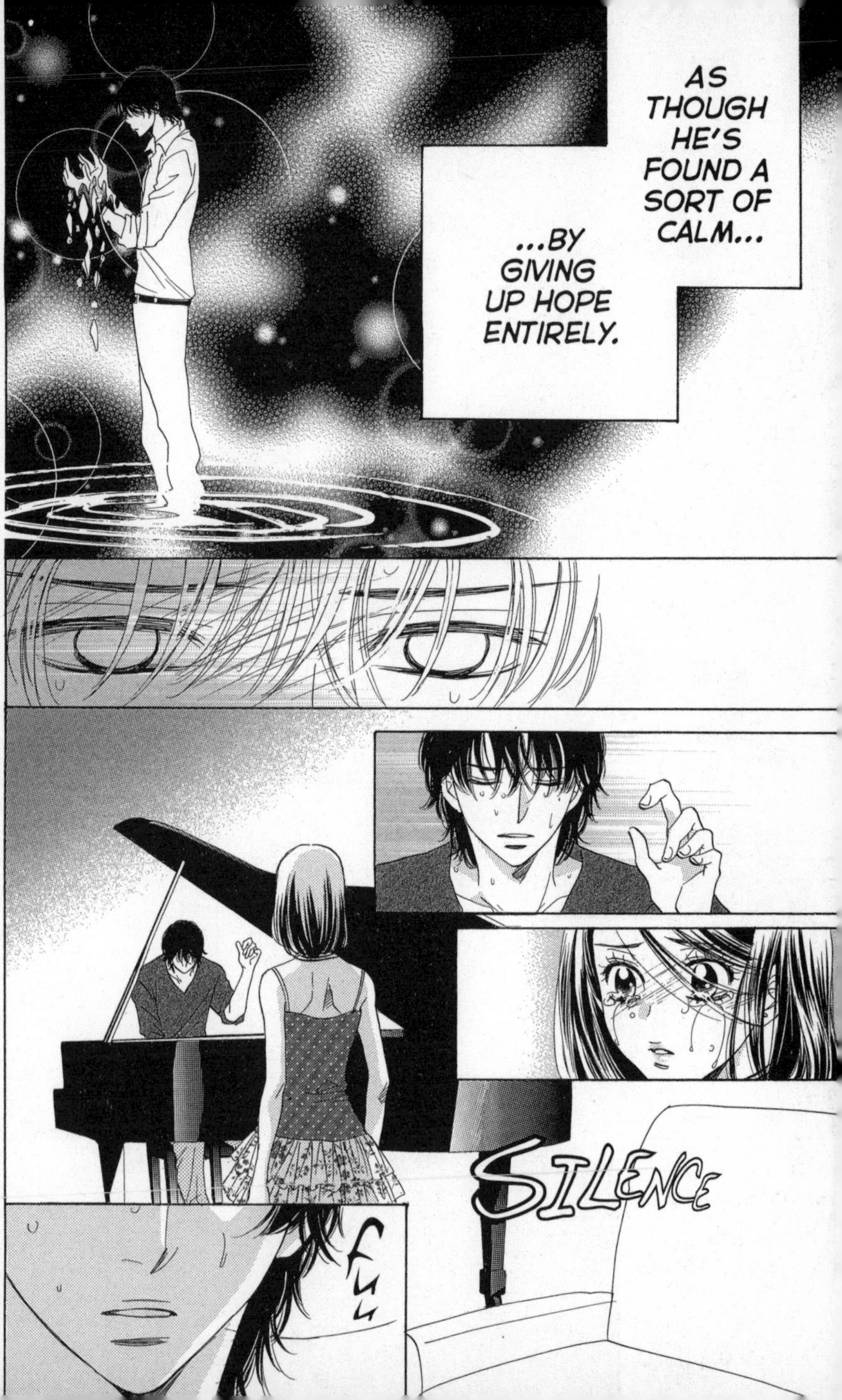
AS THOUGH HE'S FOUND A SORT OF CALM...
...BY GIVING UP HOPE ENTIRELY.
SILENCE
FUU

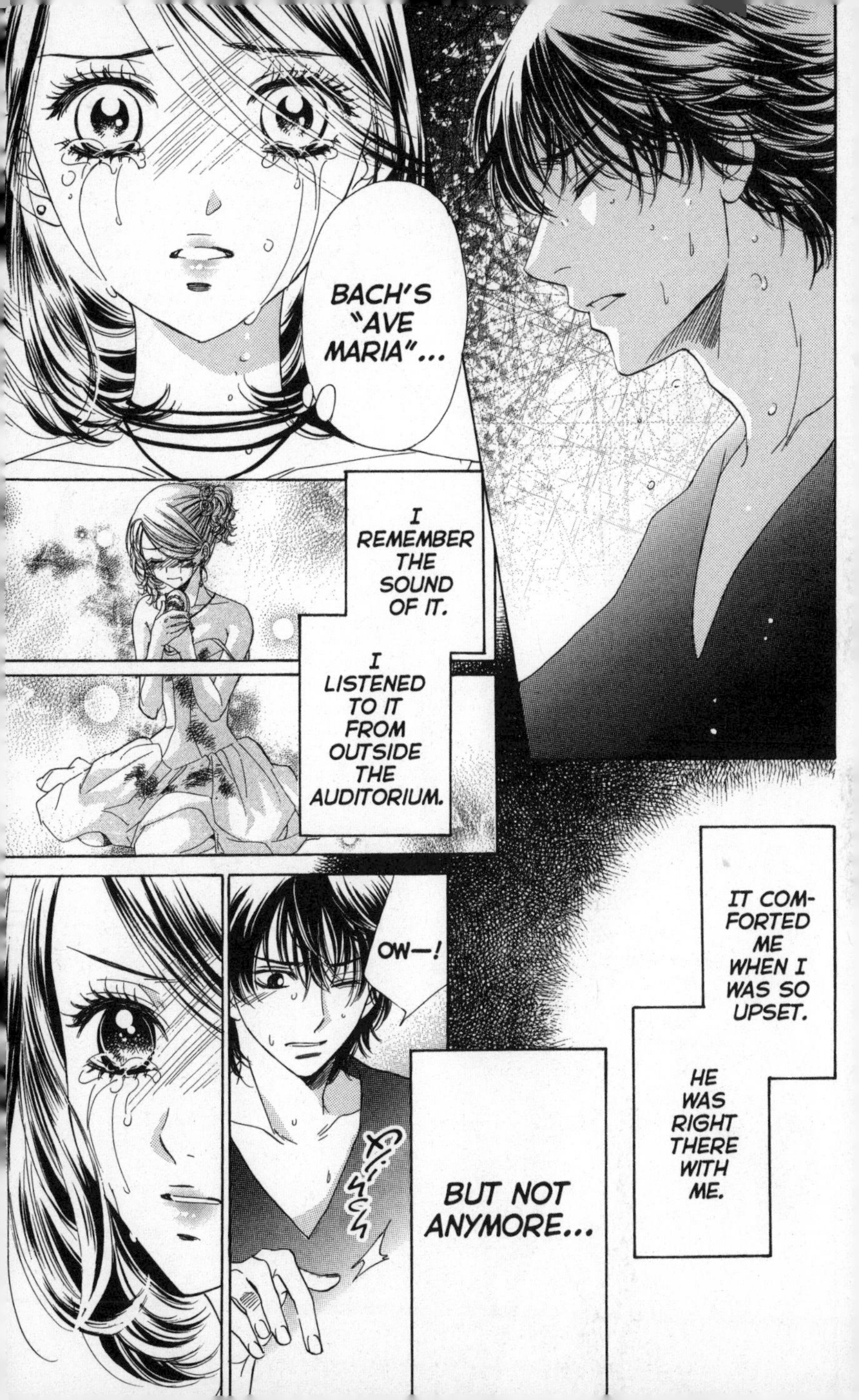
BACH'S "AVE MARIA"...
I REMEMBER THE SOUND OF IT.
I LISTENED TO IT FROM OUTSIDE THE AUDITORIUM.
IT COMFORTED ME WHEN I WAS SO UPSET.
HE WAS RIGHT THERE WITH ME.
BUT NOT ANYMORE...
OW—!

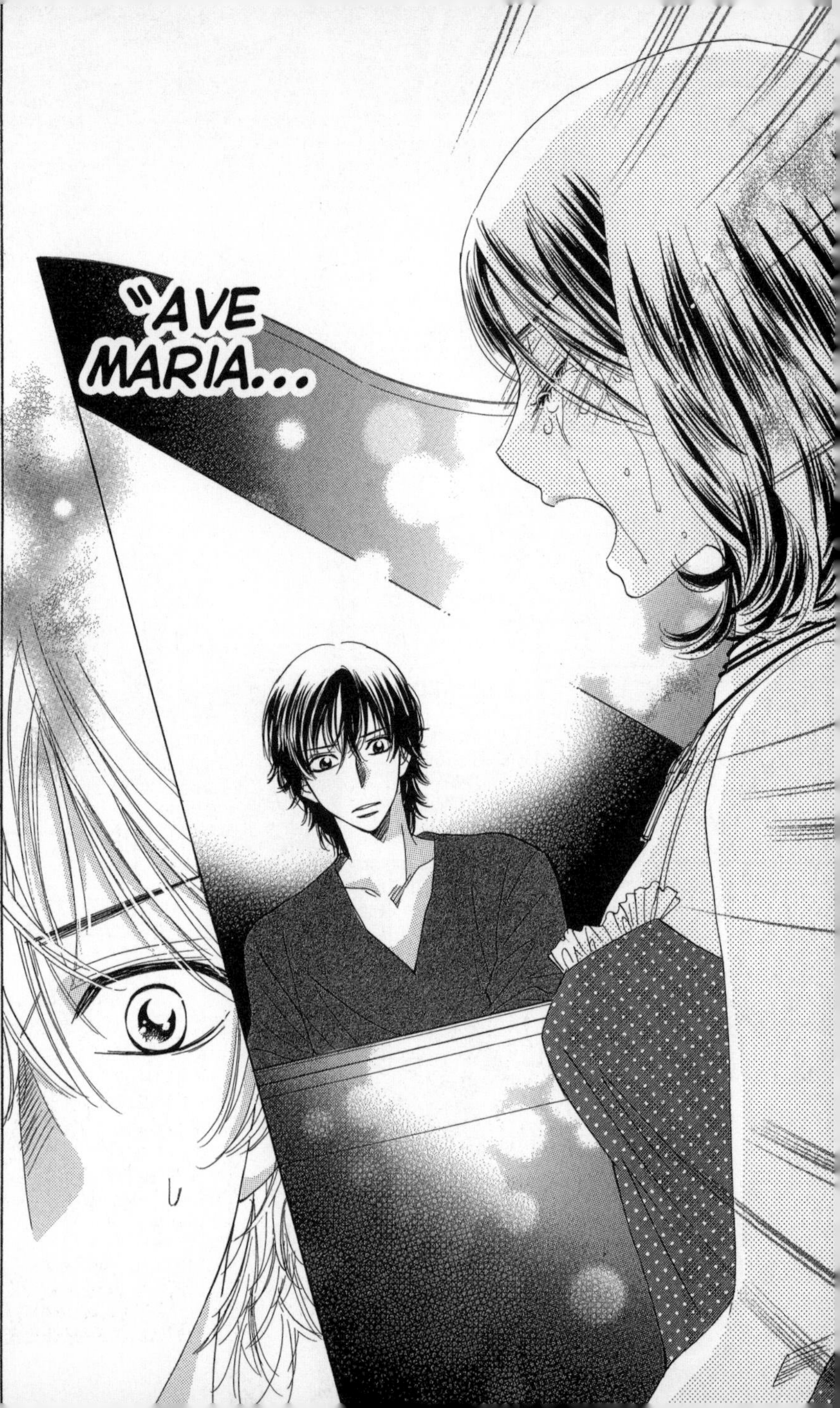
"AVE MARIA...

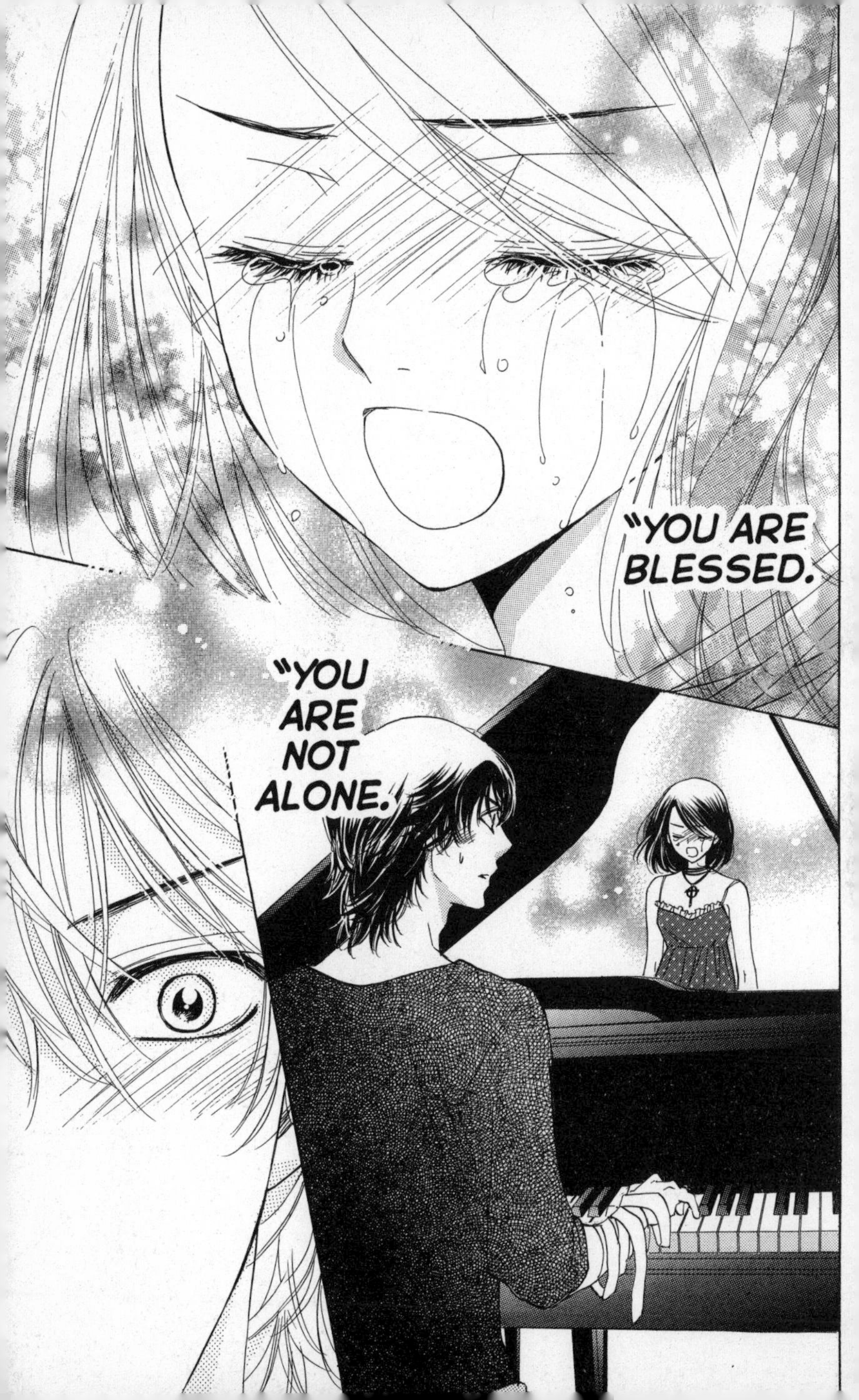
"YOU ARE BLESSED.
"YOU ARE NOT ALONE.

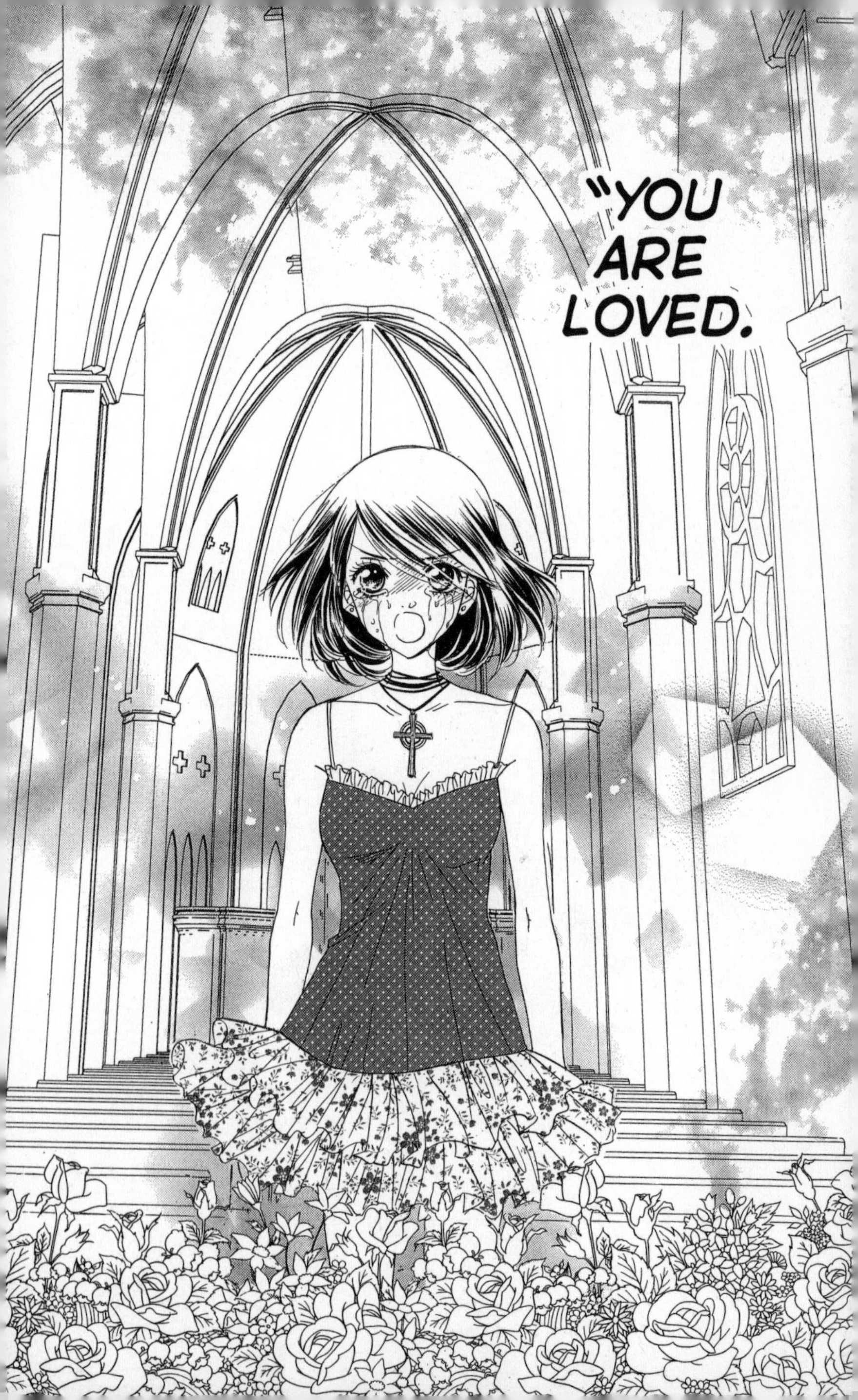
"YOU ARE LOVED.

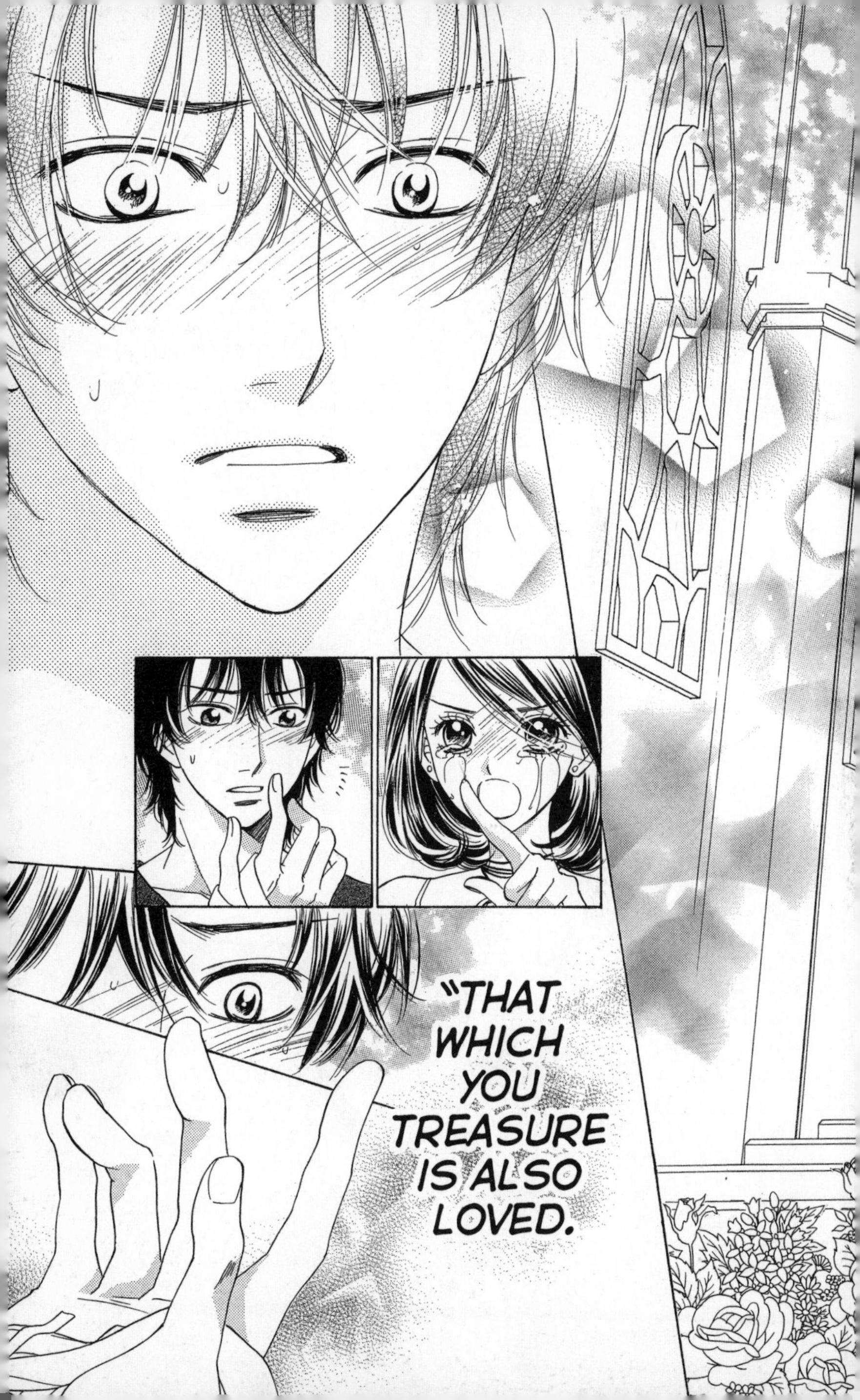
"THAT WHICH YOU TREASURE IS ALSO LOVED.

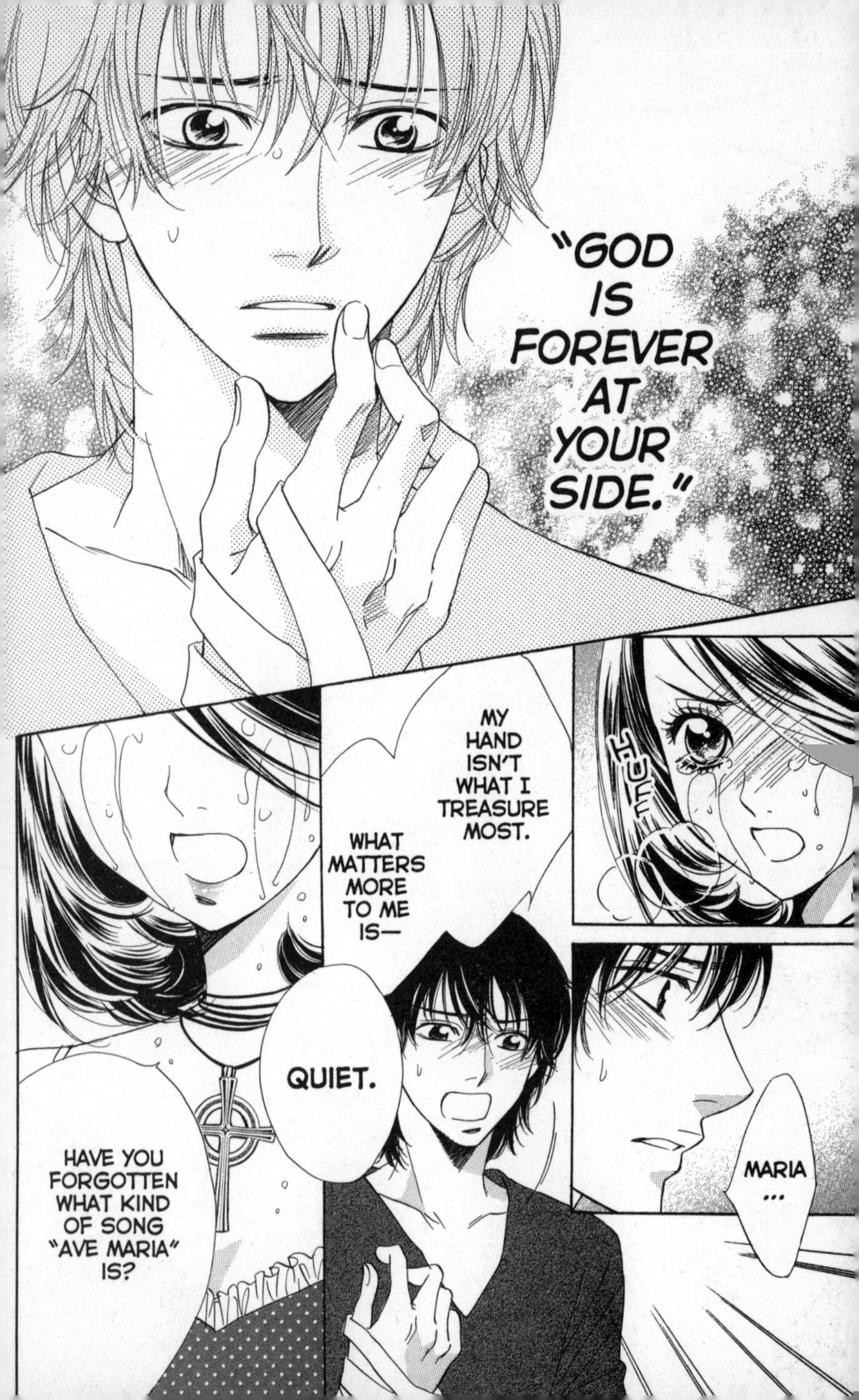
"GOD IS FOREVER AT YOUR SIDE."
HUFF
MARIA ...
MY HAND ISN'T WHAT I TREASURE MOST.
WHAT MATTERS MORE TO ME IS—
QUIET.
HAVE YOU FORGOTTEN WHAT KIND OF SONG "AVE MARIA" IS?

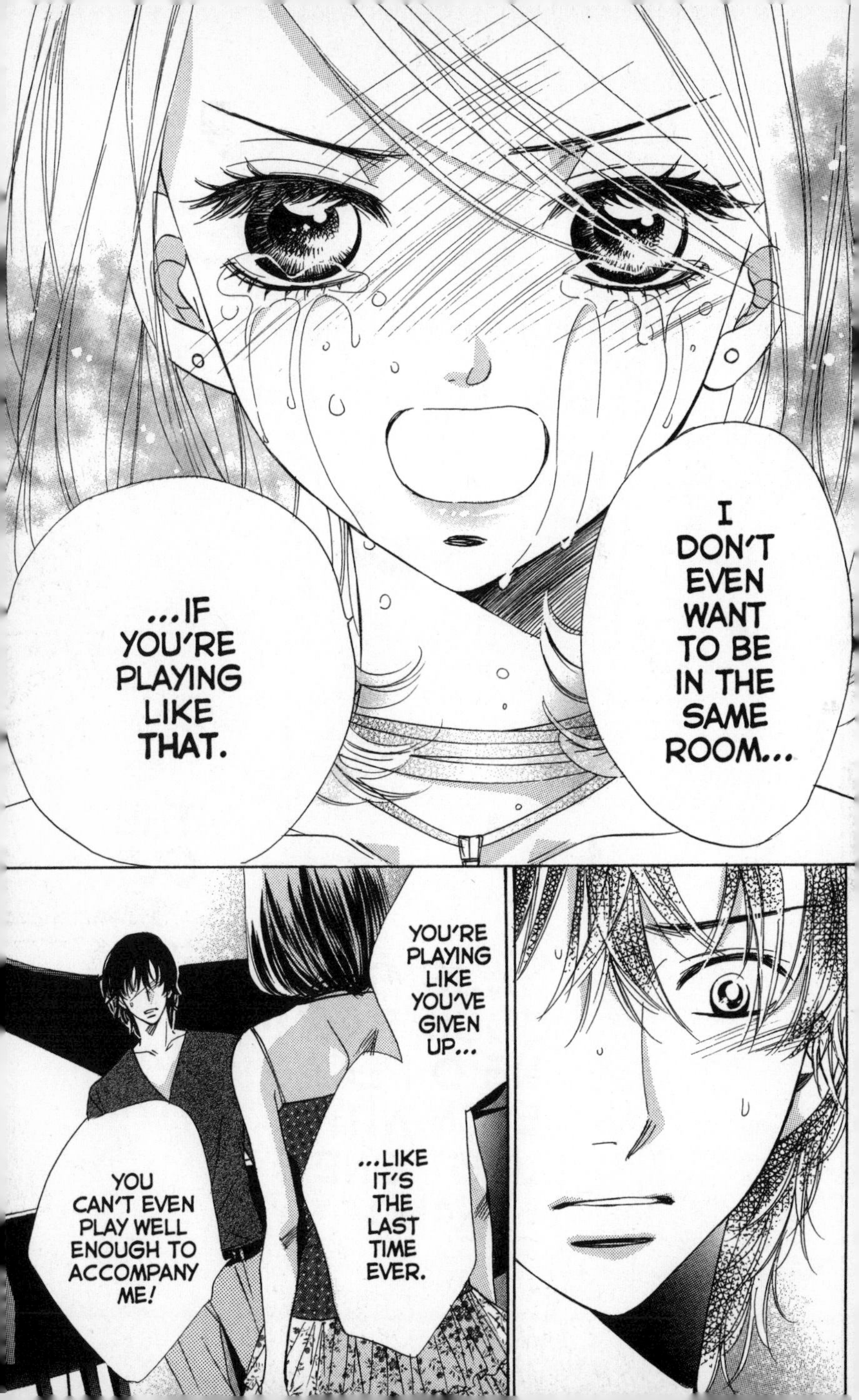
I DON'T EVEN WANT TO BE IN THE SAME ROOM...
...IF YOU'RE PLAYING LIKE THAT.
YOU'RE PLAYING LIKE YOU'VE GIVEN UP...
...LIKE IT'S THE LAST TIME EVER.
YOU CAN'T EVEN PLAY WELL ENOUGH TO ACCOMPANY ME!

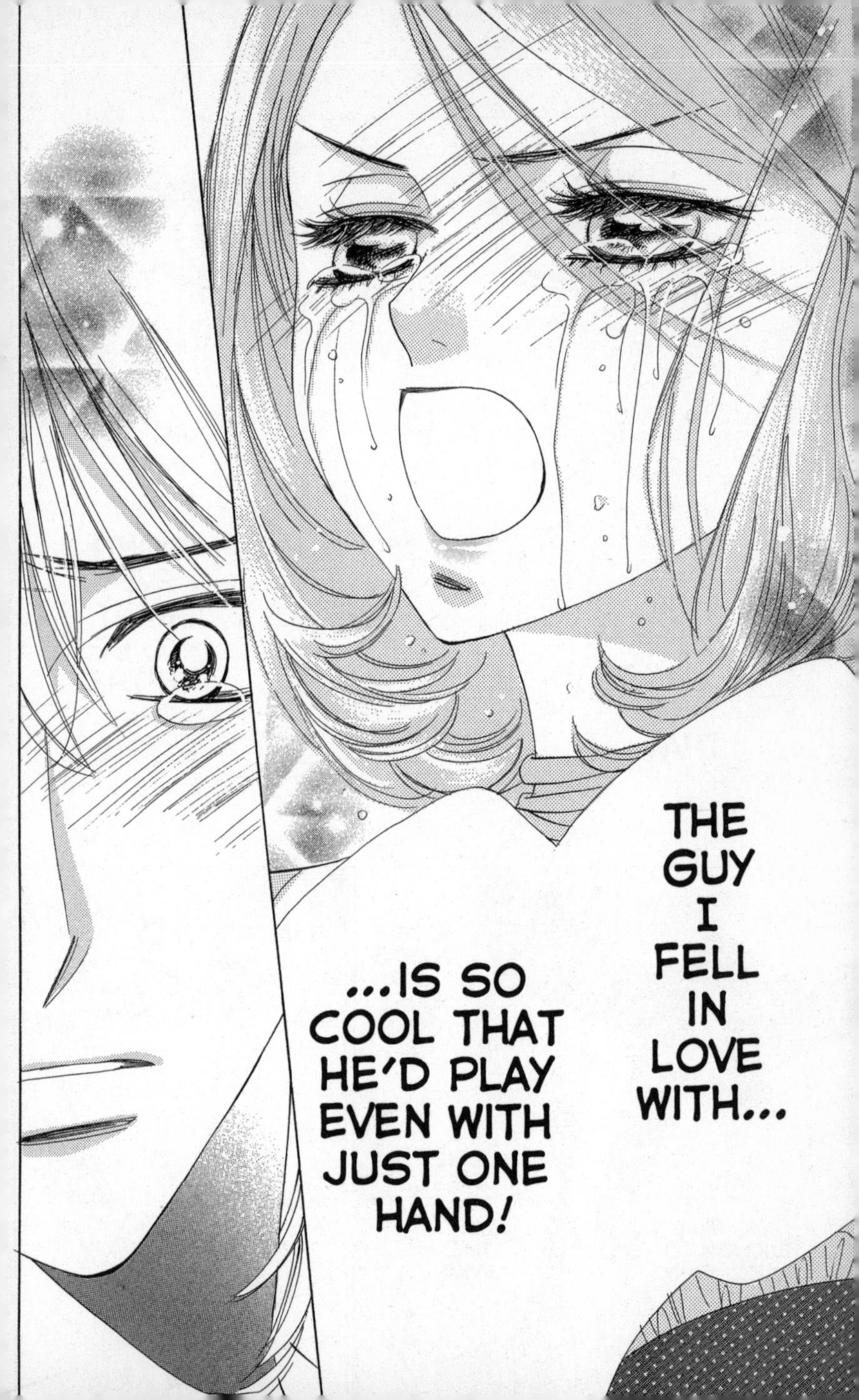
THE GUY I FELL IN LOVE WITH...
...IS SO COOL THAT HE'D PLAY EVEN WITH JUST ONE HAND!

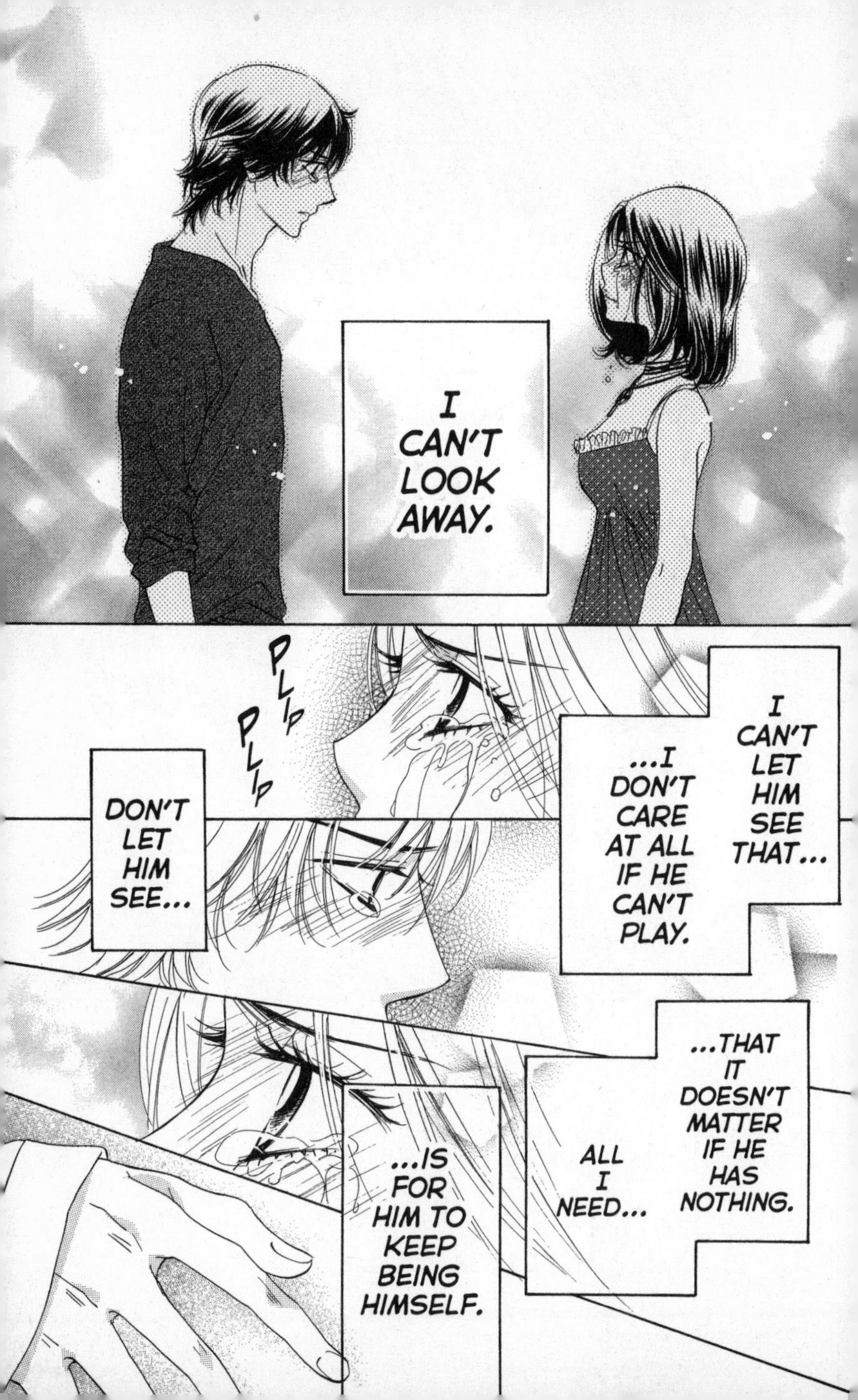
I CAN'T LOOK AWAY.
I CAN'T LET HIM SEE THAT...
...I DON'T CARE AT ALL IF HE CAN'T PLAY.
PLIP
PLIP
DON'T LET HIM SEE...
...THAT IT DOESN'T MATTER IF HE HAS NOTHING.
ALL I NEED...
...IS FOR HIM TO KEEP BEING HIMSELF.

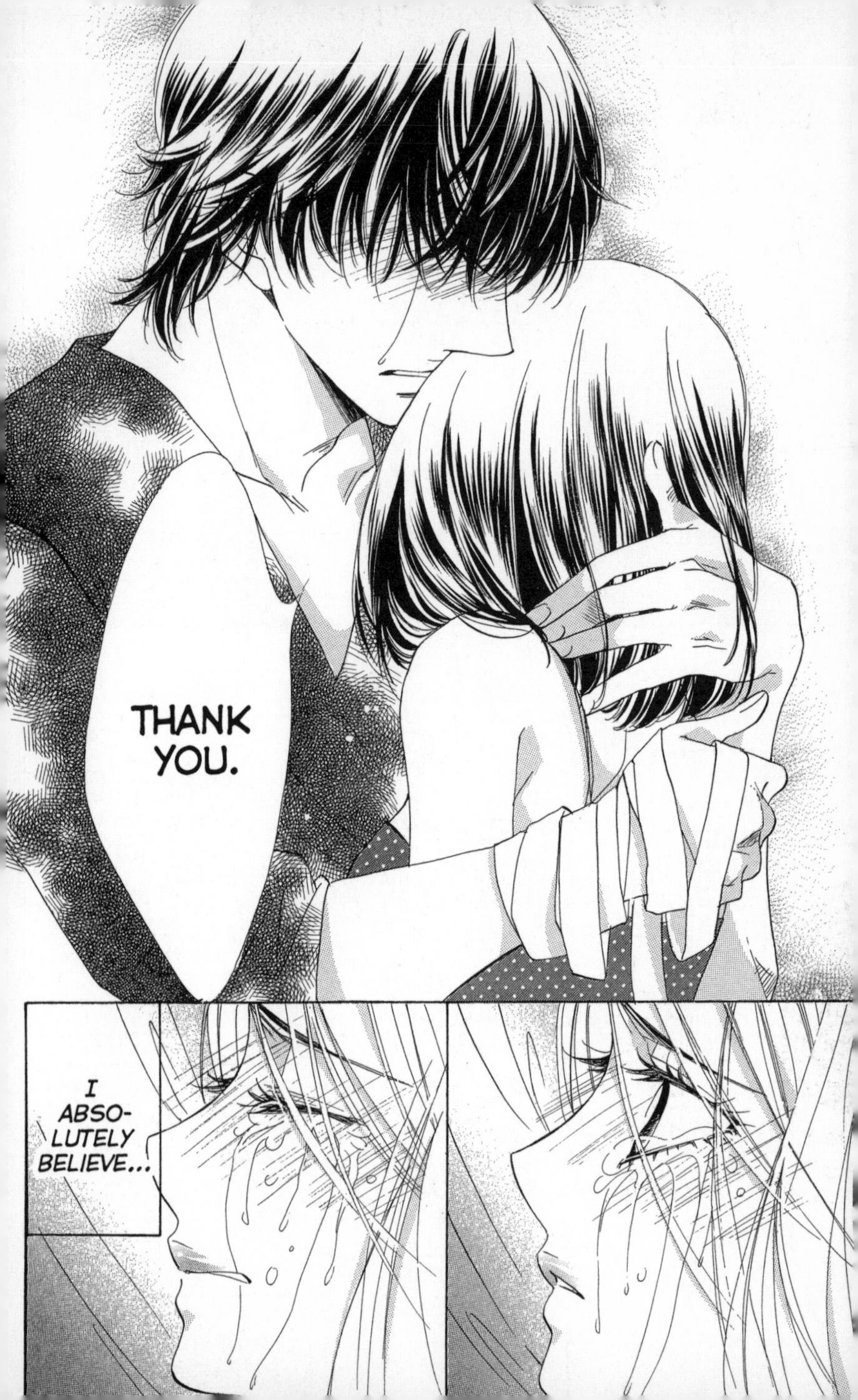
THANK YOU.
I ABSO-LUTELY BELIEVE...

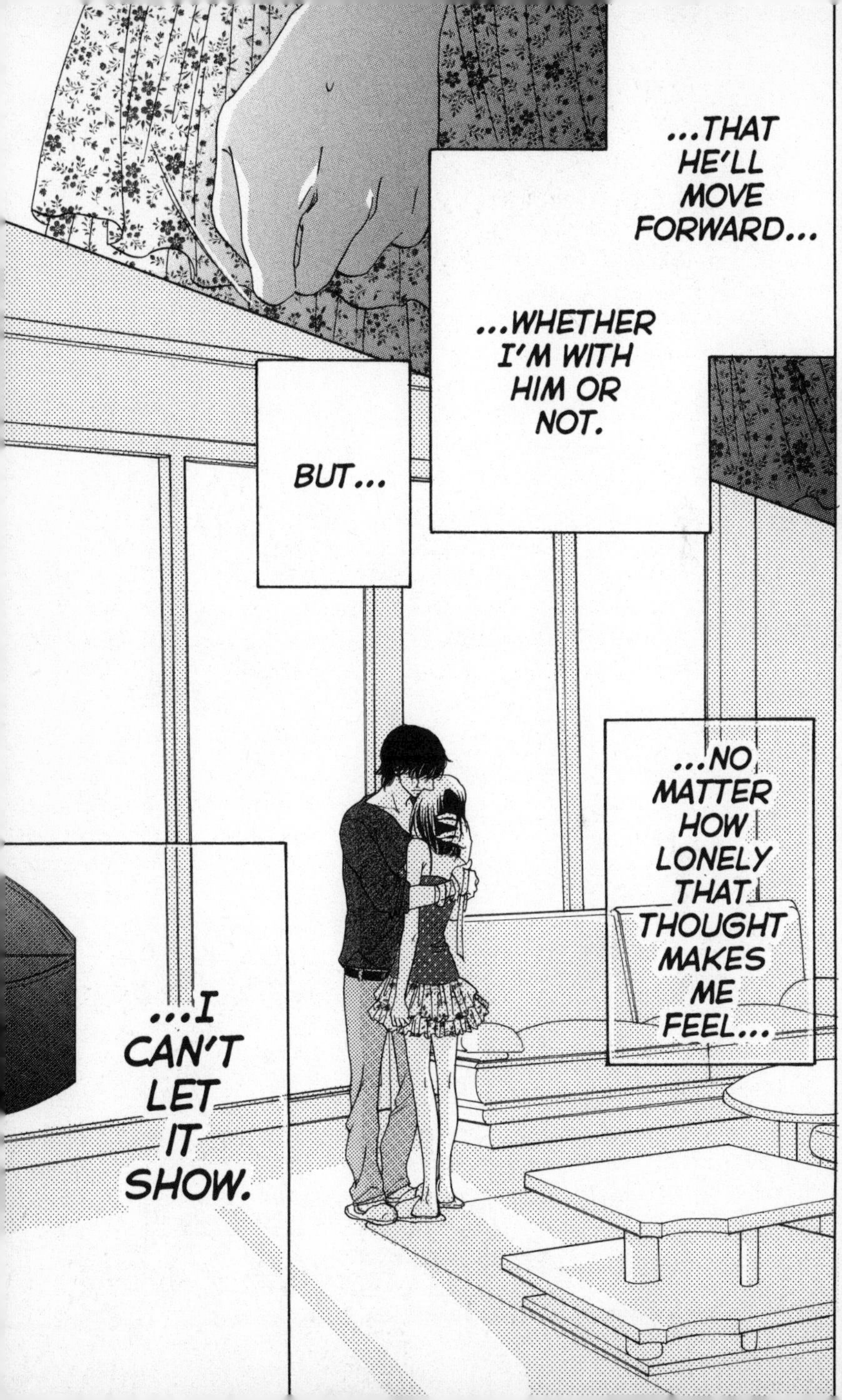
...THAT HE'LL MOVE FORWARD...
...WHETHER I'M WITH HIM OR NOT.
BUT...
...NO MATTER HOW LONELY THAT THOUGHT MAKES ME FEEL...
...I CAN'T LET IT SHOW.

A Devil and Her Love Song

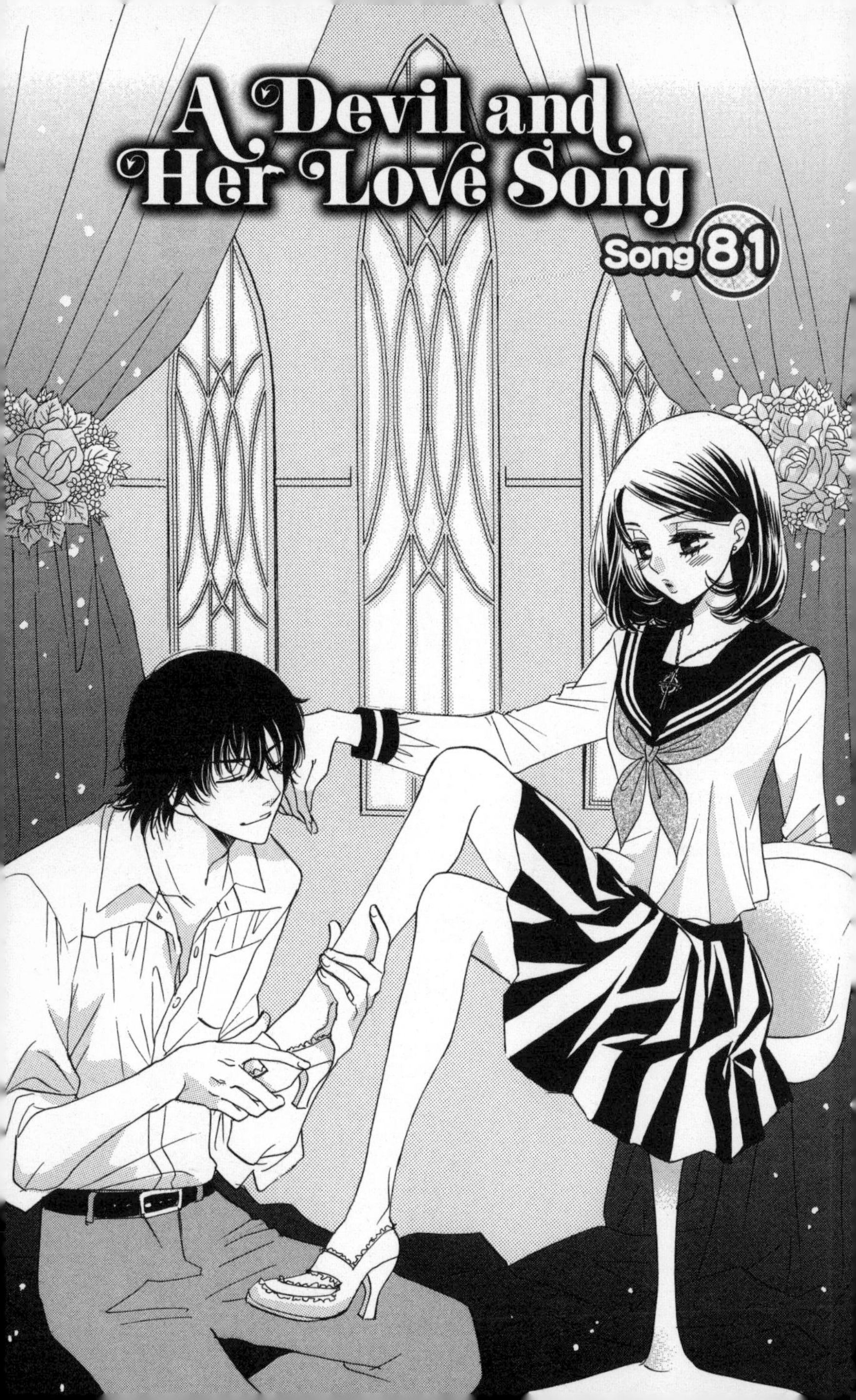
A Devil and Her Love Song
Song 81

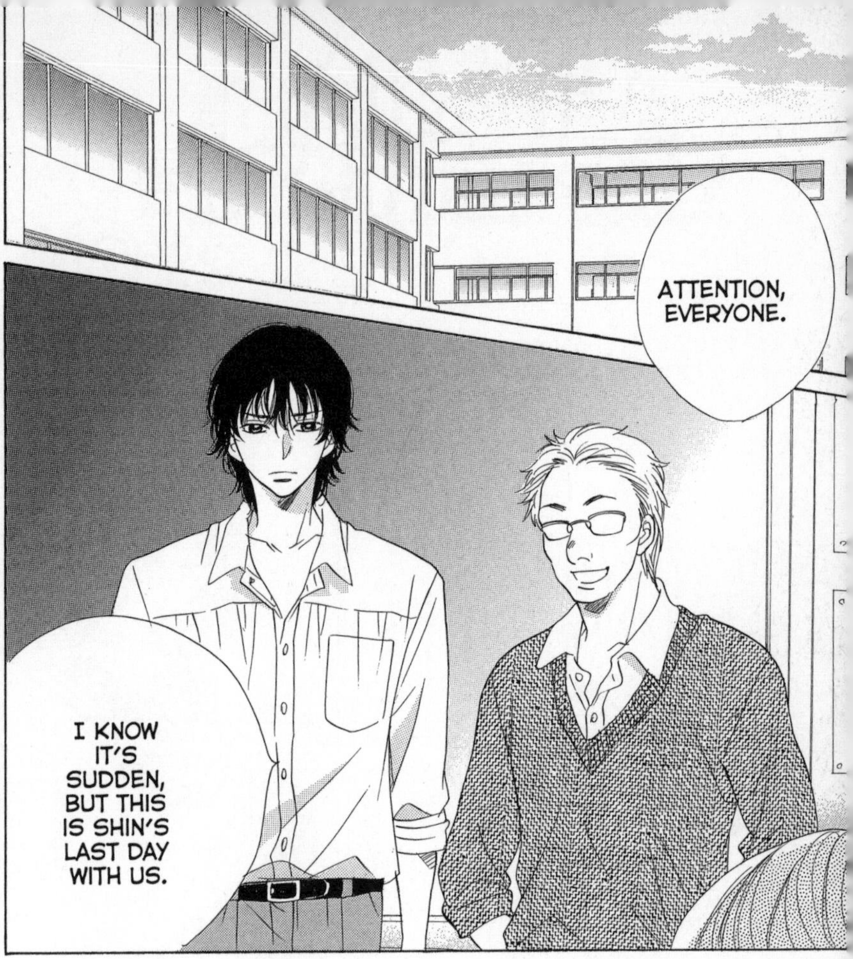
ATTENTION, EVERYONE.
I KNOW IT'S SUDDEN, BUT THIS IS SHIN'S LAST DAY WITH US.

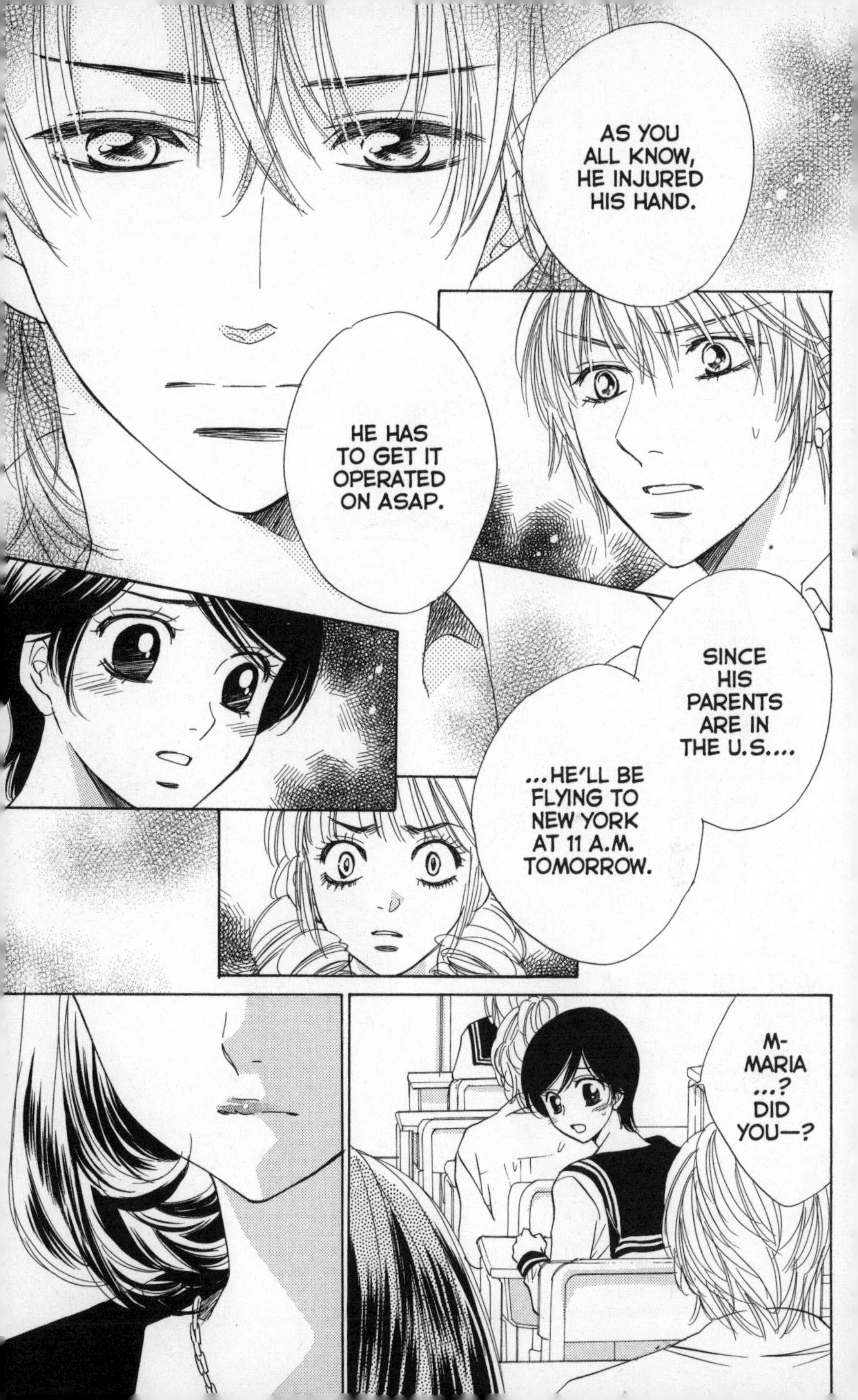
AS YOU ALL KNOW, HE INJURED HIS HAND.
HE HAS TO GET IT OPERATED ON ASAP.
SINCE HIS PARENTS ARE IN THE U.S....
...HE'LL BE FLYING TO NEW YORK AT 11 A.M. TOMORROW.
M-MARIA ...? DID YOU—?

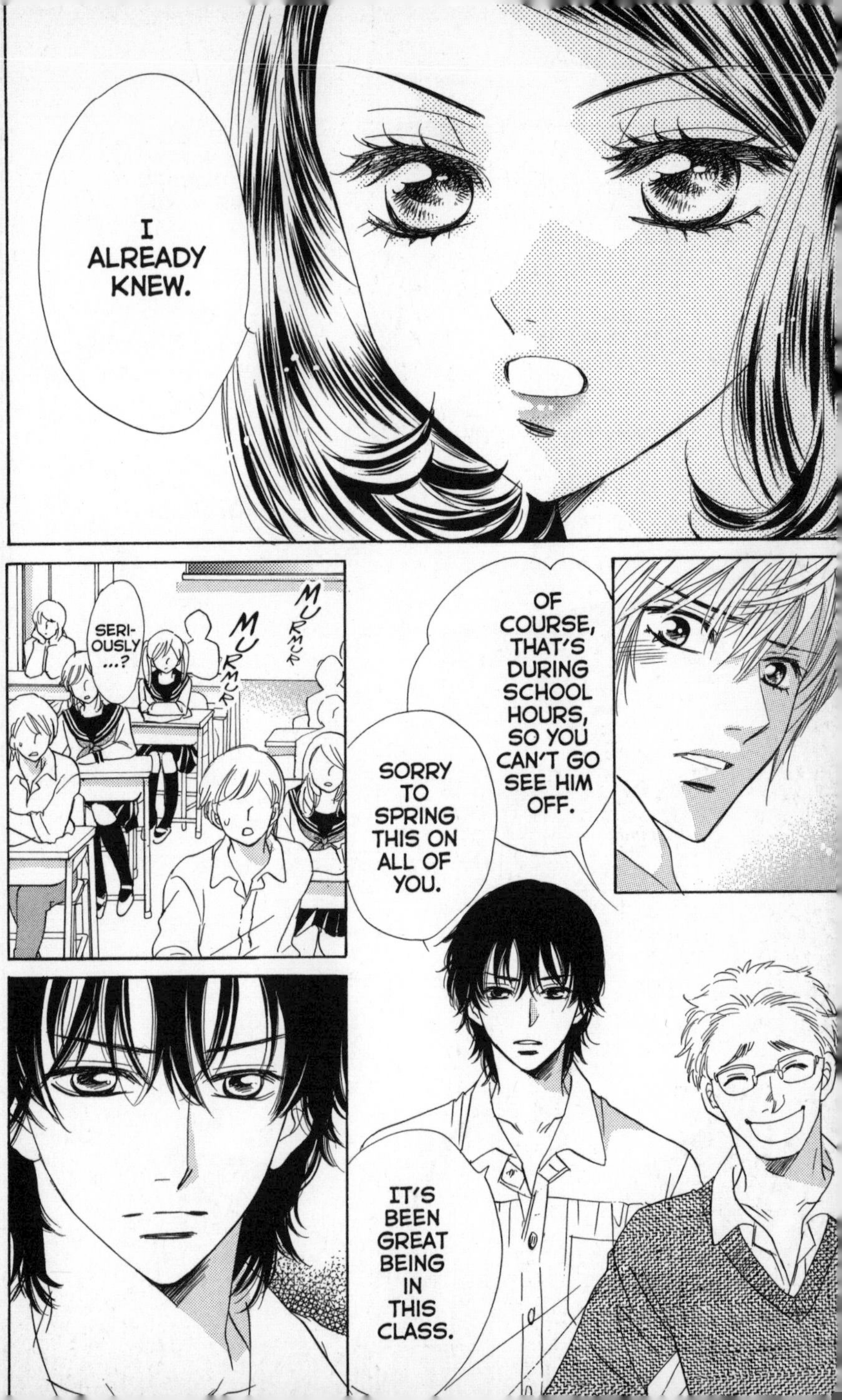
I ALREADY KNEW.
OF COURSE, THAT'S DURING SCHOOL HOURS, SO YOU CAN'T GO SEE HIM OFF.
SORRY TO SPRING THIS ON ALL OF YOU.
MURMUR
MURMUR
SERI-OUSLY ...?
IT'S BEEN GREAT BEING IN THIS CLASS.

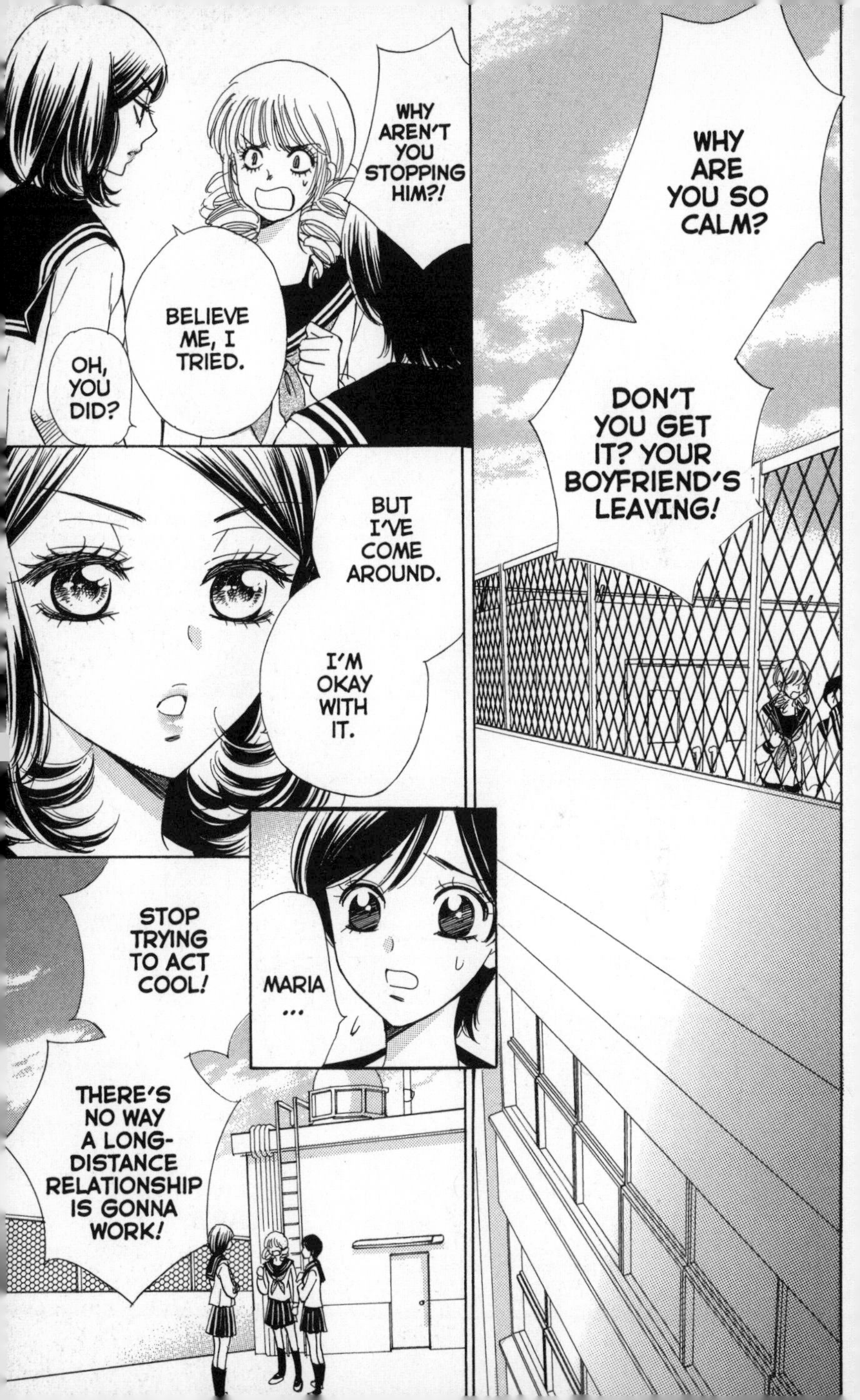
WHY ARE YOU SO CALM?
DON'T YOU GET IT? YOUR BOYFRIEND'S LEAVING!
WHY AREN'T YOU STOPPING HIM?!
BELIEVE ME, I TRIED.
OH, YOU DID?
BUT I'VE COME AROUND.
I'M OKAY WITH IT.
MARIA...
STOP TRYING TO ACT COOL!
THERE'S NO WAY A LONG-DISTANCE RELATIONSHIP IS GONNA WORK!

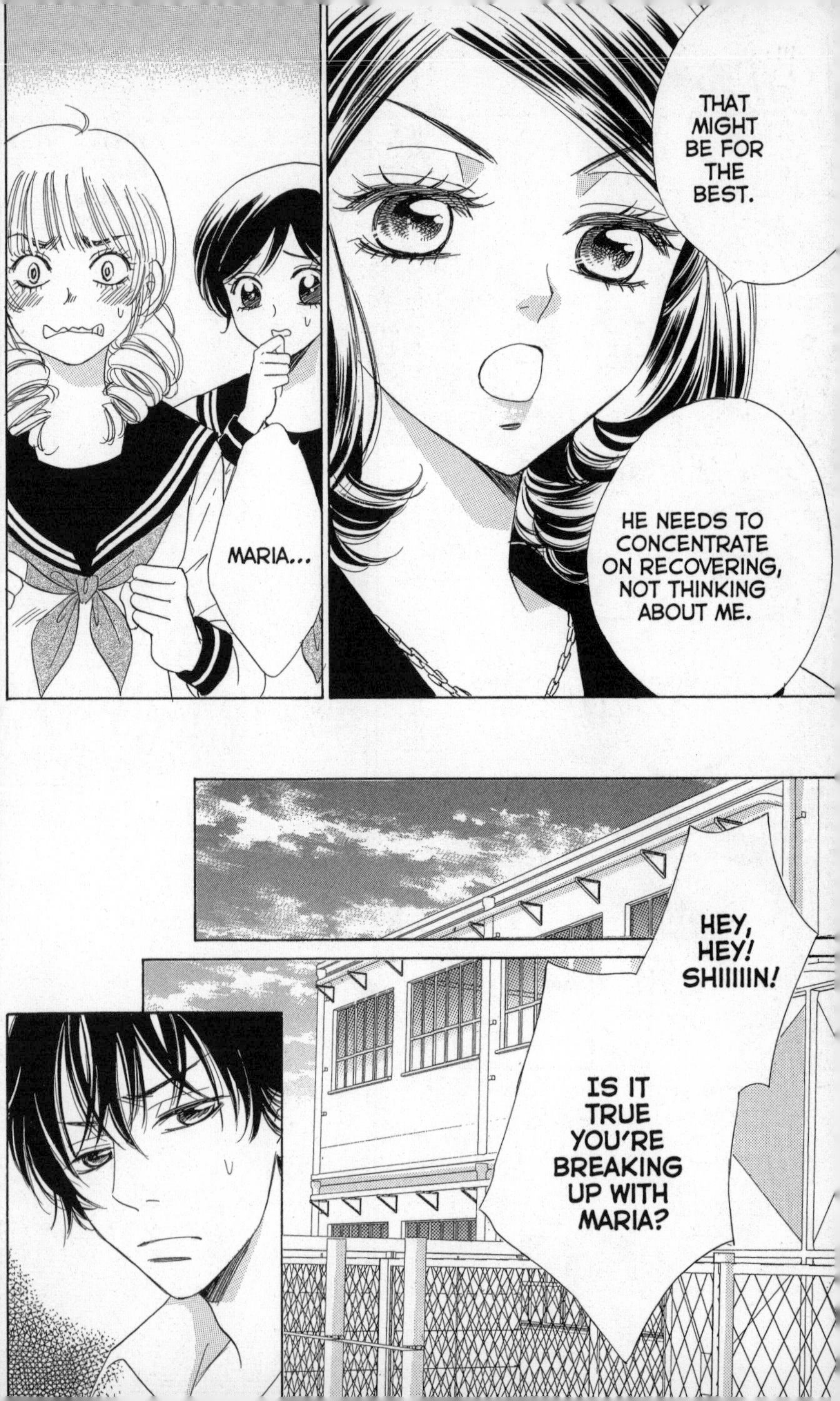
THAT MIGHT BE FOR THE BEST.
HE NEEDS TO CONCENTRATE ON RECOVERING, NOT THINKING ABOUT ME.
MARIA...
HEY, HEY! SHIIIIIN!
IS IT TRUE YOU'RE BREAKING UP WITH MARIA?

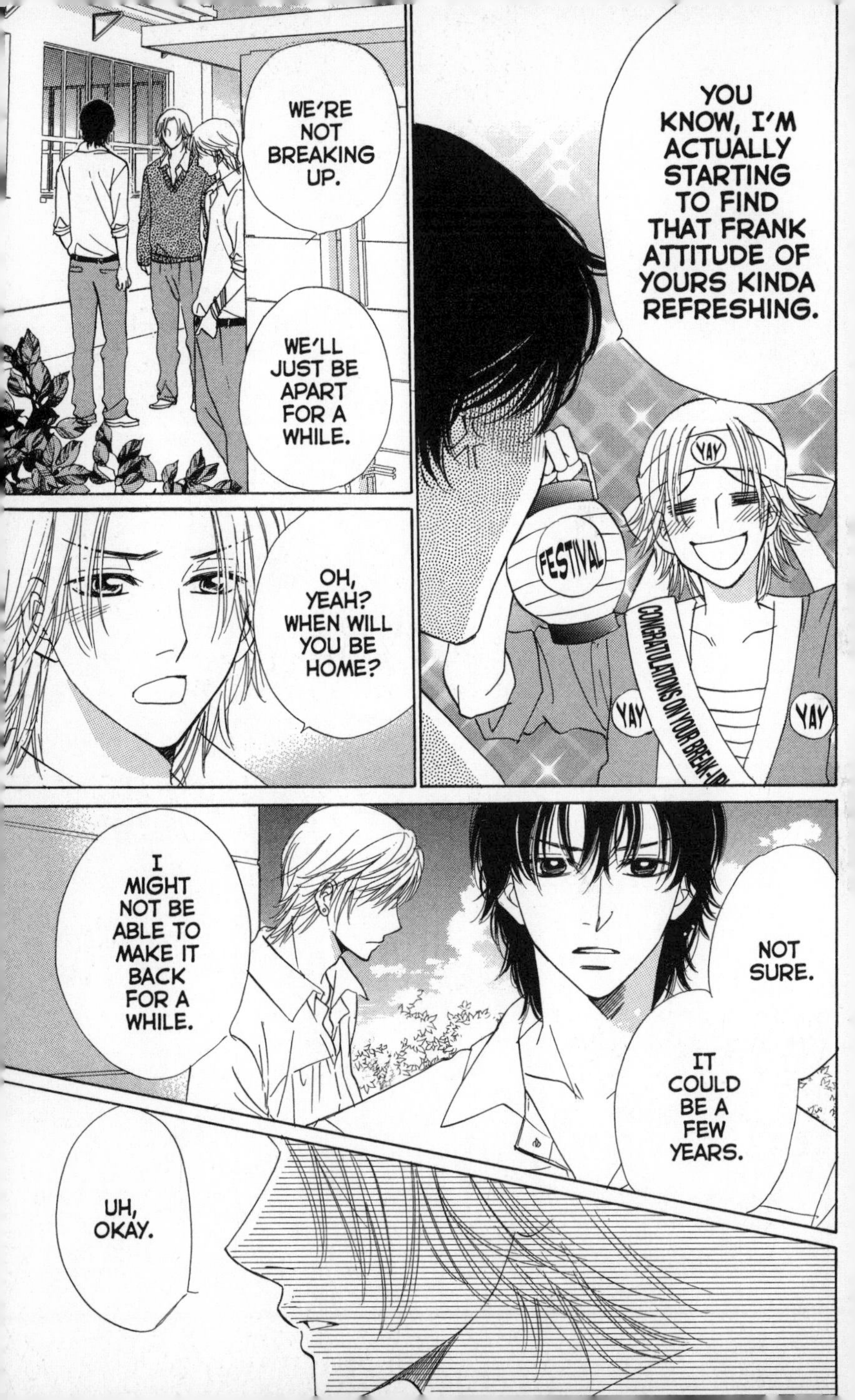
YOU KNOW, I'M ACTUALLY STARTING TO FIND THAT FRANK ATTITUDE OF YOURS KINDA REFRESHING.
YAY
FESTIVAL
CONGRATULATIONS ON YOUR BREAK-UP
YAY
YAY
WE'RE NOT BREAKING UP.
WE'LL JUST BE APART FOR A WHILE.
OH, YEAH? WHEN WILL YOU BE HOME?
NOT SURE.
IT COULD BE A FEW YEARS.
I MIGHT NOT BE ABLE TO MAKE IT BACK FOR A WHILE.
UH, OKAY.

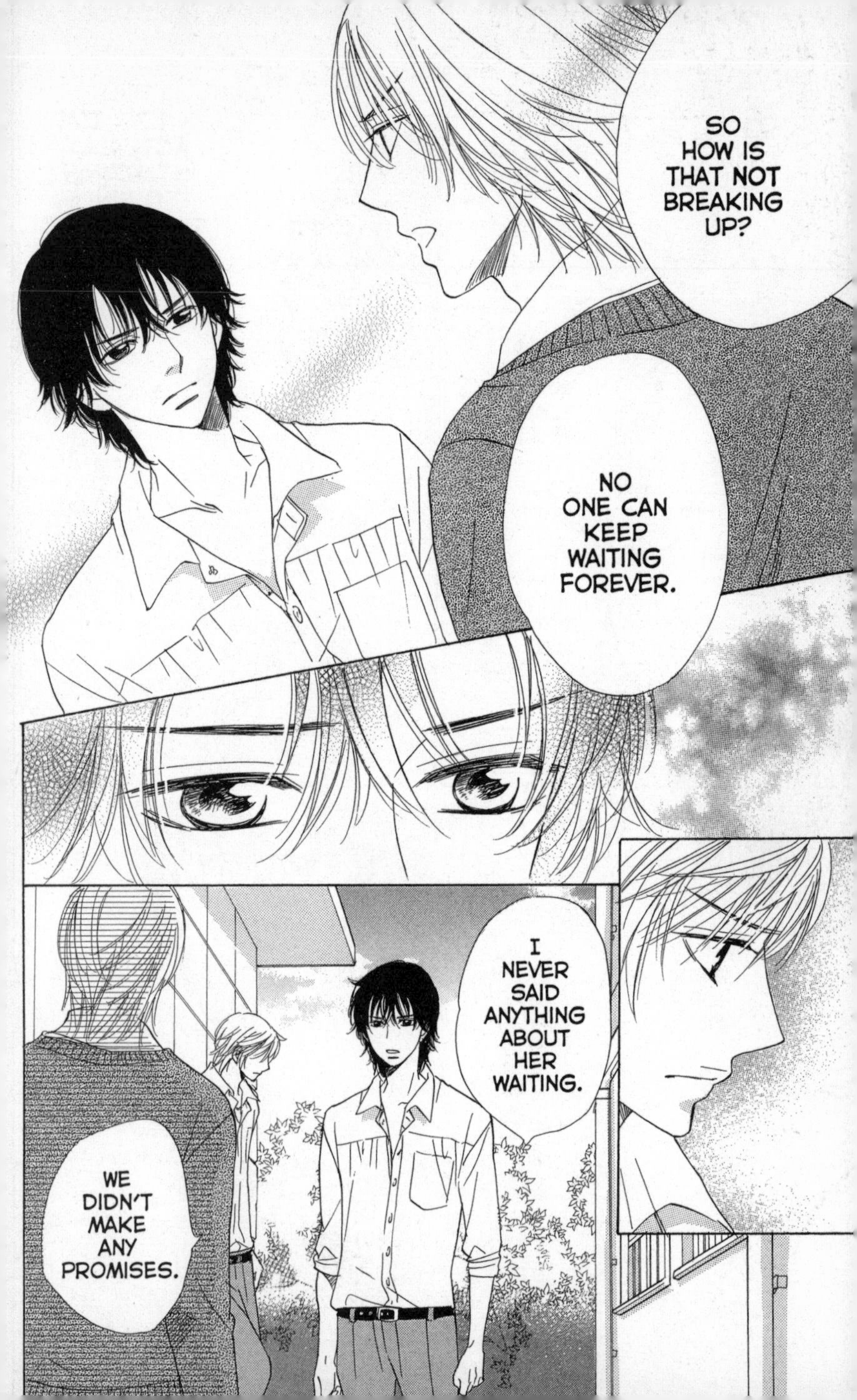
SO HOW IS THAT NOT BREAKING UP?
NO ONE CAN KEEP WAITING FOREVER.
I NEVER SAID ANYTHING ABOUT HER WAITING.
WE DIDN'T MAKE ANY PROMISES.

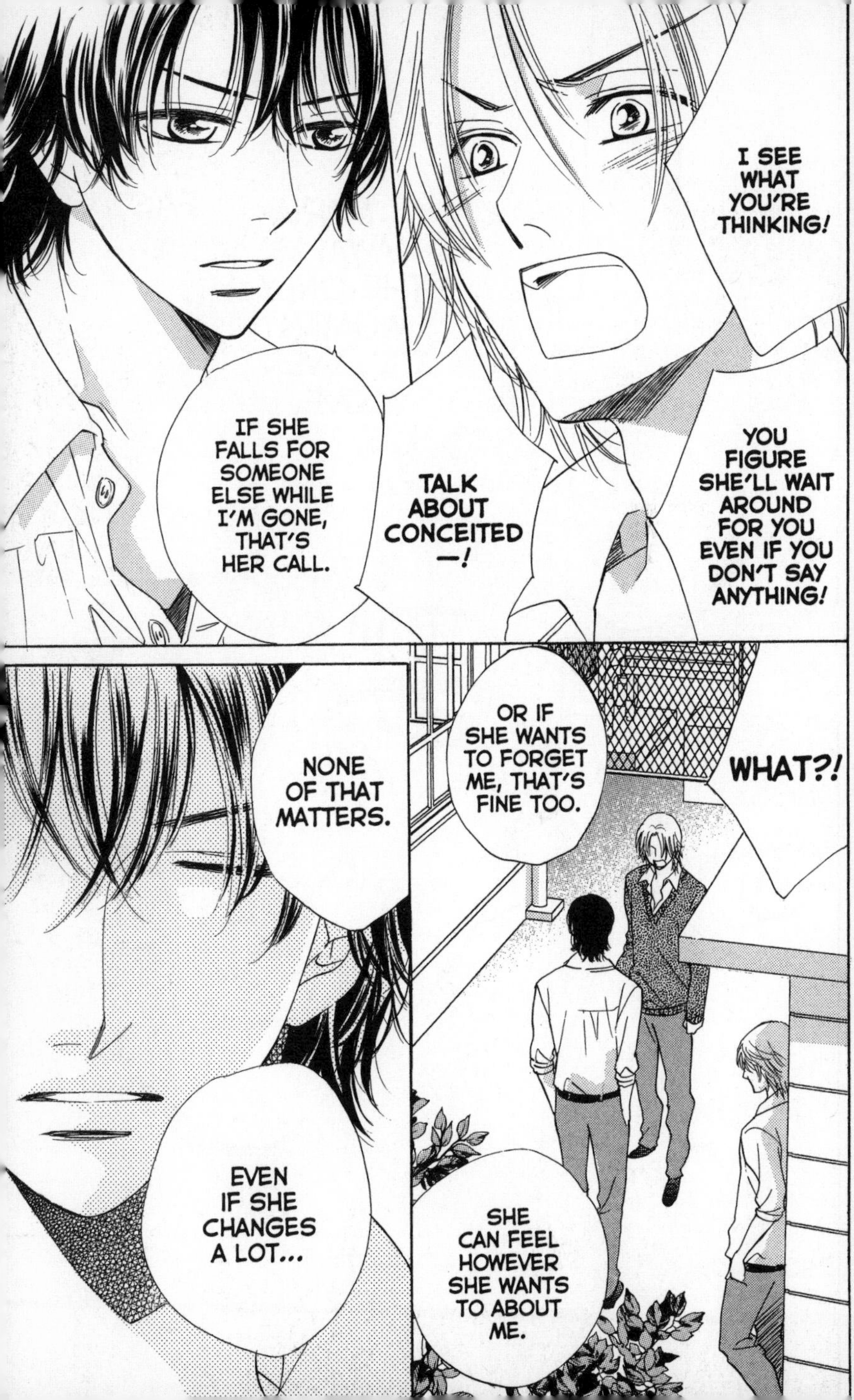
I SEE WHAT YOU'RE THINKING!
YOU FIGURE SHE'LL WAIT AROUND FOR YOU EVEN IF YOU DON'T SAY ANYTHING!
TALK ABOUT CONCEITED —!
IF SHE FALLS FOR SOMEONE ELSE WHILE I'M GONE, THAT'S HER CALL.
WHAT?!
OR IF SHE WANTS TO FORGET ME, THAT'S FINE TOO.
SHE CAN FEEL HOWEVER SHE WANTS TO ABOUT ME.
NONE OF THAT MATTERS.
EVEN IF SHE CHANGES A LOT...

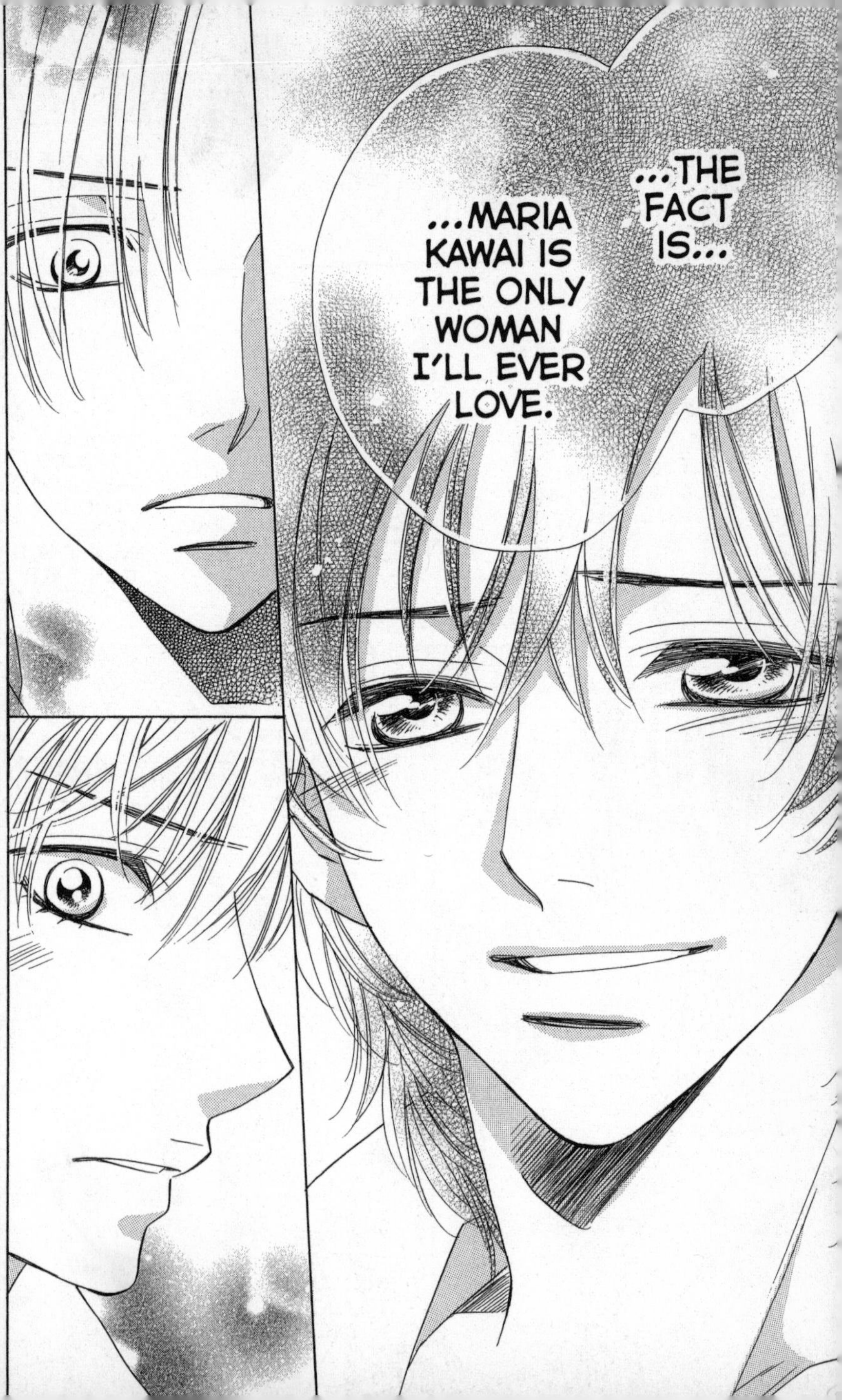
...THE FACT IS...
...MARIA KAWAI IS THE ONLY WOMAN I'LL EVER LOVE.

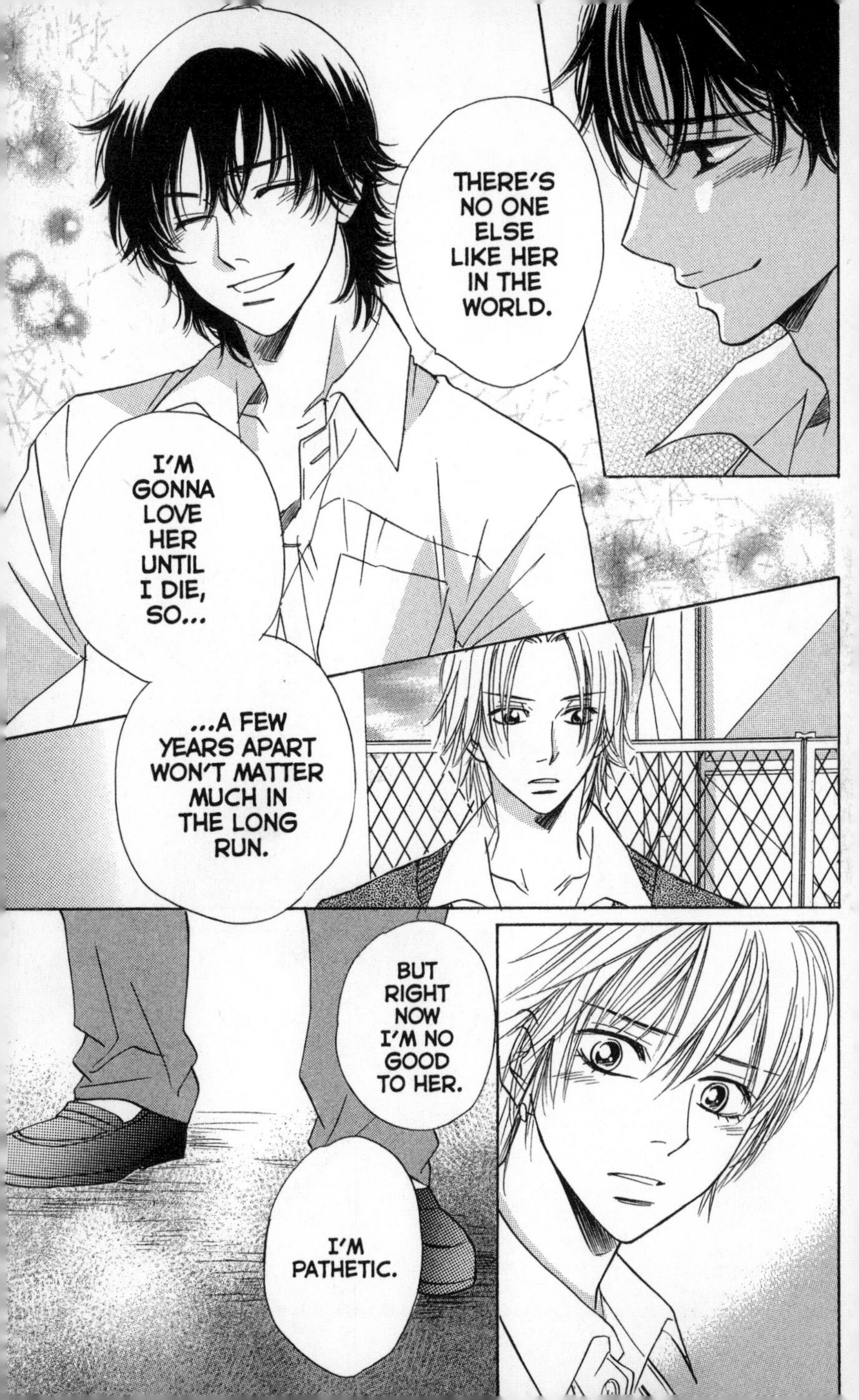
THERE'S NO ONE ELSE LIKE HER IN THE WORLD.
I'M GONNA LOVE HER UNTIL I DIE, SO...
...A FEW YEARS APART WON'T MATTER MUCH IN THE LONG RUN.
BUT RIGHT NOW I'M NO GOOD TO HER.
I'M PATHETIC.

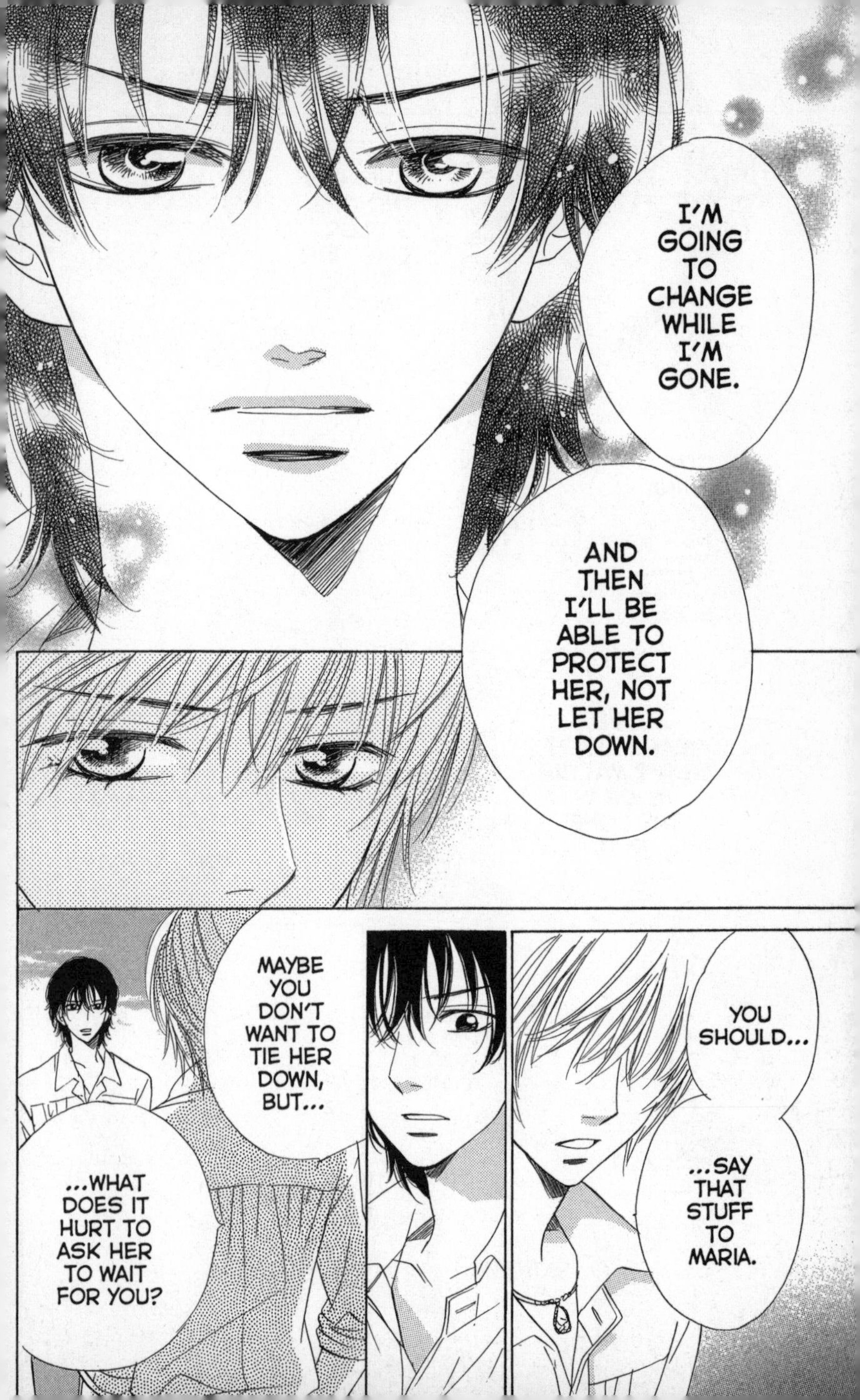
I'M GOING TO CHANGE WHILE I'M GONE.
AND THEN I'LL BE ABLE TO PROTECT HER, NOT LET HER DOWN.
YOU SHOULD...
...SAY THAT STUFF TO MARIA.
MAYBE YOU DON'T WANT TO TIE HER DOWN, BUT...
...WHAT DOES IT HURT TO ASK HER TO WAIT FOR YOU?

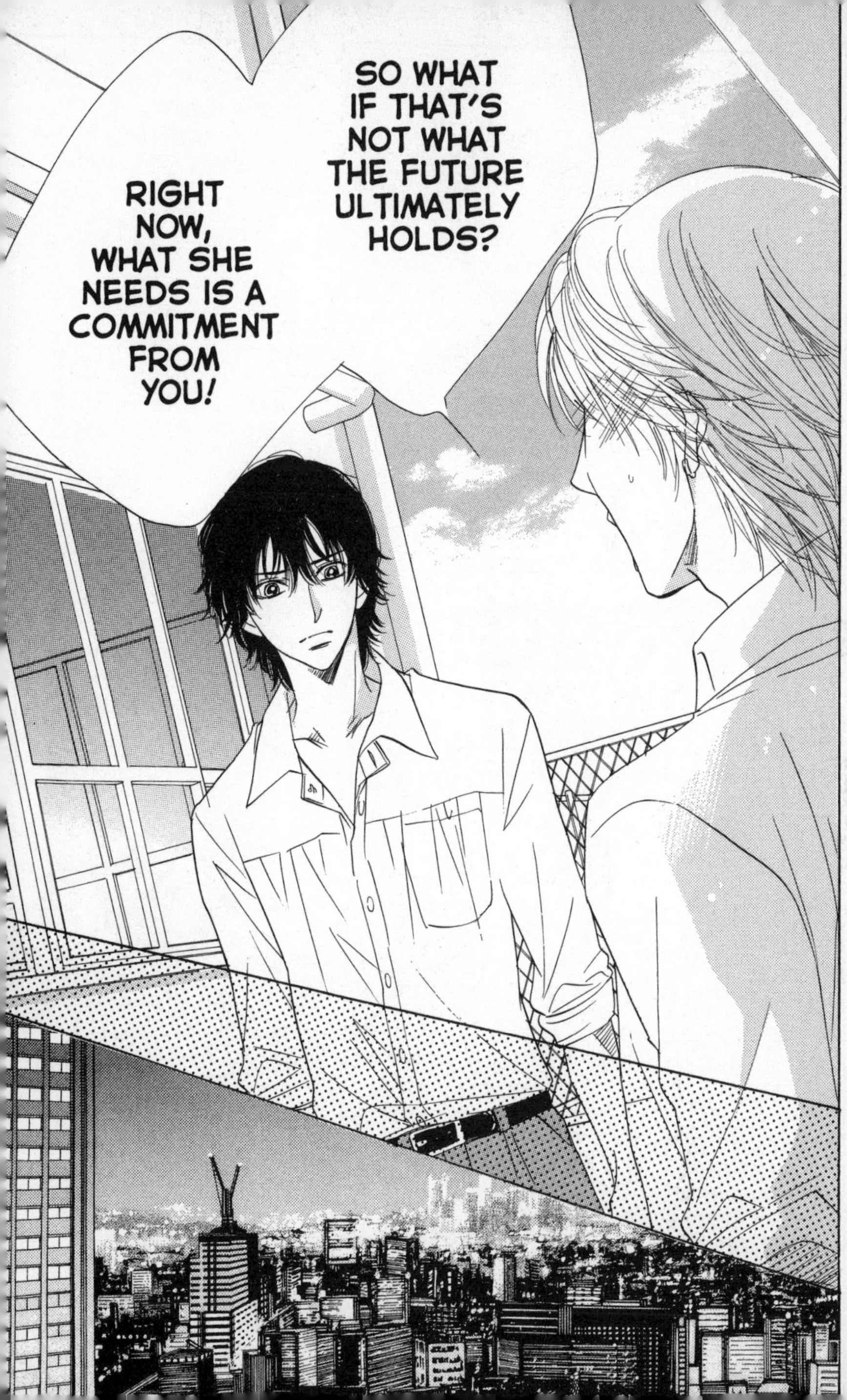
SO WHAT IF THAT'S NOT WHAT THE FUTURE ULTIMATELY HOLDS?
RIGHT NOW, WHAT SHE NEEDS IS A COMMITMENT FROM YOU!

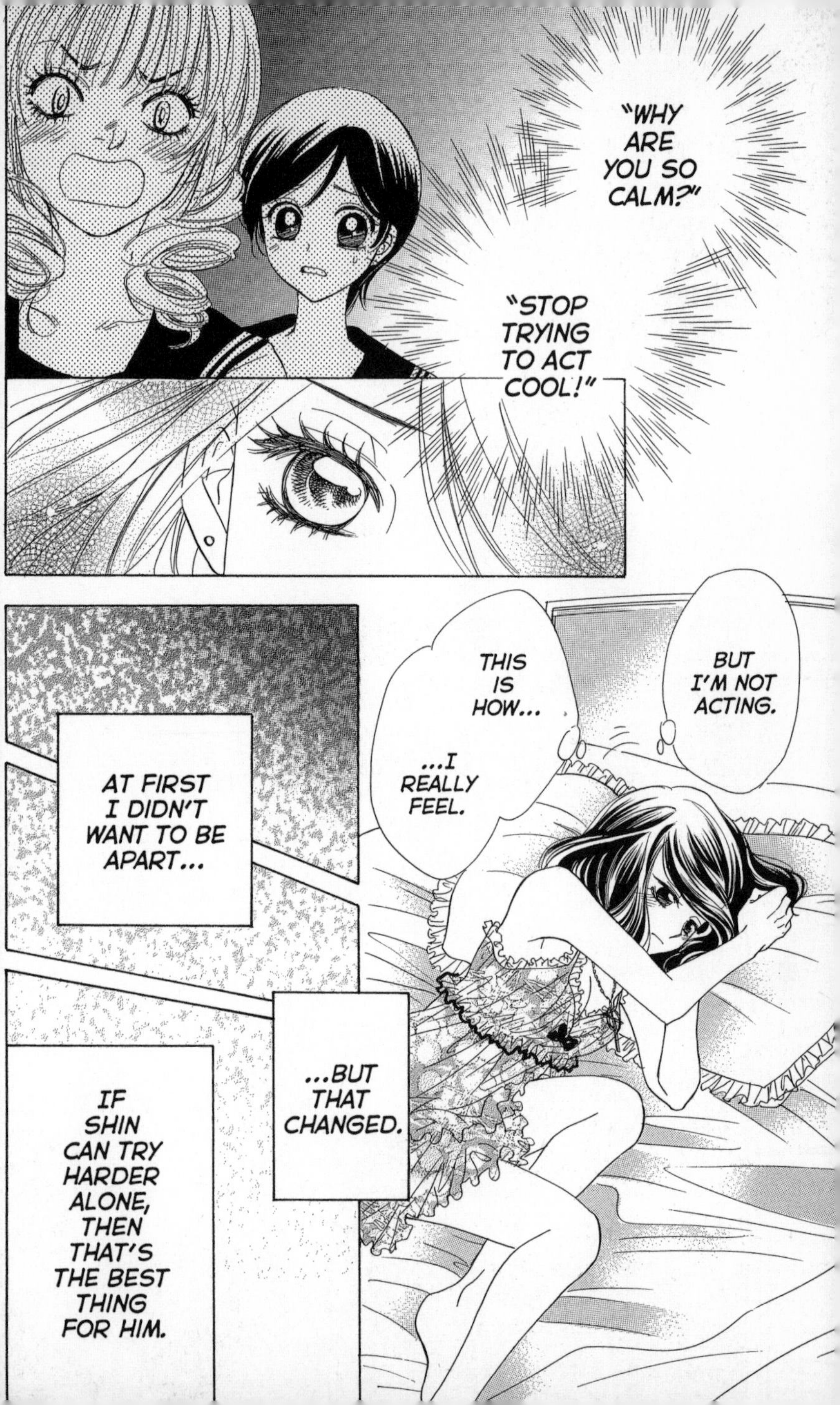
"WHY ARE YOU SO CALM?"
"STOP TRYING TO ACT COOL!"
BUT I'M NOT ACTING.
THIS IS HOW...
...I REALLY FEEL.
AT FIRST I DIDN'T WANT TO BE APART...
...BUT THAT CHANGED.
IF SHIN CAN TRY HARDER ALONE, THEN THAT'S THE BEST THING FOR HIM.

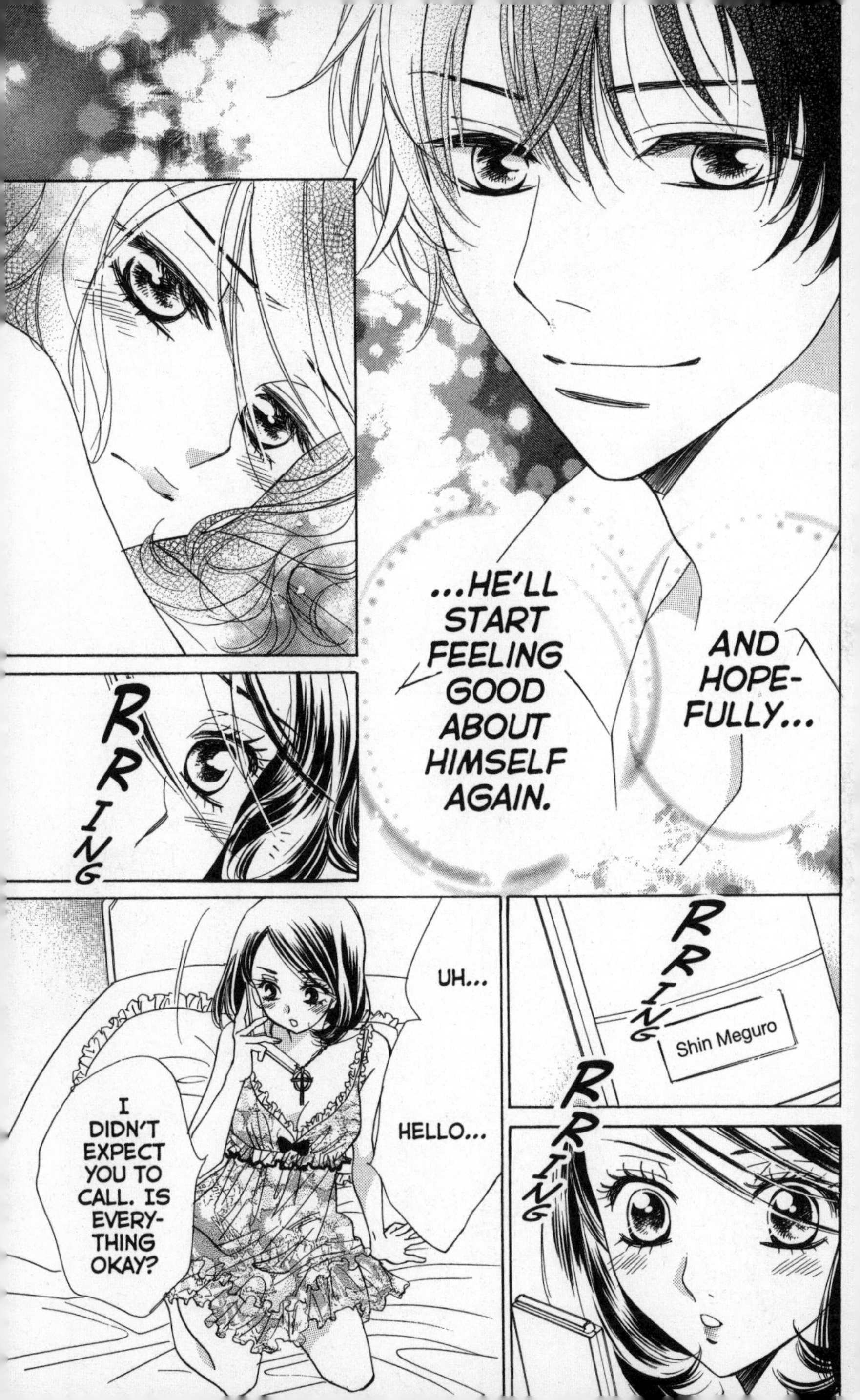
AND HOPEFULLY...
...HE'LL START FEELING GOOD ABOUT HIMSELF AGAIN.
RRING
RRING
Shin Meguro
RRING
UH...
HELLO...
I DIDN'T EXPECT YOU TO CALL. IS EVERYTHING OKAY?

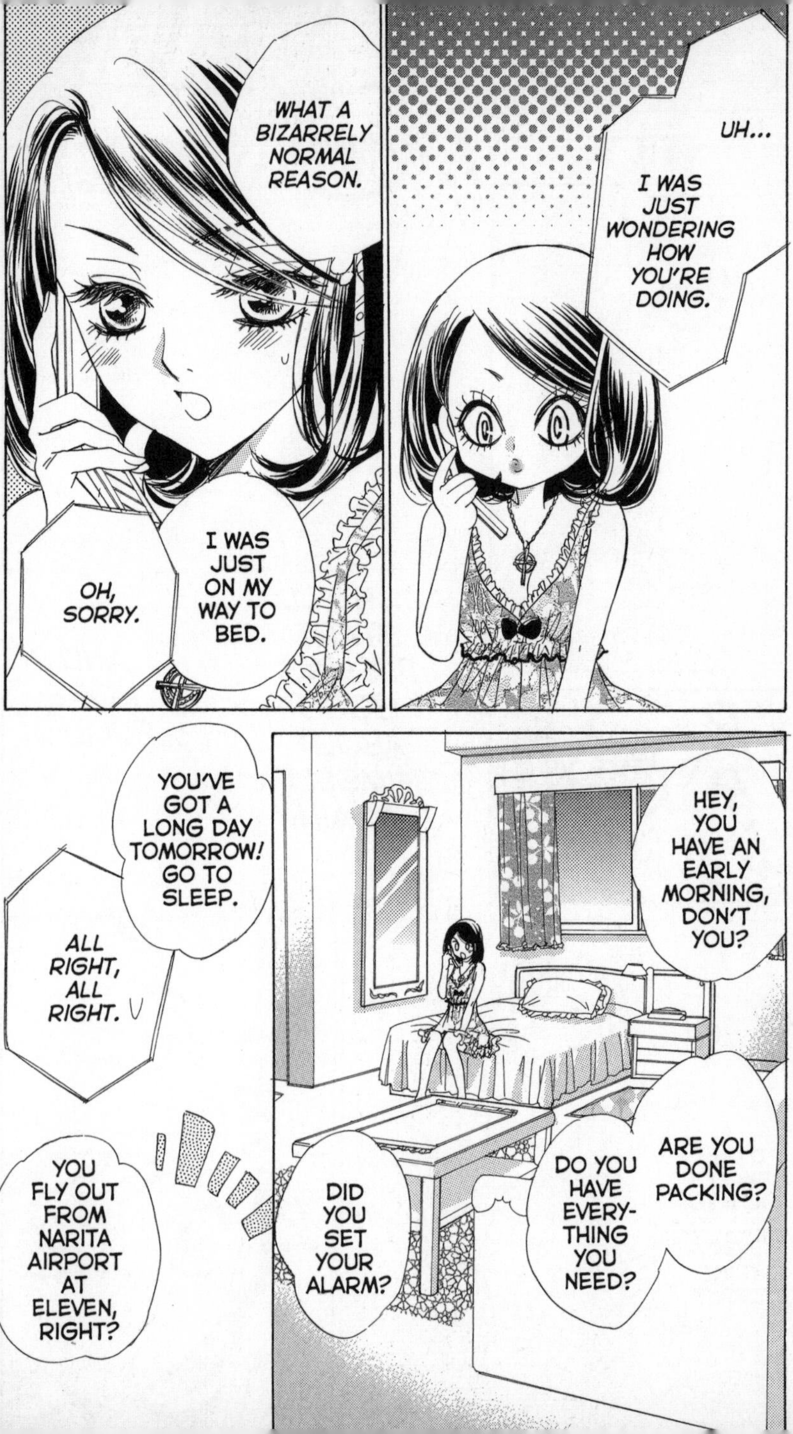
UH...
I WAS JUST WONDERING HOW YOU'RE DOING.
WHAT A BIZARRELY NORMAL REASON.
I WAS JUST ON MY WAY TO BED.
OH, SORRY.
HEY, YOU HAVE AN EARLY MORNING, DON'T YOU?
YOU'VE GOT A LONG DAY TOMORROW! GO TO SLEEP.
ALL RIGHT, ALL RIGHT.
ARE YOU DONE PACKING?
DO YOU HAVE EVERY-THING YOU NEED?
DID YOU SET YOUR ALARM?
YOU FLY OUT FROM NARITA AIRPORT AT ELEVEN, RIGHT?

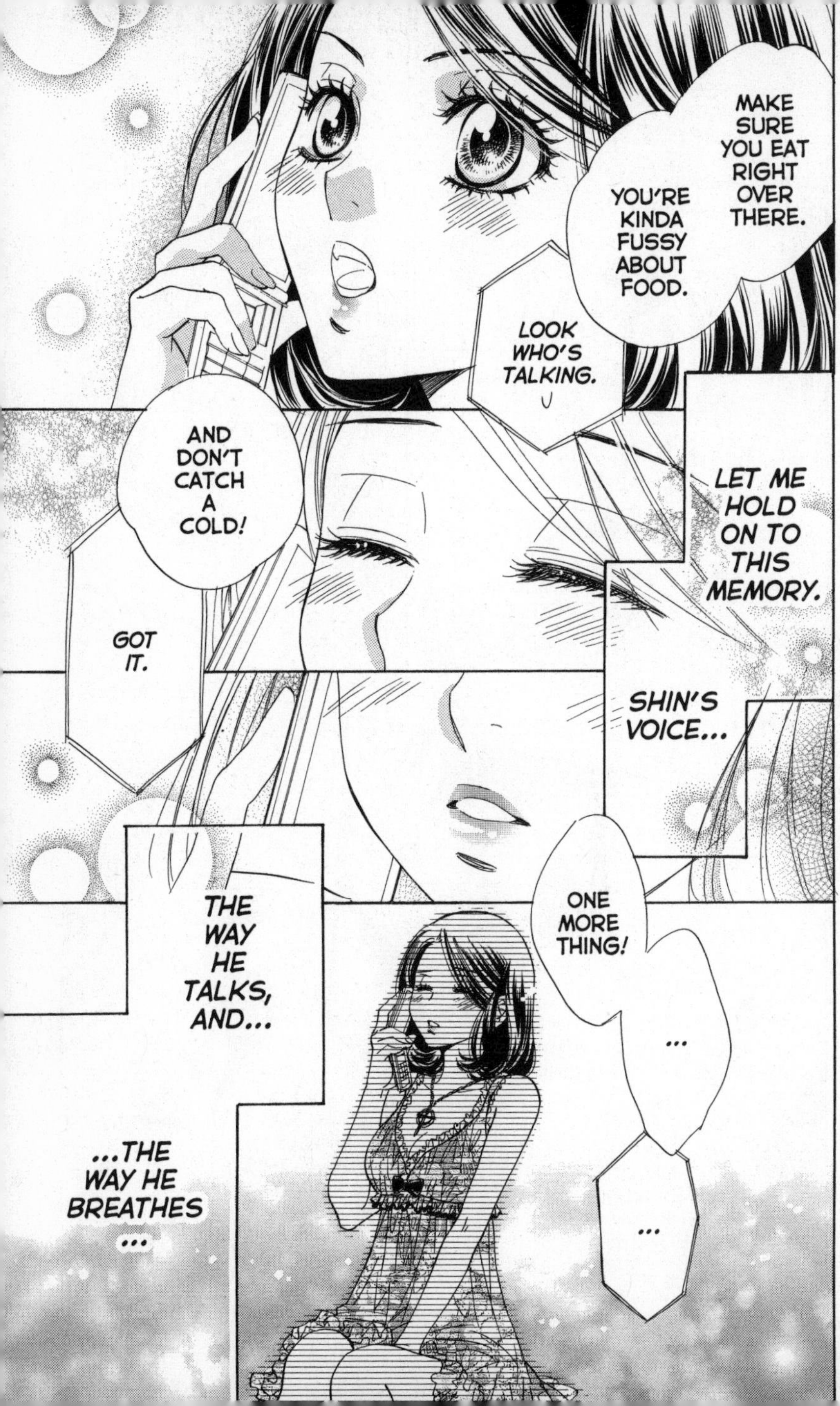
MAKE SURE YOU EAT RIGHT OVER THERE.
YOU'RE KINDA FUSSY ABOUT FOOD.
LOOK WHO'S TALKING.
LET ME HOLD ON TO THIS MEMORY.
AND DON'T CATCH A COLD!
GOT IT.
SHIN'S VOICE...
ONE MORE THING!
...
...
THE WAY HE TALKS, AND...
...THE WAY HE BREATHES...

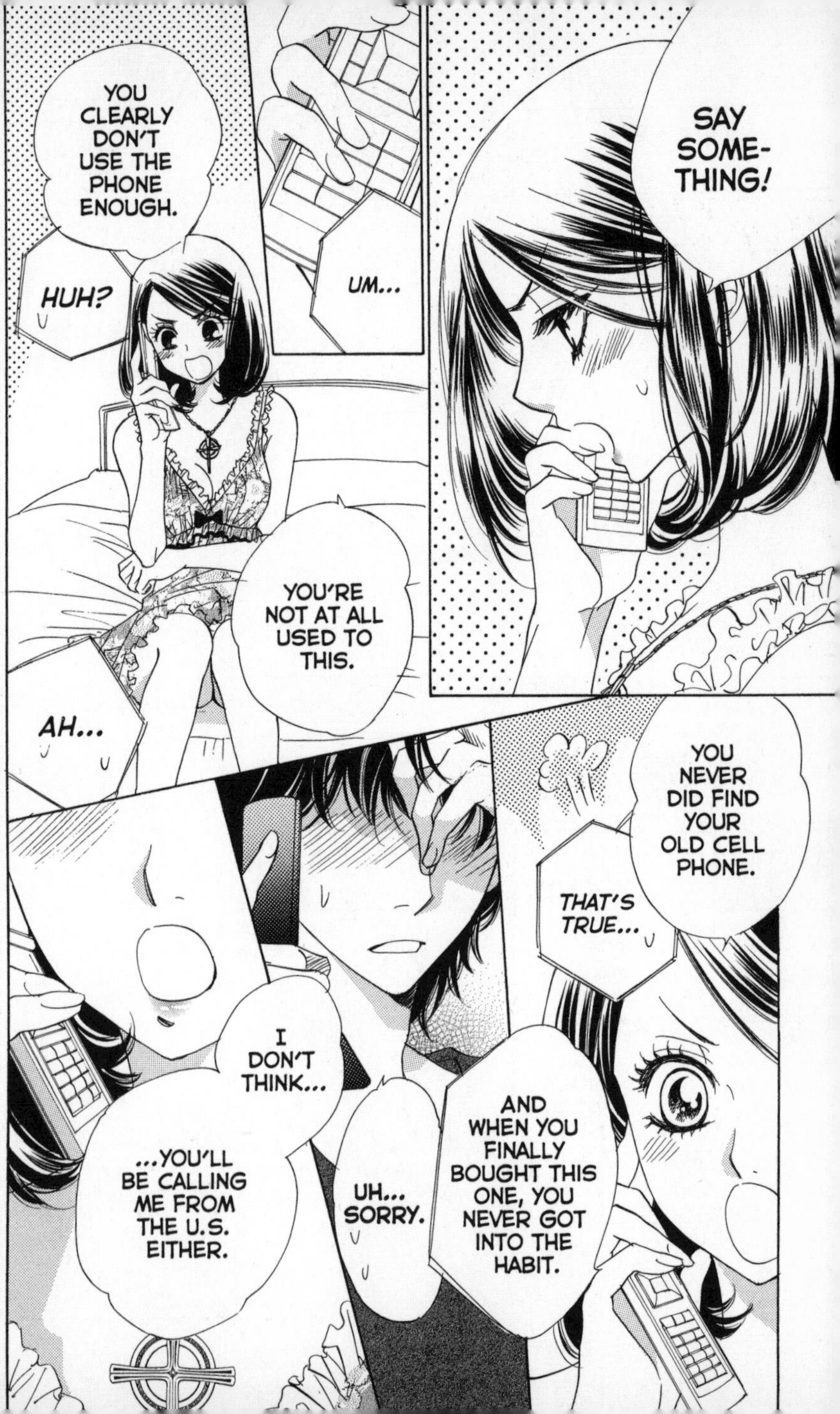

SAY SOMETHING!
UM...
YOU CLEARLY DON'T USE THE PHONE ENOUGH.
HUH?
YOU'RE NOT AT ALL USED TO THIS.
AH...
YOU NEVER DID FIND YOUR OLD CELL PHONE.
THAT'S TRUE...
AND WHEN YOU FINALLY BOUGHT THIS ONE, YOU NEVER GOT INTO THE HABIT.
UH... SORRY.
I DON'T THINK...
...YOU'LL BE CALLING ME FROM THE U.S. EITHER.

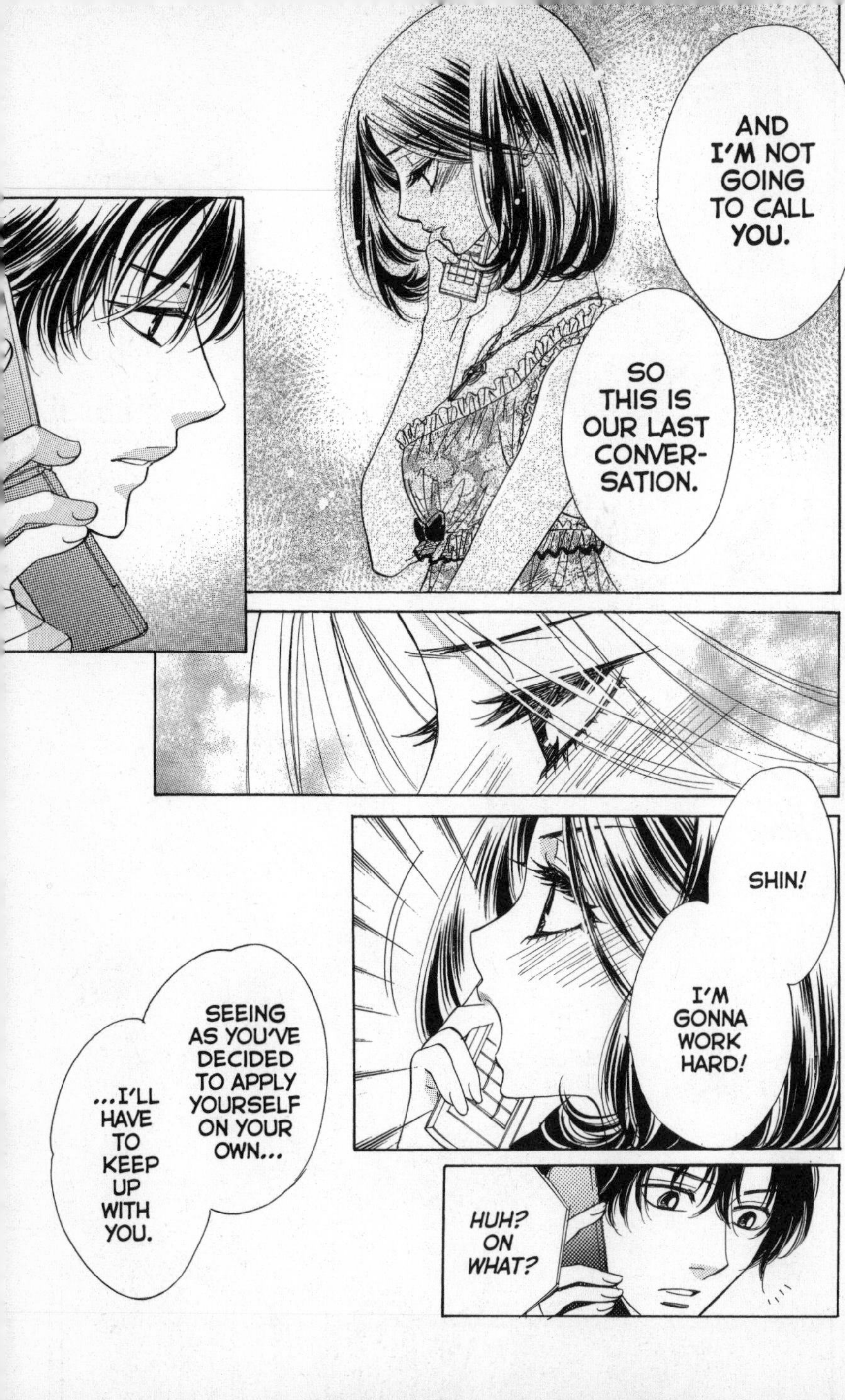
AND I'M NOT GOING TO CALL YOU.
SO THIS IS OUR LAST CONVERSATION.
SHIN!
I'M GONNA WORK HARD!
HUH? ON WHAT?
SEEING AS YOU'VE DECIDED TO APPLY YOURSELF ON YOUR OWN...
...I'LL HAVE TO KEEP UP WITH YOU.

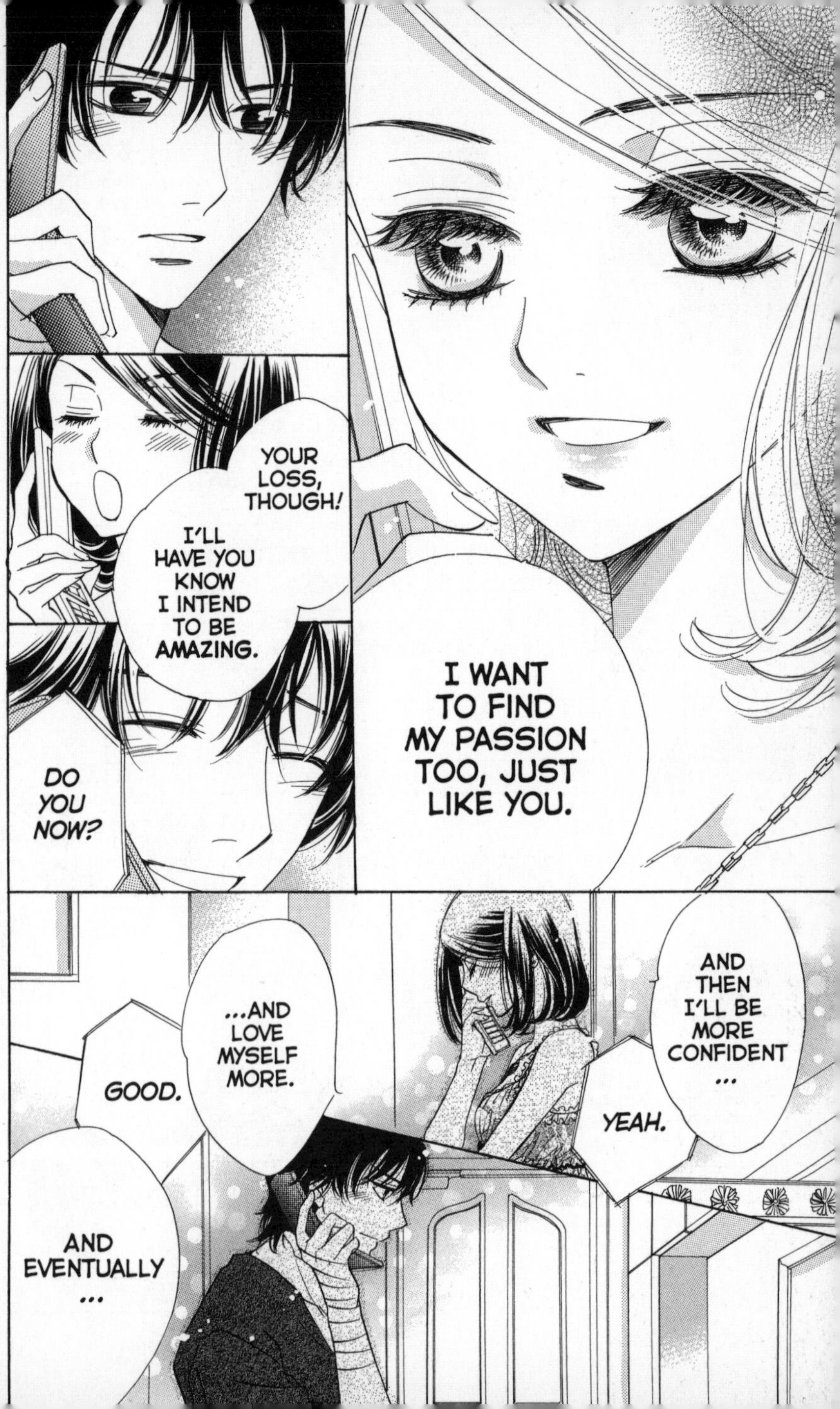
I WANT TO FIND MY PASSION TOO, JUST LIKE YOU.
YOUR LOSS, THOUGH!
I'LL HAVE YOU KNOW I INTEND TO BE AMAZING.
DO YOU NOW?
AND THEN I'LL BE MORE CONFIDENT ...
YEAH.
...AND LOVE MYSELF MORE.
GOOD.
AND EVENTUALLY ...

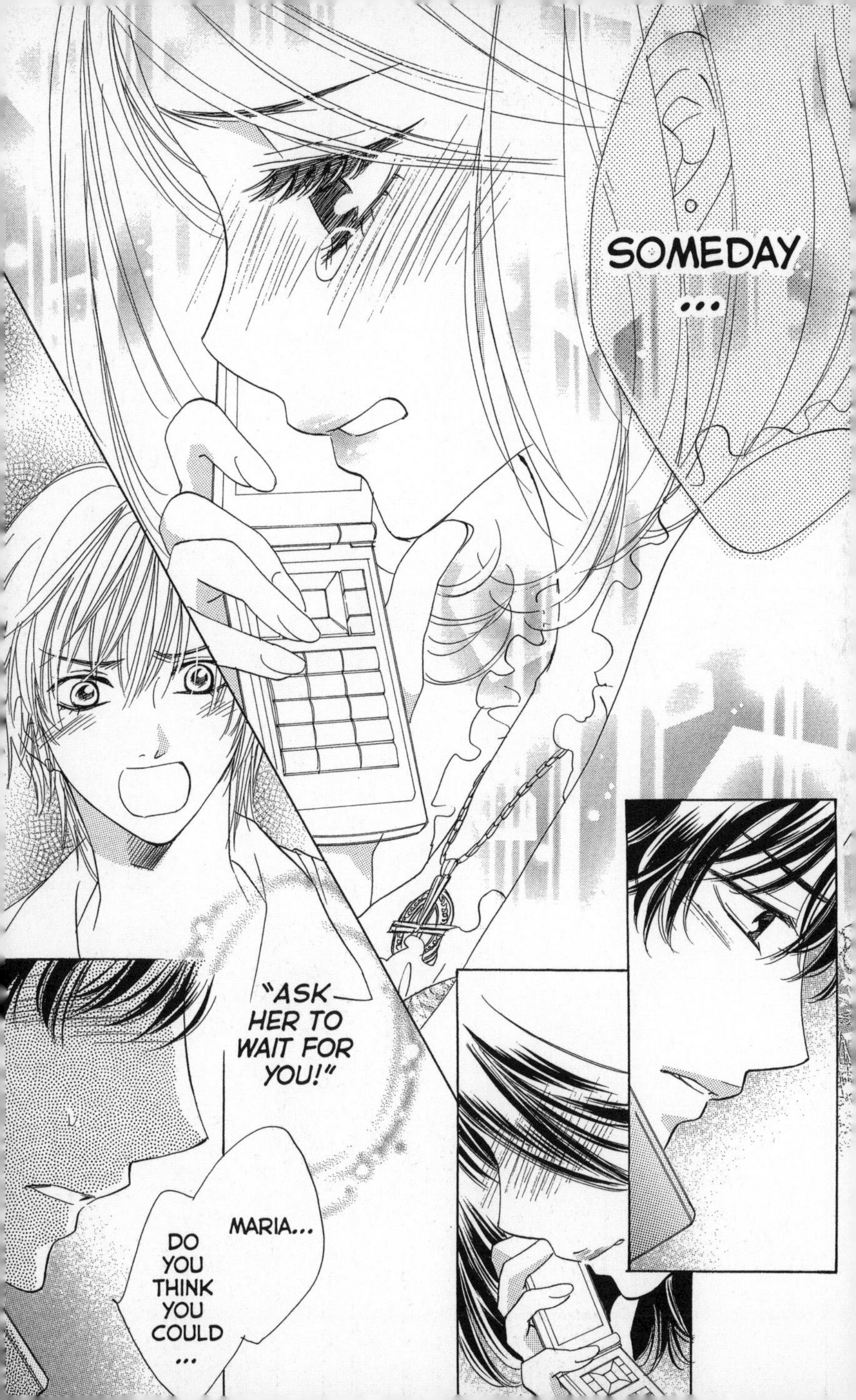
SOMEDAY...
"ASK HER TO WAIT FOR YOU!"
MARIA... DO YOU THINK YOU COULD...

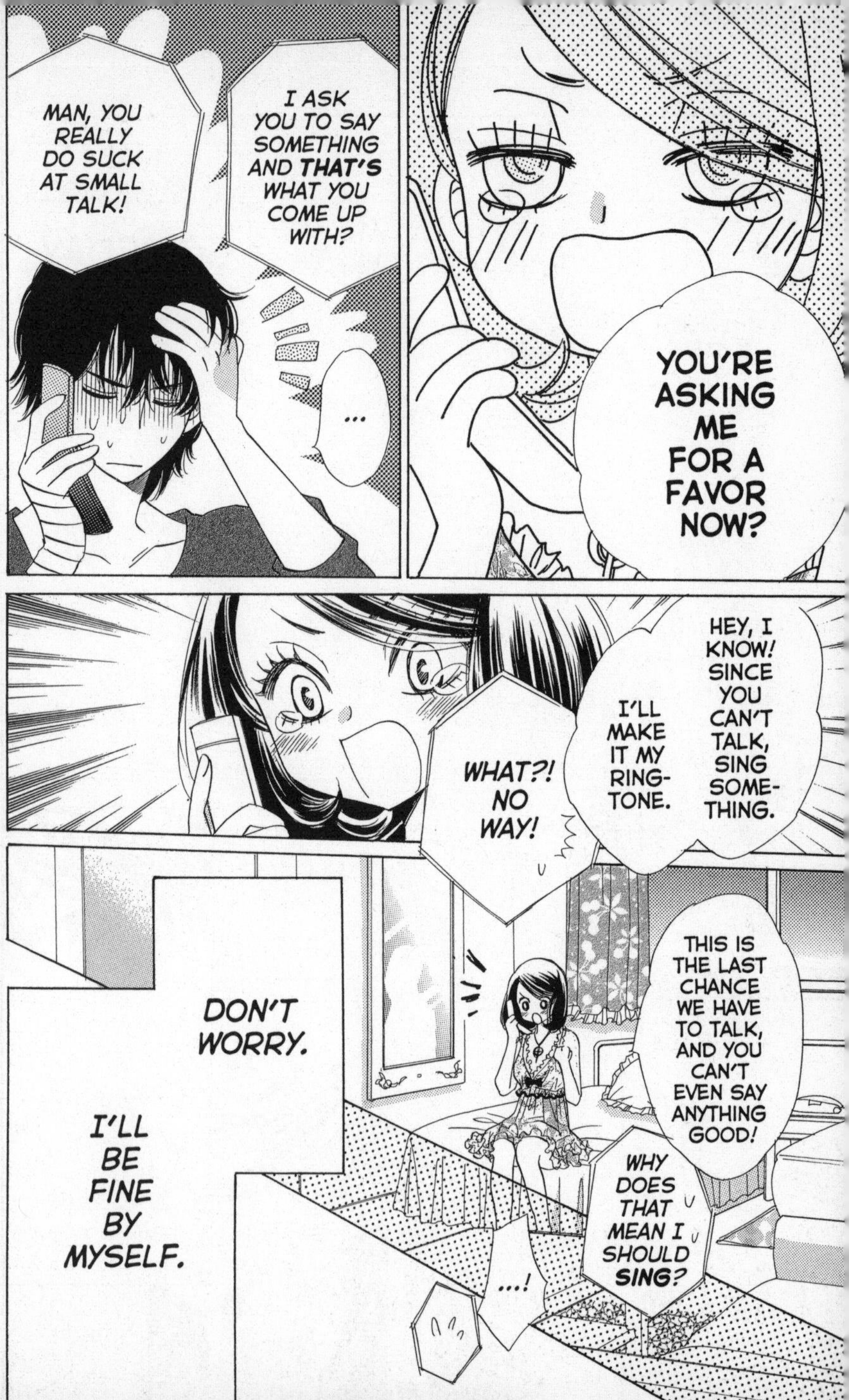
YOU'RE ASKING ME FOR A FAVOR NOW?
I ASK YOU TO SAY SOMETHING AND THAT'S WHAT YOU COME UP WITH?
MAN, YOU REALLY DO SUCK AT SMALL TALK!
...
HEY, I KNOW! SINCE YOU CAN'T TALK, SING SOME-THING.
I'LL MAKE IT MY RING-TONE.
WHAT?! NO WAY!
THIS IS THE LAST CHANCE WE HAVE TO TALK, AND YOU CAN'T EVEN SAY ANYTHING GOOD!
WHY DOES THAT MEAN I SHOULD SING?
...!
DON'T WORRY.
I'LL BE FINE BY MYSELF.

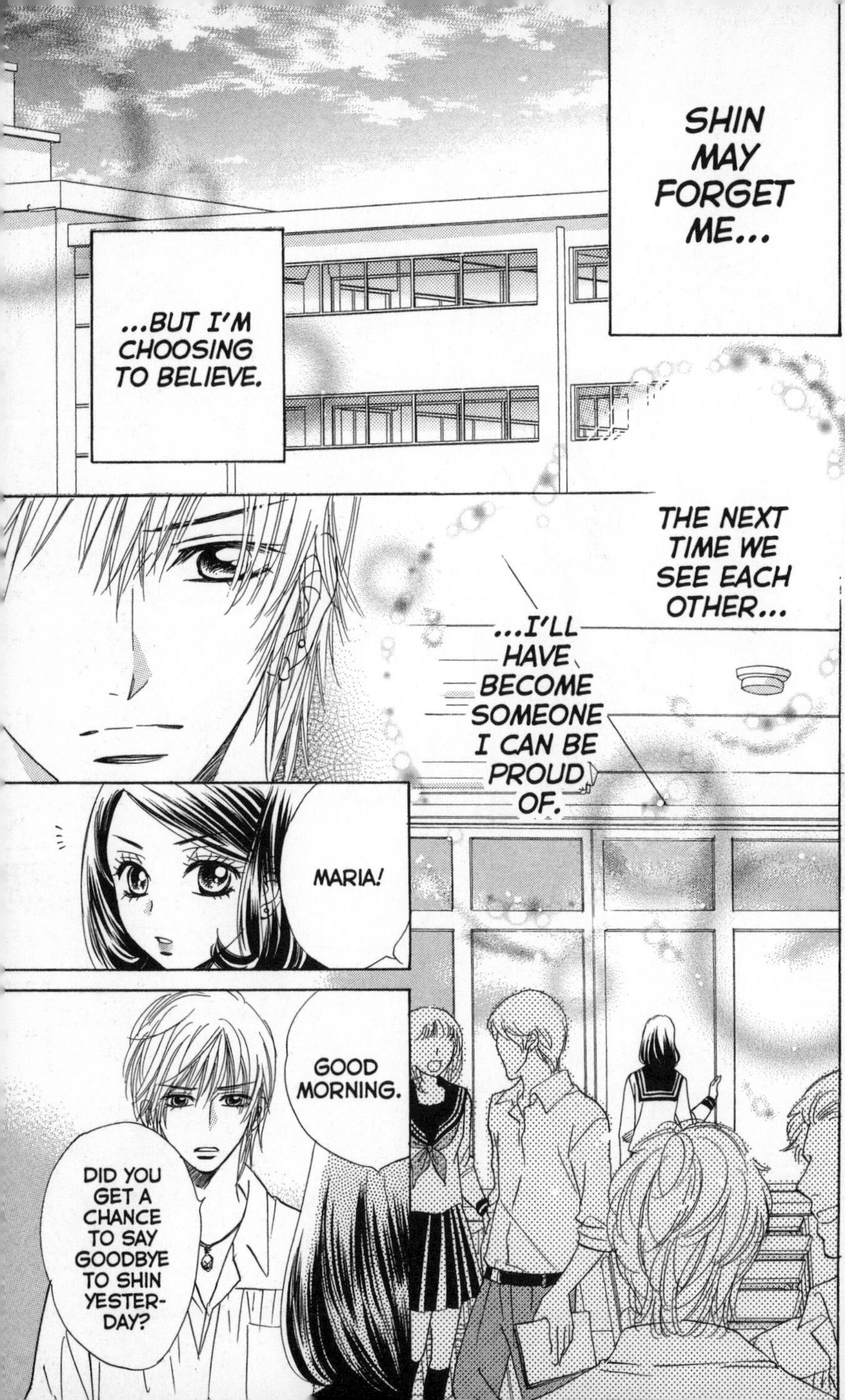
SHIN MAY FORGET ME...
...BUT I'M CHOOSING TO BELIEVE.
THE NEXT TIME WE SEE EACH OTHER...
...I'LL HAVE BECOME SOMEONE I CAN BE PROUD OF.
MARIA!
GOOD MORNING.
DID YOU GET A CHANCE TO SAY GOODBYE TO SHIN YESTER-DAY?

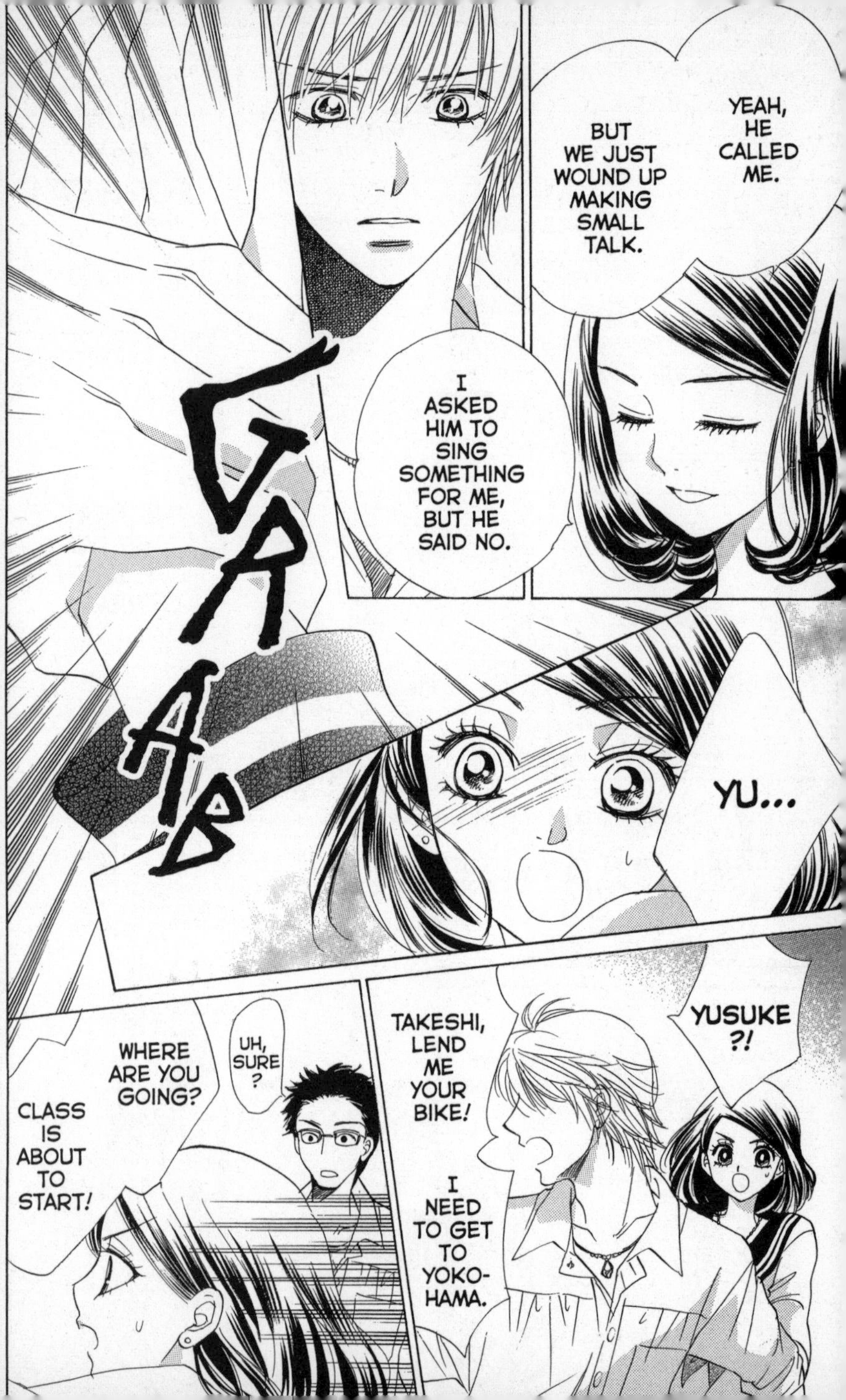
YEAH, HE CALLED ME.
BUT WE JUST WOUND UP MAKING SMALL TALK.
I ASKED HIM TO SING SOMETHING FOR ME, BUT HE SAID NO.
GRAB
YU...
YUSUKE?!
TAKESHI, LEND ME YOUR BIKE!
I NEED TO GET TO YOKOHAMA.
UH, SURE?
WHERE ARE YOU GOING?
CLASS IS ABOUT TO START!

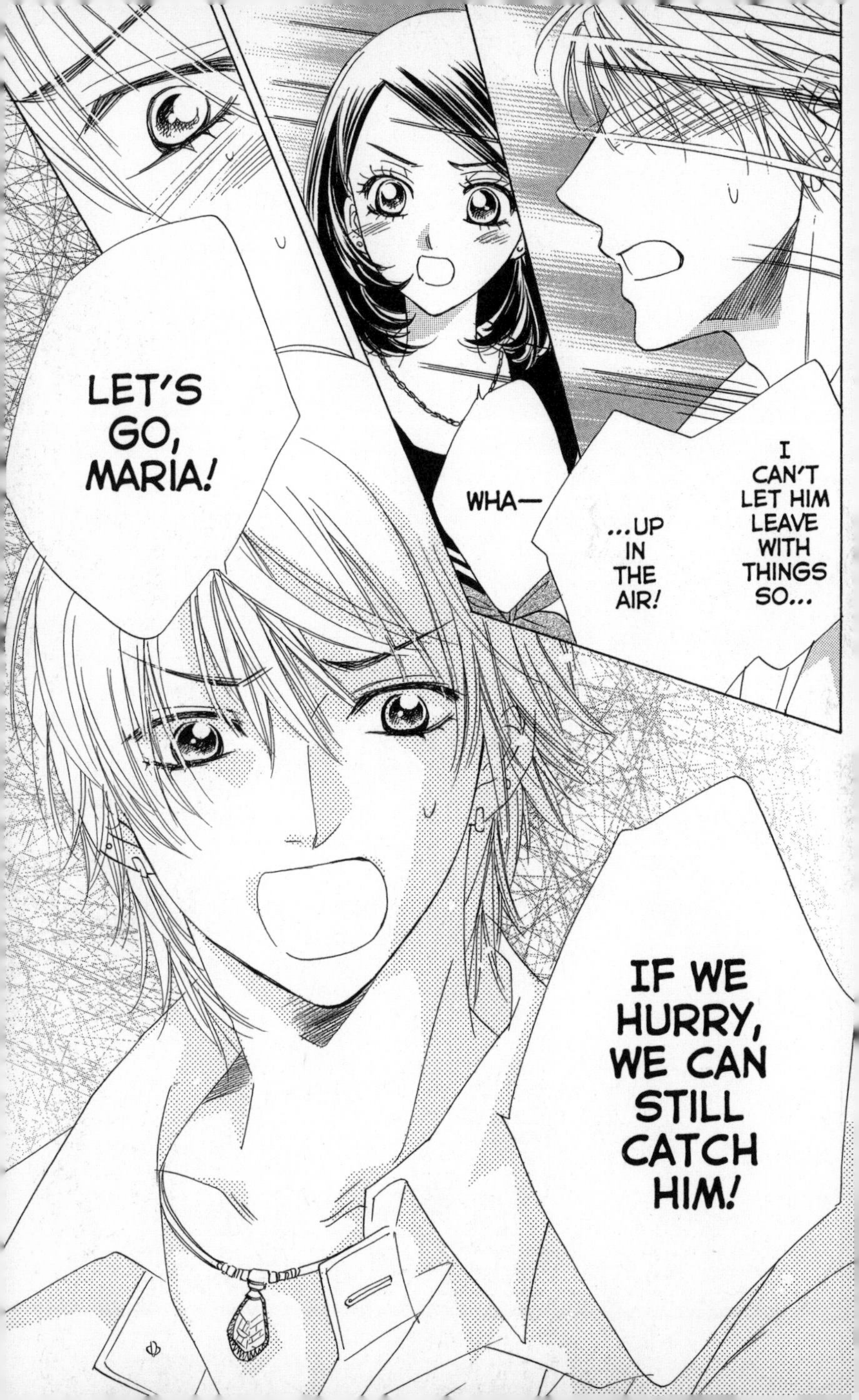
I CAN'T LET HIM LEAVE WITH THINGS SO...
...UP IN THE AIR!
WHA—
IF WE HURRY, WE CAN STILL CATCH HIM!
LET'S GO, MARIA!

A Devil and Her Love Song

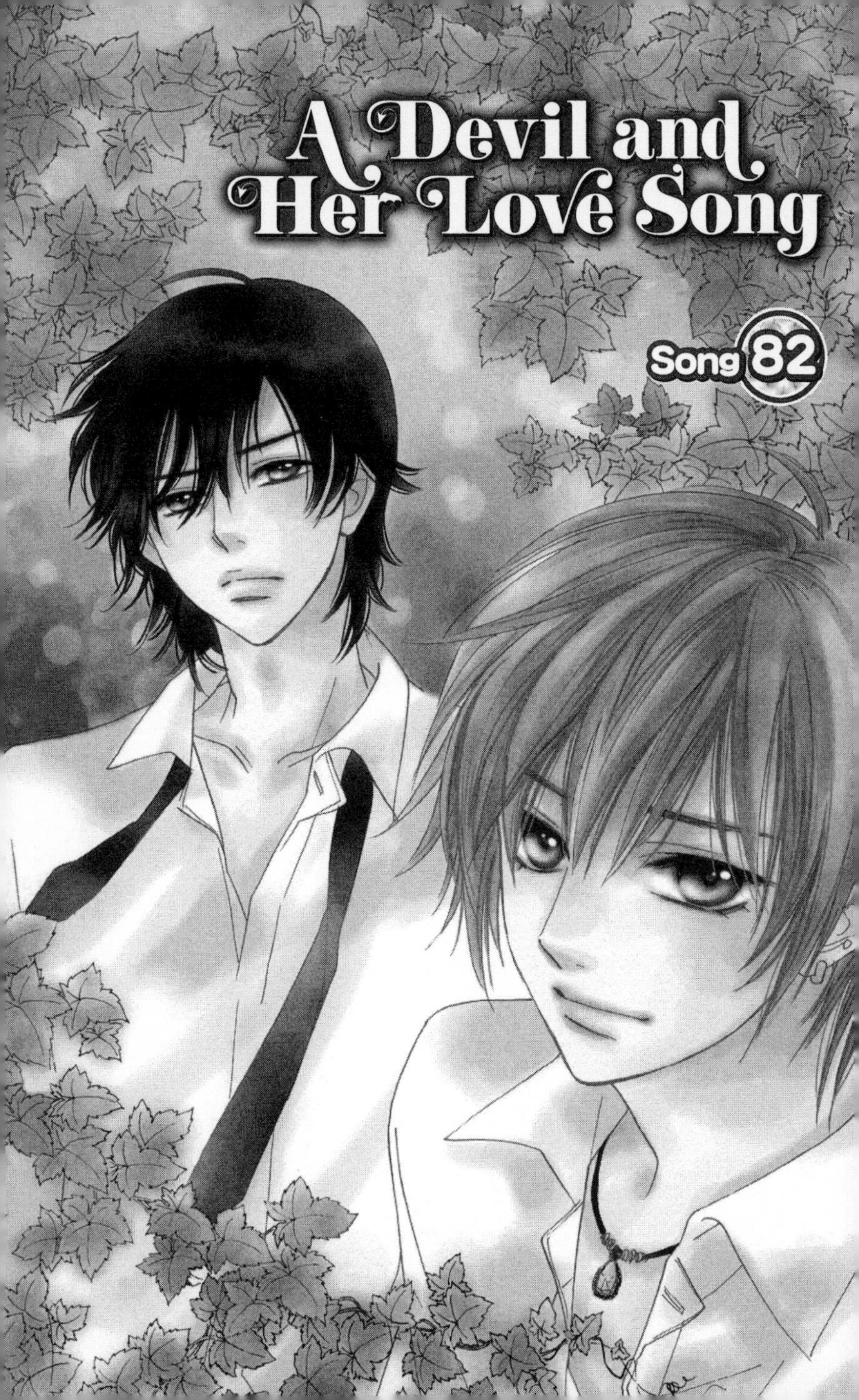
A Devil and Her Love Song
Song 82

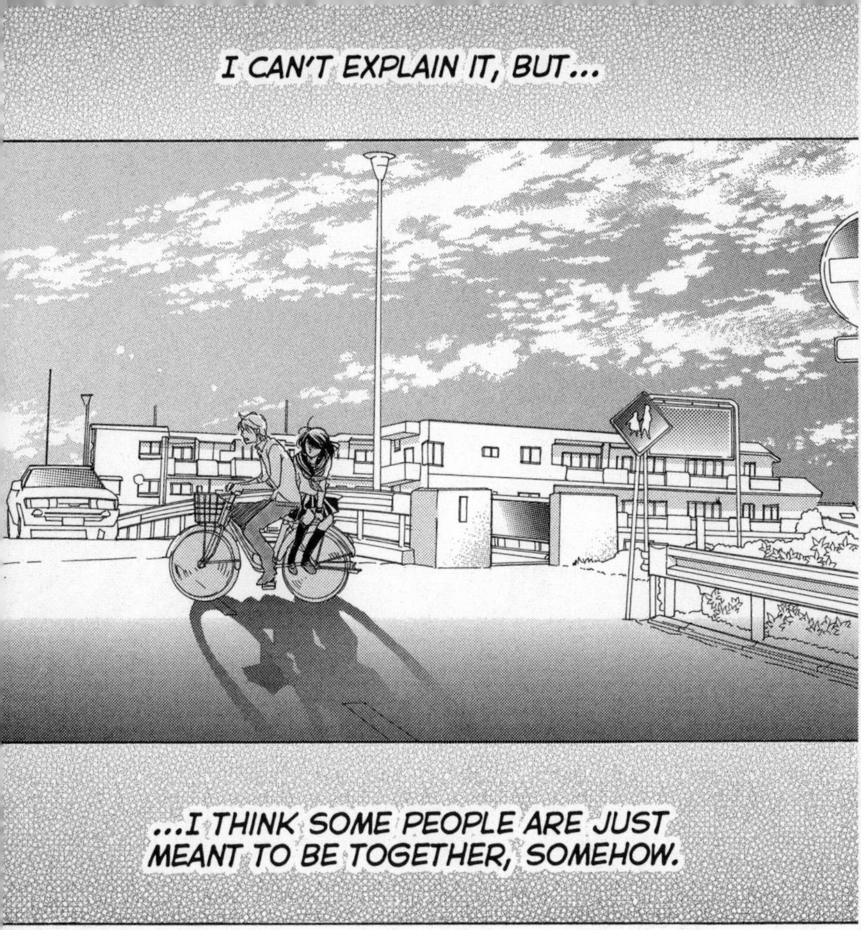
I CAN'T EXPLAIN IT, BUT...
...I THINK SOME PEOPLE ARE JUST MEANT TO BE TOGETHER, SOMEHOW.

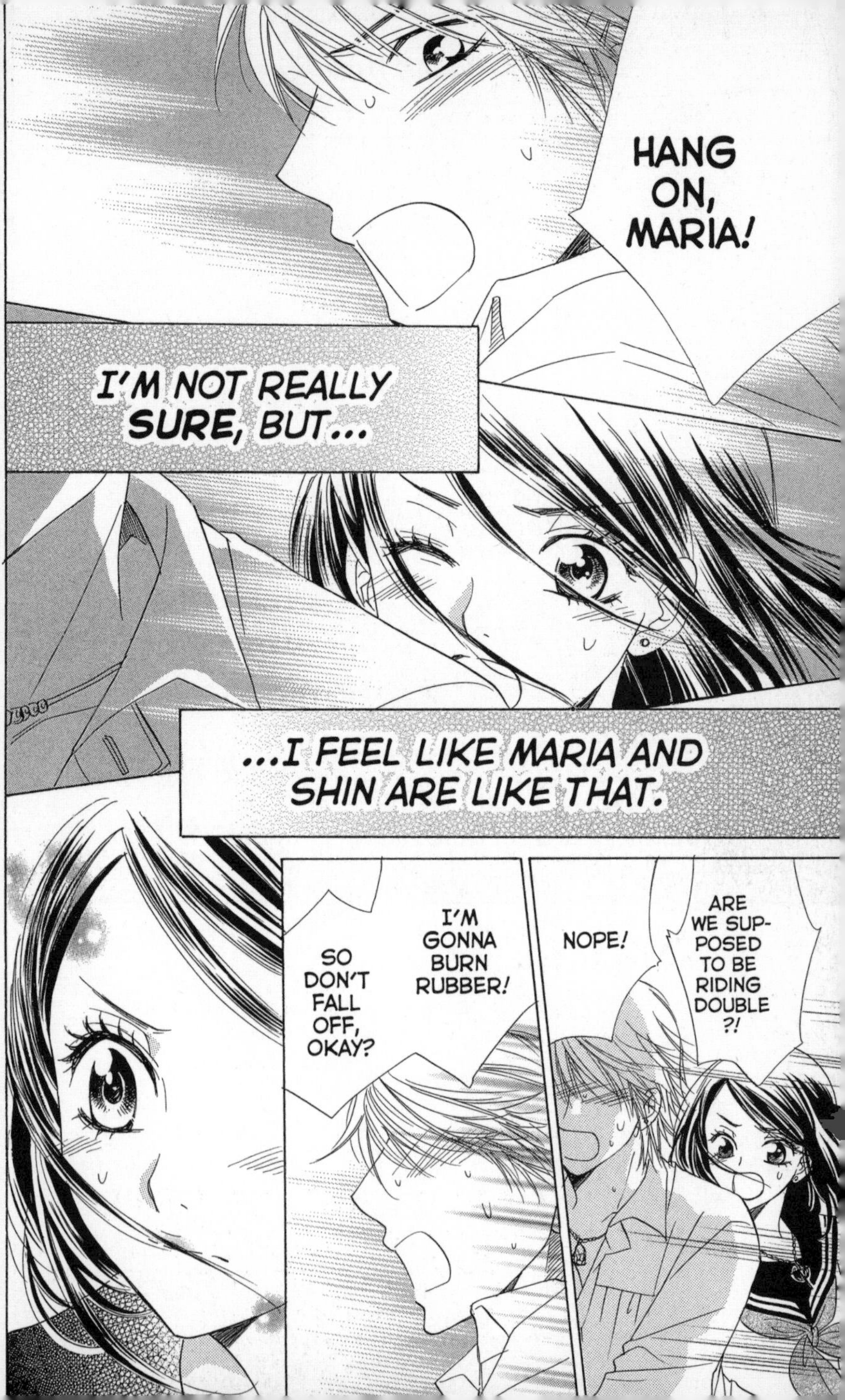
HANG ON, MARIA!
I'M NOT REALLY SURE, BUT...
...I FEEL LIKE MARIA AND SHIN ARE LIKE THAT.
ARE WE SUP-POSED TO BE RIDING DOUBLE ?!
NOPE!
I'M GONNA BURN RUBBER!
SO DON'T FALL OFF, OKAY?

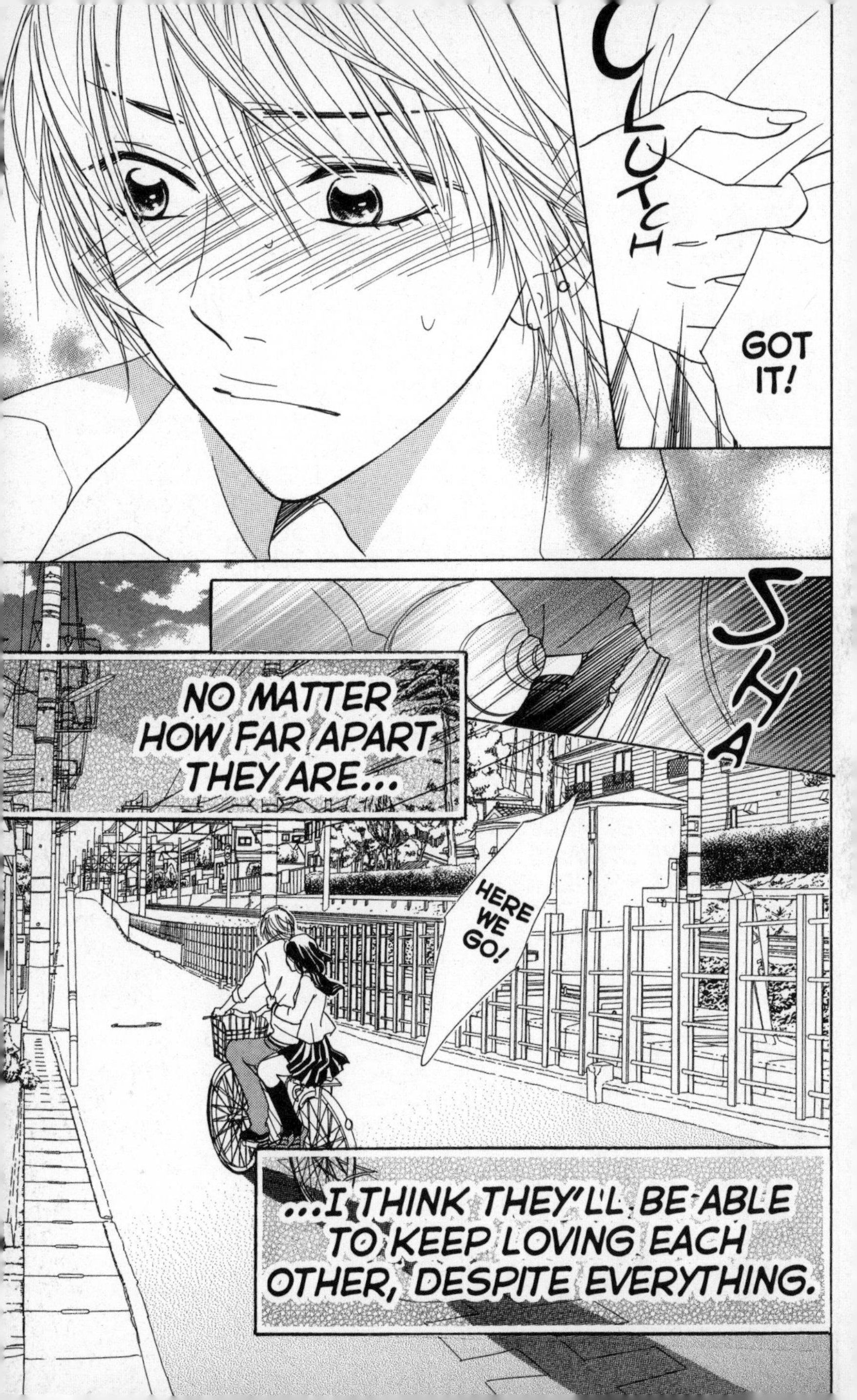
CLUTCH
GOT IT!
SHA
NO MATTER HOW FAR APART THEY ARE...
HERE WE GO!
...I THINK THEY'LL BE ABLE TO KEEP LOVING EACH OTHER, DESPITE EVERYTHING.

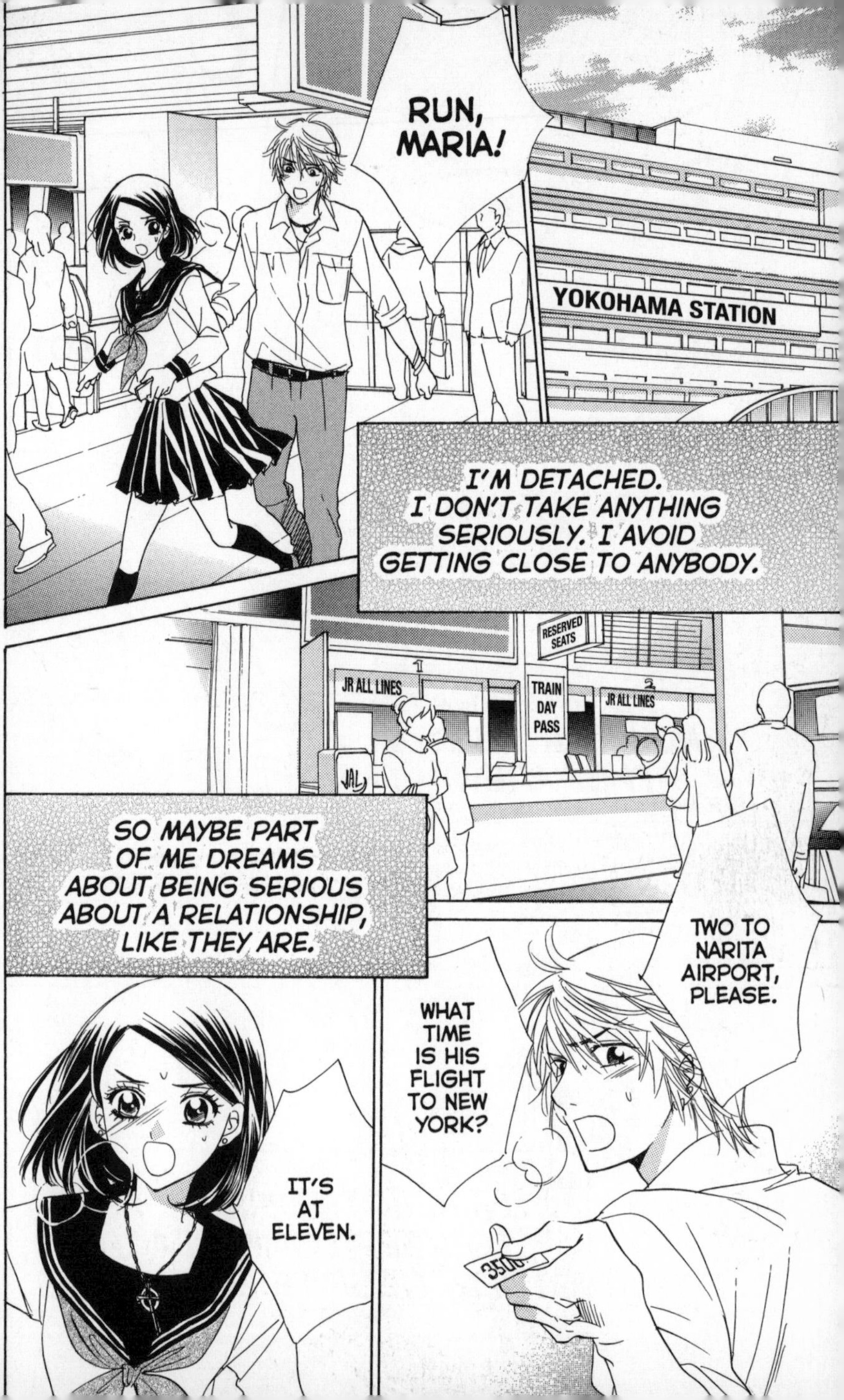
RUN, MARIA!
YOKOHAMA STATION
I'M DETACHED. I DON'T TAKE ANYTHING SERIOUSLY. I AVOID GETTING CLOSE TO ANYBODY.
RESERVED SEATS
JR ALL LINES
TRAIN DAY PASS
JR ALL LINES
JAL
SO MAYBE PART OF ME DREAMS ABOUT BEING SERIOUS ABOUT A RELATIONSHIP, LIKE THEY ARE.
TWO TO NARITA AIRPORT, PLEASE.
WHAT TIME IS HIS FLIGHT TO NEW YORK?
IT'S AT ELEVEN.

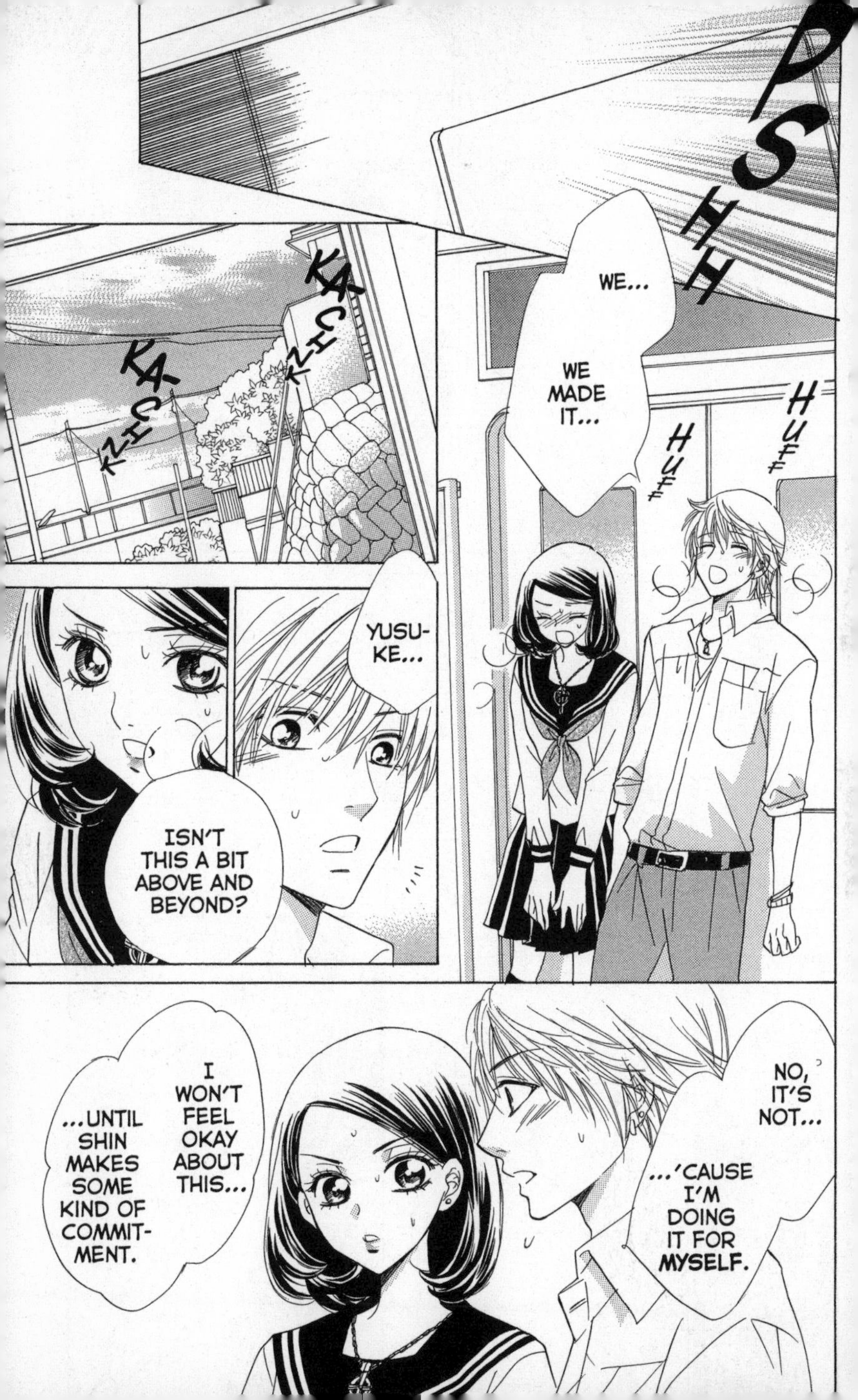
PSHH
WE...
WE MADE IT...
HUFF
HUFF
KA-CHIN
KA-CHIN
YUSU-KE...
ISN'T THIS A BIT ABOVE AND BEYOND?
NO, IT'S NOT...
...'CAUSE I'M DOING IT FOR MYSELF.
I WON'T FEEL OKAY ABOUT THIS...
...UNTIL SHIN MAKES SOME KIND OF COMMIT-MENT.

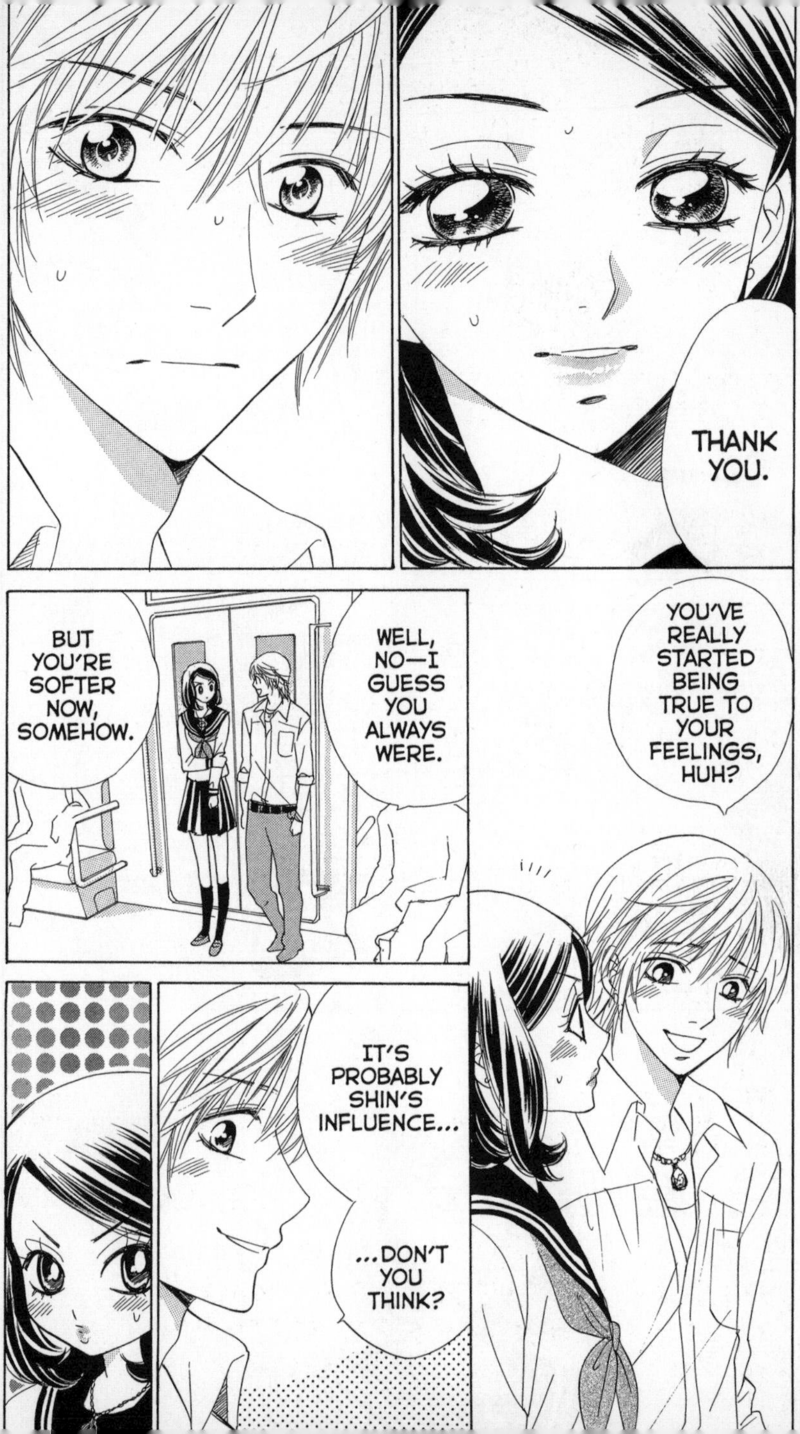
THANK YOU.
YOU'VE REALLY STARTED BEING TRUE TO YOUR FEELINGS, HUH?
WELL, NO—I GUESS YOU ALWAYS WERE.
BUT YOU'RE SOFTER NOW, SOMEHOW.
IT'S PROBABLY SHIN'S INFLUENCE...
...DON'T YOU THINK?

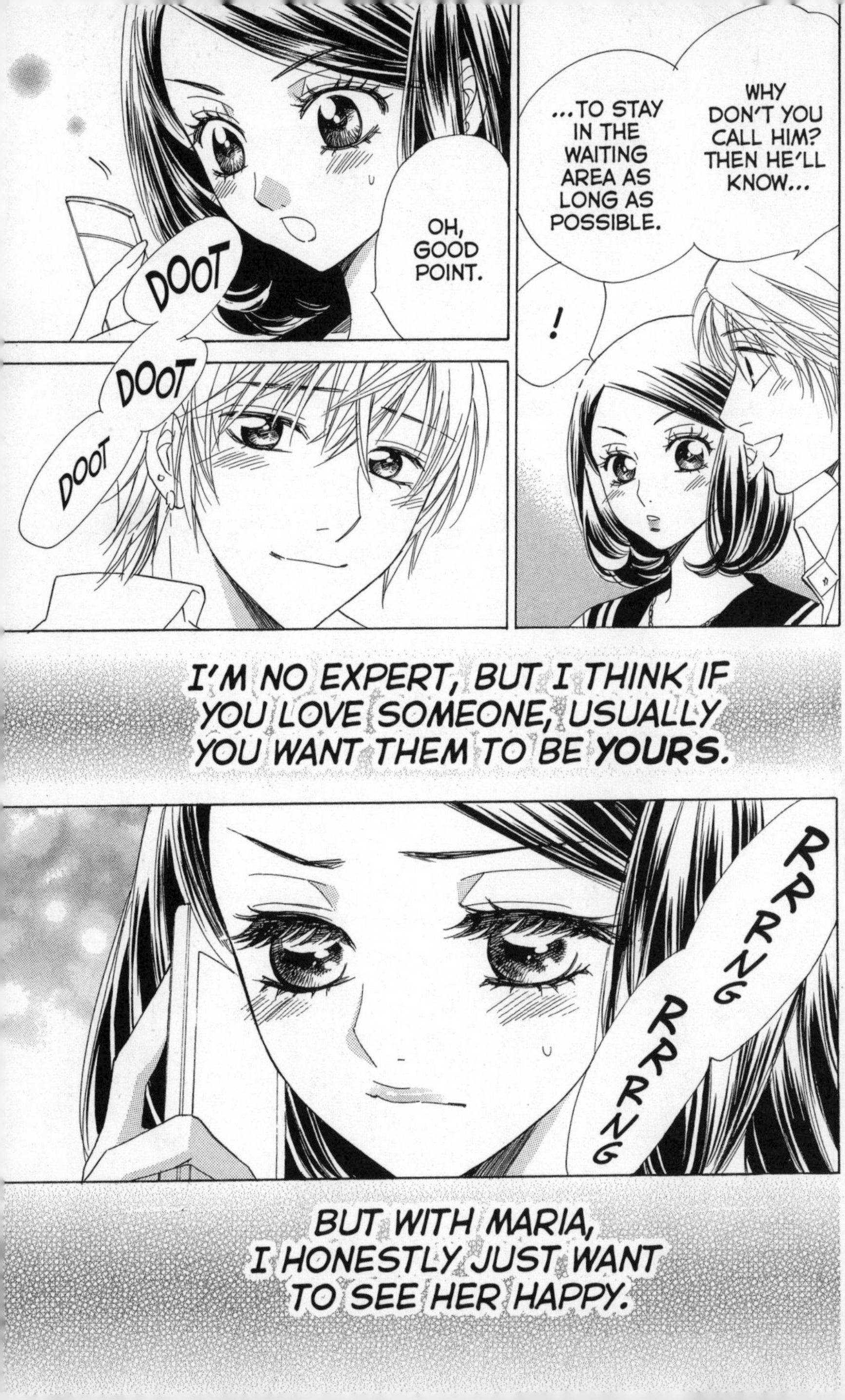

WHY DON'T YOU CALL HIM? THEN HE'LL KNOW...
...TO STAY IN THE WAITING AREA AS LONG AS POSSIBLE.
!
OH, GOOD POINT.
DOOT
DOOT
DOOT
I'M NO EXPERT, BUT I THINK IF YOU LOVE SOMEONE, USUALLY YOU WANT THEM TO BE **YOURS.**
RRRNG
RRRNG
BUT WITH MARIA, I HONESTLY JUST WANT TO SEE HER HAPPY.

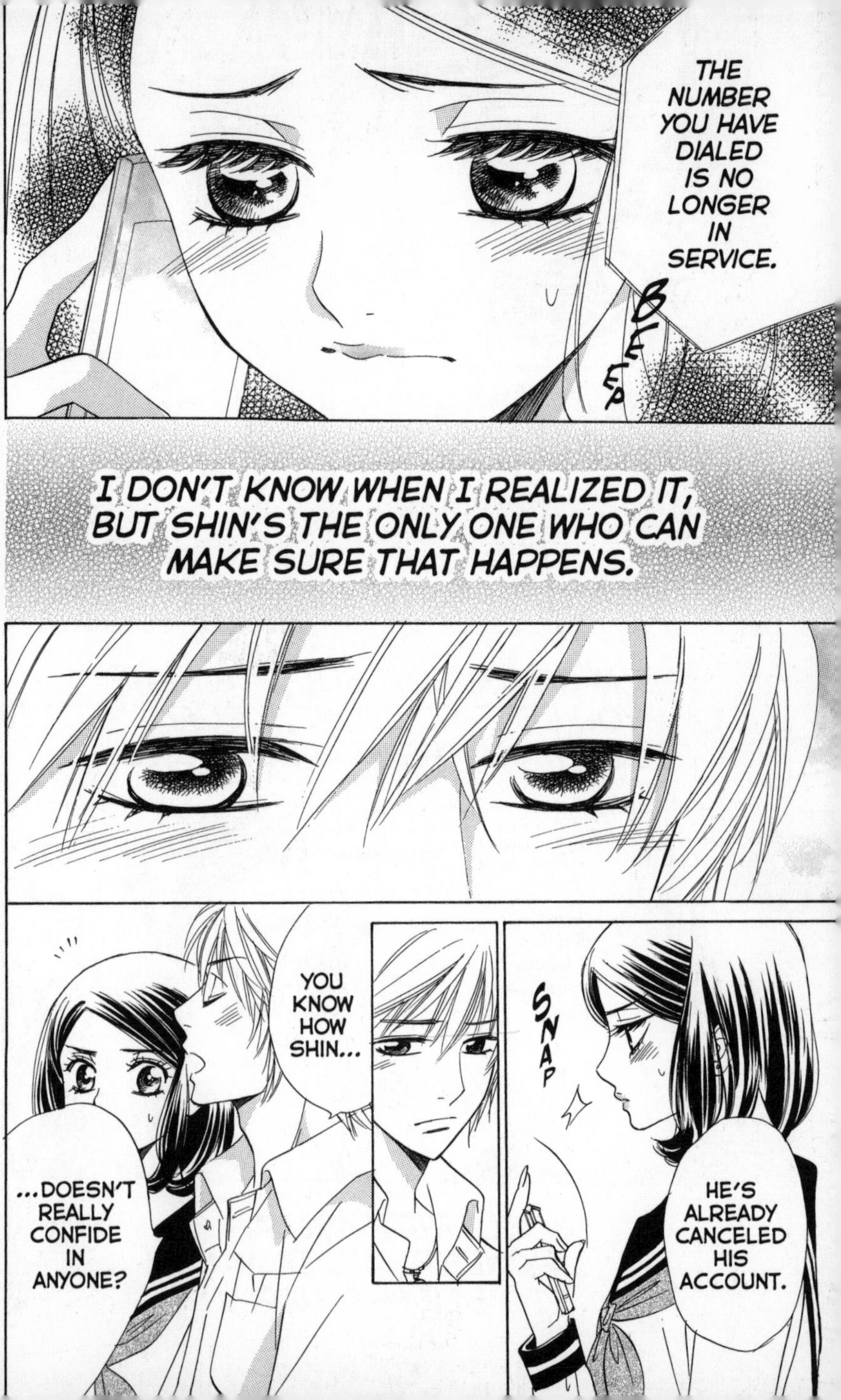
THE NUMBER YOU HAVE DIALED IS NO LONGER IN SERVICE.
BLEEP
I DON'T KNOW WHEN I REALIZED IT, BUT SHIN'S THE ONLY ONE WHO CAN MAKE SURE THAT HAPPENS.
SNAP
HE'S ALREADY CANCELED HIS ACCOUNT.
YOU KNOW HOW SHIN...
...DOESN'T REALLY CONFIDE IN ANYONE?

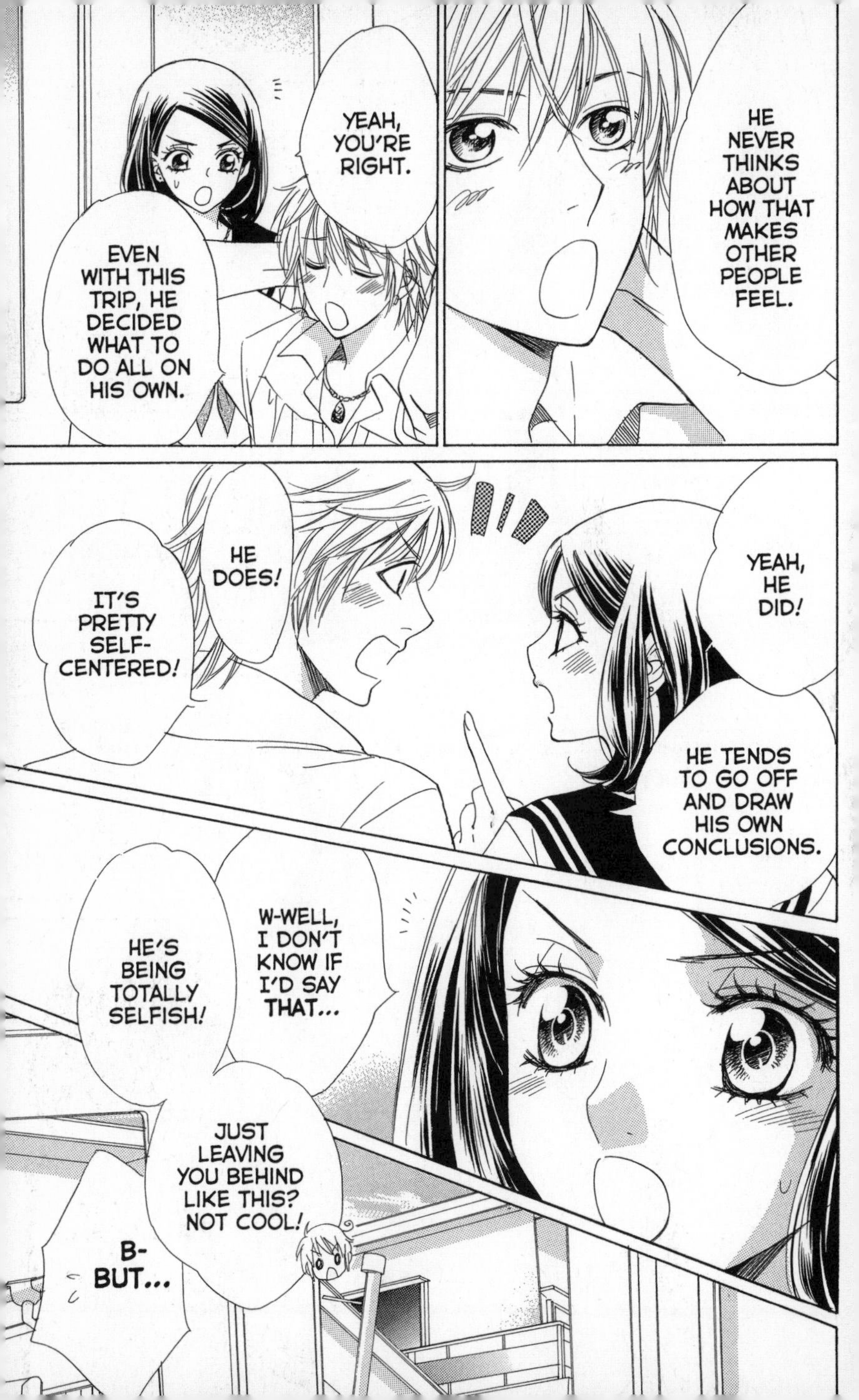
HE NEVER THINKS ABOUT HOW THAT MAKES OTHER PEOPLE FEEL.
YEAH, YOU'RE RIGHT.
EVEN WITH THIS TRIP, HE DECIDED WHAT TO DO ALL ON HIS OWN.
YEAH, HE DID!
HE TENDS TO GO OFF AND DRAW HIS OWN CONCLUSIONS.
HE DOES!
IT'S PRETTY SELF-CENTERED!
W-WELL, I DON'T KNOW IF I'D SAY THAT...
HE'S BEING TOTALLY SELFISH!
JUST LEAVING YOU BEHIND LIKE THIS? NOT COOL!
B-BUT...

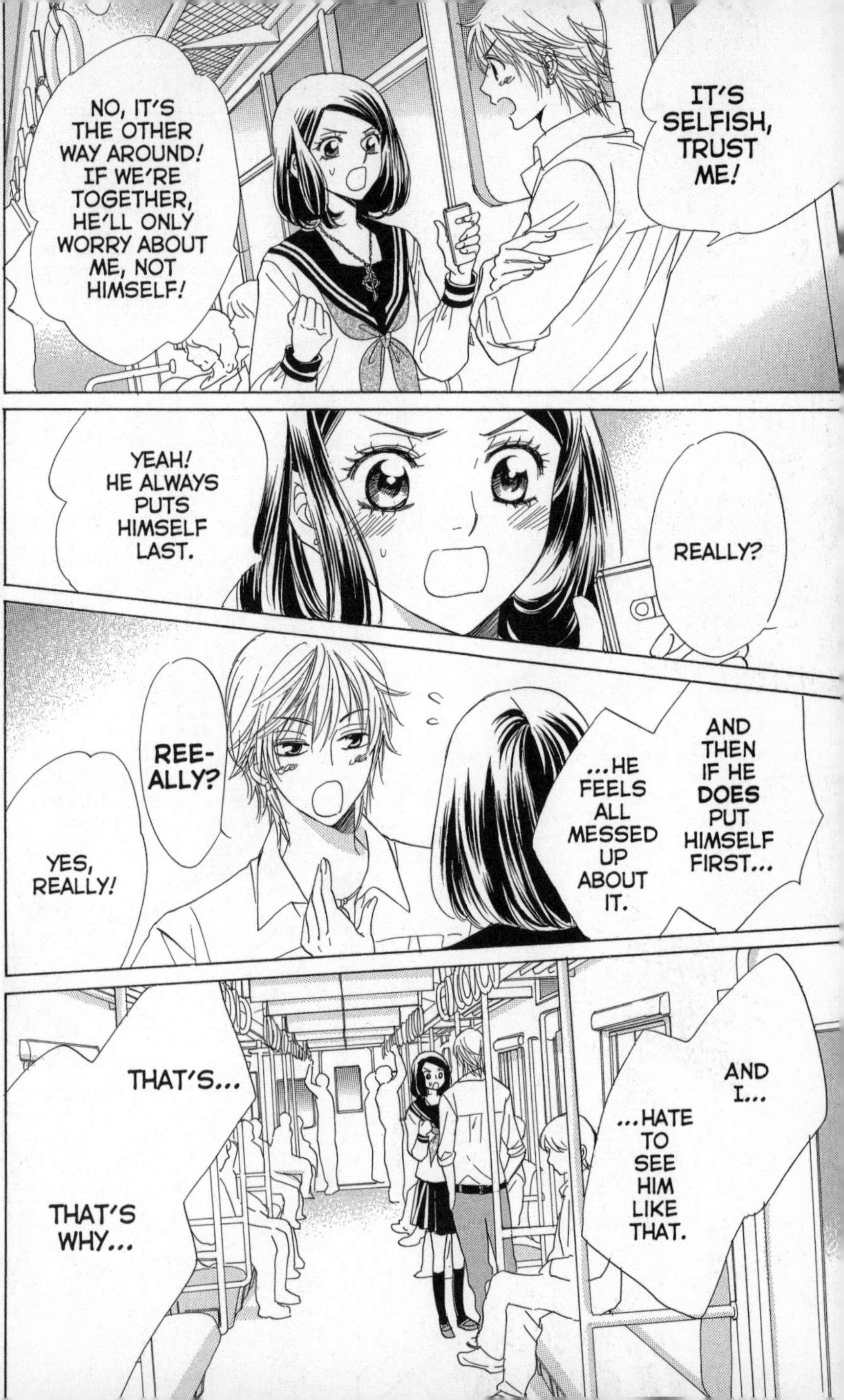
IT'S SELFISH, TRUST ME!
NO, IT'S THE OTHER WAY AROUND! IF WE'RE TOGETHER, HE'LL ONLY WORRY ABOUT ME, NOT HIMSELF!
REALLY?
YEAH! HE ALWAYS PUTS HIMSELF LAST.
AND THEN IF HE DOES PUT HIMSELF FIRST...
...HE FEELS ALL MESSED UP ABOUT IT.
REE-ALLY?
YES, REALLY!
AND I...
...HATE TO SEE HIM LIKE THAT.
THAT'S...
THAT'S WHY...

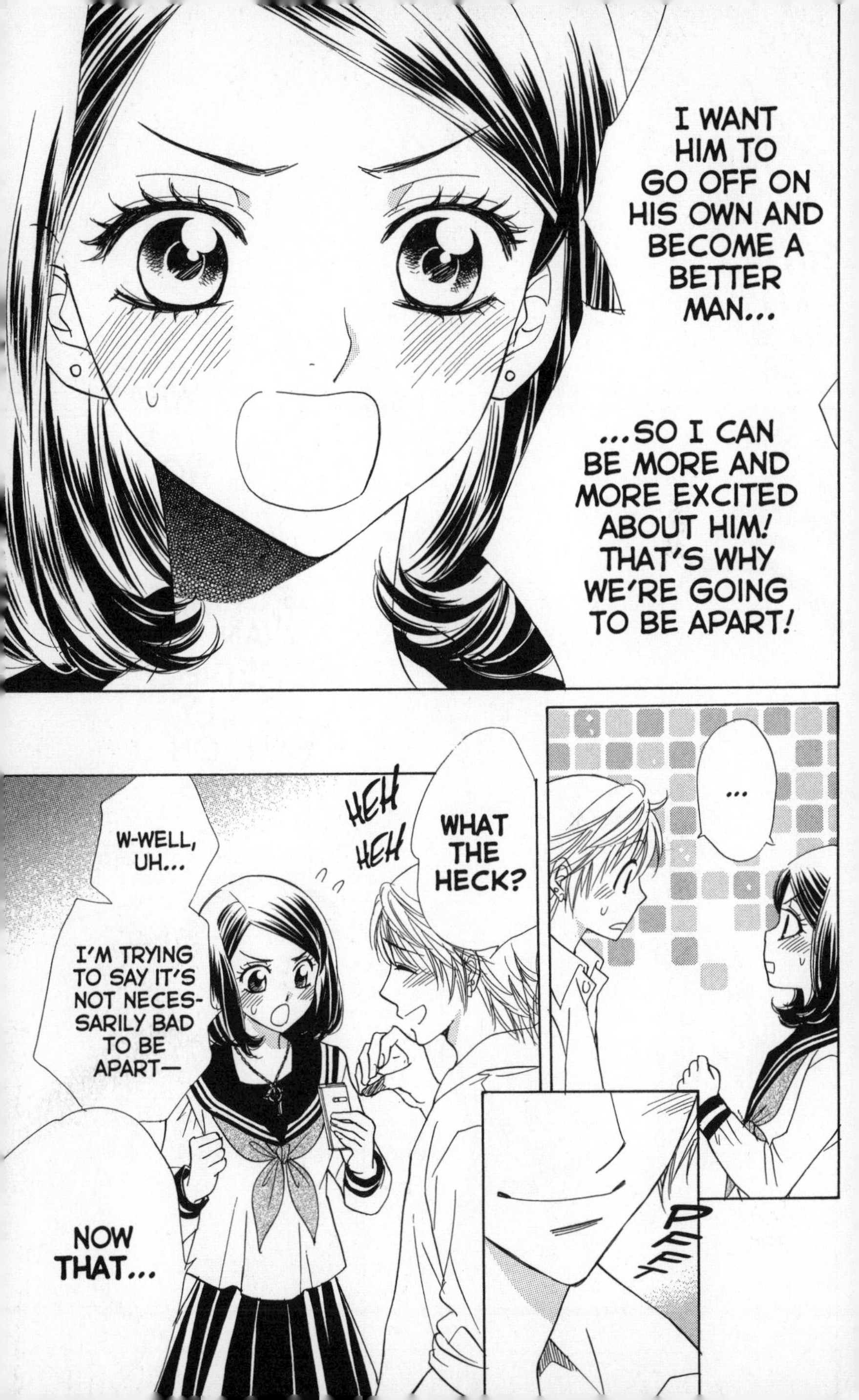
I WANT HIM TO GO OFF ON HIS OWN AND BECOME A BETTER MAN...
...SO I CAN BE MORE AND MORE EXCITED ABOUT HIM! THAT'S WHY WE'RE GOING TO BE APART!
...
PEEF
WHAT THE HECK?
HEH HEH
W-WELL, UH...
I'M TRYING TO SAY IT'S NOT NECES-SARILY BAD TO BE APART—
NOW THAT...

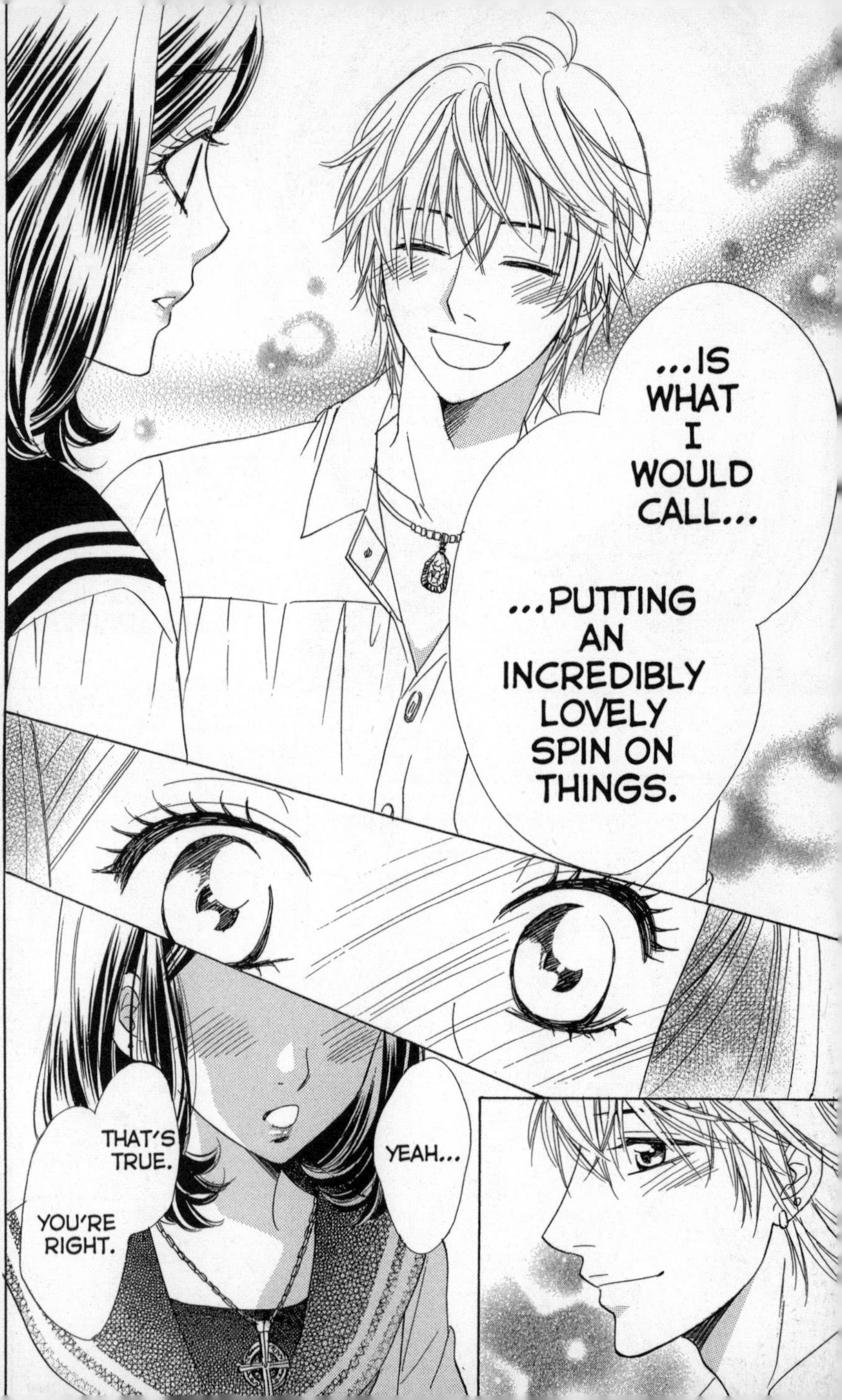
...IS WHAT I WOULD CALL...
...PUTTING AN INCREDIBLY LOVELY SPIN ON THINGS.
YEAH...
THAT'S TRUE.
YOU'RE RIGHT.

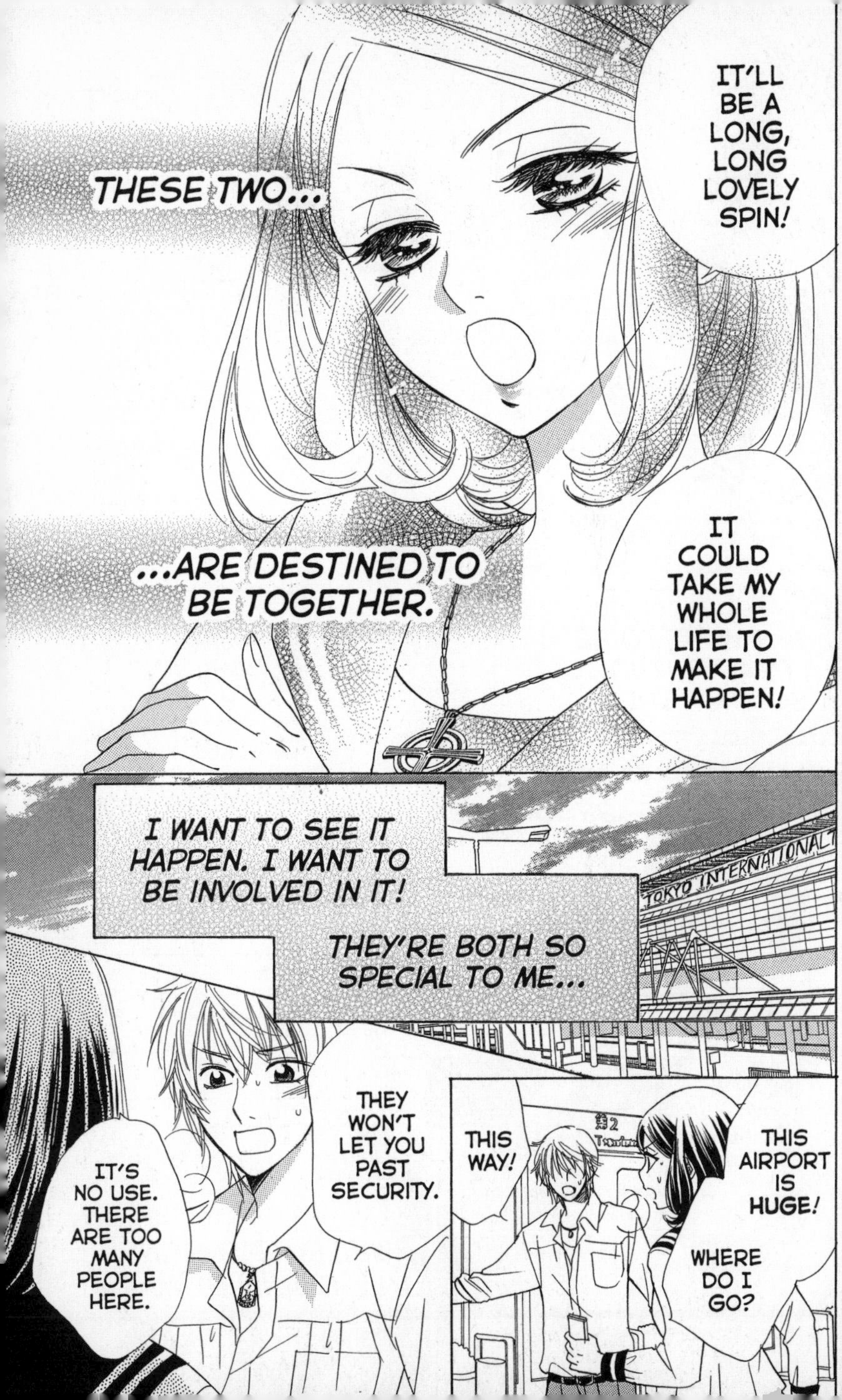
IT'LL BE A LONG, LONG LOVELY SPIN!
THESE TWO...
IT COULD TAKE MY WHOLE LIFE TO MAKE IT HAPPEN!
...ARE DESTINED TO BE TOGETHER.
I WANT TO SEE IT HAPPEN. I WANT TO BE INVOLVED IN IT!
THEY'RE BOTH SO SPECIAL TO ME...
TOKYO INTERNATIONAL
THIS AIRPORT IS HUGE!
WHERE DO I GO?
THIS WAY!
THEY WON'T LET YOU PAST SECURITY.
IT'S NO USE. THERE ARE TOO MANY PEOPLE HERE.

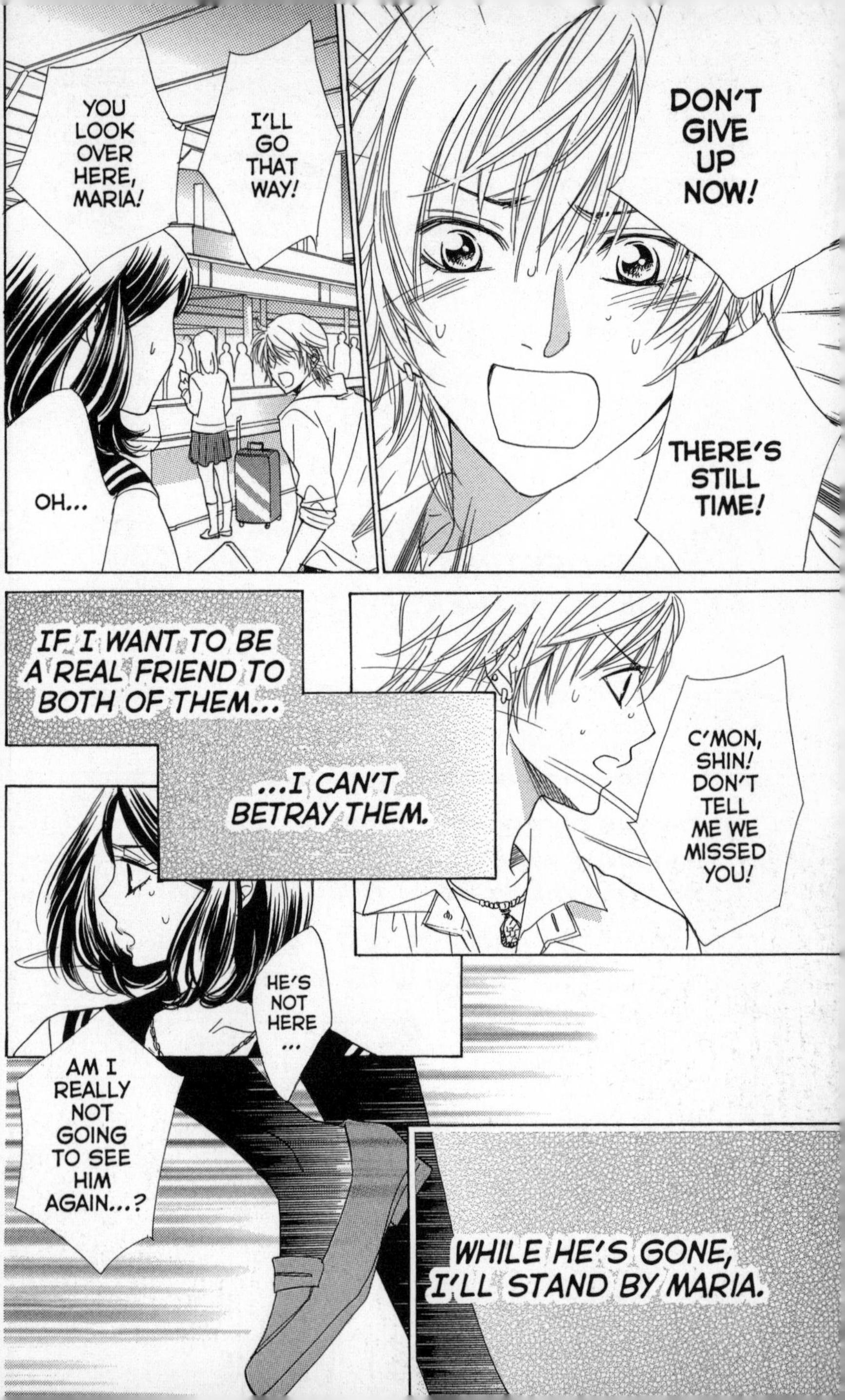
DON'T GIVE UP NOW!
THERE'S STILL TIME!
I'LL GO THAT WAY!
YOU LOOK OVER HERE, MARIA!
OH...
C'MON, SHIN! DON'T TELL ME WE MISSED YOU!
IF I WANT TO BE A REAL FRIEND TO BOTH OF THEM...
...I CAN'T BETRAY THEM.
HE'S NOT HERE...
AM I REALLY NOT GOING TO SEE HIM AGAIN...?
WHILE HE'S GONE, I'LL STAND BY MARIA.

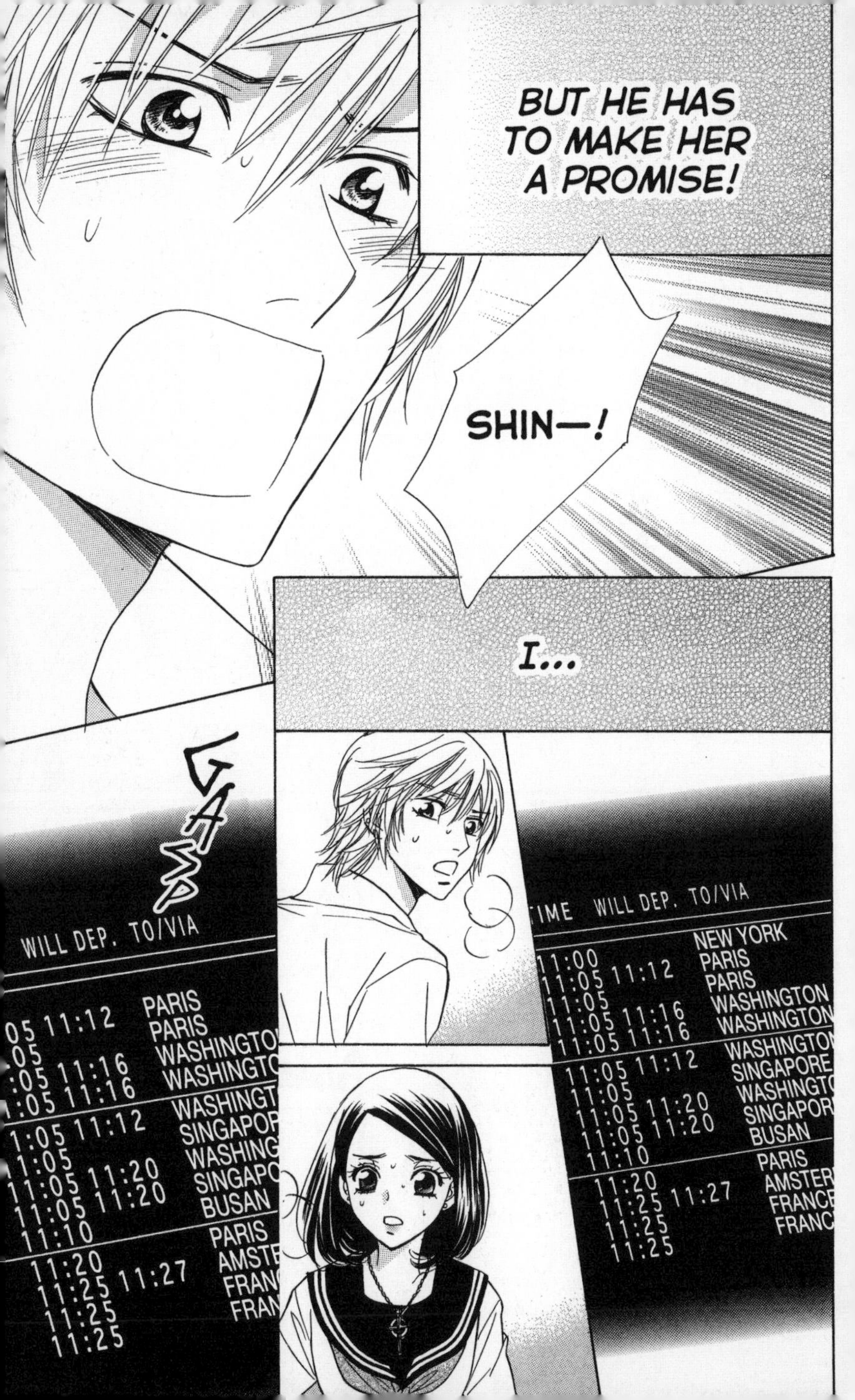
BUT HE HAS TO MAKE HER A PROMISE!
SHIN—!
I...
GASP
TIME WILL DEP. TO/VIA
WILL DEP. TO/VIA

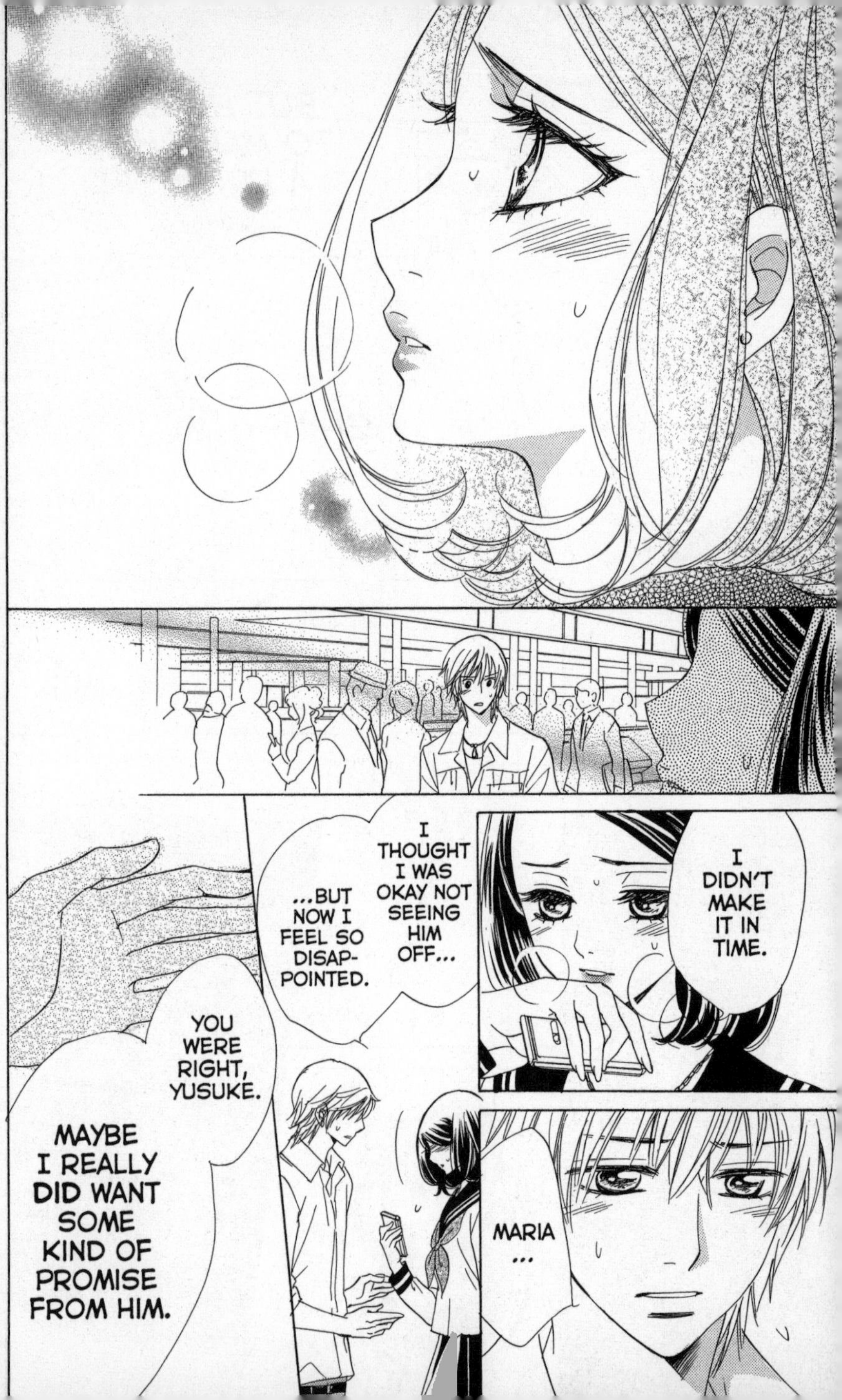
I DIDN'T MAKE IT IN TIME.
I THOUGHT I WAS OKAY NOT SEEING HIM OFF...
...BUT NOW I FEEL SO DISAPPOINTED.
YOU WERE RIGHT, YUSUKE.
MARIA ...
MAYBE I REALLY DID WANT SOME KIND OF PROMISE FROM HIM.

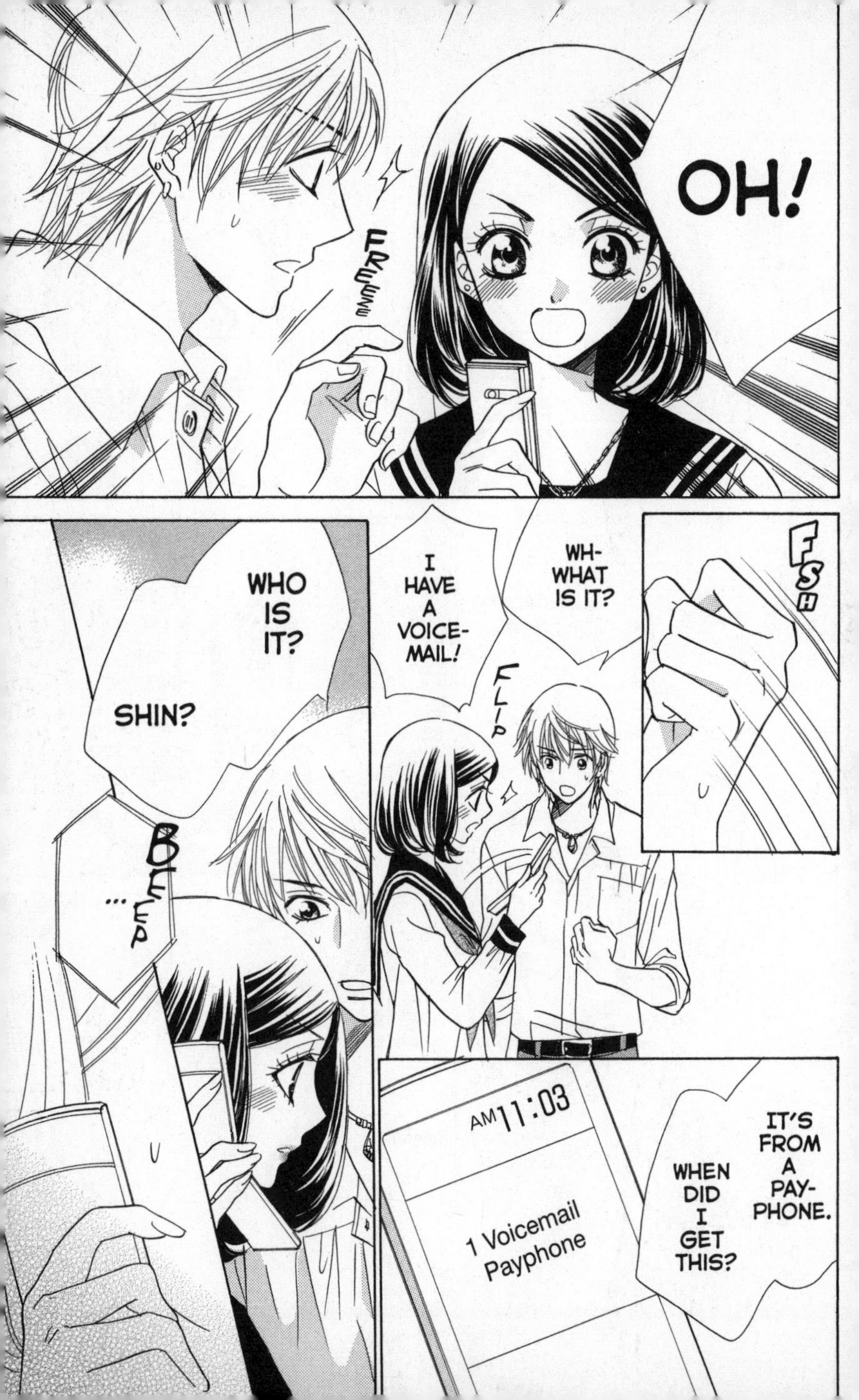

OH!
FREEZE
FSH
WH-
WHAT
IS IT?
I
HAVE
A
VOICE-
MAIL!
FLIP
IT'S
FROM
A
PAY-
PHONE.
WHEN
DID
I
GET
THIS?
AM 11:03
1 Voicemail
Payphone
WHO
IS
IT?
SHIN?
...
BLEEP

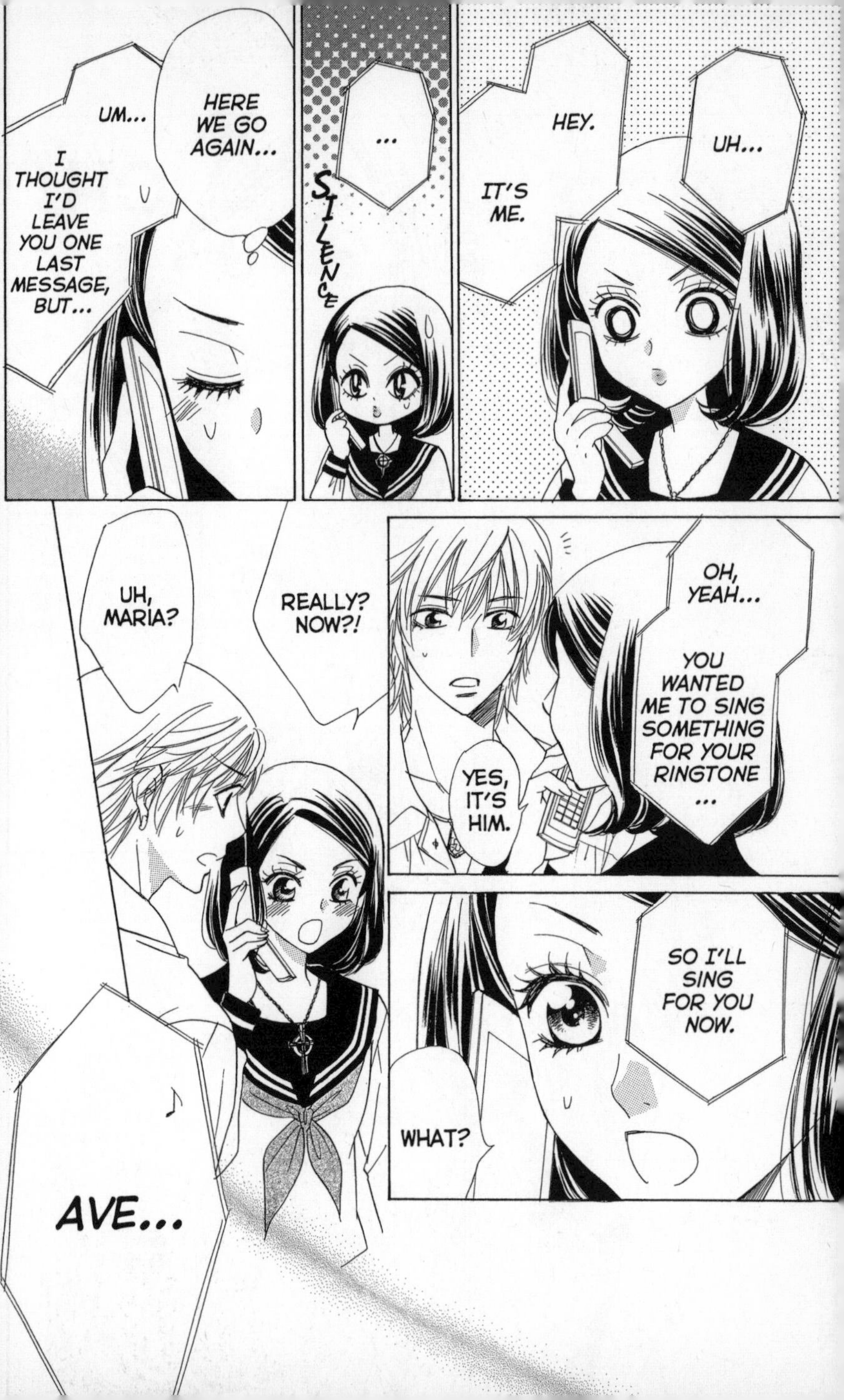
UH...
HEY. IT'S ME.
...
SILENCE
HERE WE GO AGAIN...
UM... I THOUGHT I'D LEAVE YOU ONE LAST MESSAGE, BUT...
OH, YEAH... YOU WANTED ME TO SING SOMETHING FOR YOUR RINGTONE...
YES, IT'S HIM.
SO I'LL SING FOR YOU NOW.
WHAT?
REALLY? NOW?!
UH, MARIA?
AVE...

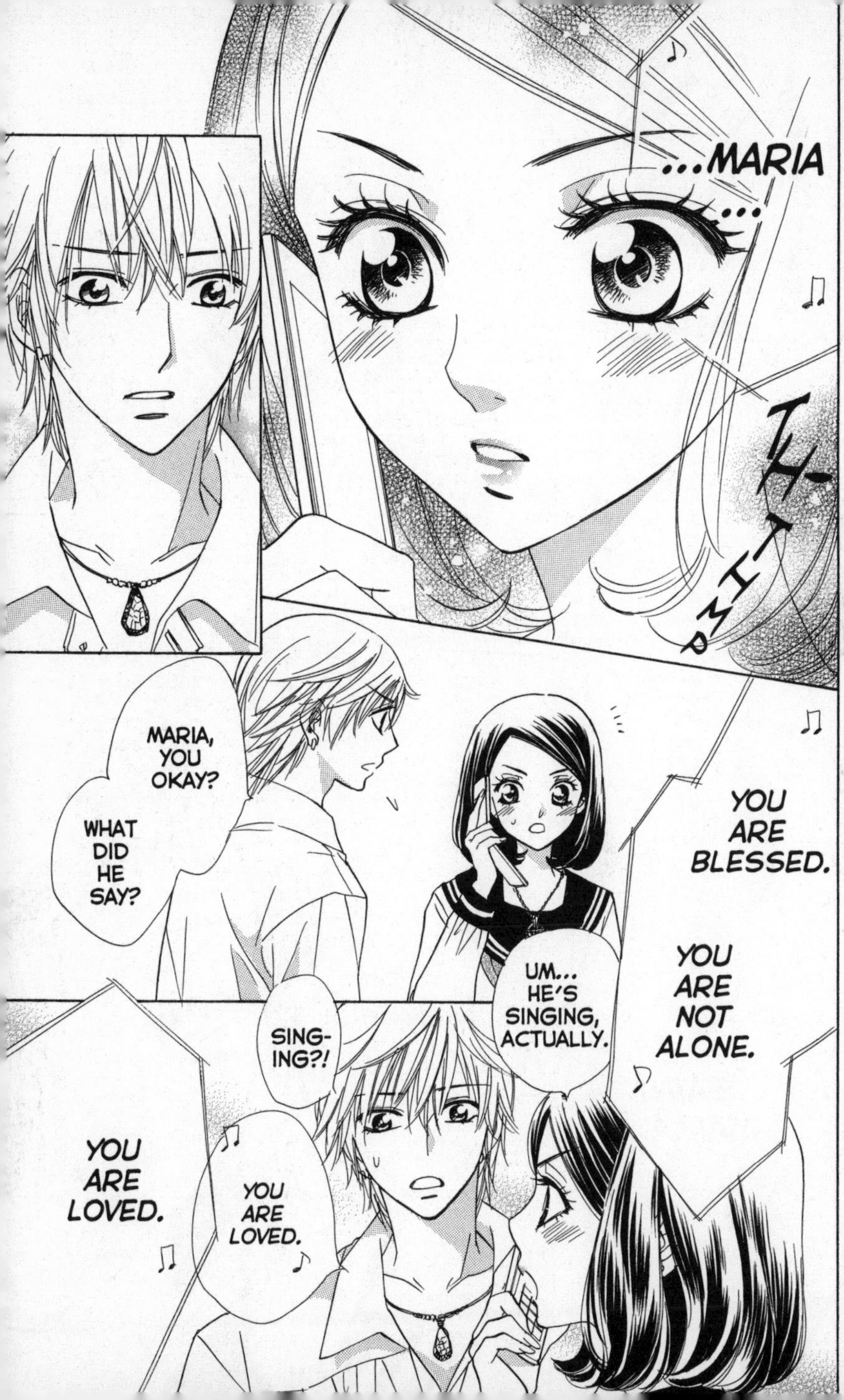
...MARIA ...
TH-THMP
YOU ARE BLESSED.
MARIA, YOU OKAY?
WHAT DID HE SAY?
YOU ARE NOT ALONE.
UM... HE'S SINGING, ACTUALLY.
SING-ING?!
YOU ARE LOVED.
YOU ARE LOVED.

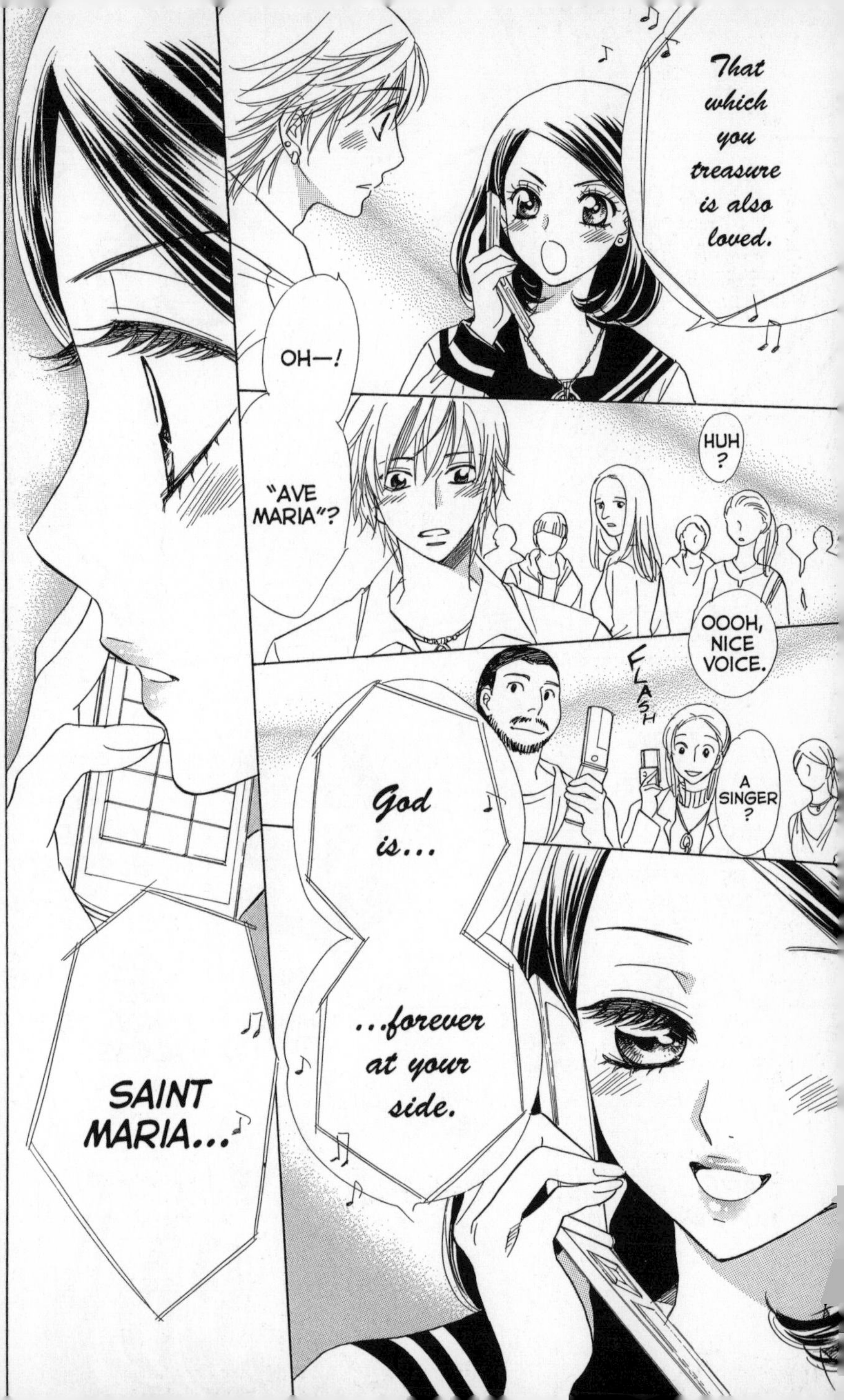
That which you treasure is also loved.
OH—!
HUH?
"AVE MARIA"?
OOOH, NICE VOICE.
FLASH
A SINGER?
God is...
...forever at your side.
SAINT MARIA...

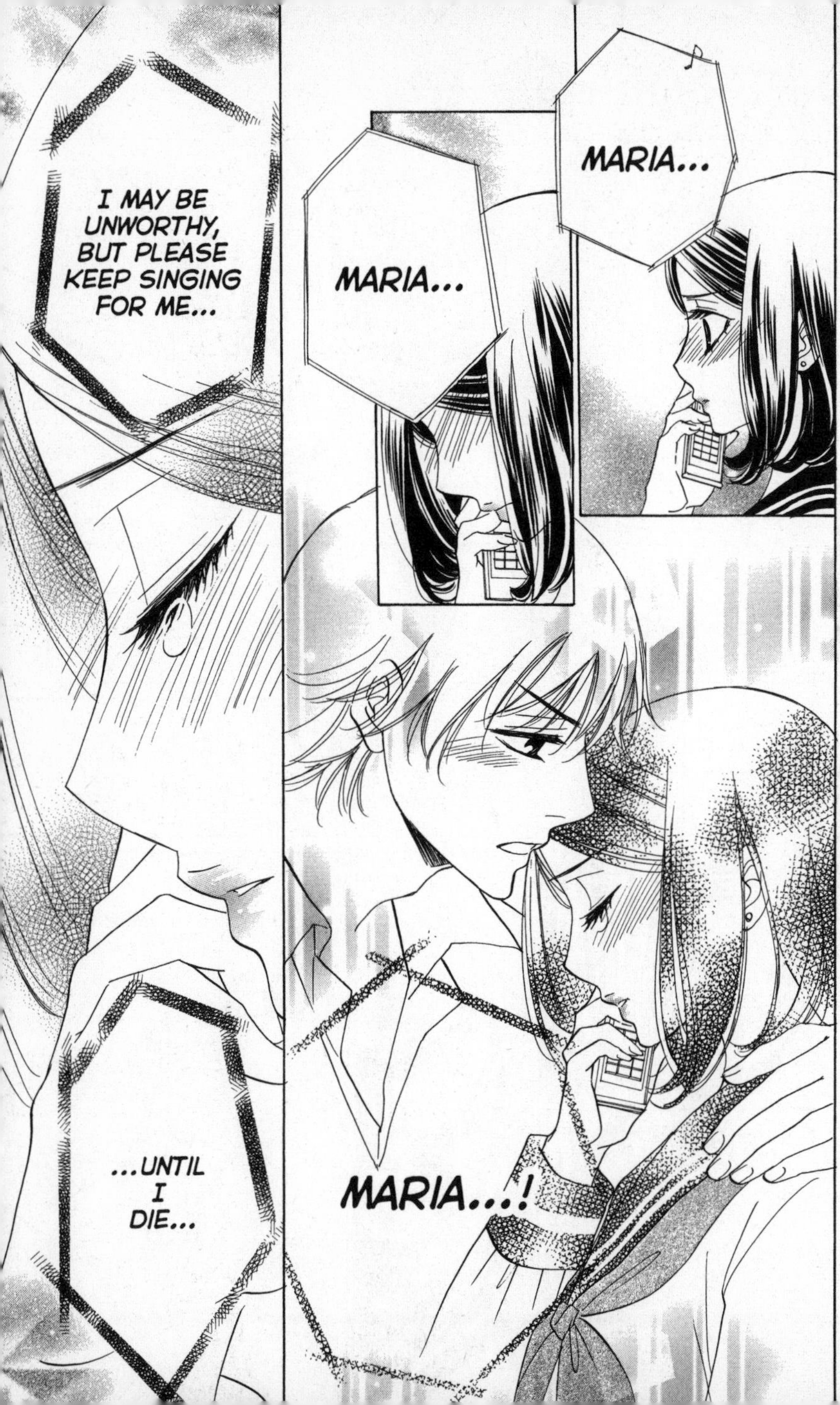
MARIA...
MARIA...
MARIA...!
I MAY BE UNWORTHY, BUT PLEASE KEEP SINGING FOR ME...
...UNTIL I DIE...

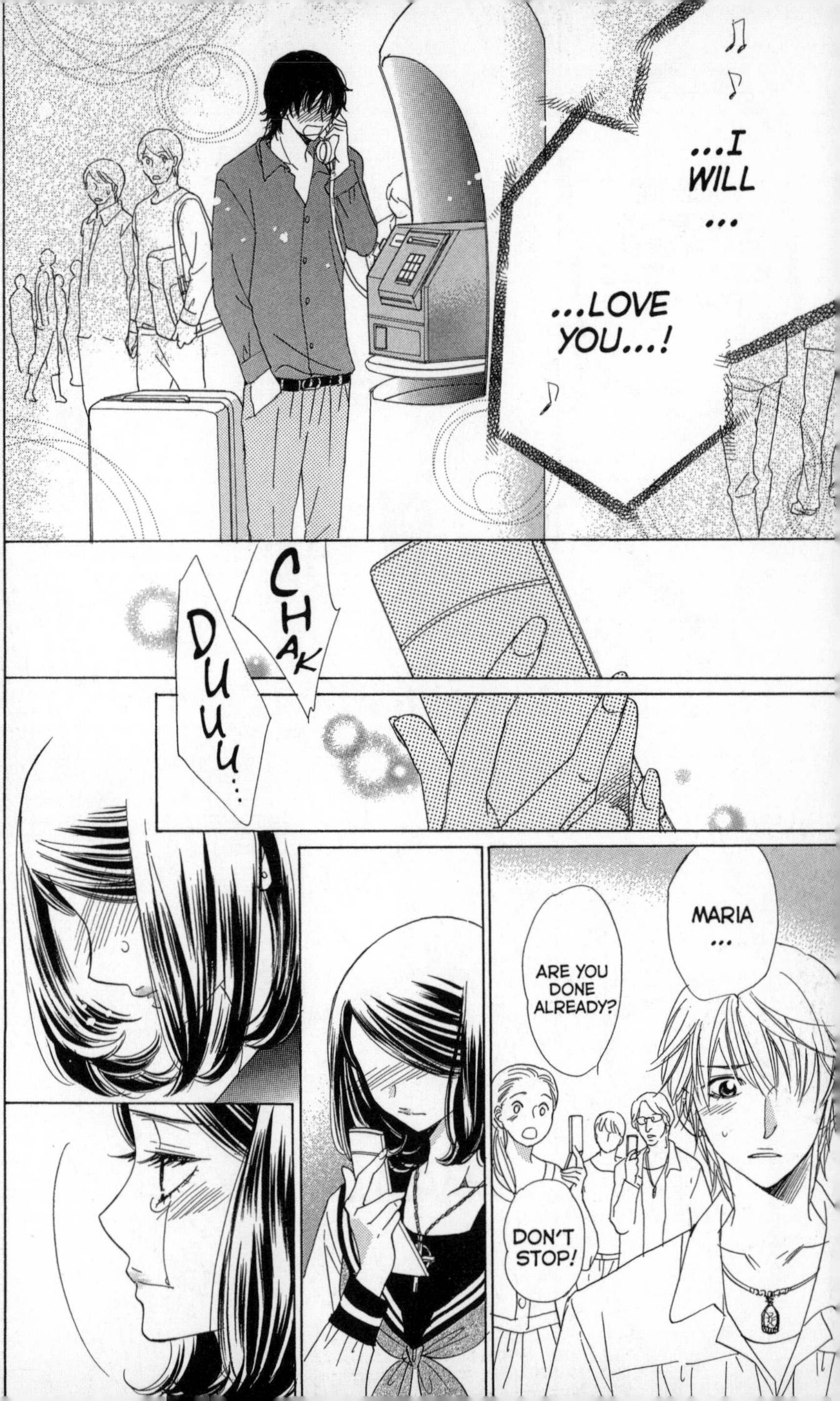
...I WILL ...
...LOVE YOU...!
CHAK
DUUU...
MARIA ...
ARE YOU DONE ALREADY?
DON'T STOP!

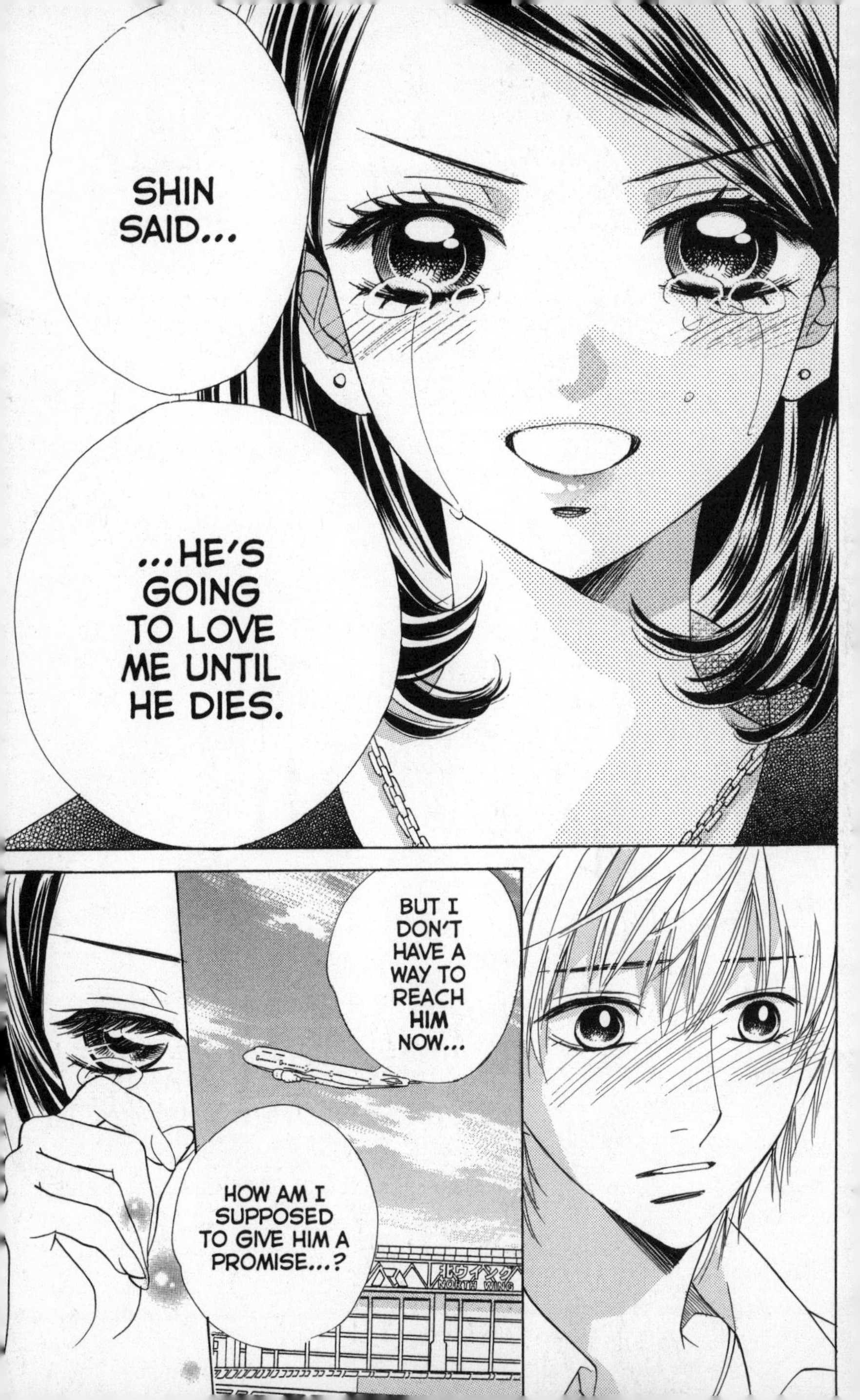
SHIN SAID...
...HE'S GOING TO LOVE ME UNTIL HE DIES.
BUT I DON'T HAVE A WAY TO REACH HIM NOW...
HOW AM I SUPPOSED TO GIVE HIM A PROMISE...?
NORTH WING

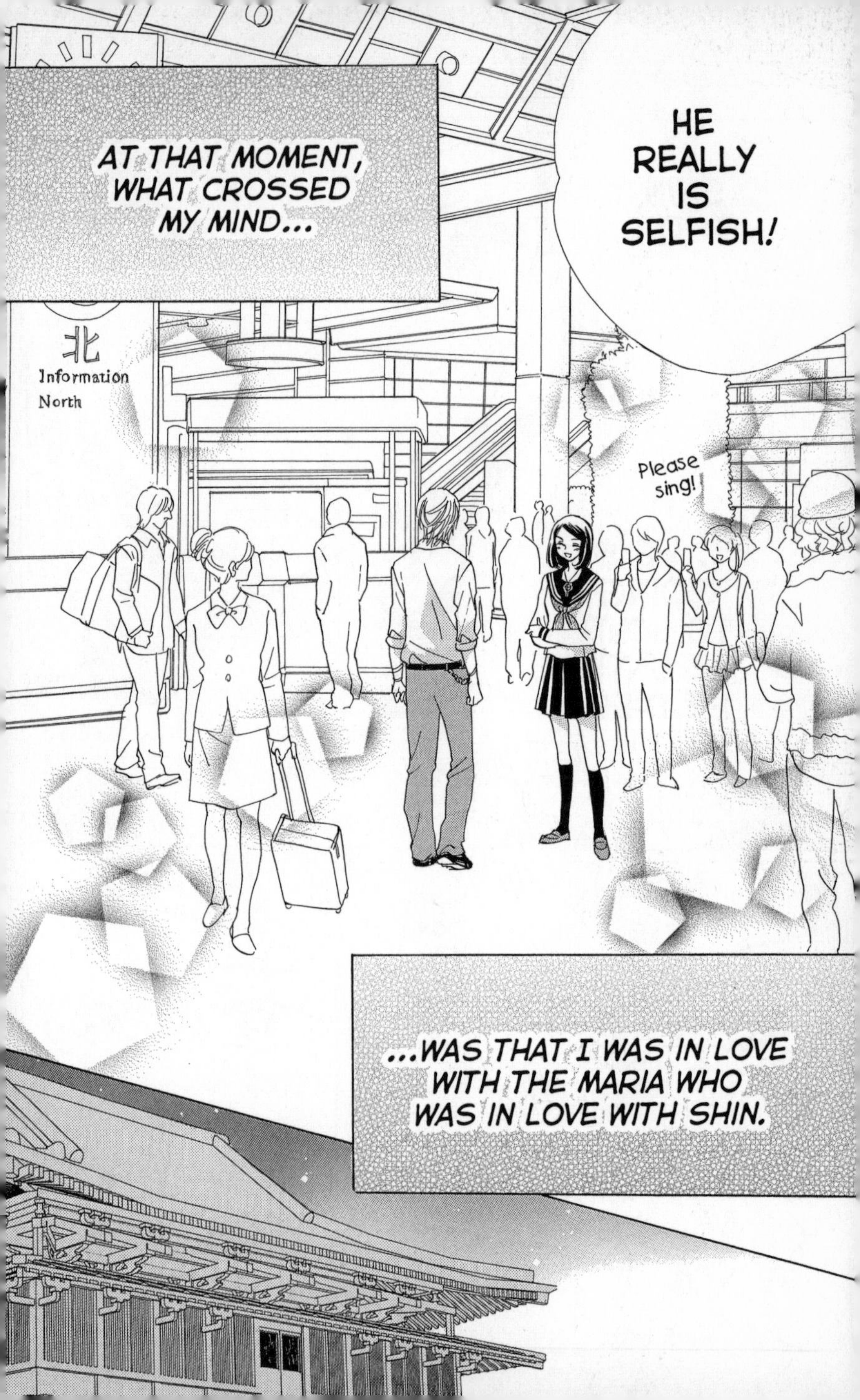
HE REALLY IS SELFISH!
AT THAT MOMENT, WHAT CROSSED MY MIND...
北
Information North
Please sing!
...WAS THAT I WAS IN LOVE WITH THE MARIA WHO WAS IN LOVE WITH SHIN.

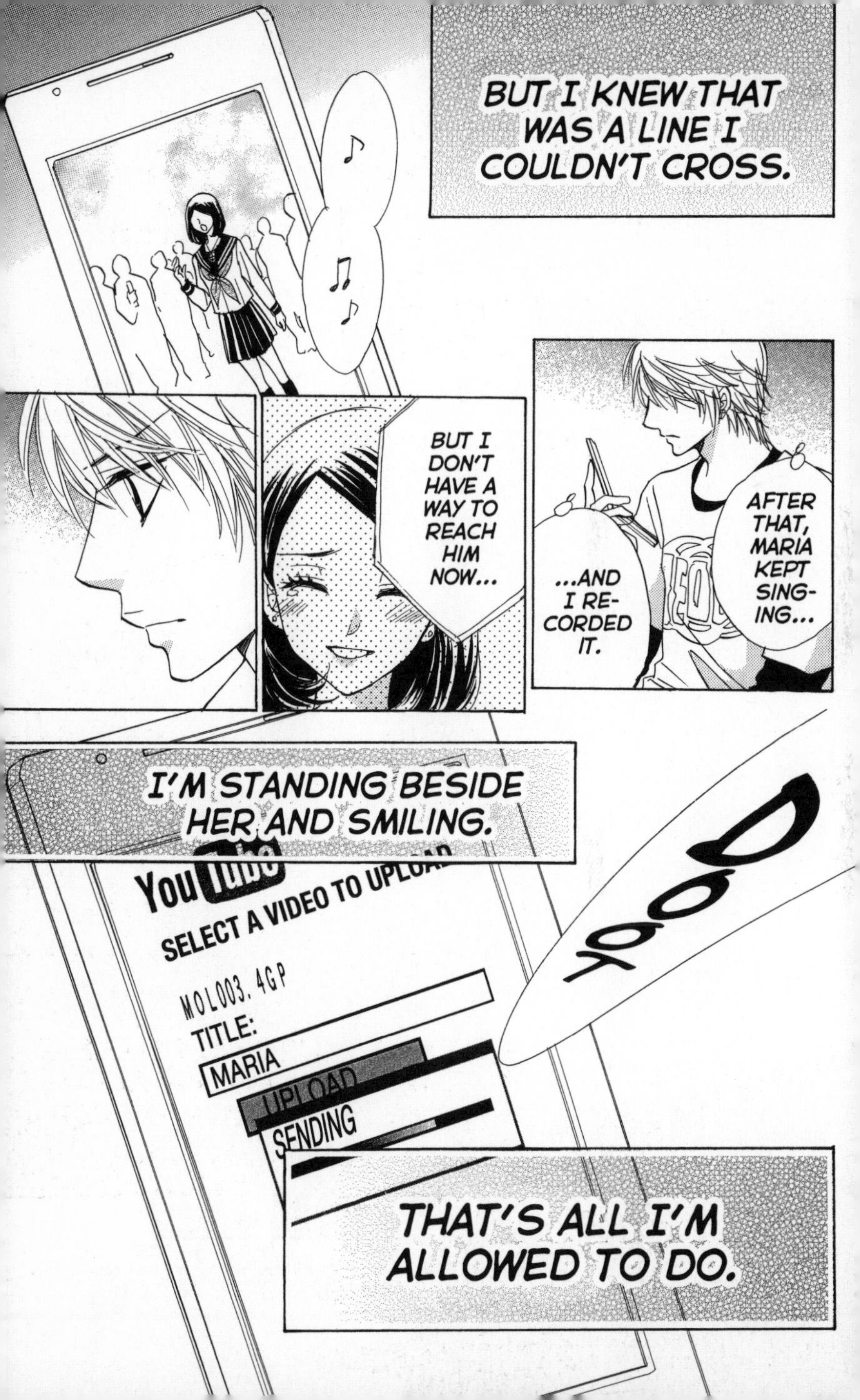

BUT I KNEW THAT WAS A LINE I COULDN'T CROSS.
♪
♫ ♪
AFTER THAT, MARIA KEPT SING-ING...
...AND I RE-CORDED IT.
BUT I DON'T HAVE A WAY TO REACH HIM NOW...
I'M STANDING BESIDE HER AND SMILING.
Doot
SELECT A VIDEO TO UPLOA
MOL003.4GP
TITLE:
MARIA
UPLOAD
SENDING
THAT'S ALL I'M ALLOWED TO DO.

A Devil and
Her Love Song

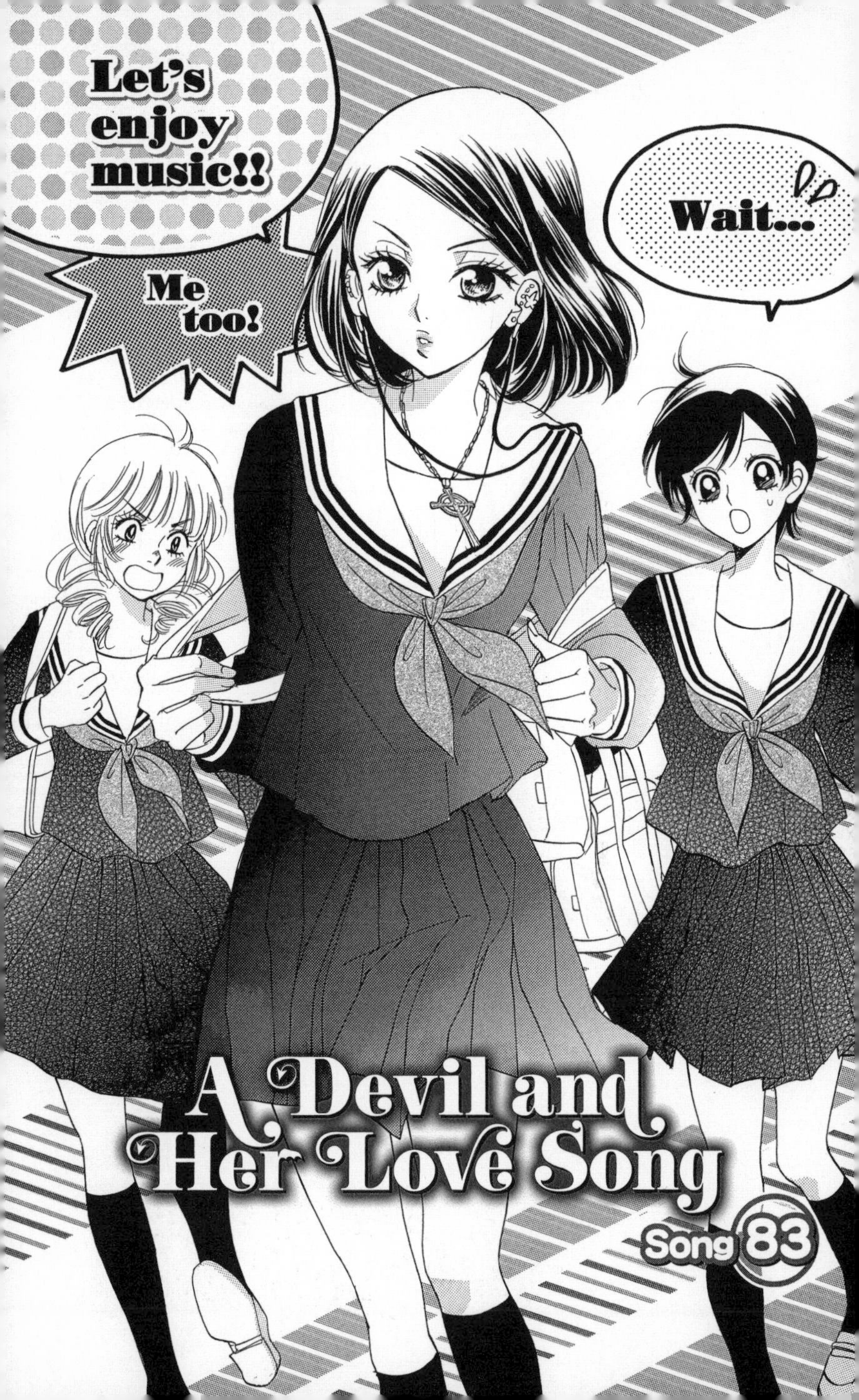
Let's enjoy music!!
Me too!
Wait...
A Devil and Her Love Song
Song 83

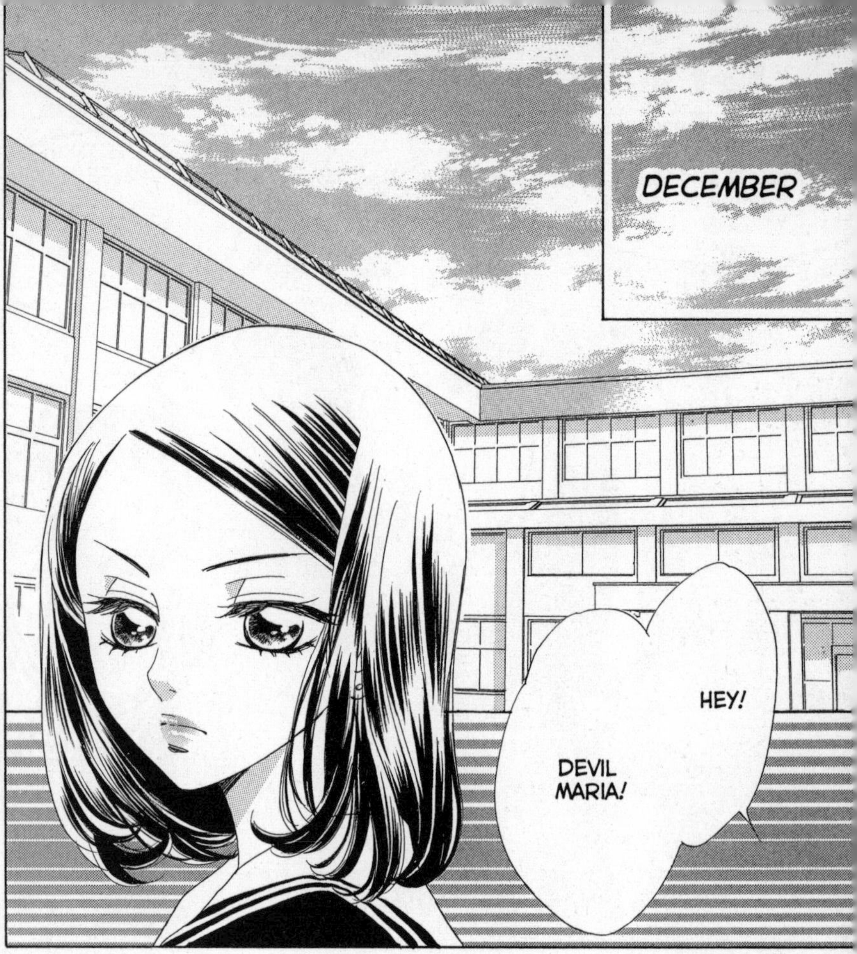
DECEMBER
HEY! DEVIL MARIA!

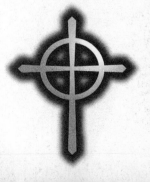

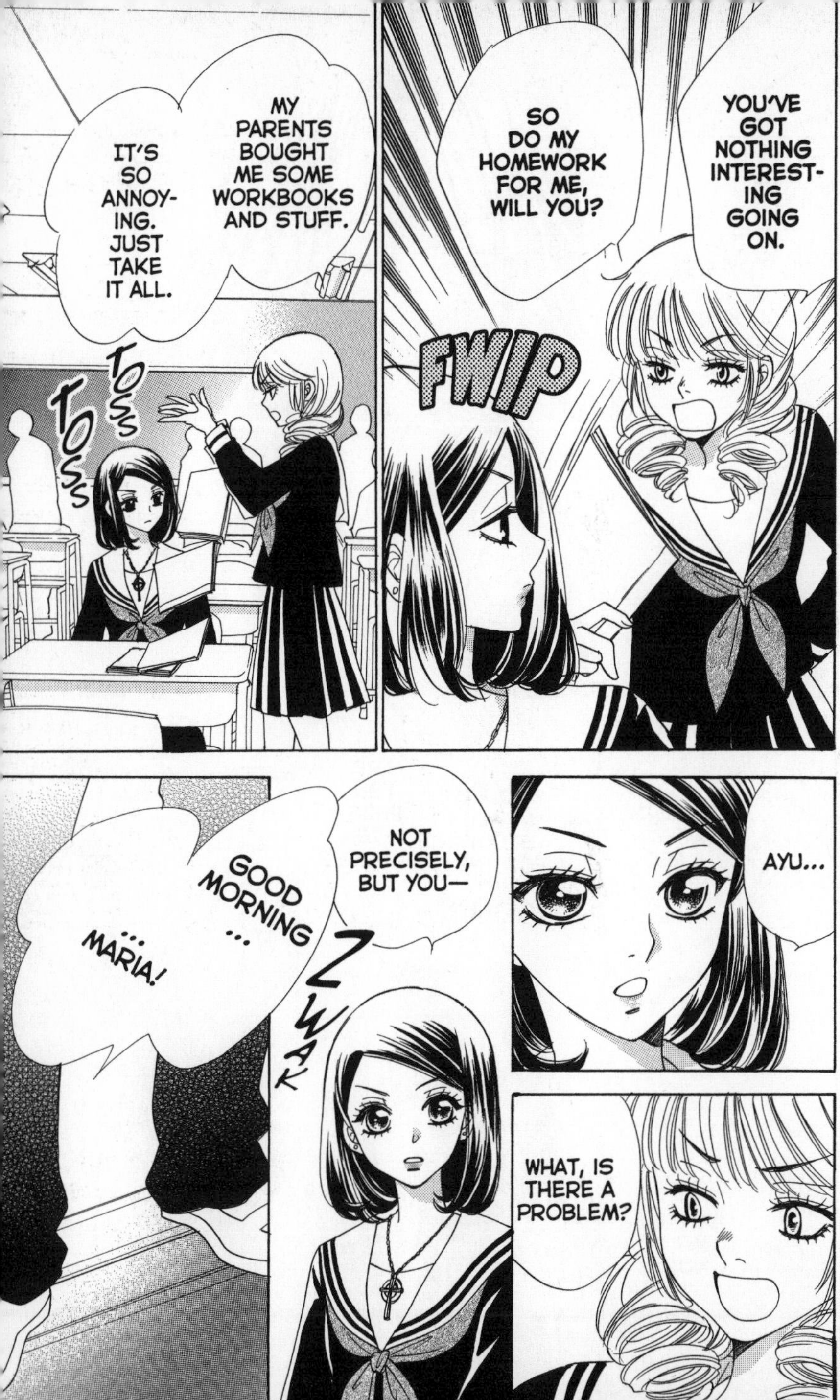
YOU'VE GOT NOTHING INTEREST-ING GOING ON.
SO DO MY HOMEWORK FOR ME, WILL YOU?
FWIP
MY PARENTS BOUGHT ME SOME WORKBOOKS AND STUFF.
IT'S SO ANNOY-ING. JUST TAKE IT ALL.
TOSS
TOSS
AYU...
WHAT, IS THERE A PROBLEM?
NOT PRECISELY, BUT YOU—
ZWAK
GOOD MORNING...
...MARIA!

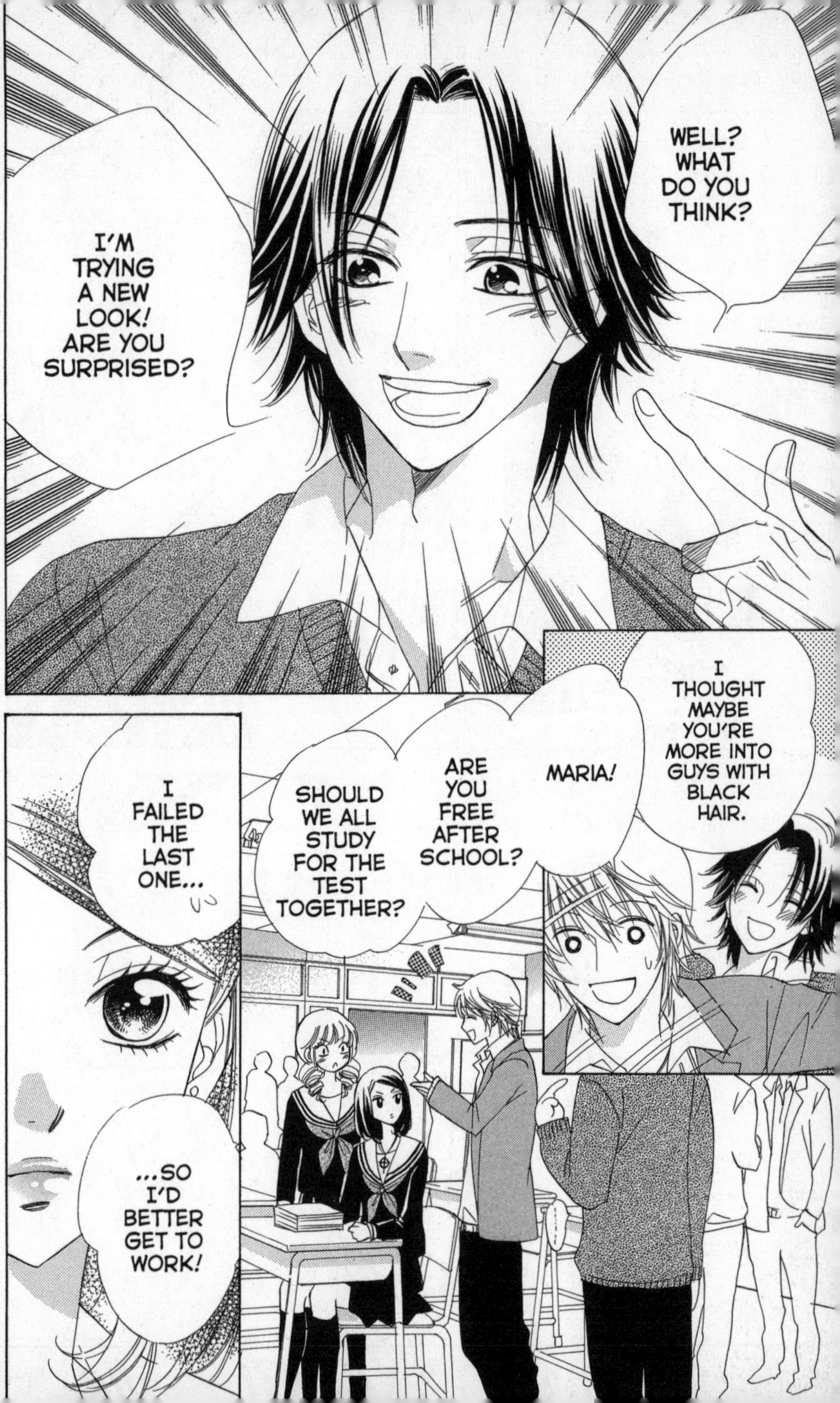
WELL? WHAT DO YOU THINK?
I'M TRYING A NEW LOOK! ARE YOU SURPRISED?
I THOUGHT MAYBE YOU'RE MORE INTO GUYS WITH BLACK HAIR.
MARIA!
ARE YOU FREE AFTER SCHOOL?
SHOULD WE ALL STUDY FOR THE TEST TOGETHER?
I FAILED THE LAST ONE...
...SO I'D BETTER GET TO WORK!

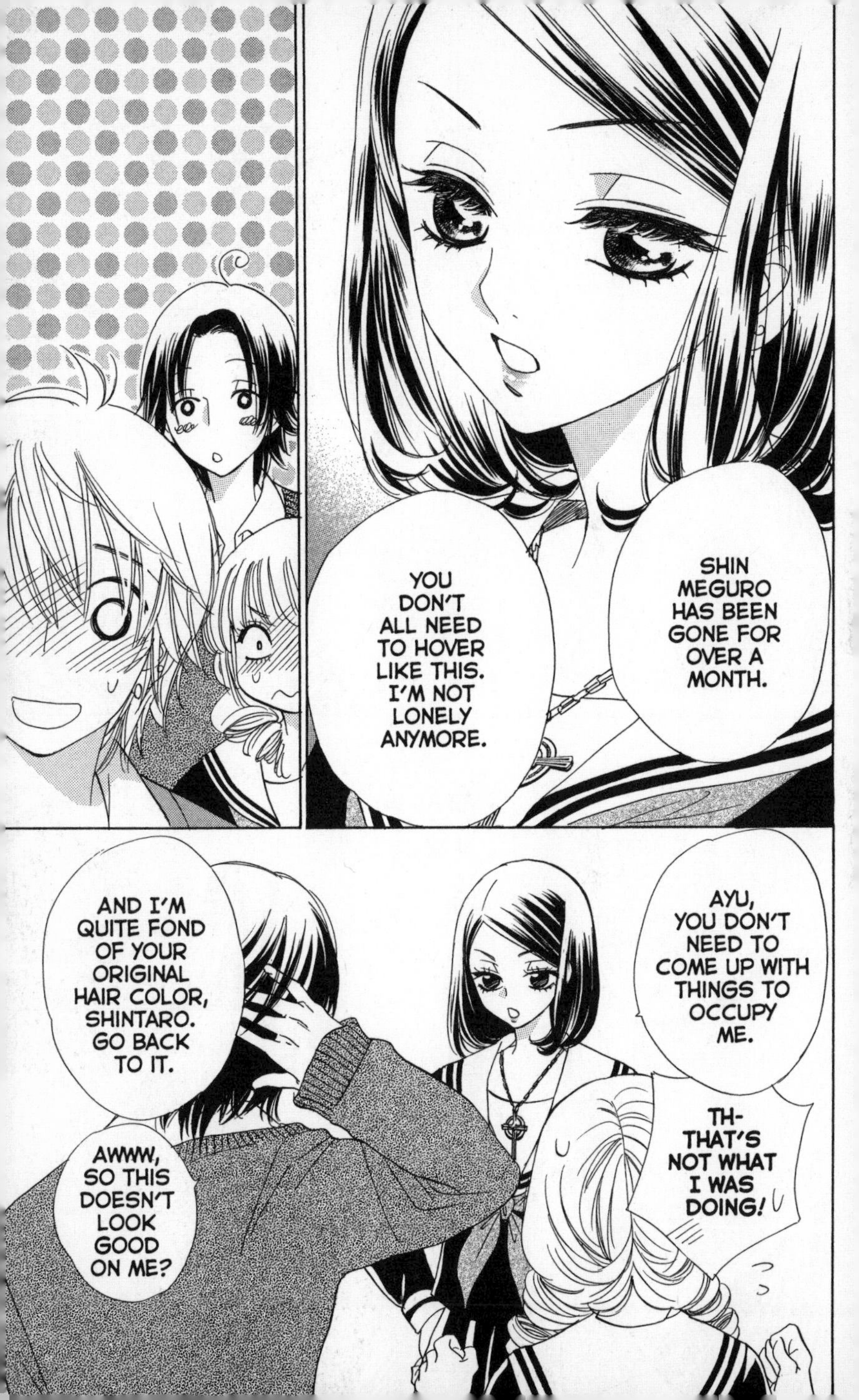
SHIN MEGURO HAS BEEN GONE FOR OVER A MONTH.
YOU DON'T ALL NEED TO HOVER LIKE THIS. I'M NOT LONELY ANYMORE.
AYU, YOU DON'T NEED TO COME UP WITH THINGS TO OCCUPY ME.
TH-THAT'S NOT WHAT I WAS DOING!
AND I'M QUITE FOND OF YOUR ORIGINAL HAIR COLOR, SHINTARO. GO BACK TO IT.
AWWW, SO THIS DOESN'T LOOK GOOD ON ME?

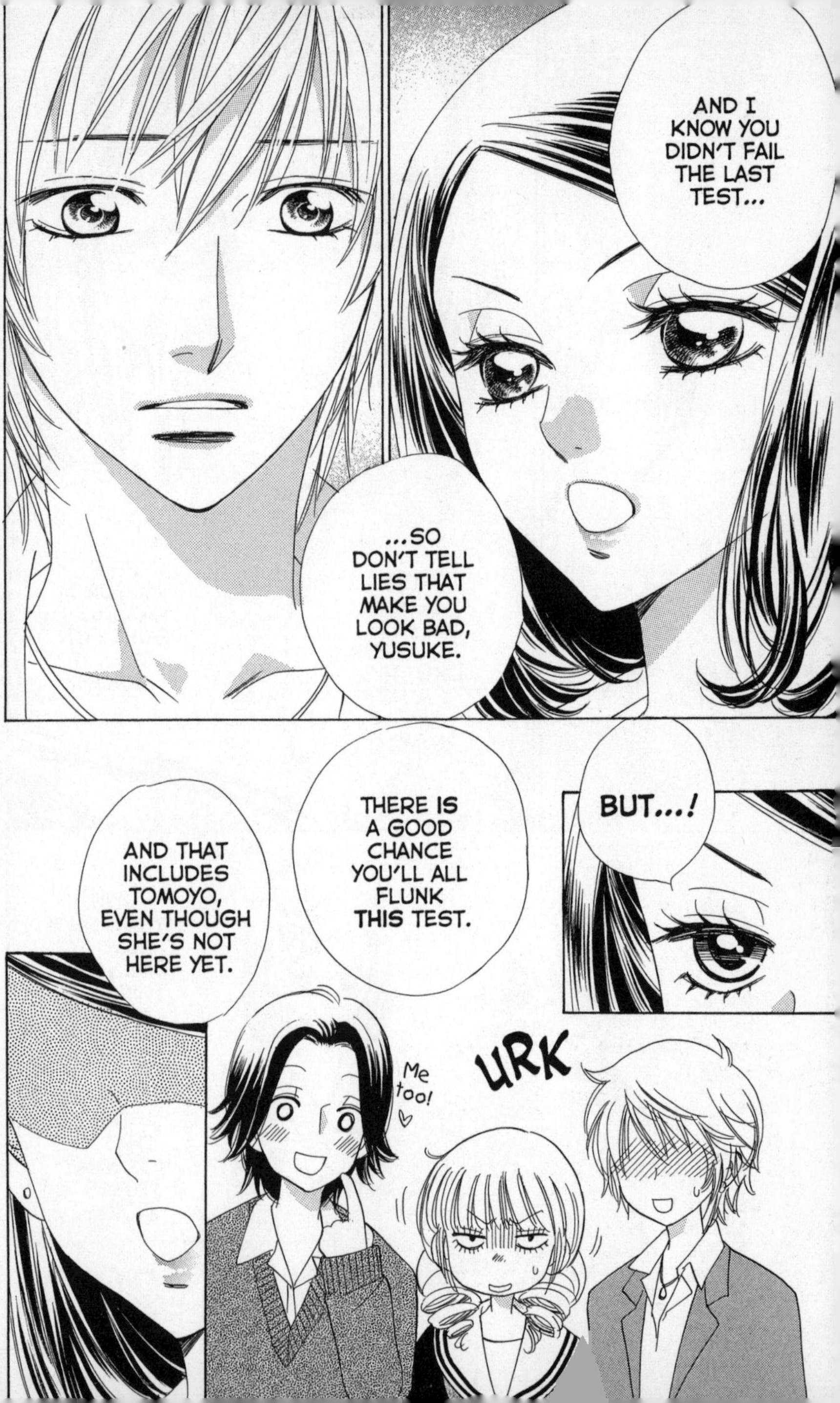
AND I KNOW YOU DIDN'T FAIL THE LAST TEST...
...SO DON'T TELL LIES THAT MAKE YOU LOOK BAD, YUSUKE.
BUT...!
THERE IS A GOOD CHANCE YOU'LL ALL FLUNK THIS TEST.
AND THAT INCLUDES TOMOYO, EVEN THOUGH SHE'S NOT HERE YET.
URK
Me too!

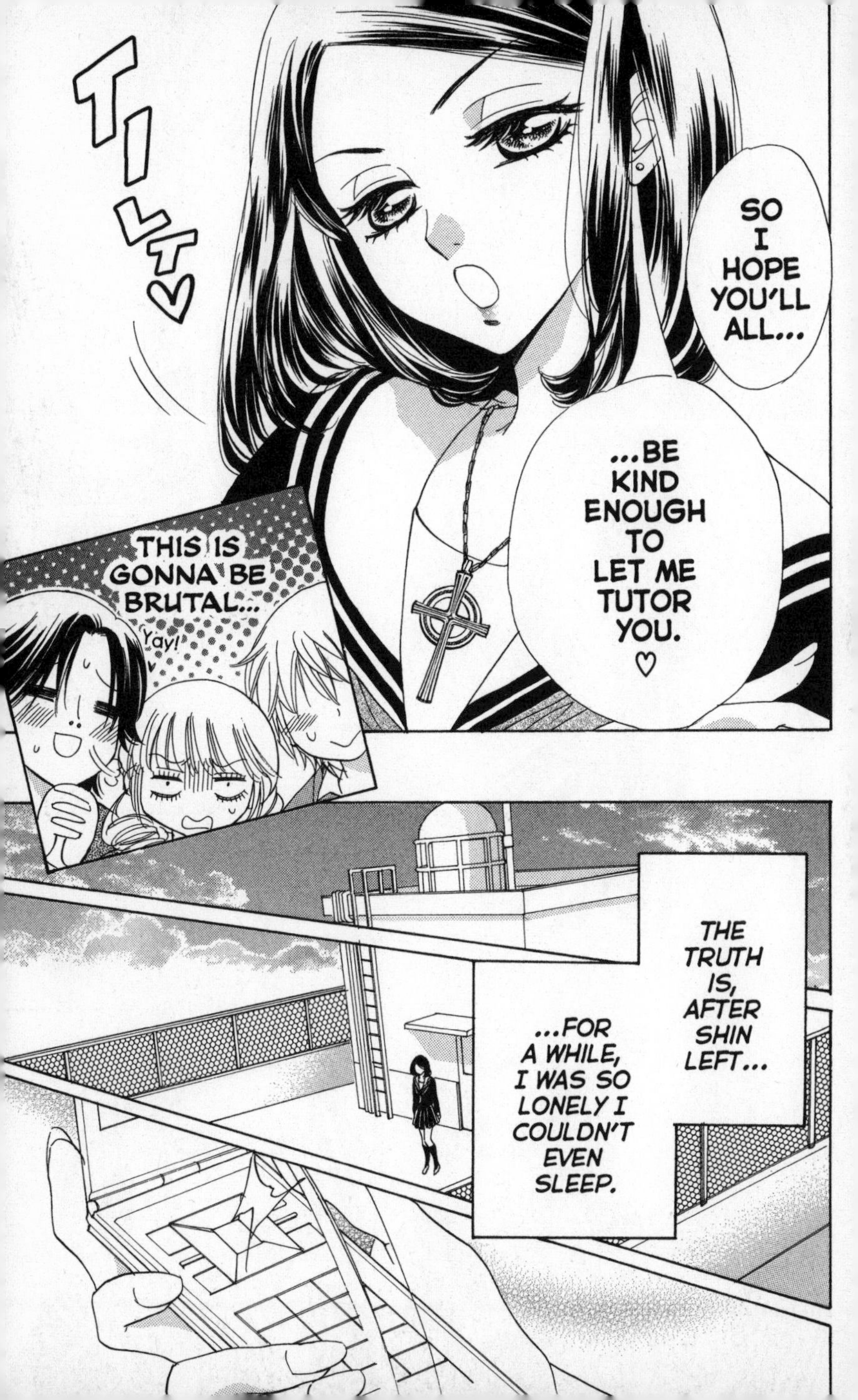
SO I HOPE YOU'LL ALL...
...BE KIND ENOUGH TO LET ME TUTOR YOU. ♥
TILT ♥
THIS IS GONNA BE BRUTAL...
Yay! ♥
THE TRUTH IS, AFTER SHIN LEFT...
...FOR A WHILE, I WAS SO LONELY I COULDN'T EVEN SLEEP.

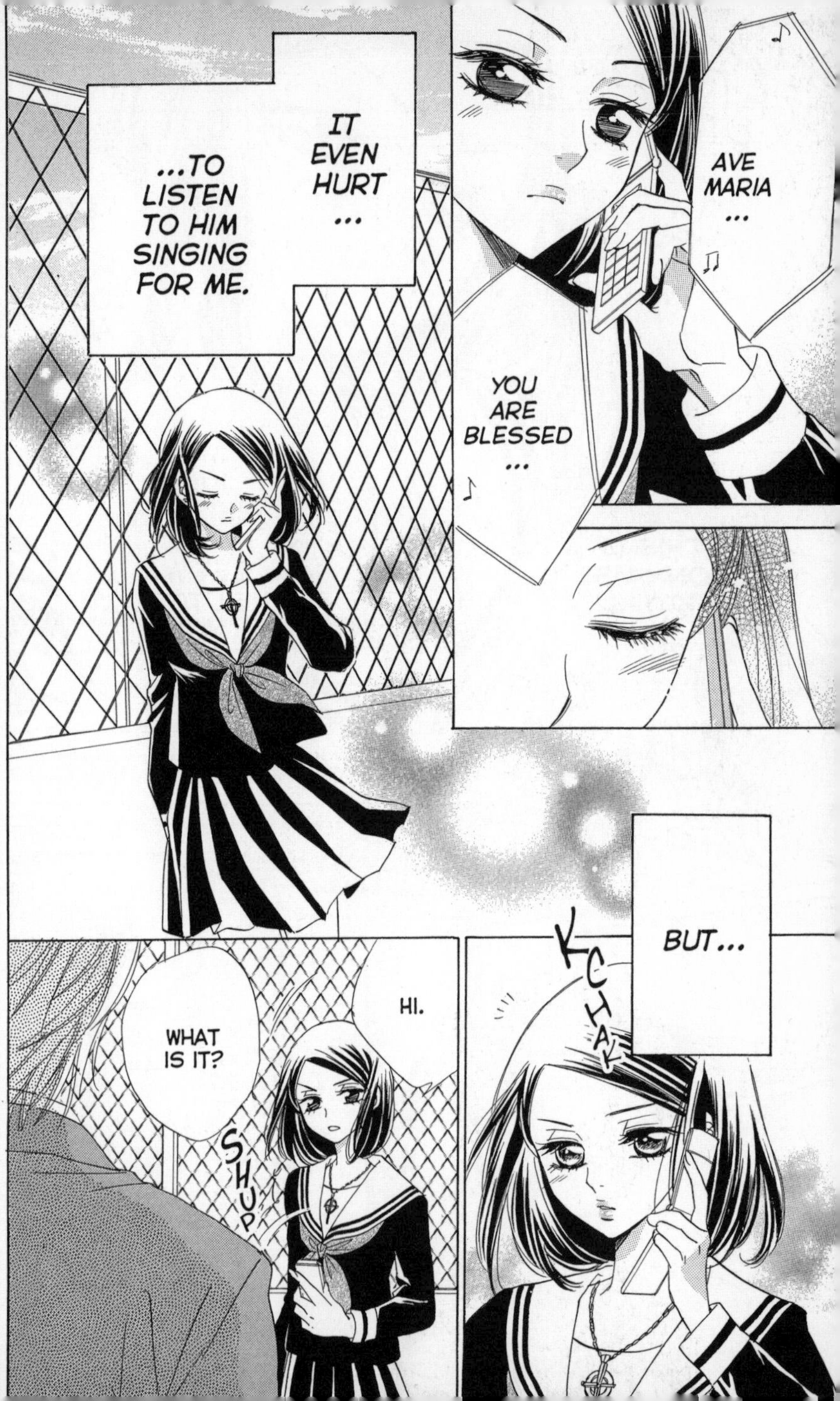
AVE MARIA ...
YOU ARE BLESSED ...
IT EVEN HURT ...
...TO LISTEN TO HIM SINGING FOR ME.
BUT...
KCHAK
HI.
WHAT IS IT?
SHUP

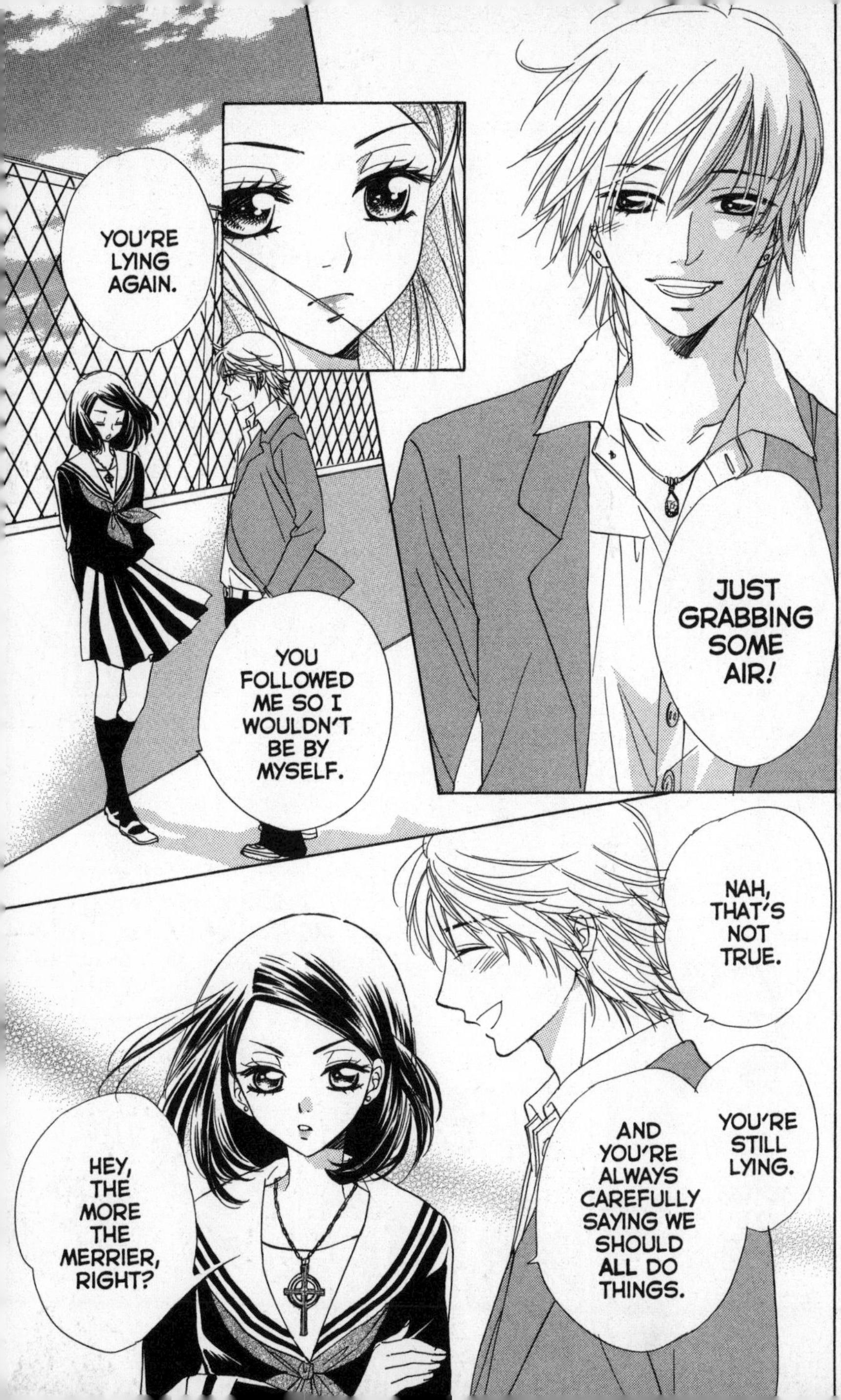
JUST GRABBING SOME AIR!
YOU'RE LYING AGAIN.
YOU FOLLOWED ME SO I WOULDN'T BE BY MYSELF.
NAH, THAT'S NOT TRUE.
YOU'RE STILL LYING.
AND YOU'RE ALWAYS CAREFULLY SAYING WE SHOULD ALL DO THINGS.
HEY, THE MORE THE MERRIER, RIGHT?

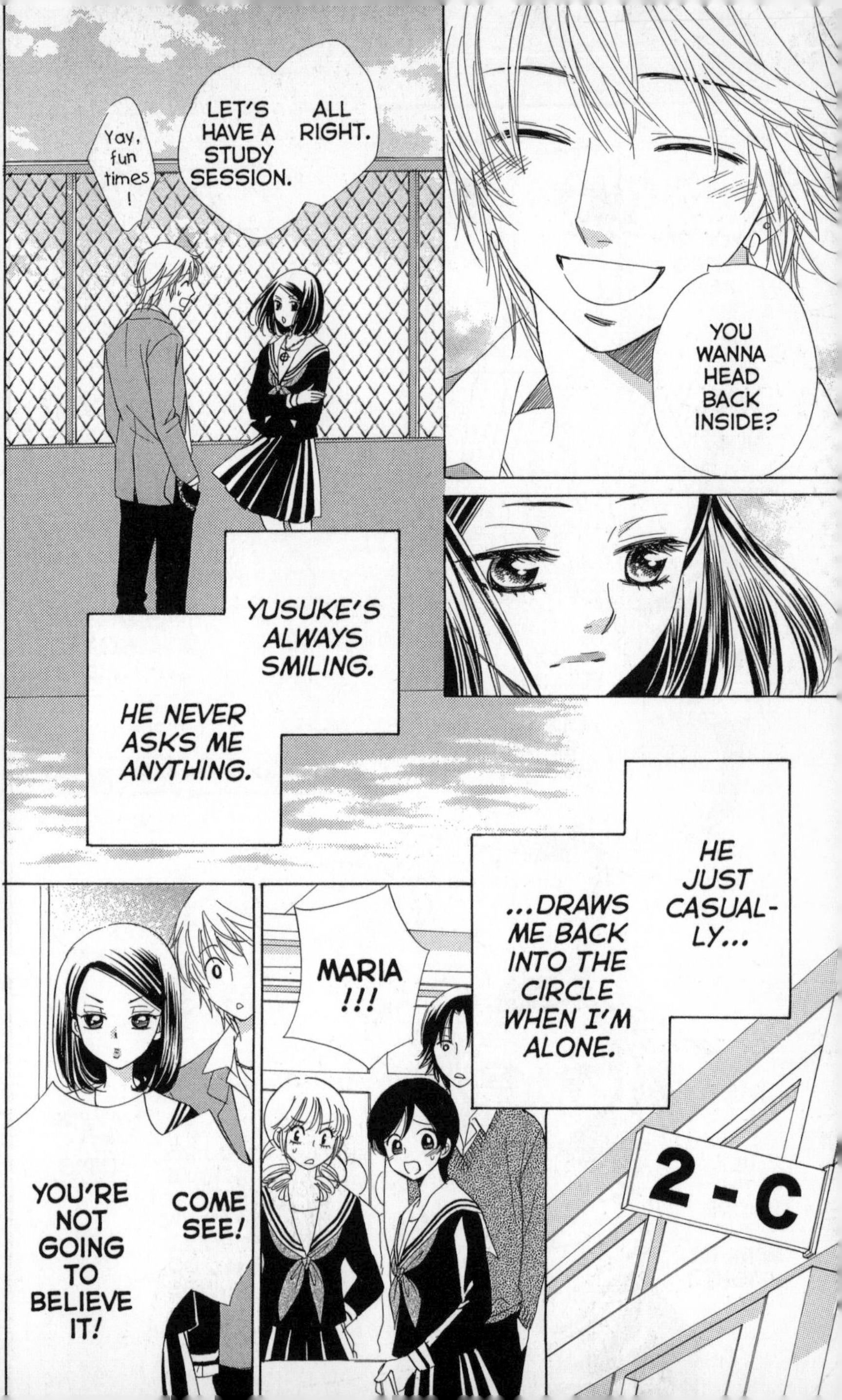
YOU WANNA HEAD BACK INSIDE?
ALL RIGHT.
LET'S HAVE A STUDY SESSION.
Yay, fun times!
YUSUKE'S ALWAYS SMILING.
HE NEVER ASKS ME ANYTHING.
HE JUST CASUAL-LY...
...DRAWS ME BACK INTO THE CIRCLE WHEN I'M ALONE.
2 - C
MARIA!!!
COME SEE!
YOU'RE NOT GOING TO BELIEVE IT!

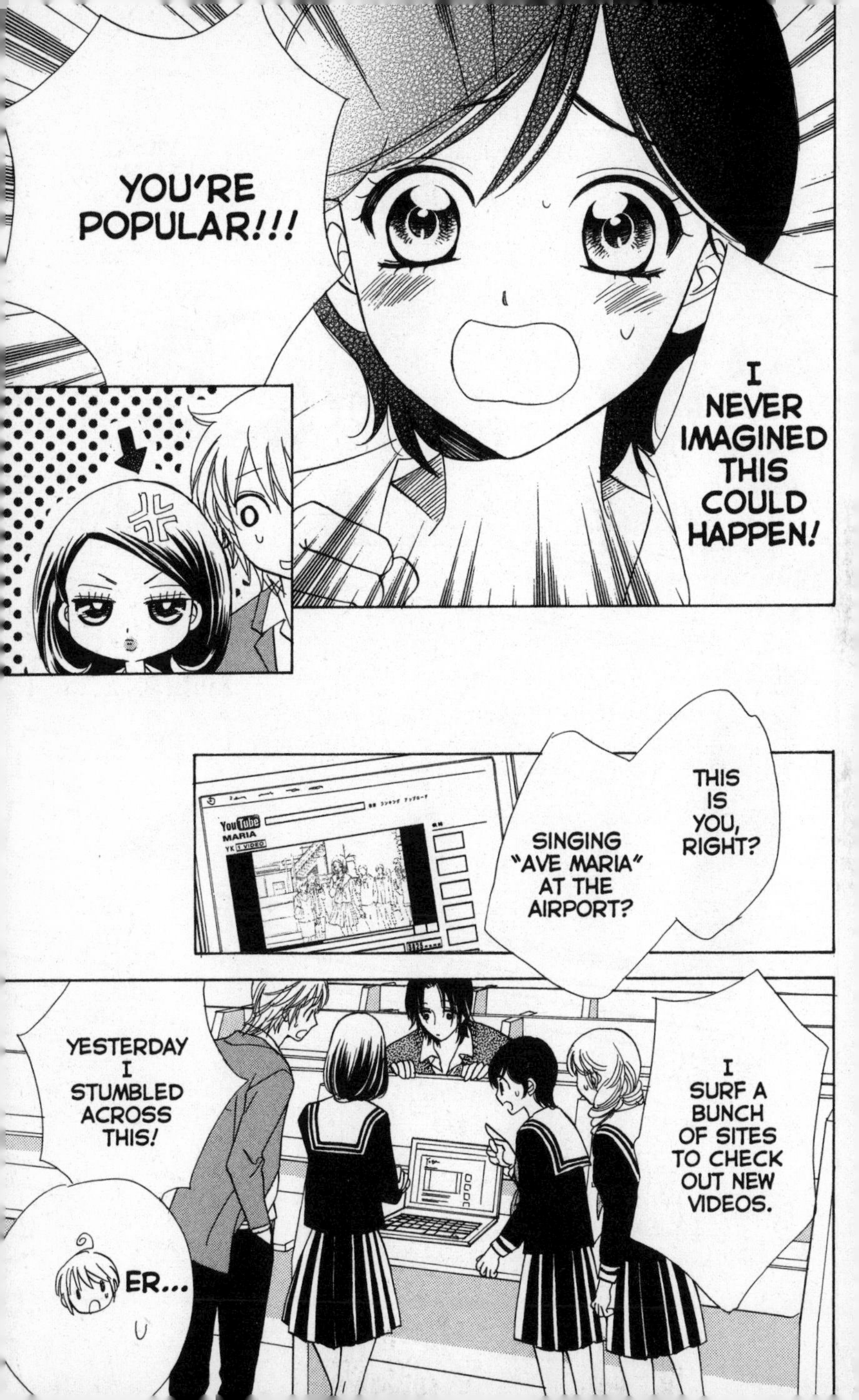
YOU'RE POPULAR!!!
I NEVER IMAGINED THIS COULD HAPPEN!
THIS IS YOU, RIGHT?
SINGING "AVE MARIA" AT THE AIRPORT?
YouTube
MARIA
I SURF A BUNCH OF SITES TO CHECK OUT NEW VIDEOS.
YESTERDAY I STUMBLED ACROSS THIS!
ER...

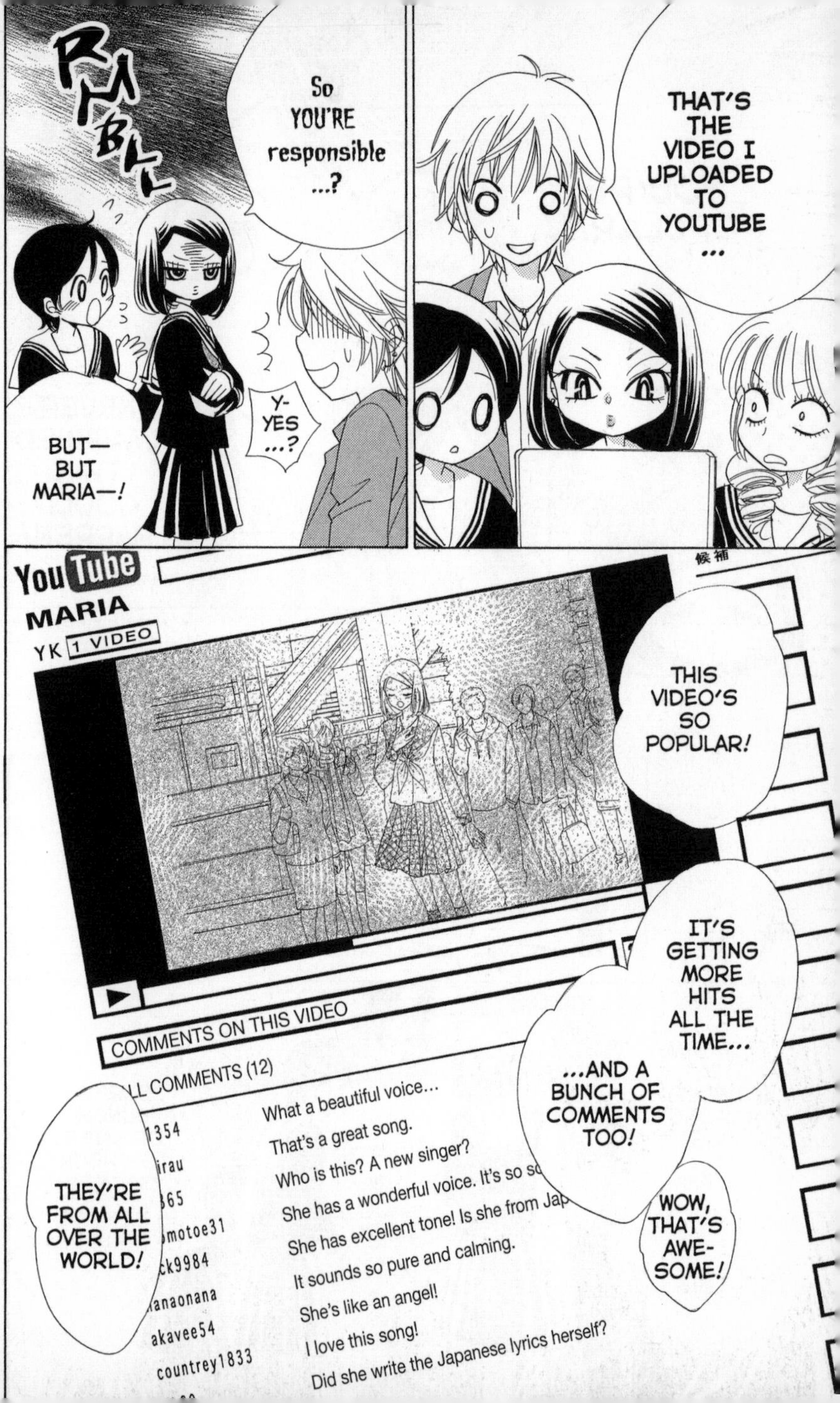
THAT'S THE VIDEO I UPLOADED TO YOUTUBE...
So YOU'RE responsible ...?
Y-YES ...?
BUT—BUT MARIA—!
YouTube
MARIA
YK 1 VIDEO
THIS VIDEO'S SO POPULAR!
IT'S GETTING MORE HITS ALL THE TIME...
...AND A BUNCH OF COMMENTS TOO!
WOW, THAT'S AWE-SOME!
THEY'RE FROM ALL OVER THE WORLD!
COMMENTS ON THIS VIDEO
What a beautiful voice...
That's a great song.
Who is this? A new singer?
It sounds so pure and calming.
She's like an angel!
akavee54
I love this song!
countrey1833
Did she write the Japanese lyrics herself?

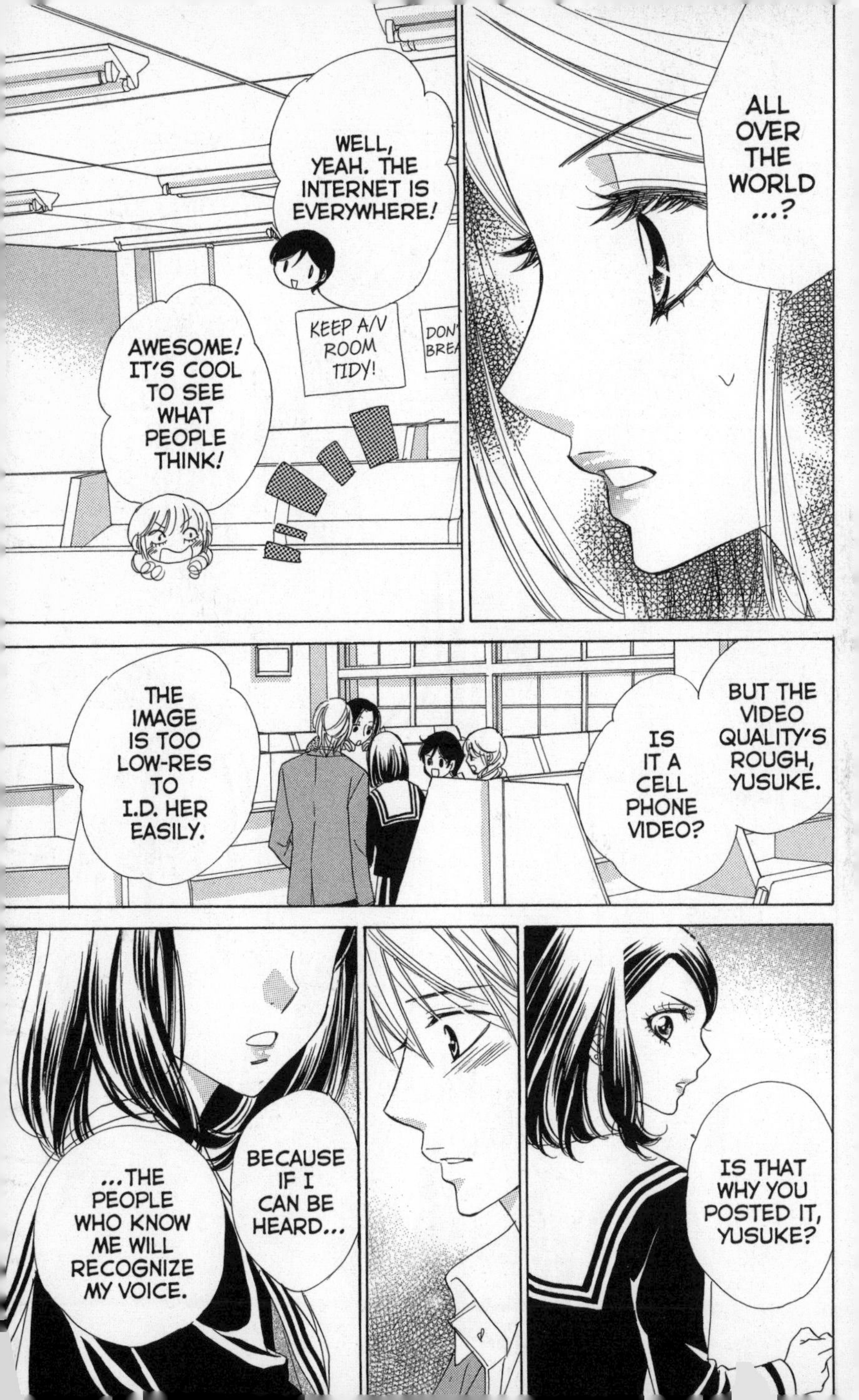
ALL OVER THE WORLD ...?
WELL, YEAH. THE INTERNET IS EVERYWHERE!
KEEP A/V ROOM TIDY!
AWESOME! IT'S COOL TO SEE WHAT PEOPLE THINK!
BUT THE VIDEO QUALITY'S ROUGH, YUSUKE.
IS IT A CELL PHONE VIDEO?
THE IMAGE IS TOO LOW-RES TO I.D. HER EASILY.
IS THAT WHY YOU POSTED IT, YUSUKE?
BECAUSE IF I CAN BE HEARD...
...THE PEOPLE WHO KNOW ME WILL RECOGNIZE MY VOICE.

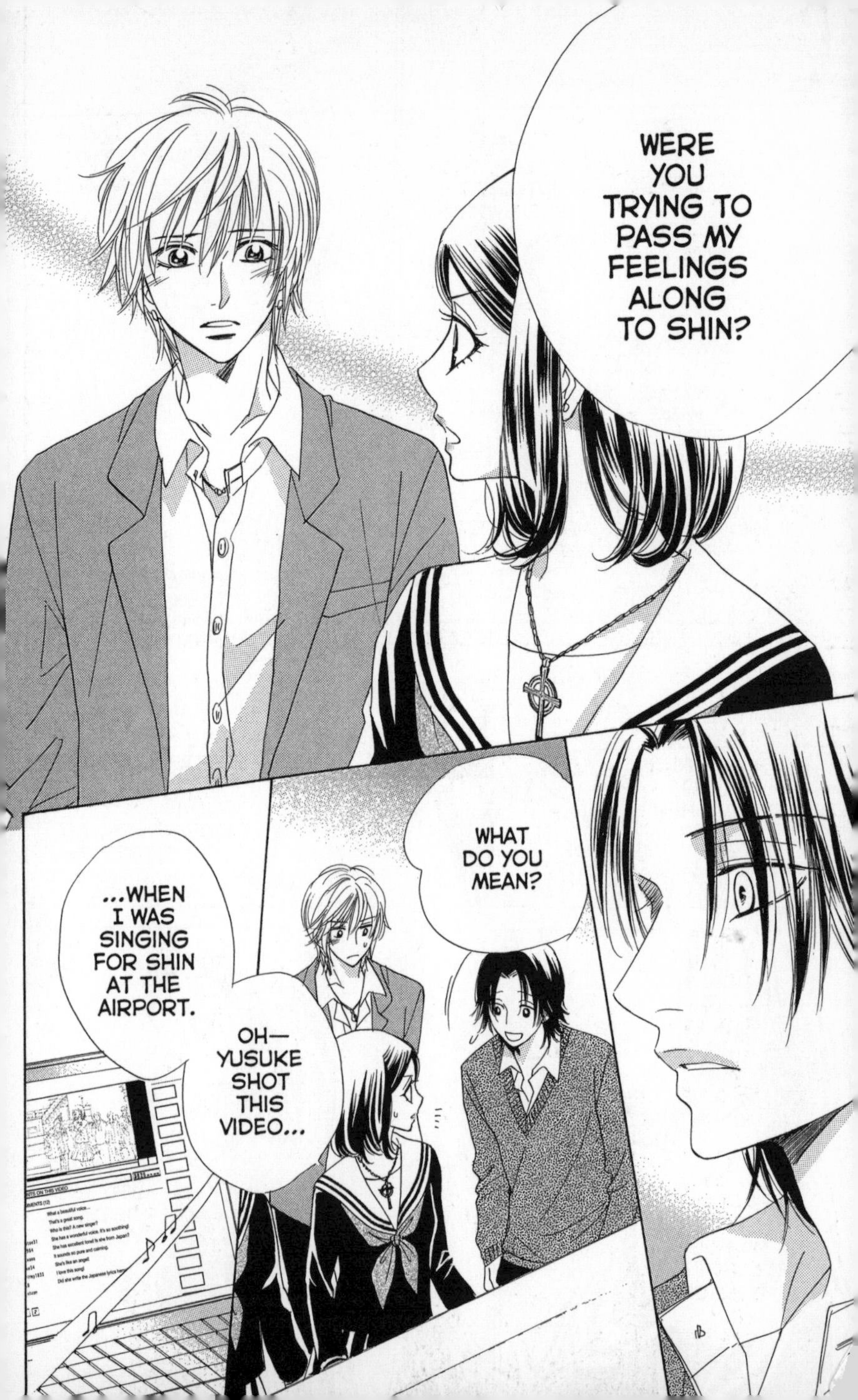
WERE YOU TRYING TO PASS MY FEELINGS ALONG TO SHIN?
WHAT DO YOU MEAN?
OH— YUSUKE SHOT THIS VIDEO...
...WHEN I WAS SINGING FOR SHIN AT THE AIRPORT.

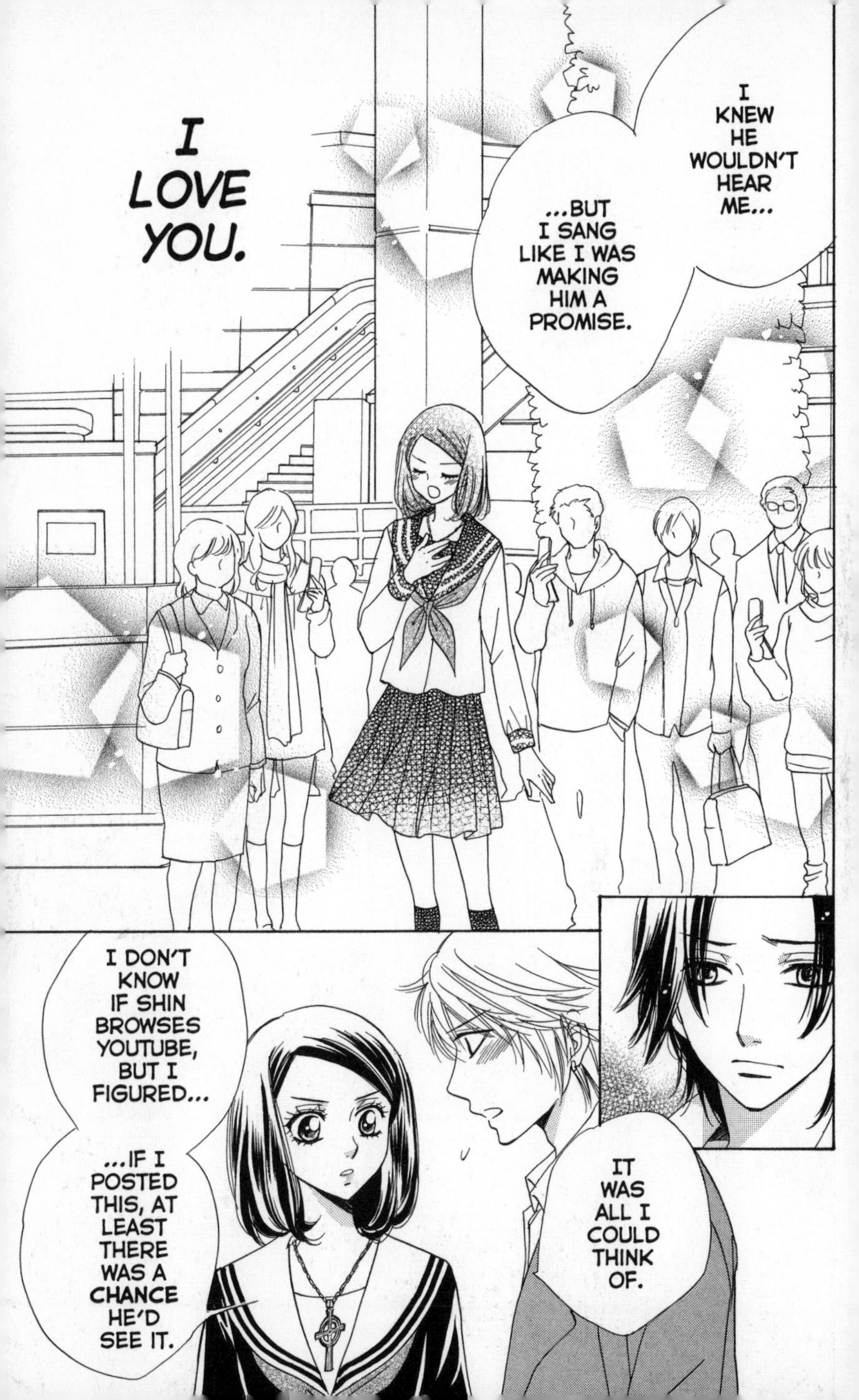
I KNEW HE WOULDN'T HEAR ME...
...BUT I SANG LIKE I WAS MAKING HIM A PROMISE.
I LOVE YOU.
I DON'T KNOW IF SHIN BROWSES YOUTUBE, BUT I FIGURED...
...IF I POSTED THIS, AT LEAST THERE WAS A CHANCE HE'D SEE IT.
IT WAS ALL I COULD THINK OF.

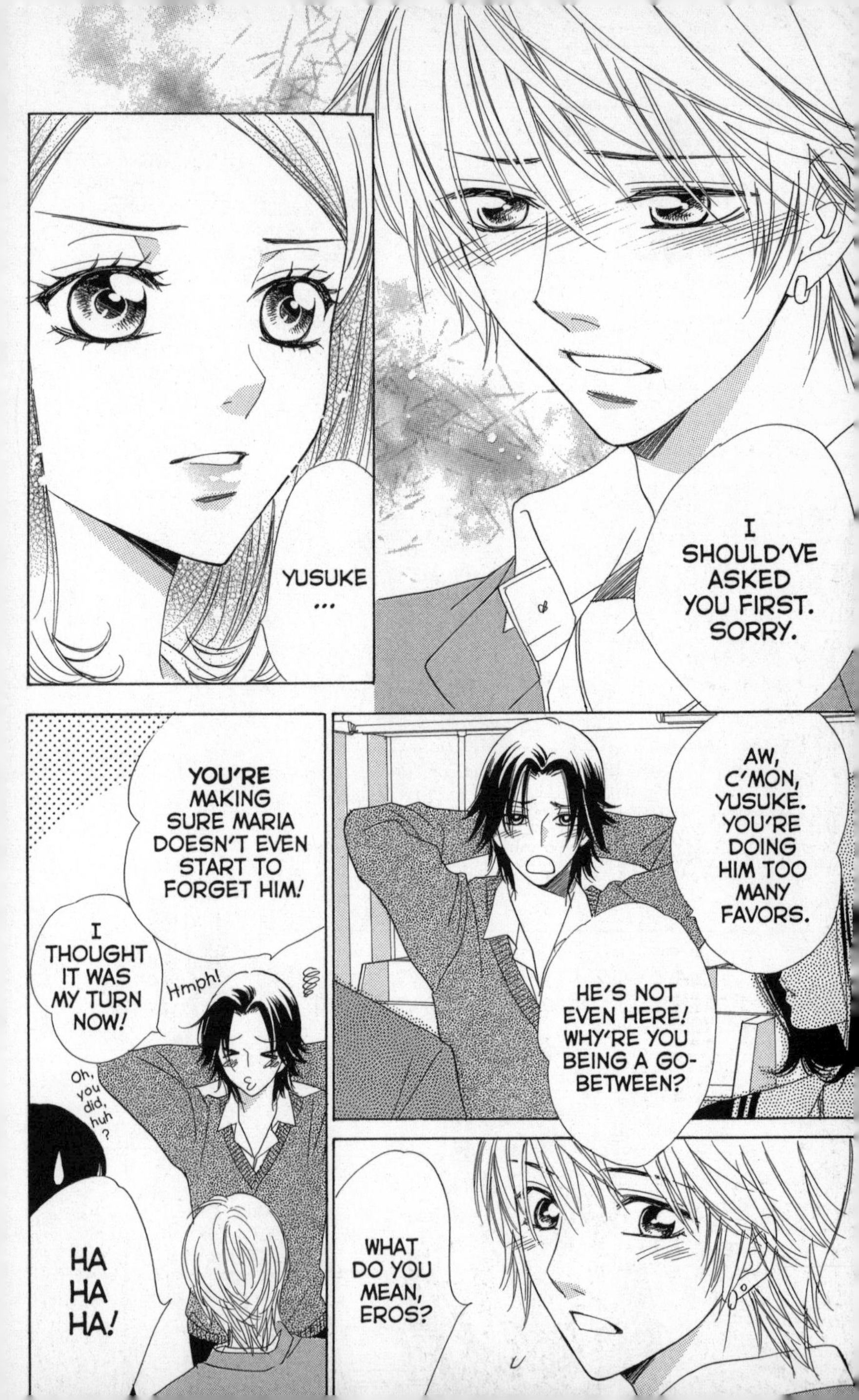
I SHOULD'VE ASKED YOU FIRST. SORRY.
YUSUKE ...
AW, C'MON, YUSUKE. YOU'RE DOING HIM TOO MANY FAVORS.
HE'S NOT EVEN HERE! WHY'RE YOU BEING A GO-BETWEEN?
WHAT DO YOU MEAN, EROS?
YOU'RE MAKING SURE MARIA DOESN'T EVEN START TO FORGET HIM!
I THOUGHT IT WAS MY TURN NOW!
Hmph!
Oh, you did, huh?
HA HA HA!

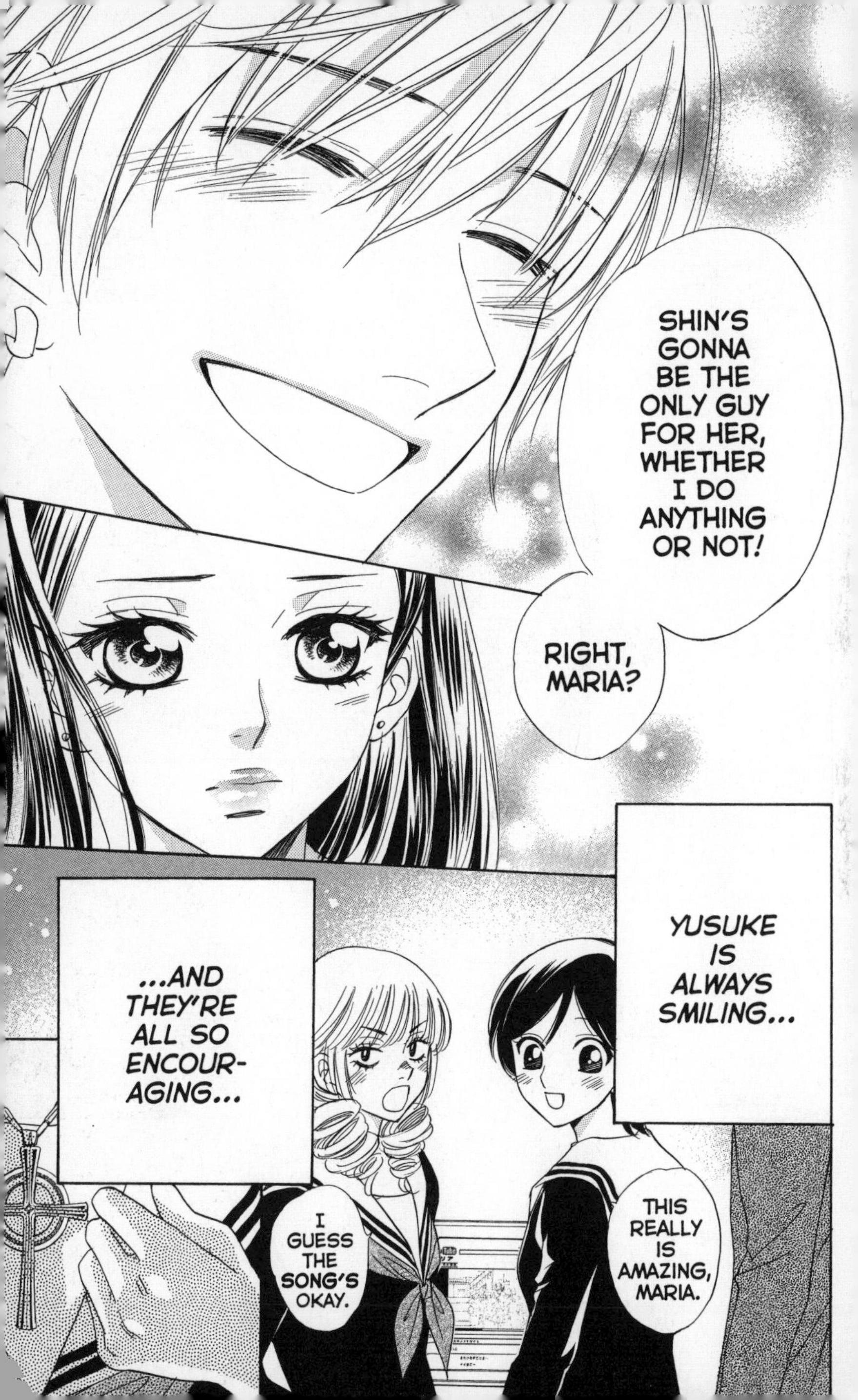
SHIN'S GONNA BE THE ONLY GUY FOR HER, WHETHER I DO ANYTHING OR NOT!
RIGHT, MARIA?
YUSUKE IS ALWAYS SMILING...
...AND THEY'RE ALL SO ENCOURAGING...
THIS REALLY IS AMAZING, MARIA.
I GUESS THE SONG'S OKAY.

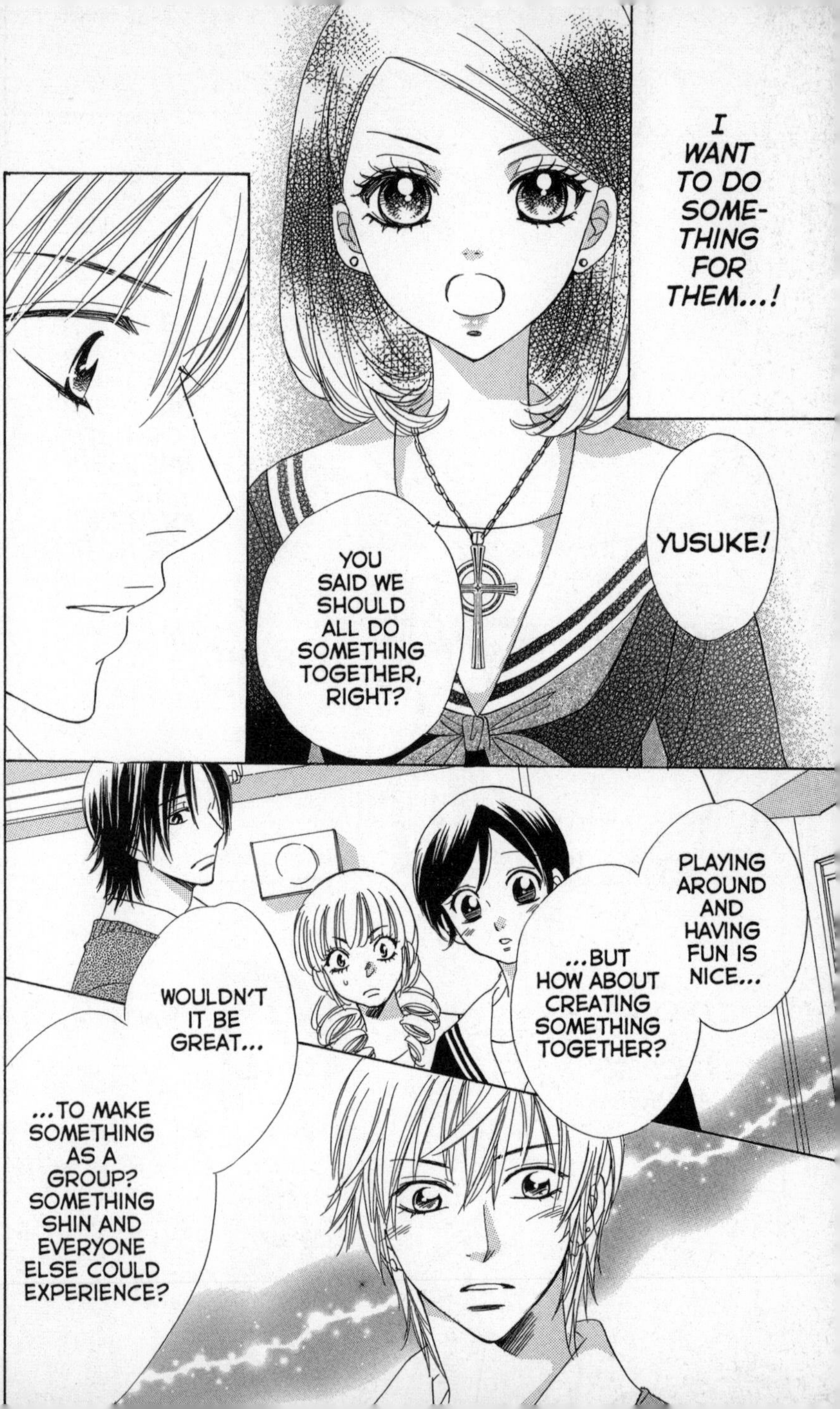
I WANT TO DO SOMETHING FOR THEM...!
YUSUKE!
YOU SAID WE SHOULD ALL DO SOMETHING TOGETHER, RIGHT?
PLAYING AROUND AND HAVING FUN IS NICE...
...BUT HOW ABOUT CREATING SOMETHING TOGETHER?
WOULDN'T IT BE GREAT...
...TO MAKE SOMETHING AS A GROUP? SOMETHING SHIN AND EVERYONE ELSE COULD EXPERIENCE?

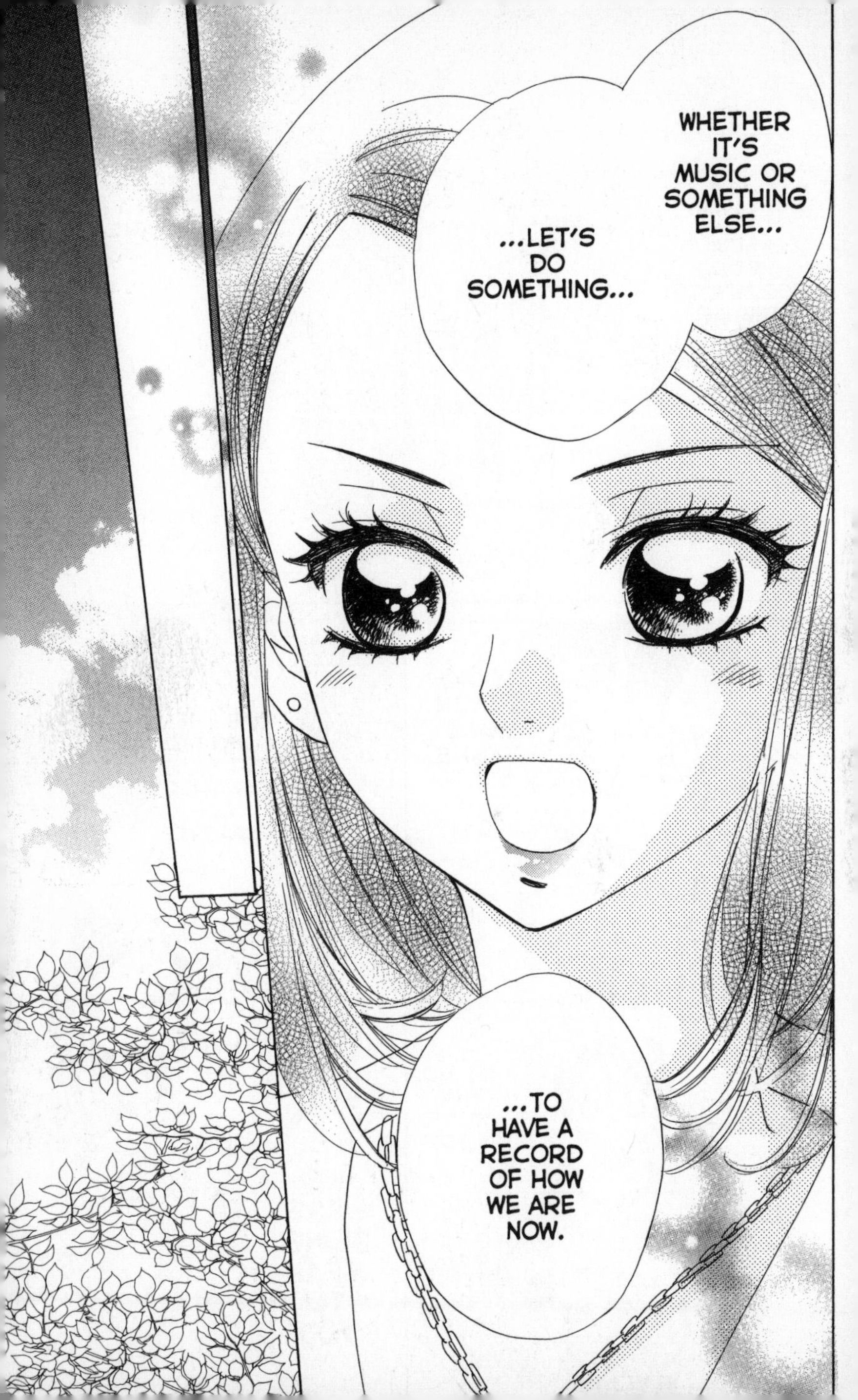
WHETHER IT'S MUSIC OR SOMETHING ELSE...
...LET'S DO SOMETHING...
...TO HAVE A RECORD OF HOW WE ARE NOW.

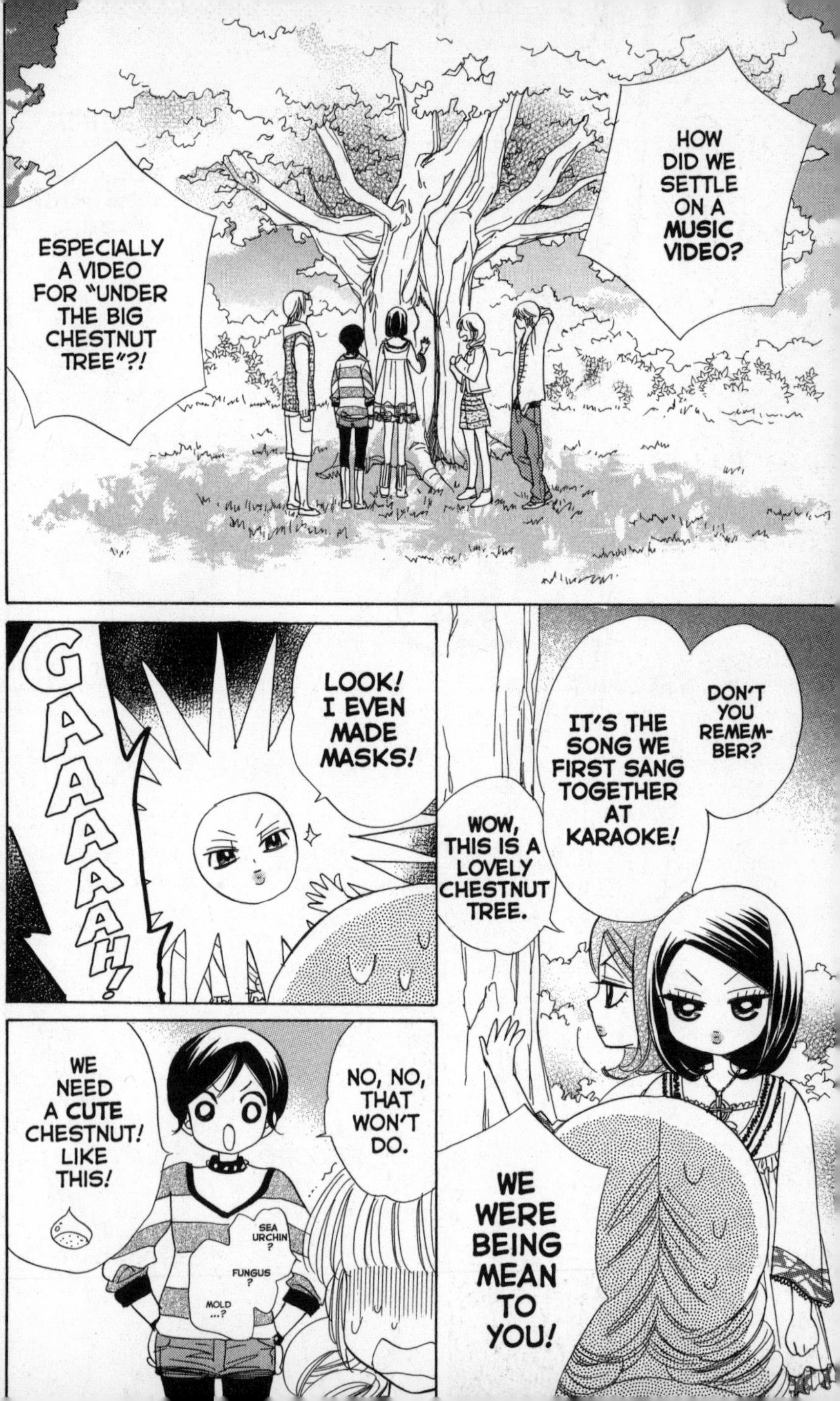
HOW DID WE SETTLE ON A MUSIC VIDEO?
ESPECIALLY A VIDEO FOR "UNDER THE BIG CHESTNUT TREE"?!
DON'T YOU REMEMBER?
IT'S THE SONG WE FIRST SANG TOGETHER AT KARAOKE!
WOW, THIS IS A LOVELY CHESTNUT TREE.
WE WERE BEING MEAN TO YOU!
LOOK! I EVEN MADE MASKS!
GAAAAAAH!
NO, NO, THAT WON'T DO.
WE NEED A CUTE CHESTNUT! LIKE THIS!
SEA URCHIN?
FUNGUS?
MOLD...?

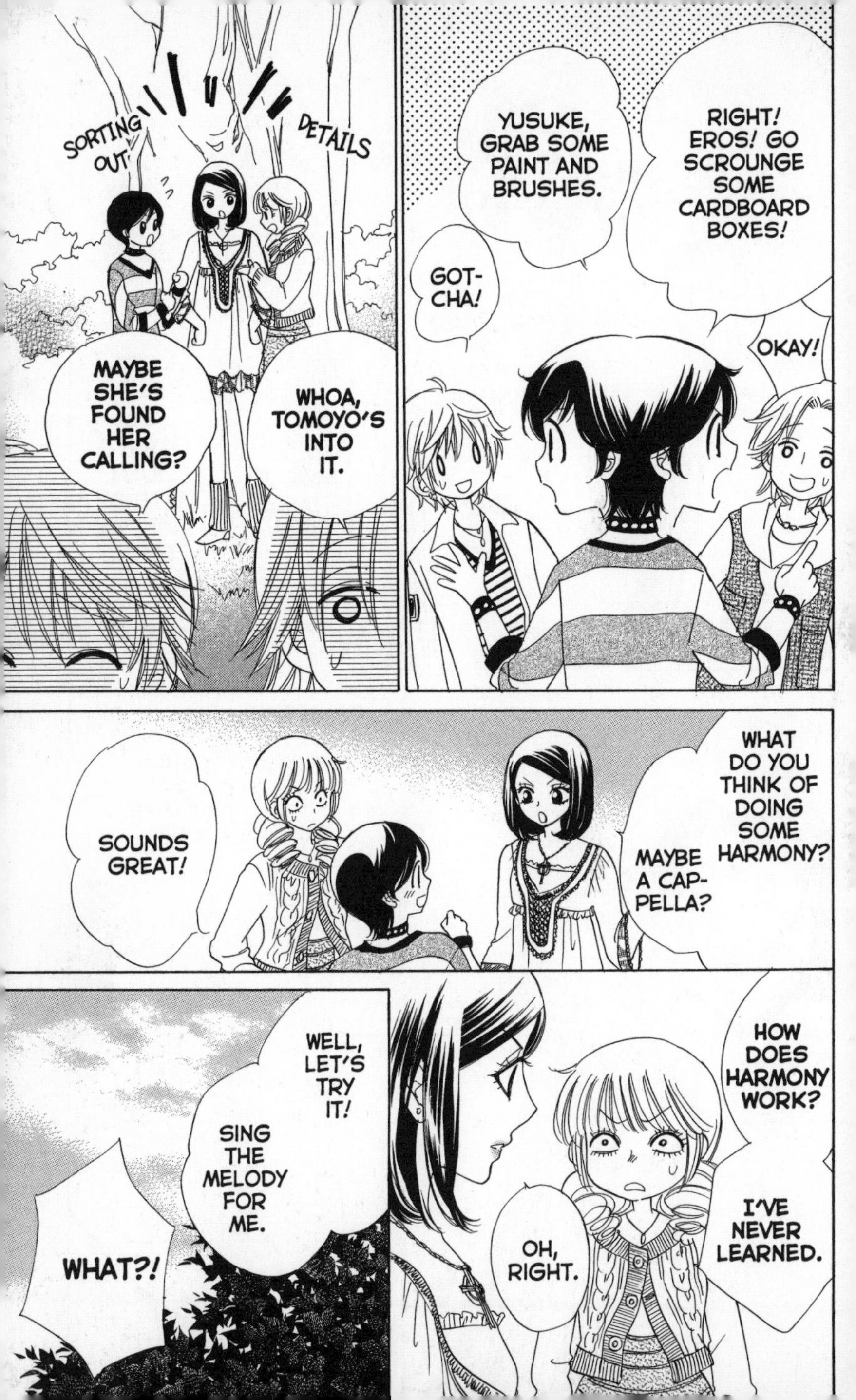
RIGHT! EROS! GO SCROUNGE SOME CARDBOARD BOXES!
YUSUKE, GRAB SOME PAINT AND BRUSHES.
OKAY!
GOT-CHA!
SORTING OUT DETAILS
WHOA, TOMOYO'S INTO IT.
MAYBE SHE'S FOUND HER CALLING?
WHAT DO YOU THINK OF DOING SOME HARMONY?
MAYBE A CAP-PELLA?
SOUNDS GREAT!
HOW DOES HARMONY WORK?
I'VE NEVER LEARNED.
OH, RIGHT.
WELL, LET'S TRY IT!
SING THE MELODY FOR ME.
WHAT?!

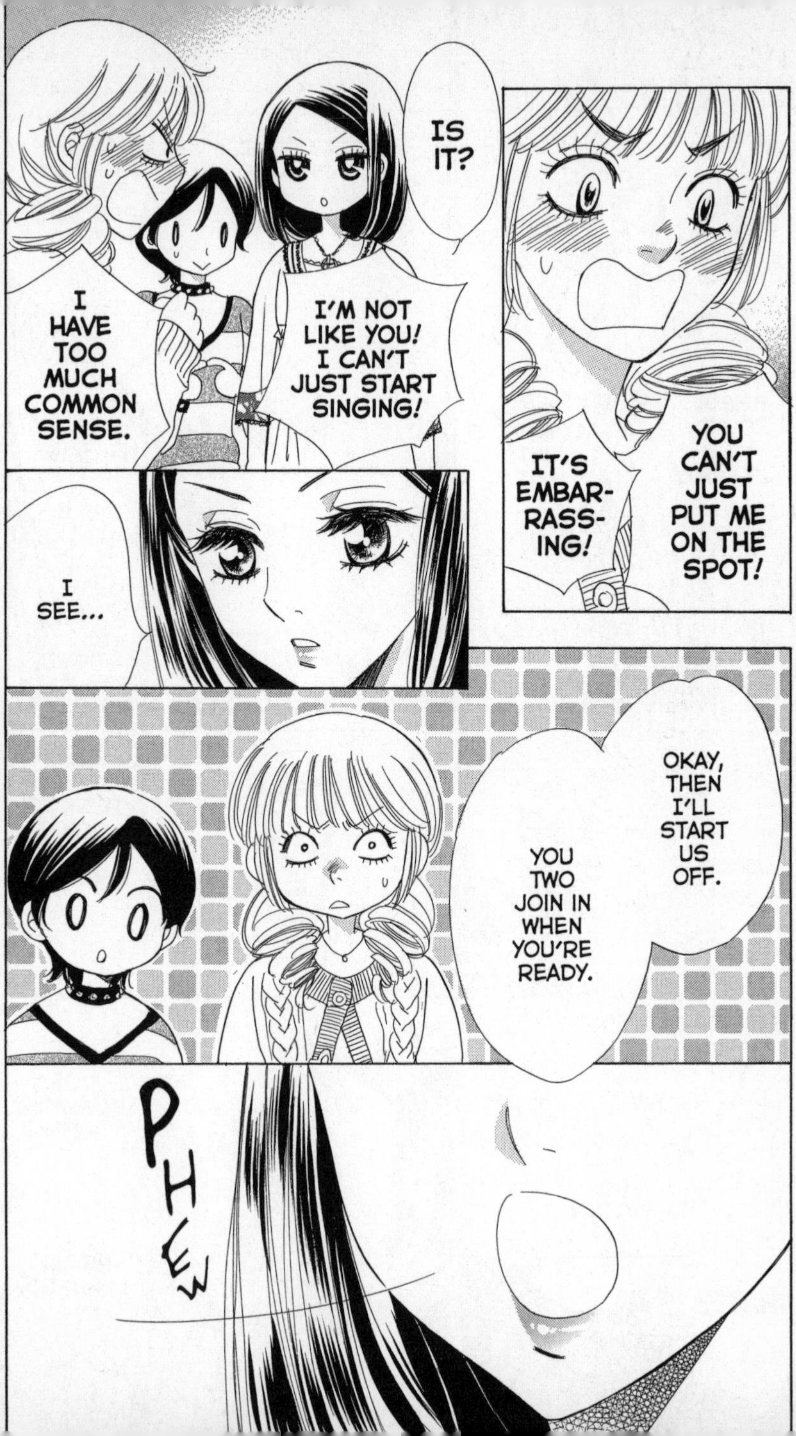
YOU CAN'T JUST PUT ME ON THE SPOT!
IT'S EMBARRASSING!
IS IT?
I'M NOT LIKE YOU! I CAN'T JUST START SINGING!
I HAVE TOO MUCH COMMON SENSE.
I SEE...
OKAY, THEN I'LL START US OFF.
YOU TWO JOIN IN WHEN YOU'RE READY.
PHEW

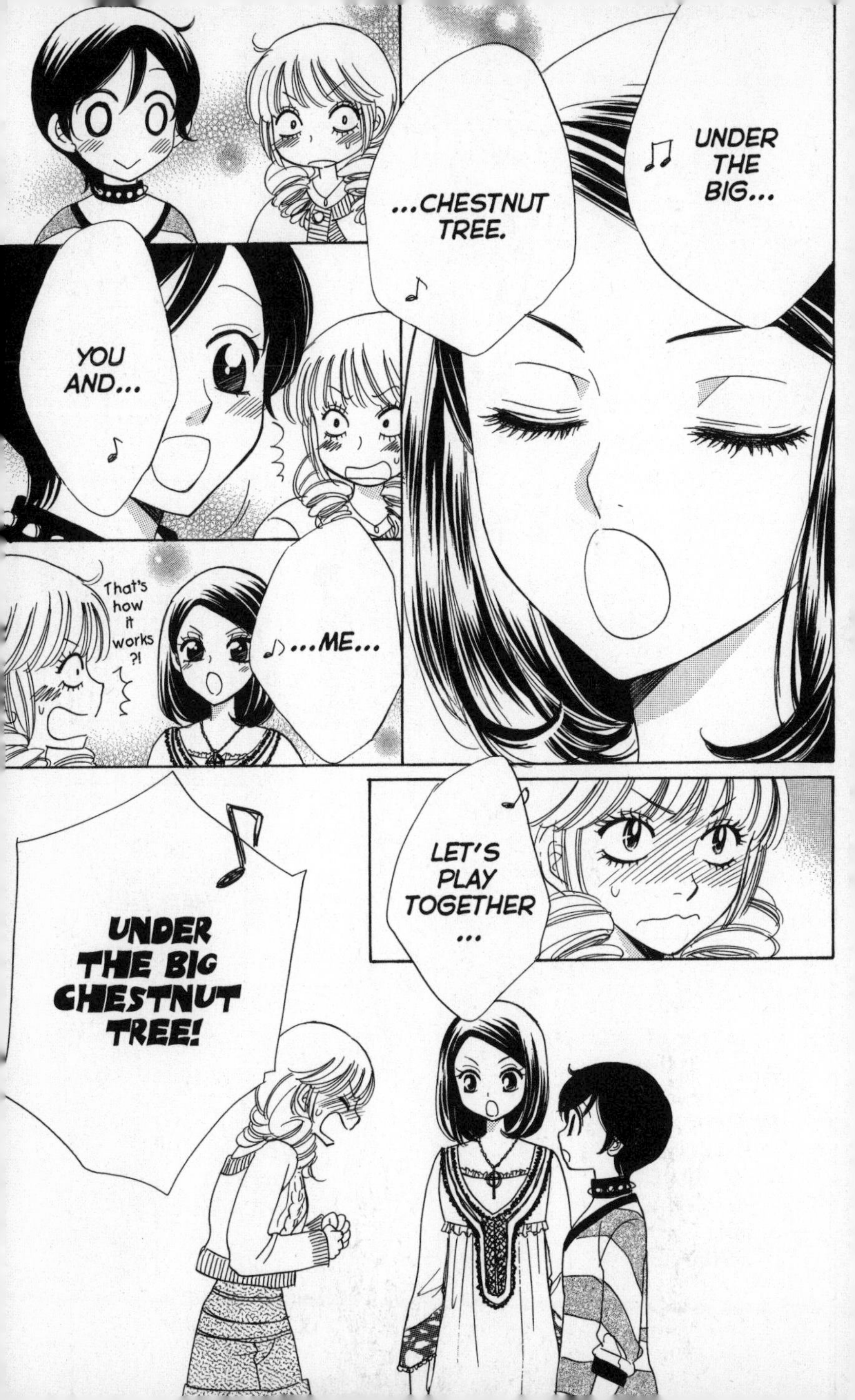
♫ UNDER THE BIG...
...CHESTNUT TREE. ♪
YOU AND... ♪
♪ ...ME...
That's how it works ?!
♪ LET'S PLAY TOGETHER ...
♪ UNDER THE BIG CHESTNUT TREE!

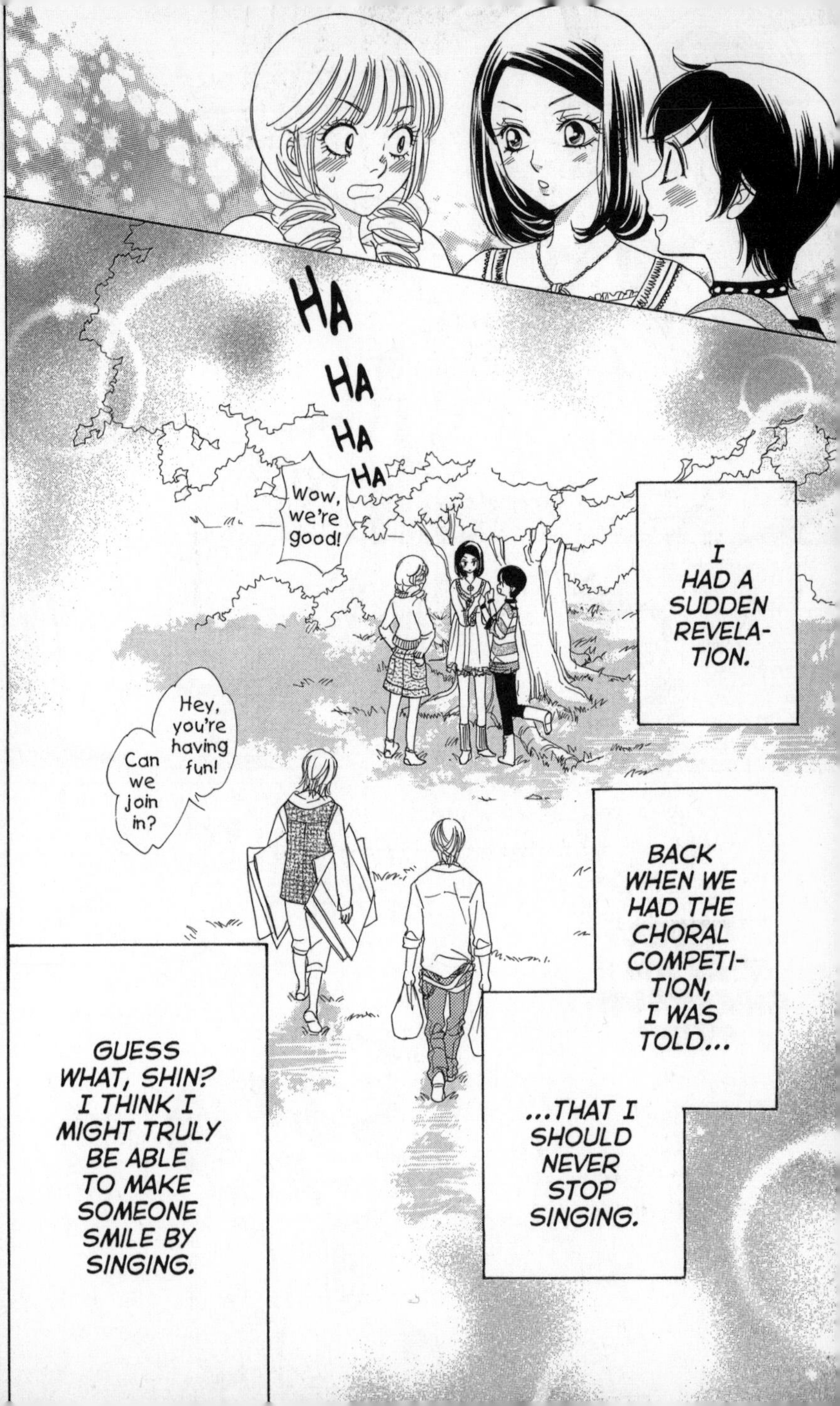
HA HA HA HA
I HAD A SUDDEN REVELATION.
Wow, we're good!
Hey, you're having fun!
Can we join in?
BACK WHEN WE HAD THE CHORAL COMPETITION, I WAS TOLD...
...THAT I SHOULD NEVER STOP SINGING.
GUESS WHAT, SHIN? I THINK I MIGHT TRULY BE ABLE TO MAKE SOMEONE SMILE BY SINGING.

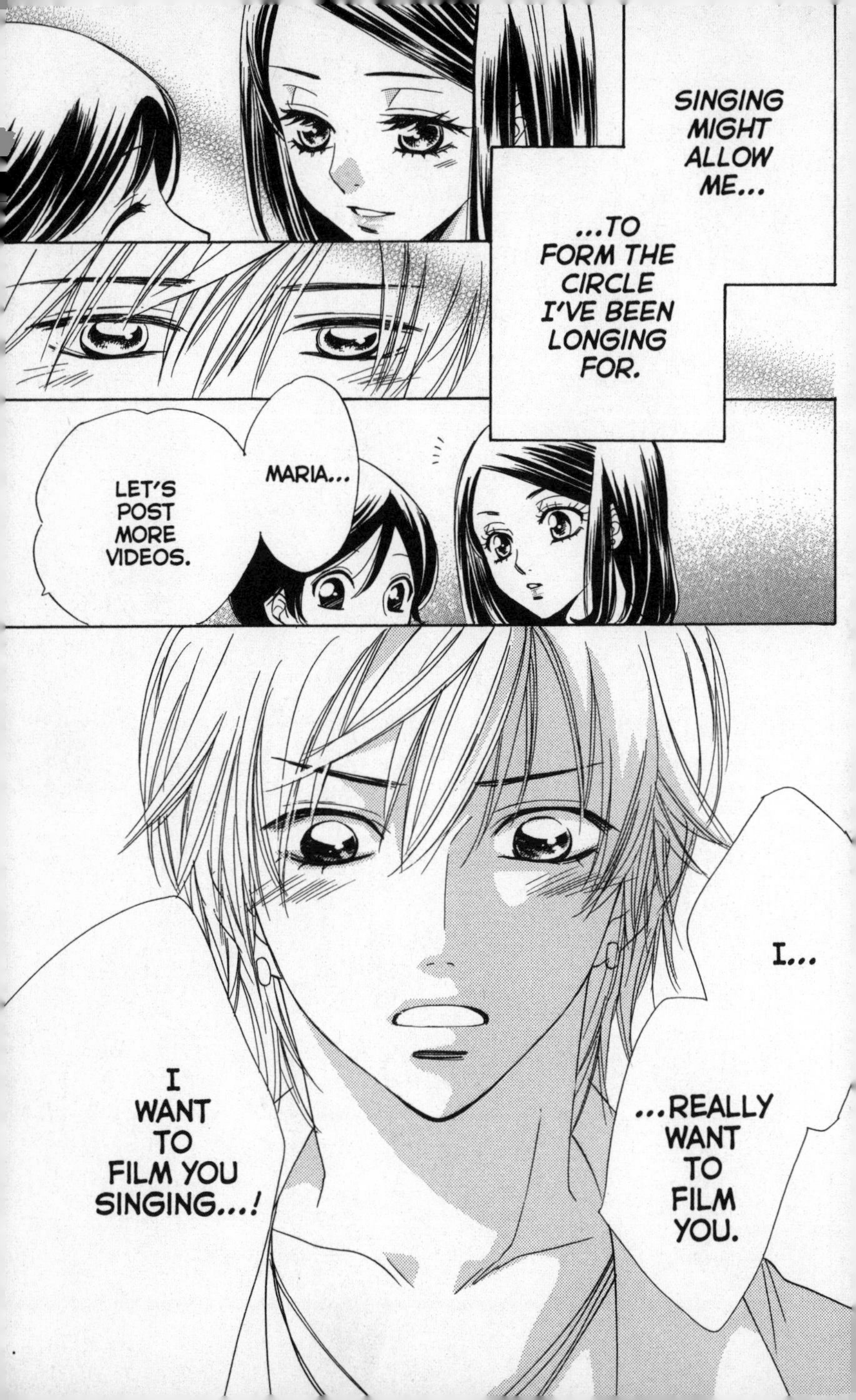
SINGING MIGHT ALLOW ME...
...TO FORM THE CIRCLE I'VE BEEN LONGING FOR.
MARIA...
LET'S POST MORE VIDEOS.
I...
...REALLY WANT TO FILM YOU.
I WANT TO FILM YOU SINGING...!

Continued
in
volume 13

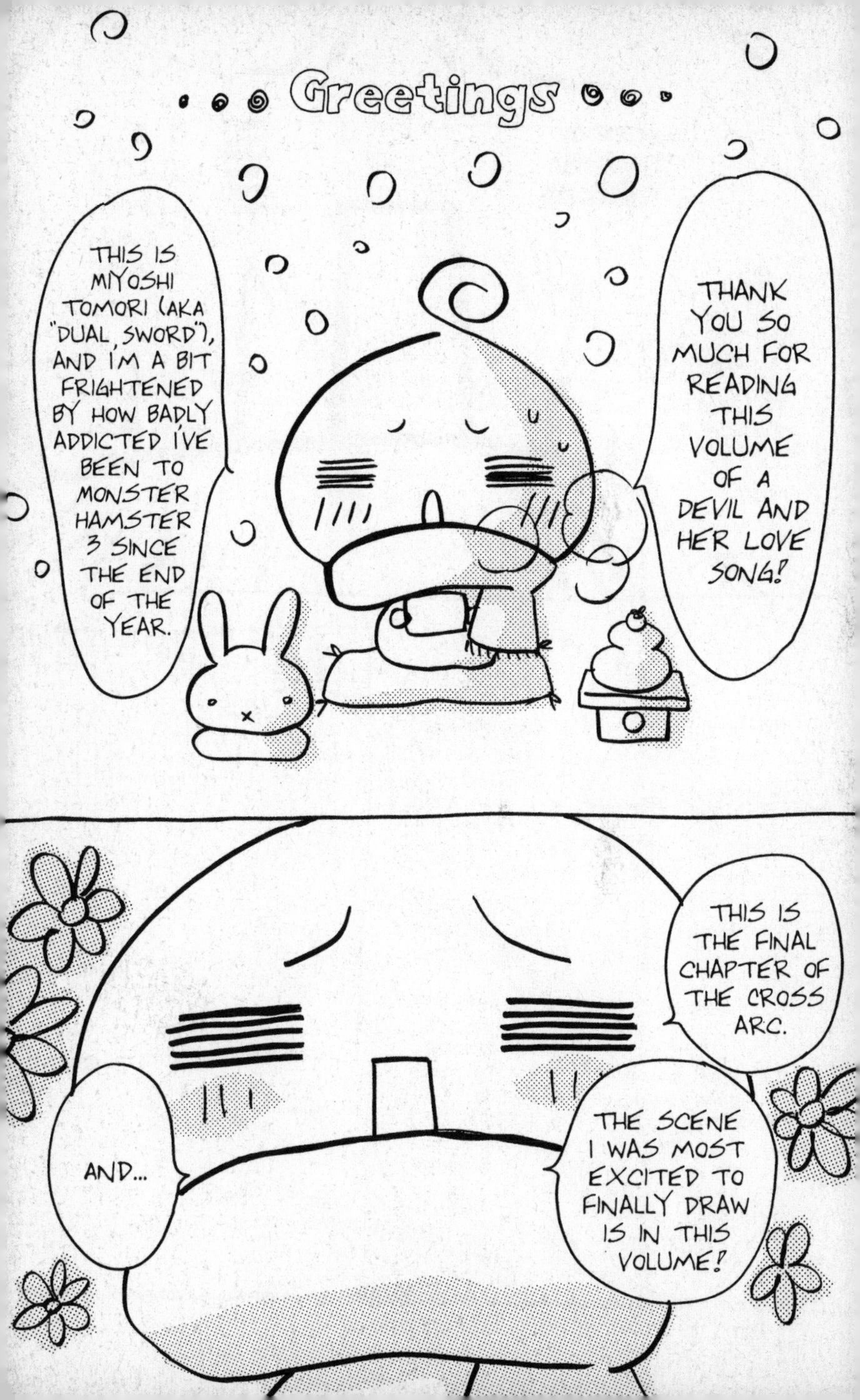
Greetings
THANK YOU SO MUCH FOR READING THIS VOLUME OF A DEVIL AND HER LOVE SONG!
THIS IS MIYOSHI TOMORI (AKA "DUAL SWORD"), AND I'M A BIT FRIGHTENED BY HOW BADLY ADDICTED I'VE BEEN TO MONSTER HAMSTER 3 SINCE THE END OF THE YEAR.
THIS IS THE FINAL CHAPTER OF THE CROSS ARC.
AND...
THE SCENE I WAS MOST EXCITED TO FINALLY DRAW IS IN THIS VOLUME!

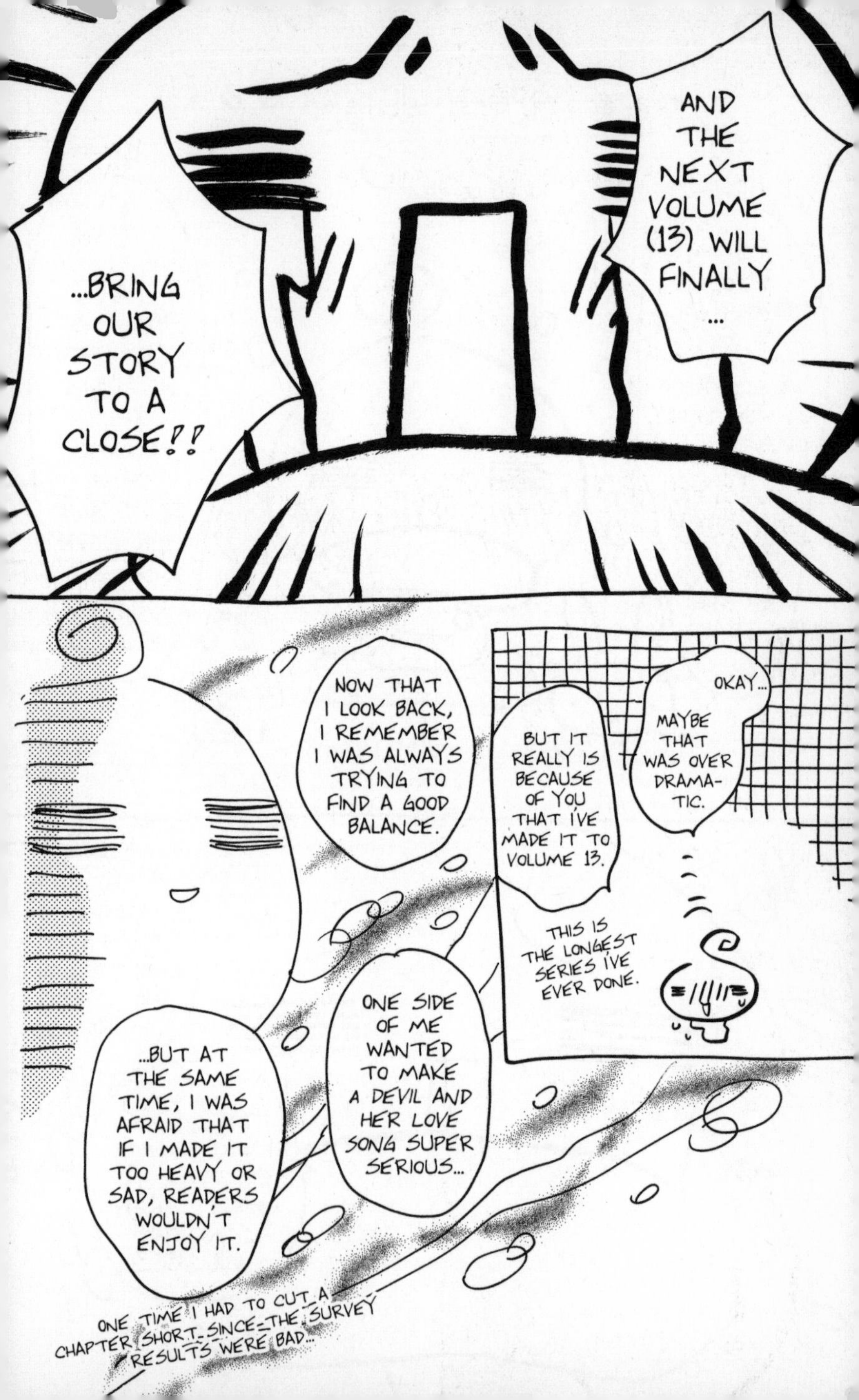
AND THE NEXT VOLUME (13) WILL FINALLY ...
...BRING OUR STORY TO A CLOSE!?!
OKAY... MAYBE THAT WAS OVER DRAMA-TIC.
BUT IT REALLY IS BECAUSE OF YOU THAT I'VE MADE IT TO VOLUME 13.
THIS IS THE LONGEST SERIES I'VE EVER DONE.
NOW THAT I LOOK BACK, I REMEMBER I WAS ALWAYS TRYING TO FIND A GOOD BALANCE.
ONE SIDE OF ME WANTED TO MAKE A DEVIL AND HER LOVE SONG SUPER SERIOUS...
...BUT AT THE SAME TIME, I WAS AFRAID THAT IF I MADE IT TOO HEAVY OR SAD, READERS WOULDN'T ENJOY IT.
ONE TIME I HAD TO CUT A CHAPTER SHORT SINCE THE SURVEY RESULTS WERE BAD...

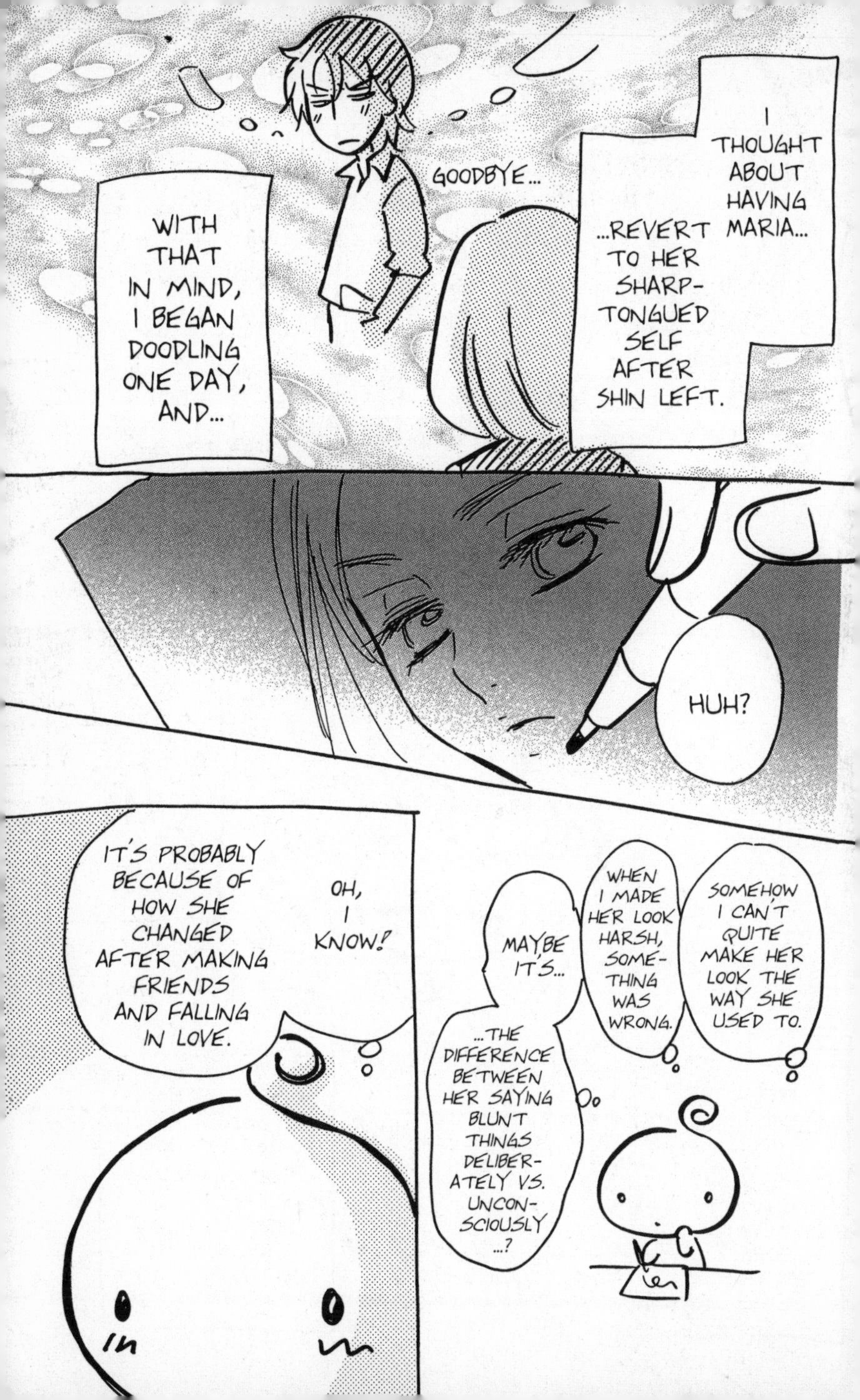
I THOUGHT ABOUT HAVING MARIA...
...REVERT TO HER SHARP-TONGUED SELF AFTER SHIN LEFT.
GOODBYE...
WITH THAT IN MIND, I BEGAN DOODLING ONE DAY, AND...
HUH?
SOMEHOW I CAN'T QUITE MAKE HER LOOK THE WAY SHE USED TO.
WHEN I MADE HER LOOK HARSH, SOMETHING WAS WRONG.
MAYBE IT'S...
...THE DIFFERENCE BETWEEN HER SAYING BLUNT THINGS DELIBERATELY VS. UNCONSCIOUSLY ...?
OH, I KNOW!
IT'S PROBABLY BECAUSE OF HOW SHE CHANGED AFTER MAKING FRIENDS AND FALLING IN LOVE.

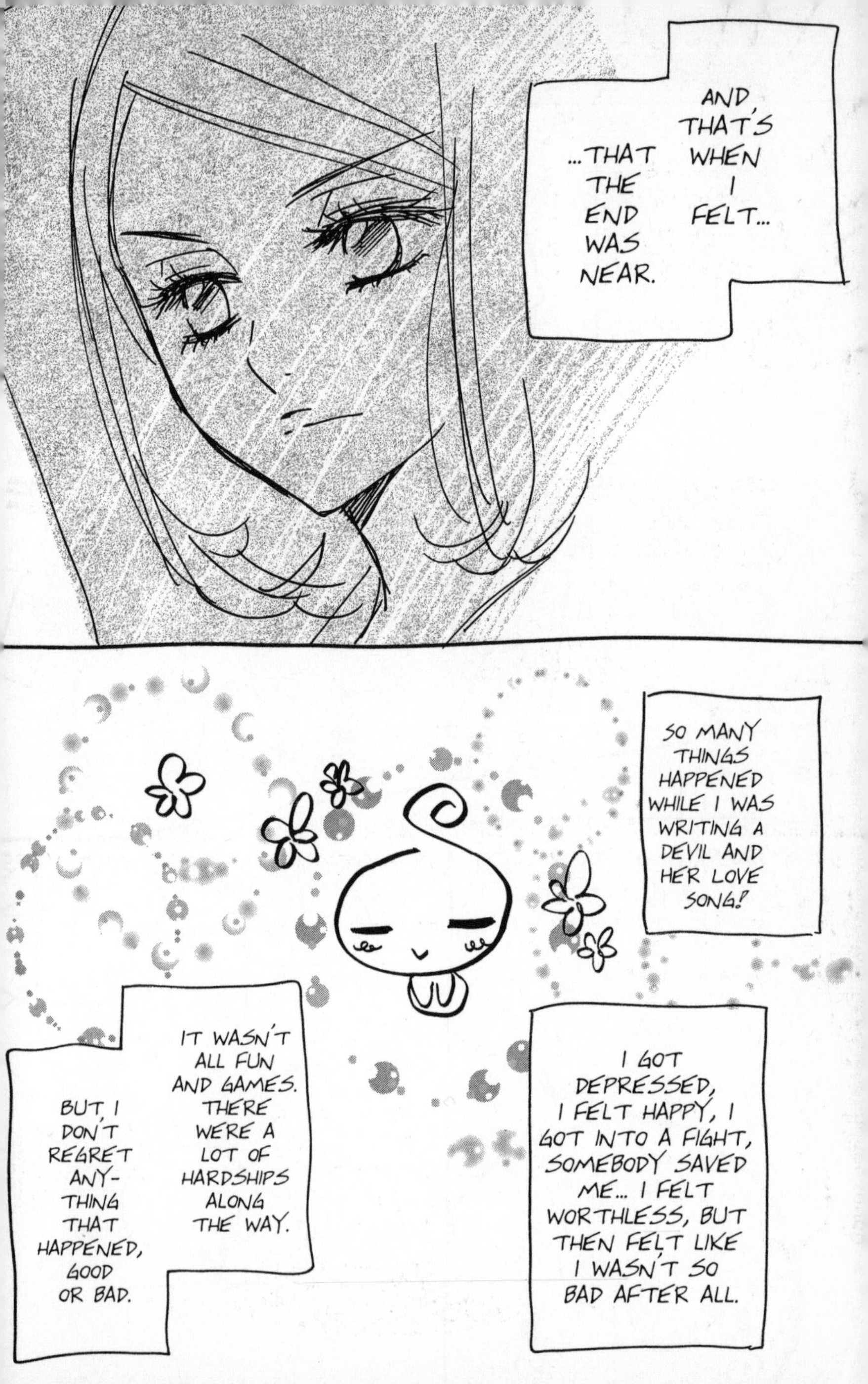
AND THAT'S WHEN I FELT...
...THAT THE END WAS NEAR.
SO MANY THINGS HAPPENED WHILE I WAS WRITING A DEVIL AND HER LOVE SONG!
I GOT DEPRESSED, I FELT HAPPY, I GOT INTO A FIGHT, SOMEBODY SAVED ME... I FELT WORTHLESS, BUT THEN FELT LIKE I WASN'T SO BAD AFTER ALL.
IT WASN'T ALL FUN AND GAMES. THERE WERE A LOT OF HARDSHIPS ALONG THE WAY.
BUT I DON'T REGRET ANYTHING THAT HAPPENED, GOOD OR BAD.

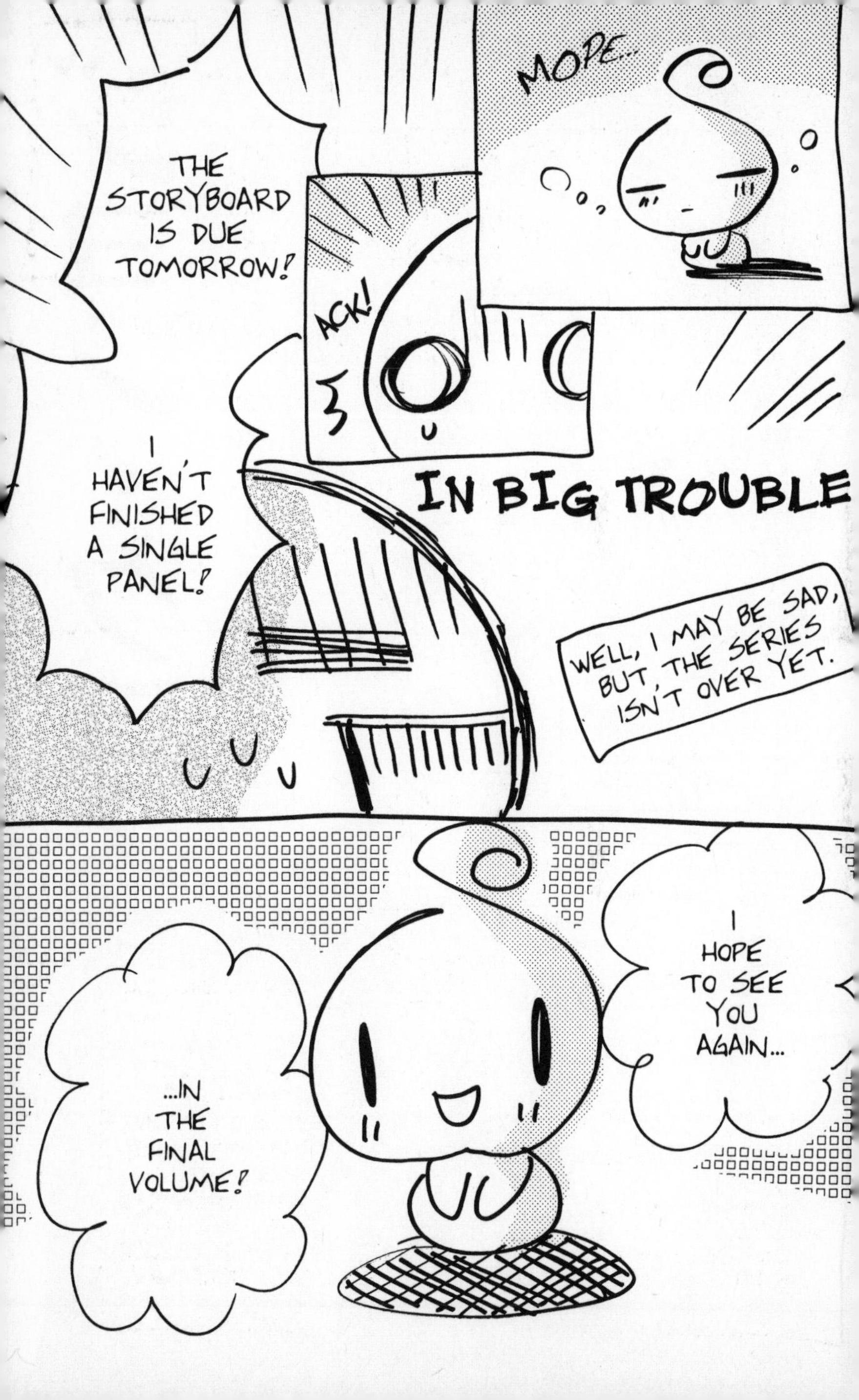
MOPE...
ACK!
THE STORYBOARD IS DUE TOMORROW!
IN BIG TROUBLE
I HAVEN'T FINISHED A SINGLE PANEL!
WELL, I MAY BE SAD, BUT THE SERIES ISN'T OVER YET.
I HOPE TO SEE YOU AGAIN...
...IN THE FINAL VOLUME!

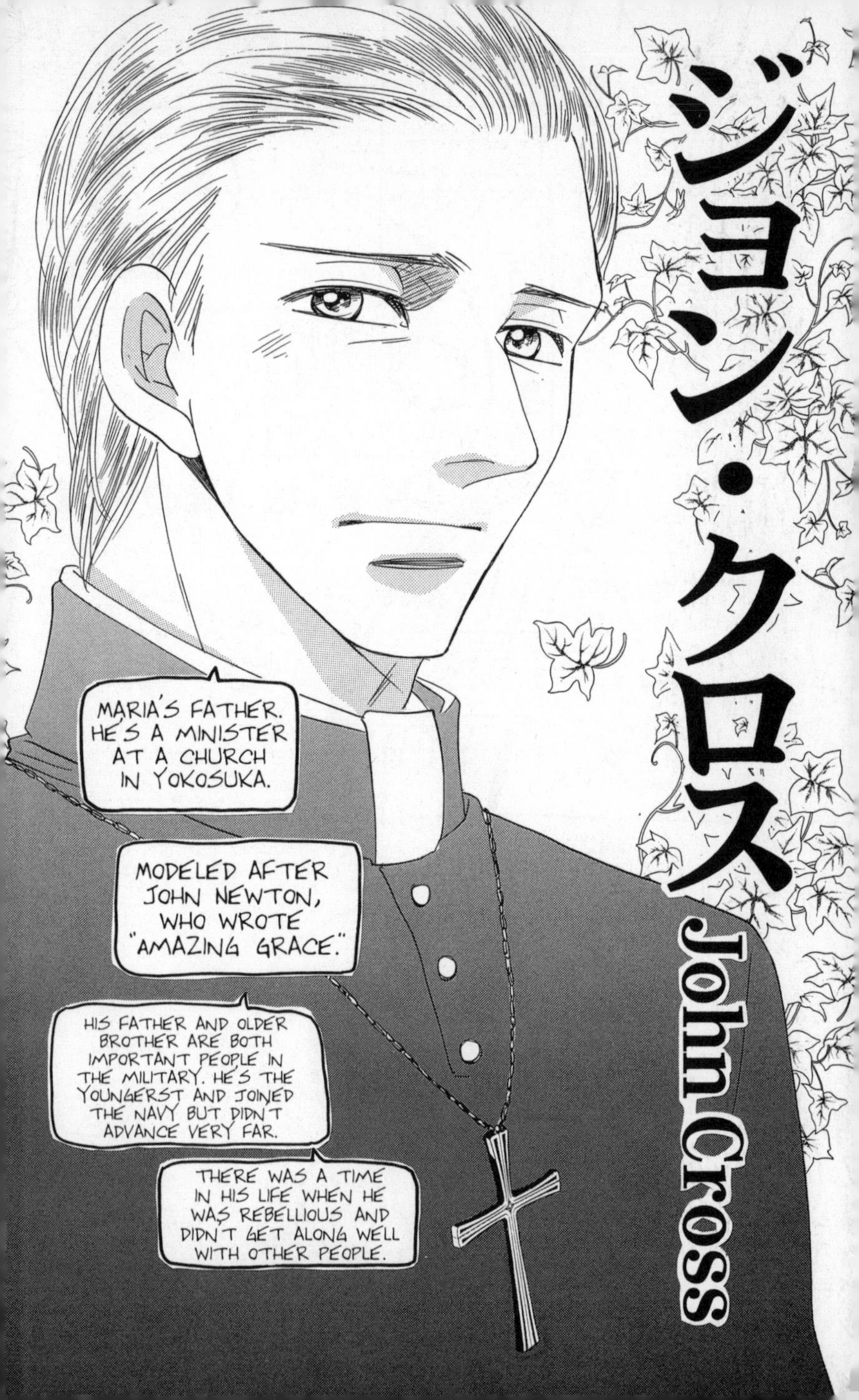
ジョン・クロス
John Cross
MARIA'S FATHER. HE'S A MINISTER AT A CHURCH IN YOKOSUKA.
MODELED AFTER JOHN NEWTON, WHO WROTE "AMAZING GRACE."
HIS FATHER AND OLDER BROTHER ARE BOTH IMPORTANT PEOPLE IN THE MILITARY. HE'S THE YOUNGERST AND JOINED THE NAVY BUT DIDN'T ADVANCE VERY FAR.
THERE WAS A TIME IN HIS LIFE WHEN HE WAS REBELLIOUS AND DIDN'T GET ALONG WELL WITH OTHER PEOPLE.

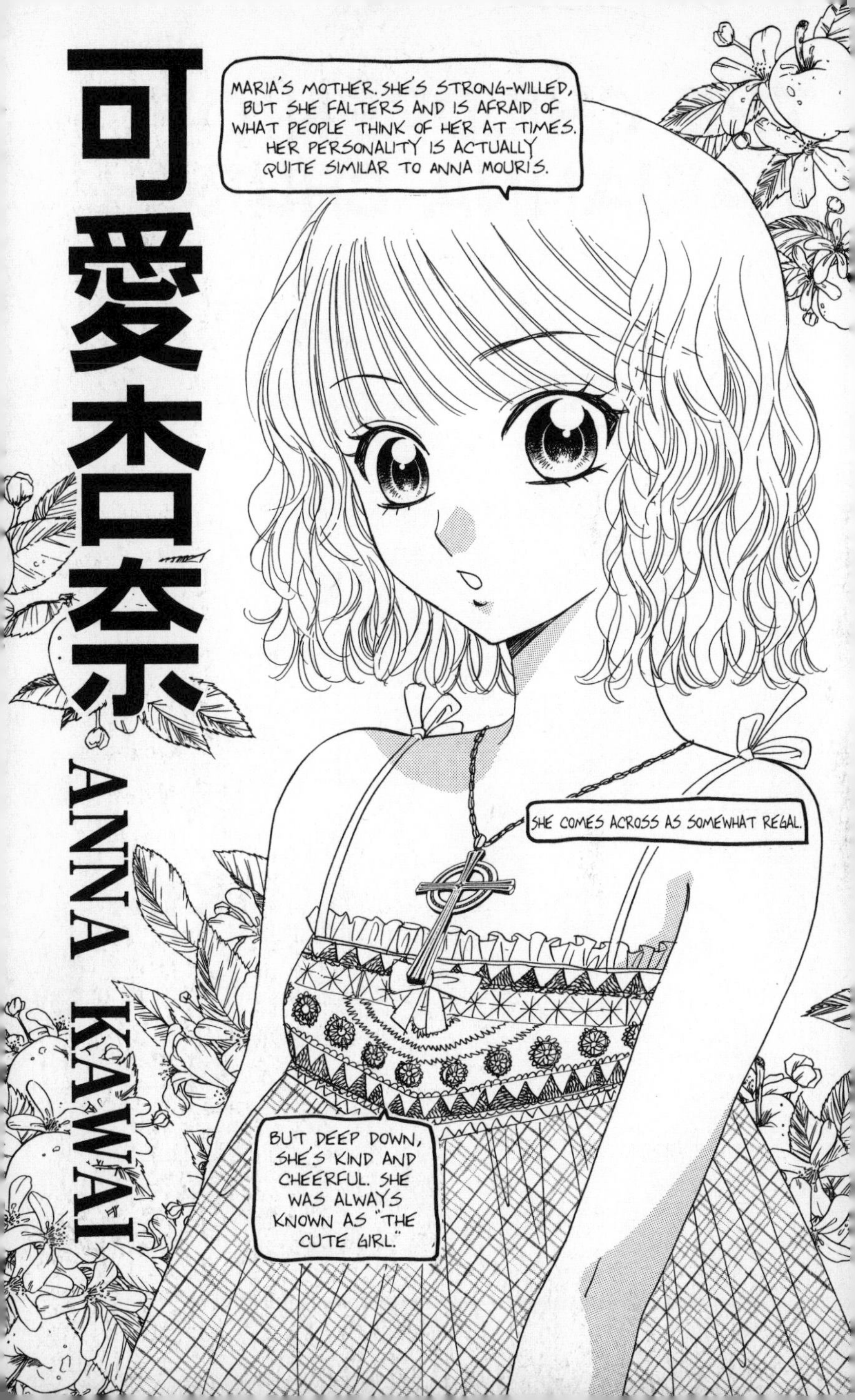
可愛杏奈
ANNA KAWAI
MARIA'S MOTHER. SHE'S STRONG-WILLED, BUT SHE FALTERS AND IS AFRAID OF WHAT PEOPLE THINK OF HER AT TIMES. HER PERSONALITY IS ACTUALLY QUITE SIMILAR TO ANNA MOURIS.
SHE COMES ACROSS AS SOMEWHAT REGAL.
BUT DEEP DOWN, SHE'S KIND AND CHEERFUL. SHE WAS ALWAYS KNOWN AS "THE CUTE GIRL."

THE CHILDREN OF MARIANNA CHURCH

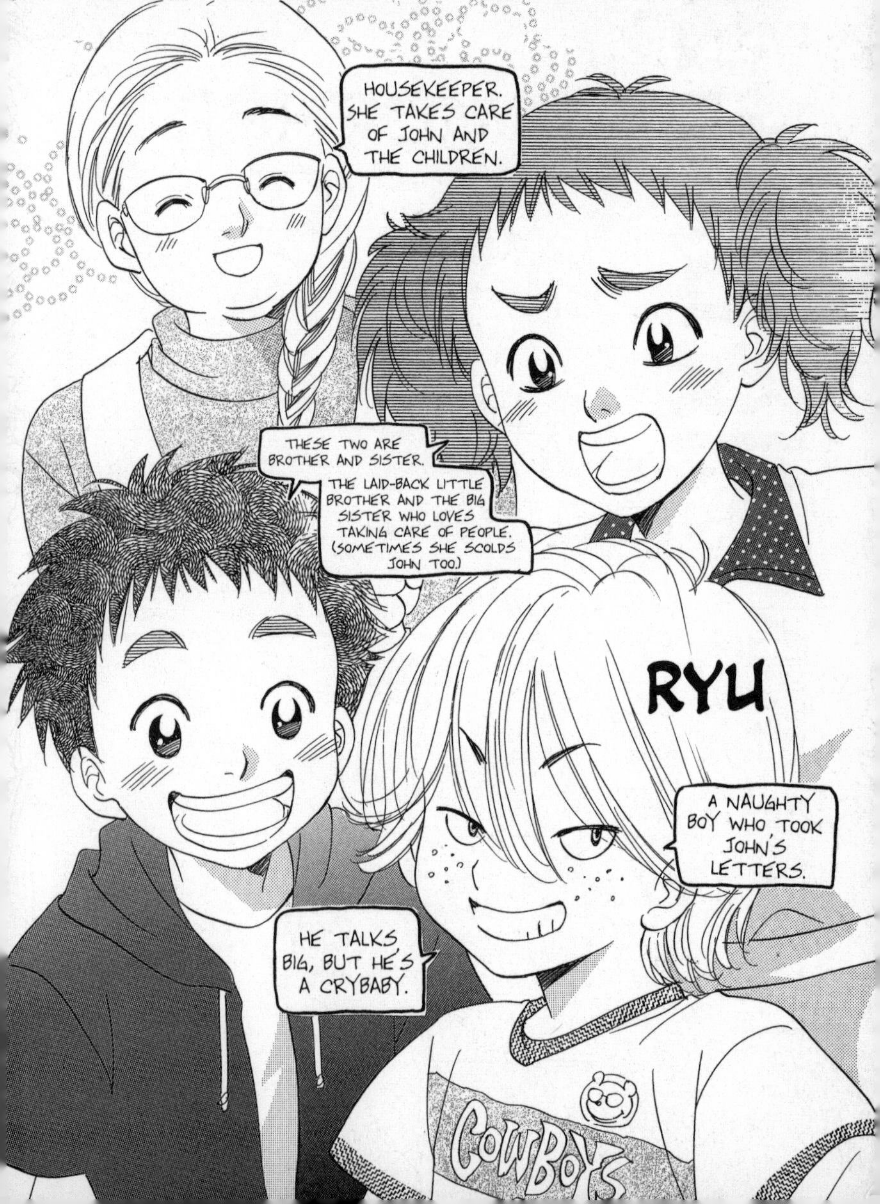
HOUSEKEEPER. SHE TAKES CARE OF JOHN AND THE CHILDREN.
THESE TWO ARE BROTHER AND SISTER.
THE LAID-BACK LITTLE BROTHER AND THE BIG SISTER WHO LOVES TAKING CARE OF PEOPLE. (SOMETIMES SHE SCOLDS JOHN TOO.)
RYU
A NAUGHTY BOY WHO TOOK JOHN'S LETTERS.
HE TALKS BIG, BUT HE'S A CRYBABY.
COWBOYS

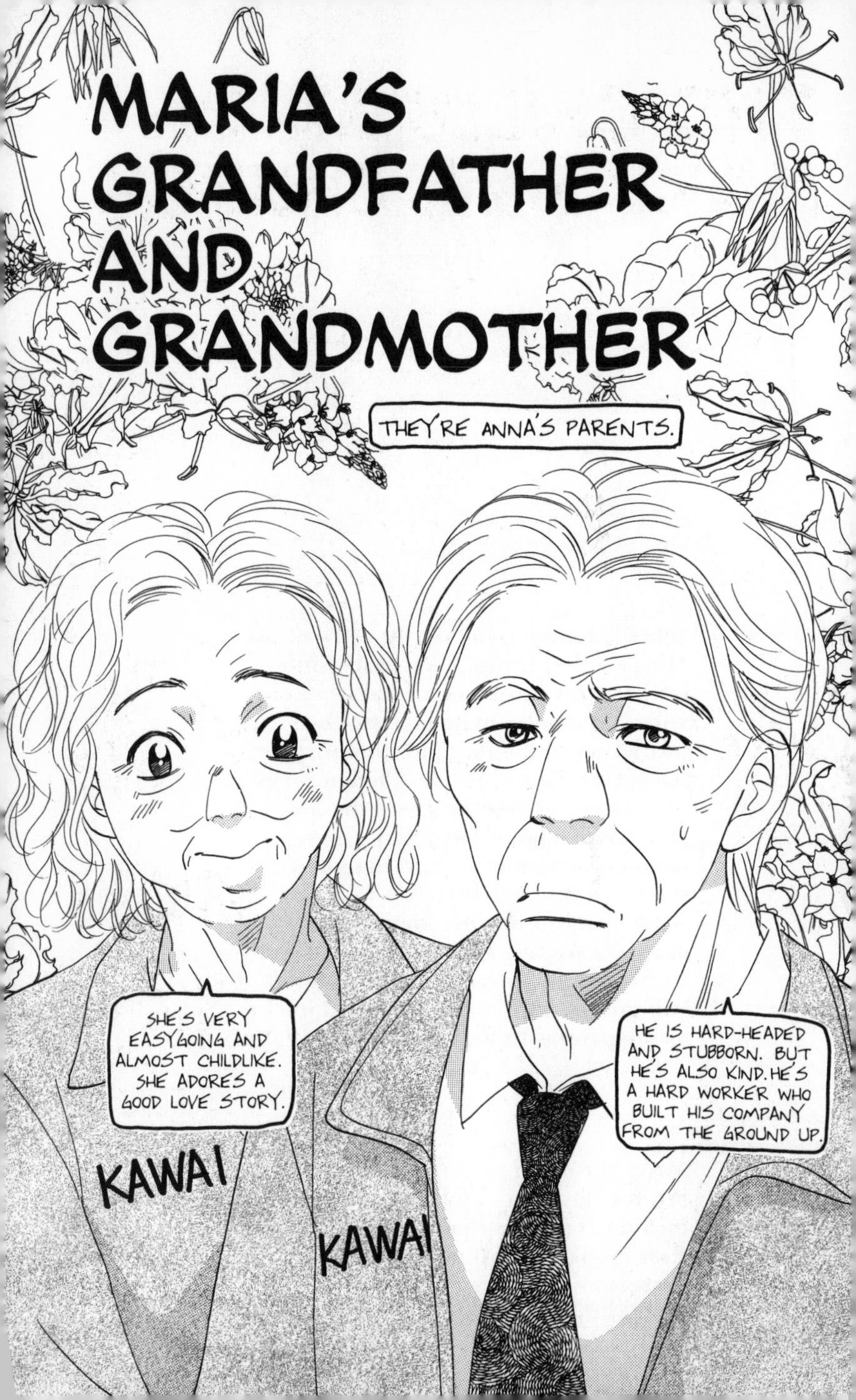
MARIA'S GRANDFATHER AND GRANDMOTHER
THEY'RE ANNA'S PARENTS.
HE IS HARD-HEADED AND STUBBORN. BUT HE'S ALSO KIND. HE'S A HARD WORKER WHO BUILT HIS COMPANY FROM THE GROUND UP.
SHE'S VERY EASYGOING AND ALMOST CHILDLIKE. SHE ADORES A GOOD LOVE STORY.
KAWAI
KAWAI

While I was working on the *A Devil and Her Love Song* series, I was really into magnets for some reason. I started out with just regular magnets, and then moved on to the pushpin-type magnets. After that, I'd collect all different types of magnet series—there was the dog-face series, the butterfly series, the Japanese sweets series and the planet series... I'd switch them up to create what is now a magnet kingdom. *A Devil and Her Love Song* is nearing its end, but I imagine my obsession with magnets will go on...as I continue to find joy in visiting stores to look for magnets.

-Miyoshi Tomori

Miyoshi Tomori made her debut as a manga creator in 2001, and her previous titles include *Hatsukare* (First Boyfriend), *Tongari Root* (Square Root), and *Brass Love!!* In her spare time she likes listening to music in the bath and playing musical instruments.

A DEVIL AND HER LOVE SONG
Volume 12
Shojo Beat Edition

STORY AND ART BY
MIYOSHI TOMORI

English Adaptation/Ysabet MacFarlane
Translation/JN Productions
Touch-up Art & Lettering/Monalisa de Asis
Design/Courtney Utt
Editor/Amy Yu

AKUMA TO LOVE SONG © 2006 by Miyoshi Tomori
All rights reserved. First published in Japan in 2006
by SHUEISHA Inc., Tokyo.
English translation rights arranged
by SHUEISHA Inc.

Printed in the U.S.A.

Published by VIZ Media, LLC
P.O. Box 77010
San Francisco, CA 94107

10 9 8 7 6 5 4 3 2 1
First printing, December 2013

www.viz.com   www.shojobeat.com

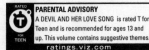

PARENTAL ADVISORY
A DEVIL AND HER LOVE SONG is rated T for
Teen and is recommended for ages 13 and
up. This volume contains suggestive themes.
ratings.viz.com

Surprise!

You may be reading the wrong way!

It's true: In keeping with the original Japanese comic format, this book reads from right to left—so action, sound effects, and word balloons are completely reversed. This preserves the orientation of the original artwork—plus, it's fun! Check out the diagram shown here to get the hang of things, and then turn to the other side of the book to get started!

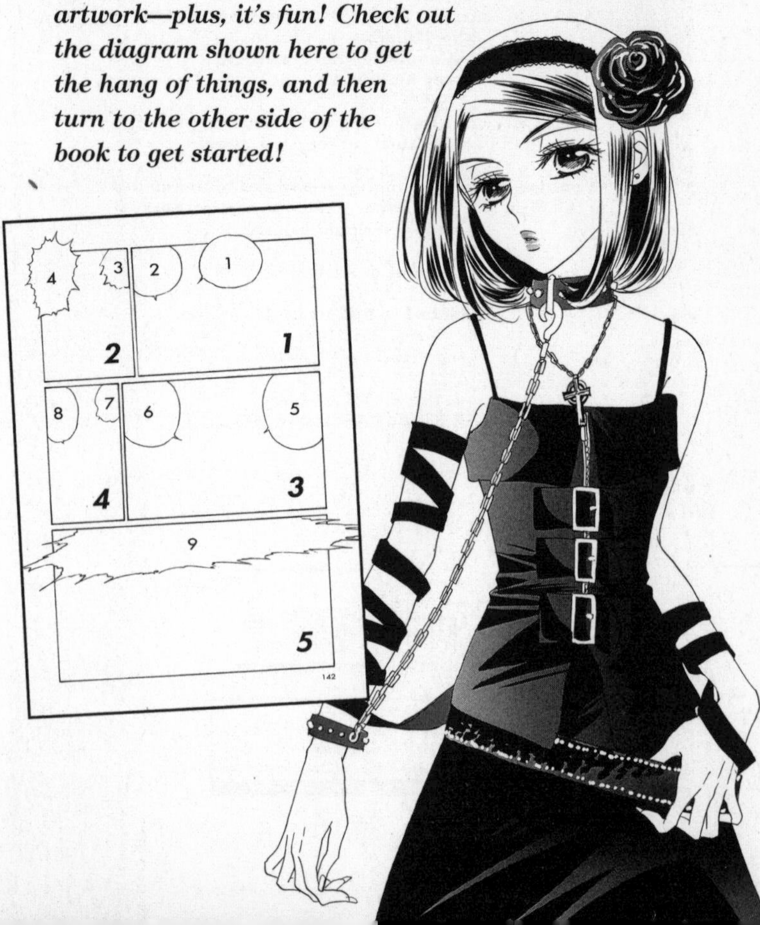
1
2
1
3
4
2
5
6
3
7
8
4
9
5
142